Business management
information technology

Business maths and information technology

M WISNIEWSKI and S SKIDMORE

The Chartered Association of Certified Accountants

Longman

PUBLISHED BY LONGMAN GROUP UK LTD IN CO-OPERATION
WITH THE CHARTERED ASSOCIATION OF CERTIFIED ACCOUNTANTS

© Longman Group UK Ltd 1988

ISBN 0 85121 4584

Published by

Longman Professional and Business Communications Division
Longman Group UK Limited
21–27 Lamb's Conduit Street, London WC1N 3NJ

Associated Offices

Australia	Longman Professional Publishing (Pty) Limited 130 Phillip Street, Sydney, NSW 2000
Hong Kong	Longman Group (Far East) Limited Cornwall House, 18th Floor, Taikoo Trading Estate, Tong Chong Street, Quarry Bay
Malaysia	Longman Malaysia Sdn Bhd No 3 Jalan Kilang A, Off Jalan Penchala, Petaling Jaya, Selangor, Malaysia
Singapore	Longman Singapore Publishers (Pte) Ltd 25 First Lok Yang Road, Singapore 2262
USA	Longman Group (USA) Inc 500 North Dearborn Street, Chicago, Illinois 60610

A CIP catalogue record for this book is available from the British Library.

Printed in Great Britain by Bell & Bain Ltd, Glasgow.

For further information and enquiries please contact your local Longman office.

Europe, Latin America, Iran
Please contact our International
Sales Department
Longman House
Burnt Mill
Harlow
Essex CM20 2JE

Arab World
Longman Arab World Centre
Butros Bustani Street
Zokak el Blat
PO Box 11-945
Beirut
Lebanon

New Sphinx Publishing Co. Ltd.
3 Shawarby Street
Kasr el Nil
Cairo
Egypt

Librairie Sayegh
Salhie Street
PO Box 704
Damaascus
Syria

Longman Arab World Centre
Al-Hajairi Building
Amir Mohammed Street
PO Box 6587
Amman
Jordan

Longman Arab World Centre
15th Street
PO Box 1391
Khartoum
Sudan

Cameroon
M A W Ngoumbah
BP 537
Limbe
Cameroon

Australia
Longman Cheshire Pty Ltd
Longman Cheshire House
Kings Gardens
91-97 Coventry Street
South Melbourne
Victoria 3205

Botswana
Longman Botswana (Pty) Ltd.
PO Box 1083
Gaborone

Canada
James D Lang
Marketing Manager
Carswell Legal Publications
2330 Midland Avenue
Agincourt
Ontario
M1S 1P7

Ghana
Sedco Publishing Co. Ltd.
Sedco House
PO Box 2051
Tabon Street
North Ridge
Accra

Hong Kong
Longman Group (Far East) Ltd.
18th Floor Cornwall House
Taikoo Trading Estate
Tong Chong Street
Quarry Bay

India
Orient Longman Limited
5-9-41/1 Bashir Bagh
Hyderabad 500 029

UBS Publishers Distributors
5, Ansari Road
PO Box 7051
New Delhi 110 002

Japan
Longman Penguin Japan Co. Ltd.
Yamaguchi Building
2-12-9 Kanda Jimbocho
Chiyoda-ku
Tokyo 101

Kenya
Longman Kenya Ltd.
PO Box 18033
Funzi Road, Industrial Area
Nairobi

Lesotho
Longman Lesotho (Pty) Ltd.
PO Box 1174
Maseru, 100

Malawi
Dzuka Publishing Co. Ltd.
Blantyre Printing & Publishing
Co. Ltd. PMB 39
Blantyre

Malaysia
Longman Malaysia Sdn, Berhad
No. 3 Jalan Kilang A
Off Jalan Penchala
Petaling Jaya
Selangor

New Zealand
Longman Paul Ltd.
Private Bag
Takapuna
Auckland 9

Nigeria
Longman Nigeria Ltd.
52 Oba Akran Avenue
Private Mail Bag 21036
Ikeja
Lagos

Pakistan
Tahir M Lodhi
Regional Manager
Butterworths
7 Jahangir Street
Islamia Park
Poonch Road
Lahore

Singapore
Longman Singapore
Publishers Pte Ltd.
25 First Lok Yang Road
Off International Road
Jurong Town
Singapore 22

South Africa
Maskew Miller Longman (Pty) Ltd.
PO Box 396
Howard Drive
Pinelands 7405
Cape Town 8000

Swaziland
Longman Swaziland Ltd.
PO Box 2207
Manzni

Tanzania
Ben & Co. Ltd.
PO Box 3164
Dar-es-Salaam

USA
Longman Trade USA.
Caroline House Inc.
520 North Dearborn Street
Chicago
Illinois 60610

Transnational Publishers, Inc.
PO Box 7282
Ardsley-on-Hudson
NY 10503

West Indies
Longman Caribbean (Trinidad) Ltd.
Boundary Road
San Juan
Trinidad

Longman Jamaica Ltd.
PO Box 489
95 Newport Boulevard
Newport West
Kingston 10
Jamaica

Mr Louis A Forde
'Suncrest'
Sunrise Drive
Pine Gardens
St Michael
Barbados

Zimbabwe
Longman Zimbabwe (PVT) Ltd
PO Box ST 125
Southerton
Harare

Contents

An introduction to this text

Students have bought this text with the hope that it will help them pass the exam that they will shortly face. The authors of this text also hope that it will help students pass their exams. A major reason for writing this book was to provide students with a comprehensive coverage of the syllabus content that is both relevant to their own studies and also easy to read and to understand.

Although the text is aimed primarily at those students intending to take professional accountancy examinations it will also be of direct relevance to all students in the business studies area, including BTEC and undergraduates in economics, accounting and finance and business studies. It is *not* directed at students whose main interest is in statistics, mathematics or computing. We assume that, like ourselves, students in the fields of accountancy, finance and business have no interest in these subject areas in their own right but rather in the practical *applications* of such topics and techniques to business. However, whilst the text was written to help students pass their exams it also has a wider purpose. The reason why all students in the business area have to take an examination in the quantitative analysis/information technology area is that a working knowledge of these topics is essential for present and future managers. In order to work effectively in a modern business organisation, whether that organisation is a private commercial company, a government agency, a state industry or whatever, a student today must be able to *use* quantitative techniques and *understand* their use and results in a confident and reliable manner.

1.1   INTRODUCTION

Today's students are striving to become tomorrow's managers. Practising accountants will make decisions based on the information relating to the financial state of the organisation. Economists will make decisions based on the information relating to the economic framework in which the organisation operates. Personnel managers will make decisions based on the information relating to the levels of employment in the organisation and so on. Such information is increasingly quantitative and it is apparent that managers (both practising and intending) need a working knowledge of the procedures and techniques appropriate for analysing and evaluating such quantitative information.

Additionally, the business information technology area is undergoing considerable change. Advice and expertise in this field is now sought from managers as well as from the IT (or computing) department within the organisation. Given the increasing emphasis on technologically based methods of storing, retrieving and analysing information it is apparent that the manager requires a detailed level of knowledge relating to the areas of computing and data processing, the area that has come to be known as 'information technology'. It is the aim of this text to provide future decision-makers in business with the necessary skills and background knowledge in these subject areas.

1.2   APPROACH OF THE TEXT

Accordingly, the material presented in the text focuses on the practical and applied areas of relevance to business organisations. Students are assumed to have no previous knowledge or use of the areas covered, either in numerical terms or in terms of computing. The necessary introduction to any techniques will be provided in the text itself. However, we do assume that students are able to deal with the elementary mathematics (in terms of arithmetic and simple algebra) that are pre-requisites for this type of material.

The text adopts a twin focus to the topics covered. On the one hand, it is necessary for you to develop the necessary skills to be able to solve a typical problem, in other words, to be able to find 'the answer' to a problem set. On the other hand, it is necessary to develop a critical understanding and awareness of the techniques and methods covered. It is plainly inadequate simply to provide the solution to a quantitative problem if you cannot also interpret and evaluate the solution in the business context in which it is set. After all, these days computers are far more efficient at finding 'the answer' than people. A computer system cannot, however, formulate the problem, decide which method of analysis is appropriate, assess the business relevance of the solution and interpret the 'answer' in terms that the managing director can understand!

Accordingly, we hope that you will not use this text simply to be able to work out the solution to a problem but also to gain a wider awareness of the role and function of quantitative analysis in business.

1.3   CONTENT OF THE TEXT

The text adopts the following structure:

Section A covers the major elements of descriptive statistics: that is, those statistical techniques that can be used to describe numerical information and form the basis for reaching conclusions and making decisions. This section covers data presentation, the aggregation of raw data, the calculation of averages and measures of variation, the use of index numbers and an introduction to probability.

Section B covers the major elements of business mathematics and presents simple linear equations, the use of matrix algebra in representing linear relationships, linear programming, simple linear regression, the analysis of time series data, non-linear equations, the use of calculus in business mathematics and simple stock control techniques.

Section C covers the main elements of financial mathematics looking at interest rate calculations, the use of mathematical series, present value and the use of discounting and introduces the major applications of these to financial problems.

Section D introduces the major elements of information technology looking at hardware, software and communication systems, introducing the principles of systems modelling and design, investigating software construction and computer languages and reviewing the needs of business systems.

1.4   ORGANISATION OF THE TEXT

Each chapter in the text takes the following general format:

First, each chapter introduces the relevant topic and places it in a typical business context.

Second, an example problem is thoroughly investigated and discussed both in terms of determining a solution to the problem and discussing the wider business applications of the technique.

Third, a summary of the major points in the chapter is presented.

Fourth, a series of Self-test questions are presented which allow you to test your own understanding of the topic covered. The relevant answers to these questions are to be found in the chapter itself.

Lastly, a set of student exercises are presented. These fulfil two functions. First, they develop ideas and applications introduced in the chapter. Second, they provide practice at the type of question you may well face in the examination.

1.5   THE CONTEXT OF THE BOOK

To help students appreciate the relevance and importance of the topics to business, a case study approach has been adopted where practical in the various chapters. We have assumed that you are working for a large national organisation involved primarily in the retail sector. The organisation is called the Mega Trading Group (MTG) and is a public company that has expanded considerably over the last few years. Such expansion has taken place largely through the company's having an aggressive policy of opening new shops and stores in towns and cities throughout the country and also by takeover of existing smaller companies.

MTG are involved in five major retail areas:

Food
Clothing
Footwear
Furniture
Electrical Goods

Their turnover in 1987 was approximately £160m and has increased considerably over the past five years or so. MTG employ a considerable number of staff in a variety of categories: sales, administrative and clerical and managerial.

The operations of MTG are based around a regional structure. The country is divided into a number of regions and the day-to-day management of stores and shops in that region is the responsibility of the Regional Office and the Regional Manager. There is also a national headquarters which acts in a group coordinating role and is concerned with strategic and long-term planning and decision making.

We shall be introducing topics and techniques in the context of MTG so that you can appreciate *why* the development of a particular technique is necessary and place the technique and its analysis and solution in a typical business context.

1.6   USING THE TEXT

The text has been written in such a way that is effectively self-contained. It may, therefore, be used by the student working alone or by a student receiving tuition in this subject.

It is essential, however, that the text is used in the correct way if you are to gain the most from it in your studies. Much of the material is presented in sequential order and it is, therefore, important that you thoroughly understand one chapter in a section before progressing to the next. To this end it is also essential that you attempt both the Self-test questions and the exercises at the end of each chapter to ensure that you have understood both the major concepts and the methods of solution. The exercises in particular are designed to supplement the material presented in the chapter and to encourage you to think about the wider implications of the topics in business.

1.7   COMPUTERS

The text has been written in such a way that direct access to computing facilities is not essential in following the material presented. However, you will find your knowledge and understanding of business computing systems considerably enhanced if you can gain access to such equipment through college, through a business or through the promotional literature supplied by many computer companies.

Because of the rapid development of information technology no textbook can hope to keep pace. It is essential, therefore, that students keep abreast of such developments via both professional and popular media sources.

The quantitative elements of the text are also presented such that use of computing facilities is not required, but again the use of appropriate systems will considerably increase your understanding of the techniques. If at all possible you should access and use relevant computer software. This may simply be general business software that can be adapted for use in mathematics and statistics—computer spreadsheets are ideal for many of the repetitive calculations required. Alternatively, you may have access to purpose-written software designed for use with these techniques. There are a variety of such packages available, for example, QUANTASS (Quantitative Analysis for the Social Sciences), written by Mik Wisniewski. This is directly related to the material presented in the text and is available for use with the BBC microcomputer. For more information, write to:

> Social Science Software
> Richard Ball Publishing
> Shrewsbury Road
> Claughton
> Birkenhead
> Merseyside   L43 8SP

This software covers the main quantitative topics covered in this text and many of the end-of-chapter exercises are suitable for analysis using this software.

Steve Skidmore would like to thank Edward Arnold (the educational, academic and medical publishing division of Hodder and Stoughton) for allowing him to use some of the material originally published in his book *Business Computing* (Edward Arnold 1987). He would also like to acknowledge the help of Mike Crawford and Martin Abram of the Assist Partnership who contributed to the Information Technology section of this text.

Section A: Statistical techniques and probability

Statistical techniques and probability

All business organisations, using the term 'business' in its widest sense, generate, collect and use vast quantities of information. Such information may relate to levels of production, to manpower, to profits, to sales and so on. To the statistician and to the business analyst who uses statistical techniques such information is referred to as 'data'. The focus of *business* statistics is clearly on the methods and techniques by which such data can be collected and presented in a comprehensible form and analysed in a way that is potentially useful to the people in the business who have to make decisions about the future. This section is concerned primarily with introducing such methods and techniques.

Chapter 2 looks at the specialised vocabulary of statistics and reviews some basic mathematical principles.

Chapter 3 looks at how data can be presented effectively in the form of tables, diagrams and graphs.

Chapter 4 adds to these visual methods of data presentation by introducing frequency tables and their graphical counterpart, histograms.

Chapter 5 introduces the first group of summary statistics that can be used to describe and analyse a set of data—measures of average.

Chapter 6 supplements these statistical measures by introducing the concept of dispersion and the appropriate statistical measures.

Chapter 7 introduces the main approaches in constructing an index, which is a typical business application of averages.

After the methods of presenting and describing data have been discussed, *Chapter 8* looks at the main methods of collecting data and the relevant sampling methods frequently used in data collection.

Business decision-making typically takes place under conditions of uncertainty. The effect of decisions taken and their outcomes are not known for certain. For example, if a business raises the price charged for a particular product it does not know the effect this will have on sales, revenue and profit with absolute certainty.

Accordingly, *Chapters 9 and 10* are concerned with the concepts and techniques related to probability. The first covers the basic principles of probability and the second introduces three typical probability distributions often used in business decision making.

Introduction and review of basic principles

Like most academic disciplines statistics has its own specialised vocabulary and terminology, the main elements of which are introduced in this section.

2.1 STATISTICAL TERMINOLOGY

2.1.1 Variables

In statistics the 'variable' is simply the thing we are measuring or analysing, for example, company sales, profits or income. A variable will normally fall into one of three types:

DISCRETE

A variable is discrete if it can take only certain specific, fixed values. A variable such as the number of customers in a store, for example, is discrete. A store may have 1500 customers or 2322 but it cannot have 1500.6 customers or 2322.1.

CONTINUOUS

A continuous variable, on the other hand, is one which can take any numerical value. So, for example, a person's height or weight is a continuous variable as we can measure the variable to any degree of accuracy.

ATTRIBUTE

An attribute variable is one that is not expressed in numerical terms. So, for example, a person's sex or marital status is not measured in number form.

2.1.2 Primary and secondary data

Primary data are data which have been collected and, usually, analysed at first hand by the person or organisation directly involved. Secondary data, on the other hand, are data which are being used for a purpose other than that for which they were initially collected, or by someone other than the person who collected them.

As an illustration, MTG may decide to collect and analyse data on the profitability of its various stores up and down the country. Such data would be collected by the firm itself and would, therefore, be primary data. The firm may also commission a market research firm to undertake an investigation into the type of customers attracted to the stores. Such data, for MTG, would be secondary data as the company would not have the information collected at first hand.

By implication, analysis of secondary data is potentially less reliable because we may not be sure how it was collected, for what purposes it was originally collected or in what ways it may already have been processed before we are able to use it.

2.1.3   Raw and aggregated data

Raw data are data in their original form where the individual numbers are available for analysis. Aggregated data relates to data which have, in some way, already been summarised. Analysis based on raw data is generally more accurate and reliable than that based on aggregated data.

2.1.4   Populations and samples

A population refers to the entire set of data that exists for a variable whilst a sample refers to a selected part of the population. So in the example of a market research firm collecting data on the company's customers, the population would refer to all customers while a sample would be a carefully selected group of customers intended to represent the population. For reasons of time, cost and availability data on the population are rarely available for analysis. Analysis is more usually undertaken on a representative sub-set of the population—a sample.

2.1.5   Descriptive and inferential statistics

Descriptive statistics are concerned with summarising data in order to describe its main features. The intention behind the related techniques and calculations is to identify the key elements of a data set in order to build up a picture of its characteristics in a concise and accurate manner.

Inferential statistics, on the other hand, are concerned with using the descriptive information derived from a sample to determine the likely characteristics of the population. Typically such inferential statistical techniques take place under conditions of uncertainty and are therefore based around the major concepts of probability.

2.2   REVIEW OF BASIC MATHEMATICS

In order to understand fully what follows in the rest of this section (and, indeed the rest of the text) it is necessary to review the fundamental principles of basic arithmetic and mathematical calculations.

2.2.1   Use of symbols

In both statistics and mathematics it is common to use symbols to represent variables and their data. The use of symbols, particularly in statistical formulae, is simply a convenient way of saving space and time. For example, rather than refer continually to the price of a particular item a symbol such as 'P' may be used instead, or we may use the symbol 'Q' as a convenient shorthand way of referring to the quantity or number of units of a product produced by some company.

2.2.2   Significant digits

When presenting data for some variable a choice must often be made as to the level of accuracy of the numbers given. If data on, say, company profits were being presented these could be shown to the nearest £m (eg £10m) or to the nearest £100,000 (£10.2m) and so on down to the nearest pound or even the nearest penny if desired. A distinction is made, therefore, in a number between those digits representing accurate information and those which provide information only about the size, or magnitude of the number.

For example, both the numbers below have two significant digits:

$$10m$$
$$10,000,000$$

In either case, the number is reliable only to the nearest million.

If, however, the numbers were calculated to the nearest £100,000 then they would have 3 significant figures:

10.2m
10,200,000

2.2.3 Rounding

The importance of determining the number of significant digits associated with a particular set of numbers becomes important when considering the rounding of numbers. Frequently figures are rounded (to the nearest whole unit, to the nearest thousand, to the nearest million and so on) to simplify the numbers that have to be dealt with. It is, after all, much easier to appreciate that profit was £10m (to the nearest £1m) than to say that profit was £10,191,345.37.

To round a number to the nearest unit we must determine the number of significant digits we require. Examples of rounding are shown in Table 2.1.

TABLE 2.1 **Rounding £10,191,345.37:**

To the nearest (£)	Number (£)	Significant digits (£)
1	10,191,345	8
10	10,191,340	7
100	10,191,300	6
1,000	10,191,000	5
10,000	10,190,000	4
100,000	10,200,000	3
1,000,000	10,000,000	2

Note that when we round the number 5 the convention is to round to the nearest even whole number. Thus, 345 was rounded to 340. If the number had been 355 it would be rounded to 360.

2.2.4 Accuracy

The importance of significant digits and rounding becomes apparent in the calculation of statistical measures and their presentation. With the advent of pocket calculators (and computers) that can perform the relevant calculations to five, six or more decimal places, the danger is that the person seeing such a long string of digits can easily forget that the data being analysed is significant to far fewer digits than shown on the calculator or computer printout.

As a general rule when performing calculations you should use as many significant digits as possible in the intermediate stages of the calculation and only perform the appropriate rounding at the end of the calculation.

2.2.5 Powers and exponents

The ability to deal with variables expressed in power terms is essential in both mathematics and statistics. If we have some variable, A, then A^2 is simply $A \times A$. Correspondingly, $A^3 = A \times A \times A$ and so on. Thus the term 10^2 would be $10 \times 10 = 100$ and 10^3 is $10 \times 10 \times 10 = 1000$.

It is frequently the case that arithmetic is performed on such power terms. In general, this will involve two types of such arithmetic: multiplication and division.

For multiplication we might encounter the expression

$$A^2 \times A^3$$

This can be re-written as

$$(A \times A) \times (A \times A \times A) = A \times A \times A \times A \times A = A^5$$

In general, for an expression in the form:

$$A^b \times A^c$$

the result can be expressed as:

$$A^{(b+c)}$$

For division the equivalent rule is:

$$\frac{A^b}{A^c} = A^{(b-c)}$$

The counterpart of a variable raised to some power is the root value of that variable. In business statistics and mathematics square roots are frequently encountered. Most pocket calculators will have a square root key available so the answer can be readily obtained. However, it is important to understand the meaning of the result.

If we wish to find $\sqrt{25}$ we calculate an answer of 5. This number is the square root of 25. The meaning of the square root is that, when multiplied by itself, it will produce the original number. Thus $5 \times 5 = 25$. The same principle can be applied to numbers where we wish to determine the third root, or fourth root and so on.

2.2.6   Logarithms

Frequently, the arithmetical calculations necessary in some computation—and this is especially the case in the calculation of many financial statistics—are extremely time-consuming and tedious using ordinary arithmetic. Using a particular type of arithmetic—that relating to logarithms—such calculations can be performed easily and quickly.

In the section that follows we shall focus on the use of logarithms to the base 10 and we shall assume that you have available a pocket calculator which has such logarithmic functions available. An alternative would be to make use of logarithmic tables but this will not be covered here.

Logarithmic arithmetic is based on the principles covered in the section on Powers and Exponents.

If we denote the number 100 in the form 10^2 then we define the logarithm of 100 as 2.0. That is, we define the logarithm of a number as the exponent of 10 which equates to that number. Similarly:

log (1,000)   3.0 (given that $10^3 = 1,000$)
log (10,000) = 4.0 (given that $10^4 = 10,000$)

and so on.

In general any number can have its logarithm defined in this way, eg:

log (5)   = 0.699   (given that $10^{0.699} = 5$)
log (17.9) = 1.2529 (given that $10^{1.2529} = 17.9$)

We can also define the anti-logarithm as the exact opposite:

antilog (0.699)   = 5
antilog (1.2529) = 17.9

Using the ideas introduced in the section on Powers we can now use logarithms to undertake a variety of forms of arithmetic.

Suppose we wished to determine:

$$5 \times 17.9$$

Using logarithms this would become:

$$0.699 + 1.2529 \text{ (that is } 10^{0.599} \times 10^{1.2529})$$

giving log $(5 \times 17.9) = 1.9519$

and taking antilog (1.9519) we have 89.5 which, if you check using normal arithmetic, is the product of 5×17.9.

In general, there will be four main types of logarithmic calculations that we wish to undertake:

Multiplication
Division
Obtaining powers
Obtaining roots

Most arithmetic via the use of logarithms is straightforward:

MULTIPLICATION

1   Find the logarithm of each of the numbers to be multiplied together
2   Add the logarithms together
3   Find the anti-log of this total
4   The resulting number is the product of the multiplication

Example:

18756 × 13.567 × 1987.1 × 0.98

$$\begin{aligned}
\log(18756) &= 4.273140224 \\
\log(13.567) &= 1.132483825 \\
\log(1987.1) &= 3.298219723 \\
\log(0.98) &= -0.008773924308
\end{aligned}$$

Totalling gives: 8.695069848

Taking the antilog gives the result 495529880.9.
Note two points:

1   The importance of using as many significant digits as possible
2   The fact that an answer derived via the use of logarithms will almost invariably be slightly less accurate than using normal arithmetic

DIVISION

1   Find the logarithm of each of the numbers to be divided
2   Subtract the logarithm of the number at the bottom of the division from that on the top (the denominator from the numerator)
3   Find the antilog of this total
4   The resulting number is the product of the division

Example:

$$\frac{1276.58}{32.59}$$

$$\begin{aligned}
\log(1276.58) &= 3.106048036 \\
\log(32.59) &= 1.51308436 \\
\log(1276.58) - \log(32.59) &= 3.106048036 - 1.51308436 = 1.592963676 \\
\text{Antilog } (1.592963676) &= 39.171
\end{aligned}$$

OBTAINING POWERS

1   Find the logarithm of the number which is to be raised to some power
2   Multiply the logarithm by the power number
3   Find the antilog of this total
4   The resulting number is the original number raised to the stated power

Example:

$$14.78^6$$

log (14.78)	= 1.169674434
6 × log (14.78)	= 6 × 1.169674434 = 7.018046604
antilog (7.018046604)	= 10424292.86 which is the result

OBTAINING ROOTS

1   Find the logarithm of the number for which the root is to be found
2   Divide the logarithm by the root value
3   Find the antilog of the result
4   This number is the answer

Example:

$$\sqrt[5]{6.358}$$

Log (6.358)	= 0.803320523
$\frac{\text{Log (6.358)}}{5}$	= $\frac{0.803320523}{5}$ = 0.160664104
Antilog (0.160664104)	= 1.44765

2.3   SUMMATION

As we shall soon see, we frequently require to determine the total value of a series of numbers. To assist in providing a brief summary of the arithmetical operation a special symbol is frequently used: Σ pronounced 'sigma'. This symbol is used to indicate the summation of the relevant variable.

Assume the following figures:

$$5, 8, 9, 12, 15$$

We can refer to these numbers as variable X and use the Σ symbol to write

$$\Sigma X$$

rather than say 'add the five numbers together and determine the total'. The result will be found by:

$$\Sigma X = 5 + 8 + 9 + 12 + 15 = 49$$

More complex operations can be carried out with reference to the Σ term. Thus,

$$\Sigma X^2$$

would indicate 'to square the X numbers then add them together' (giving a result here of 539). Equally, the term

$$(\Sigma X)^2$$

would refer instead to finding the total of X terms and *then* squaring (giving a result of 2401).

SUMMARY

This chapter has summarised the key elements of the statistical terminology that the student will need to be familiar with and has briefly reviewed the major elements of arithmetic and mathematics which the student is assumed to understand in order to follow the rest of this Section. The exercises which follow are intended to allow the student to determine whether he or she has an adequate grasp of these areas before proceeding further.

Briefly, the important points to note are:

1   A variable is defined as the characteristic under investigation.

2   In general a variable will fall into one of three types: discrete, continuous, attribute.

3   Primary data have been collected at first hand.

4   Secondary data are data which are being used for some other purpose than that for which they were originally collected.

5   Raw data are data which have not yet been aggregated or summarised.

6   Descriptive statistics are concerned with identifying the major features of the data set.

7   Inferential statistics are concerned with determining the probable characteristics of a statistical population based on the characteristics of a representative sample of the population.

SELF-TEST QUESTIONS

1   **Explain the difference between raw and aggregated data** (*Refer to page 10*)

2   **Explain why it is preferable to use primary data in statistical analysis** (*Refer to page 9*)

3   **Give an example of each of the three types of variable** (*Refer to page 9*)

4   **Why is it frequently necessary to analyse a sample rather than a statistical population?** (*Refer to page 10*)

5   **What is the distinction between descriptive and inferential statistics?** (*Refer to page 10*)

EXERCISES

1   A store has collected data on the following two variables for last week:

No of units sold	Price per unit
11	£2.25
5	£2.30
17	£1.67
23	£0.95
14	£1.23

Let the number of units sold = Q and the price per unit = P

  (a)   Is the variable Q
      —discrete?
      —continuous?
      —attribute?

  (b)   Give examples of each of the three general types of variable

  (c)   Determine the value of the following:
      i) ΣQ
      ii) ΣP
      iii) $\Sigma(Q \times P)$
      What will the answers to i and iii represent to the store?

  (d)   How many significant digits does your answer to iii have?

  (e)   Write your answer to iii with:
      4 significant digits
      3 significant digits
      2 significant digits
      1 significant digit

  (f)   Are the data raw or aggregated data?

  (g)   Are the data primary or secondary data?

2   Calculate the following: (check your answers by raising the result to the appropriate power)
      (a) $\sqrt{49}$
      (b) $\sqrt{100}$
      (c) $\sqrt[3]{17.6}$
      (d) $\sqrt[10]{1587}$

3   Calculate the following using logarithms: (check your answer by using normal arithmetic)

      (a) $124 \times 19.7 \times 2564.387$
      (b) $132^2 \times .765 \times 1983.5$
      (c) $134.2/23.8$
      (d) $(98.1/.75) \times 12.6 \times 923.6$

Answers on page 295.

Data presentation

The initial focus in terms of any form of quantitative analysis is to determine and describe the key features of the data set under investigation. There are a number of alternative ways of undertaking such description and this chapter introduces the main elementary visual methods that begin this process.

Statistical data can usually be presented initially either in the form of a table or in the form of a graph or chart. The key elements of constructing and presenting information in the form of a table are covered. The alternative methods of presenting the equivalent data graphically are also discussed in turn.

3.1 GENERAL PRINCIPLES

The presentation of data in the form of a table is probably the most common method used in business and one that is relatively easy to understand even by those with no formal background in quantitative techniques. Frequently, however, the information presented in a table is difficult to understand quickly and fails to make an immediate impact. Far better, in terms of making such an immediate impression, is to present the same information in a visual form. Most people find it easier to understand information presented as a simple diagram and at this stage this is the basic objective: to convey information about the data set easily, quickly and reasonably accurately.

We shall see, however, that whilst diagrams have the advantage in terms of immediate impact they suffer in that it is difficult to extract precise and accurate information from a diagrammatic representation of the data set.

It is impossible to provide any absolute guidelines as to the 'best' form of presenting numerical information. Much depends on the form and type of the data, for what reasons the analysis is being undertaken, who will see the results of the analysis and so on. It makes a considerable difference, for example, as to whether the tables/diagrams are simply for internal use in the organisation or whether they are for publication in the annual report to be distributed to shareholders. The question that must be asked is simply: does the table/diagram convey information in an understandable and reasonably accurate way? If the answer is 'yes' then that form of data presentation is serving its purpose.

If the answer is 'no' then an alternative method of presenting the same data must be sought by amending the presentation or trying another type of chart or diagram.

This construction of charts and diagrams through trial and error is both tedious and time consuming when performed by hand. Today, however, with the increasing availability of computer-based systems of data presentation it is relatively straightforward to examine the alternative methods quickly and easily and to choose whichever is felt to be most appropriate to the circumstances. Business spreadsheet packages such as Lotus 1–2–3 or SuperCalc, for example, offer a variety of graphical data presentation methods.

3.2 TABLE CONSTRUCTION

Constructing a table from a set of data is a straightforward process. Table 3.1 illustrates the main features of a tabular format. The table shows annual turnover of MTG Plc for the last five years.

A table like this contains a large amount of detailed information. Not only can we determine total turnover for the company for each of the last five years but we can also examine in detail the turnover figures for each sector of the company's operations. So, if we wished to

TABLE 3.1   **MTG Plc annual turnover 1983–87 by market sector**
(figures shown are in £m)

Year	1987	1986	1985	1984	1983
Sector					
Food	13.4	12.4	11.5	11.2	10.2
Clothing	87.6	79.0	71.5	63.2	56.1
Footwear	5.8	4.1	3.6	3.6	3.3
Furniture	23.6	22.9	21.5	21.2	20.4
Electrical goods	31.2	27.7	25.9	23.2	19.9
Total	161.6	146.1	134.0	122.4	109.9

Source: *Annual company reports*

compare the performance of the furniture sector with that of the electrical goods sector, for example, the Table contains all the relevant information.

By its very nature tabulation is extremely flexible. We could have presented the information contained in Table 3.1 in a variety of alternative ways. One frequently useful method is to include relevant percentage figures, as in Table 3.2.

TABLE 3.2   **MTG Plc annual turnover 1983–87 by market sector**
(Turnover figures shown are in £m. Percentage figures shown are as a percentage of total annual turnover.)

Year	1987		1986		1985		1984		1983	
Sector	£m	%	£m	%	£m	%	£m	%	£m	%
Food	13.4	8.3	12.4	8.5	11.5	8.6	11.2	9.2	10.2	9.3
Clothing	87.6	54.2	79.0	54.1	71.5	53.4	63.2	51.6	56.1	51.0
Footwear	5.8	3.6	4.1	2.8	3.6	2.7	3.6	2.9	3.3	3.0
Furniture	23.6	14.6	22.9	15.7	21.5	16.0	21.2	17.3	20.4	18.6
Electrical goods	31.2	19.3	27.7	18.9	25.9	19.3	23.2	19.0	19.9	18.1
Total	161.6		146.1		134.0		122.4		109.9	

Source: *Annual company reports*

It is evident from Table 3.2 that, used correctly, data presented in percentage form helps comparison and provides a quick reference particularly when the absolute figures vary considerably as in this case.

Whilst there are no strict rules about how such tables should be constructed, there are a number of points which should be noted:

1   You should have a clear idea of exactly what information you are trying to convey. The table must have a clear purpose otherwise there is no use showing it.
2   The table should have an explanatory title indicating the major features covered. The title should be brief but, at the same time, provide a reasonable description of the table's contents.
3   The table should clearly indicate the units of measurement of the data.

4   The table should clearly indicate the source of the data used.
5   Lines should be used where appropriate to divide the table into sections to aid legibility and use.
6   Where appropriate show row and column totals.
7   Finally, do not try to include too much information in a single table. It is better to use two simple tables rather than a single complex one.

In short, it is up to the person constructing the table to use their experience and judgment in order to present the data in a way that is clear, understandable and presentable.

However, data presented in the form of a table often fails to make an immediate impact on an audience. Simply, a table often contains too much information. Accordingly we may wish to present the same information in graphical form.

3.3 BAR CHARTS

A bar chart is one of the more common methods of presenting data graphically and can be used across a variety of areas and in a number of different forms:

> simple bar chart
> multiple bar chart
> component bar chart

3.3.1 Simple bar chart

A simple bar chart showing the data from Table 3.1 on total turnover is shown in Figure 3.1.

It is evident that, although the diagram is based on exactly the same data in Table 3.1, a more immediate impression is given. It is readily seen that the company's turnover has been rising steadily over the last five years. It should also be noted, however, that precise, detailed information cannot be obtained from the bar chart, for example, it is impossible to determine what the company's exact turnover in 1983 was. For this reason it is often advisable to provide an appropriate table to accompany the chart.

The construction of such a chart is straightforward. The vertical axis shows the appropriate scale for the variable under examination (turnover) and the height of the bar for each year represents the appropriate turnover figure. As with the construction of tables there are a number of points to note about the construction of such charts:

1   The vertical axis *must* be continuous and not broken as is frequently done on other forms of graphs. Such a broken axis makes it virtually impossible to assess the relative heights of the bars
2   The vertical scale chosen should make the best use of the space available
3   The widths of the bars should be the same
4   As with all presentations, titles, units of measurement etc must be clearly indicated
5   The bar chart could equally well show the data in percentage terms rather than in absolute terms
6   The chart could equally have been drawn with turnover on the horizontal scale and the bars shown horizontally rather than vertically.

3.3.2 Multiple bar chart

A multiple (or compound) bar chart is constructed along the same lines as the simple bar chart. Rather than showing *one* variable a multiple bar chart, as the name suggests, shows *several* to facilitate comparison. Assume that, rather than looking at Total Turnover over the five year period we wished to see the turnover for each sector of the company's operations. Such a multiple bar chart is shown in Figure 3.2.

Two features of the company's turnover are now immediately apparent from Figure 3.2:

B

FIGURE 3.1 **Simple bar chart**

MTG: Total annual turnover £m 1983–87

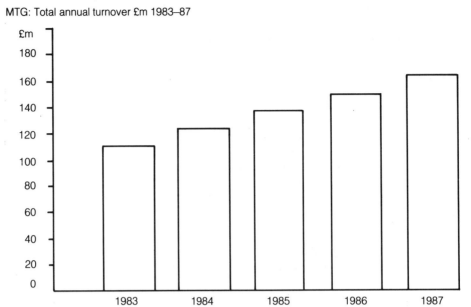

1 The clothing sector is by far the largest sector in the company's operations
2 Turnover in the various sectors has changed at different rates over this period. Footwear and food, for example, have altered relatively little since 1983. Electrical goods, on the other hand, has experienced a relatively rapid increase particularly when compared to the furniture sector.

FIGURE 3.2 **Multiple bar chart**

Annual turnover by sector £m 1983–87

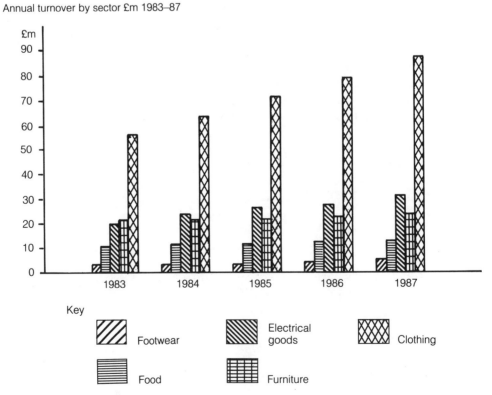

If you refer back to Table 3.1, which contained the data with which the multiple bar chart was constructed, you will realise that such patterns are far less obvious from the Table. Once again, as with the simple bar chart, we could have used percentage data rather than absolute figures to facilitate the comparison.

3.3.3 Component bar chart

The last variant of bar chart is the component bar chart where we show the various parts, or components, of some total figure in a single bar. Figure 3.3 shows such a chart for the data in Table 3.2.

This shows the percentage of total annual turnover contributed by each particular sector of the company's operations. Again, features which are not readily apparent from the original table become apparent, notably the decline in the furniture sector and the increase in the clothing sector contribution.

Figure 3.3 is a percentage component chart and, accordingly, the heights of all the bars are equal (as they must total 100%). It is also possible to construct such a chart using the actual turnover figures. In such a case the heights of the bars would not be the same but would relate to the change in total annual turnover as in Figure 3.4. Such diagrams are less useful than percentage charts because direct comparison between the various components becomes more difficult.

FIGURE 3.3 **Component bar chart**

Percentage of annual turnover by sector 1983–87

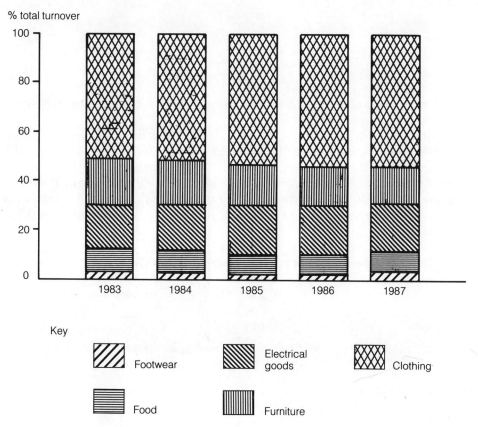

3.4 THE PIE CHART

As with the component bar chart the pie chart is used to show the various parts of a group of data. A circle is drawn to represent the total of the data and the circle is then divided into sections. Each section shows the relative importance of a particular part. Manual construction of

FIGURE 3.4   **Component bar chart**

Annual turnover by sector 1983–87

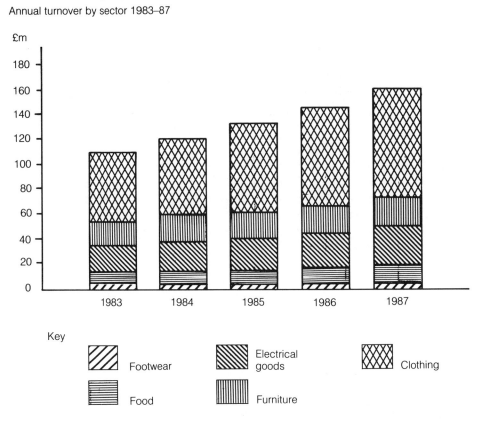

pie charts is both tedious and time consuming although it is a common feature of computer-based data presentation methods.

Let us assume that we wish to construct a pie chart to show the relative importance of each sector in total turnover for 1987. Given that there are a total of 360 degrees in a circle we have to present each sector's contribution to total turnover as a percentage of 360. From Table 3.2 we already have the percentage contribution of each sector to total turnover in 1987. Food, for example, represents 8.3% of total turnover so, in the pie chart would have a segment of 30 degrees (8.3% of 360 degrees). Similar calculations for the other sectors in the company would give the results shown in Table 3.3.

TABLE 3.3   **Sector turnover as a percentage of total turnover in 1987**

	% of total	Corresponding degrees
Food	8.3	30
Clothing	54.2	195
Footwear	3.6	13
Furniture	14.6	53
Electrical goods	19.3	69
Total	100	360

The resulting pie chart is shown in Figure 3.5.

FIGURE 3.5 **Pie chart**
1987 turnover by sector

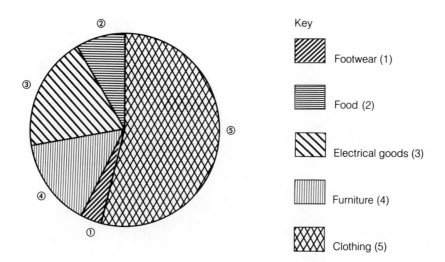

The use of pie charts in presenting such business information is widespread although their use from a practical viewpoint is limited. Not only are they difficult to construct they are also difficult to compare directly.

3.5 TIME SERIES GRAPHS

As the name suggests this is simply a graph of a variable (or variables) over a period of time. It is particularly useful for identifying trends in a variable over some period of time or for comparing two or more variables over the same period. In general, the horizontal axis will be used to show time and the vertical axis to show the variable in question. Frequently such graphs show two or more variables and both the left-hand and right-hand vertical axes are used. This is illustrated in Figure 3.6.

Two time series are shown on the same graph. The first shows the share price for MTG over this six-year period. The scale for the share price is shown on the left-hand axis and is measured in pence per share. The long-term movement in the share price is readily observed. The second series shows an index of the share prices of 10 of MTG's major competitors. (Index numbers are covered in more detail in a later chapter. For the present an index can be viewed as an average.) Because the units of measurement for this variable are different from the first variable we cannot show both scales on the same axis. Accordingly the scale for this variable is shown on the right-hand axis.

In this way two different but related variables can be shown on the same graph. Figure 3.6 allows us to compare relative movements in share prices between MTG and its major competitors. It can be seen that in 1983 and 1984 MTG's share price tended to perform badly compared with the competition. Since mid-1984 the share price has out-performed that of MTG's competitors. Both share prices were dramatically affected by the stock market crash at the end of 1987.

With careful use, such time series graphs can convey an immediate and dramatic impression of trends in the movement of variables but considerable care must be taken in their construction, particularly when using two different vertical axes.

Naturally, it is not always necessary to use two vertical axes if the time series variables to be plotted have the same units of measurement.

FIGURE 3.6 **Time series graph**

Comparison of share prices on the Stock Exchange:
MTG share price versus index of average share price of competitors

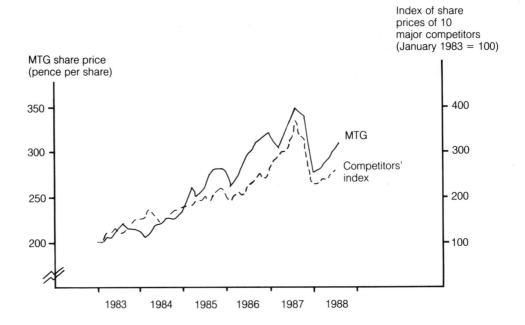

3.6 Z CHARTS

The final form of diagrammatic representation of data covered in this chapter is the Z chart. As we shall see the chart takes its name from the fact that the resulting diagram is in the shape of the letter Z. The chart is, in effect, a form of time series graph and is intended to be used and updated frequently in order to provide management with information about the progress of some variable. We shall illustrate its construction and use with a simple example. Assume that we are monitoring the monthly sales figures of a particular store in the MTG group. Relevant data are shown in Table 3.5.

TABLE 3.5 **Monthly sales of Store X (Figures are shown in £000s)**

Month	Sales 1986	Sales 1987	Moving total for last 12 months (for 1986 = 457)	Cumulative total for 1987
Jan	21	25	461	25
Feb	25	28	464	53
Mar	28	31	467	84
Apr	50	54	471	138
May	65	68	474	206
June	33	34	475	240
July	32	34	477	274
Aug	28	30	479	304
Sept	29	30	480	334
Oct	29	31	482	365
Nov	48	51	485	416
Dec	69	75	491	491

Source: *Company accounts*

The first column of figures shows monthly sales for 1986 whilst the second column shows equivalent data for 1987. The final column shows the cumulative total of monthly sales for the current year, 1987. The remaining column shows total sales for the last 12 months. The figure in the heading in this column (of 457) is total sales for Jan to Dec 1986. The next figure, 461, shows total sales for the 12 month period from Feb 1986 to Jan 1987. We methodically move through the data series with the value of 464 representing sales from Mar 1986 to Feb 1987 and so on through the rest of the column.

We now plot each of these three series, 1987 monthly sales, the moving total and the cumulative total, on one graph as in Figure 3.7.

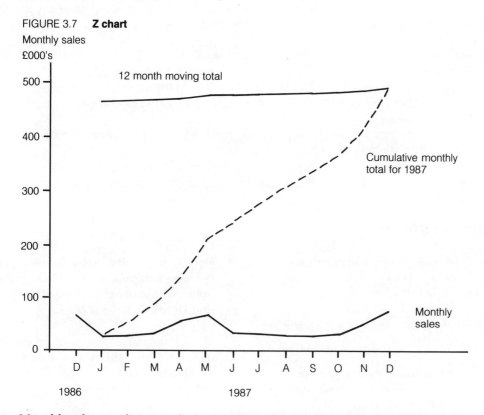

FIGURE 3.7   **Z chart**

Monthly sales are shown as the bottom line, the moving total as the top line and cumulative sales as the diagonal line (hence the Z shape and name). The diagram contains a large amount of useful management information.

The *monthly sales* can be easily monitored to identify any patterns in sales that occur. In the case of store X it is apparent that sales increase in April/May and again in November/December.

The twelve-month *moving total* allows us to compare directly performance this year with performance at the same time last year. A rising line indicates that monthly sales are increasing compared with the same period last year, whilst a downward sloping line would indicate a deteriorating performance. In the case of store X the line is gradually sloping upwards indicating a steady increase in this year's sales.

Finally, the *Cumulative Monthly Total* allows us to monitor progress to date. A common addition in business is to superimpose a line showing expected or targeted performance and comparison of the actual cumulative total with this line allows us to determine whether sales are meeting expectations.

Such a Z chart has many possible applications. It can be applied to the calendar year, as in this case, and to the financial year, on a monthly basis or on a weekly or daily basis as required.

One final point to note is that we would not normally draw a Z chart for the whole of one year as in this example. Rather, all three parts of the chart would be updated each month through the year as sales figures were recorded. The Z chart is, therefore, a diagram for operational use by management and not simply for description as with the other diagrams available.

SUMMARY

1   The purpose of both tabular and graphical methods of data presentation is to provide a clear, concise and reasonably accurate description of a data set.

2   Tables provide a considerable amount of detailed information but are frequently too complex to provide an immediate impression.

3   Bar charts are probably one of the most useful methods of graphical presentation. They are easy to construct and to interpret.

4   Bar charts offer a variety of alternative methods of presenting a data set. Simple bar charts are useful for looking at one variable, multiple bar charts for comparing several variables and component bar charts for illustrating the major elements making up a particular variable.

5   Pie charts are extremely common but are less useful in that it is difficult to extract accurate data from them and it is difficult to compare portions of different pie charts.

6   Time series graphs are useful for illustrating a long-term movement on one or more variables over some period of time. They are often useful when examining several related variables over the same period of time.

7   Z charts are useful to management in monitoring progress in some variable over a period of time (usually 12 months).

8   Care should be taken for all diagrammatic forms of representing data to ensure that definitions are clear and unambiguous and that scales used are not misleading.

SELF-TEST QUESTIONS

1   **What is the main purpose in constructing a diagram rather than showing data in a table?** (*Refer to page 19*)

2   **What are the three parts of a Z chart?** (*Refer to page 25*)

3   **Under what circumstances are percentages more useful in a table than the original figures?** (*Refer to page 18*)

4   **What are the disadvantages of a pie chart?** (*Refer to page 23*)

5   **When would it be better to use a time series graph rather than a bar chart?** (*Refer to page 23*)

6   **Why is it usually better to use a percentage component bar chart rather than a component bar chart of the original figures?** (*Refer to page 21*)

7   **What alternative diagrams could you use to show the total number of employees each year for the last 10 years?** (*Refer to pages 19 and 23*)

8   **What are the main items of information that should appear on every table or diagram?** (*Refer to page 18*)

9   **On which axis do you plot time on a time series graph?** (*Refer to page 23*)

10   **How do you work out the size of each section in a pie chart?** (*Refer to page 22*)

EXERCISES

1   Table 3.1 showed MTG's turnover by sector for the last five years. The figures below show the corresponding profit figures (all measured in £m) per sector for the same period.
Food 1987 £1.07m: Electrical goods 1985 £4.14m: Clothing 1983 £6.73m
Footwear 1987 £0.29m: Furniture 1986 £2.04m: Food 1984 £0.99m
Electrical goods 1987 £5.62m: Clothing 1987 £10.51m: Furniture 1983 £1.63m
Electrical goods 1986 £4.49m: Furniture 1987 £2.12m: Food 1986 £1.19m
Clothing 1986 £10.05m: Electrical Goods 1983 £2.39m: Food 1983 £1.02m
Food 1985 £1.01m: Clothing 1985 £8.19m: Footwear 1986 £0.24m

Furniture 1985 £1.81m: Electrical goods 1984 £3.29m: Clothing 1984 £7.98m
Footwear 1985 £0.19m: Furniture 1984 £1.72m: Footwear 1984 £0.21m
Footwear 1983 £0.20m

Required:
(a) Construct a suitable table to show profits per year per sector
(b) What comments can you make about any trends in profitability over this period?
(c) Construct a suitable table to show profit as a percentage of turnover per sector per year
(d) What trends are now apparent in profitability?
(e) Construct a simple bar chart to show total profit per year
(f) Construct suitable component bar charts for profit per year
(g) Construct a pie chart to show profit per sector for 1987 and for 1983

2 Following the Z chart illustrated in the chapter the following monthly sales figures have been obtained for Store X for 1988.

	Monthly sales £000s
Jan	27
Feb	29
Mar	35
Apr	59
May	73
Jun	36
Jul	37
Aug	33

Headquarters have set the store a sales target of £500,000 for 1988 (averaged over the 12 months at approximately £42,000 per month).

Required:
(a) Construct a suitable Z chart for the monthly sales recorded so far for 1988
(b) On the same chart draw a line showing cumulative monthly sales if the average monthly target of £42,000 is to be achieved
(c) You have been asked to advise the management of Store X as to whether the sales target is likely to be achieved by the end of 1988. Using last year's monthly sales as a guide decide whether you think the overall target will be achieved or not.

Answers on page 296.

Frequency tables and histograms

The methods of data presentation outlined in the previous chapter are frequently useful as a means of highlighting features of a data set. They are purely graphical and descriptive, however, and offer little opportunity for further *numerical* analysis. There are methods of data presentation which do provide opportunities for such quantitative analysis. The method of tabulating data into the form of a frequency table, the graphical presentation of such a table in the form of a histogram and the use of cumulative frequencies to begin the process of quantifying the key elements of a data set are detailed in this chapter.

4.1 FREQUENCY TABLES

Let us assume that, having seen the various results of presenting the annual company turnover data outlined in Chapter 3, MTG are undertaking further analysis into particular aspects of their operations. The manager of the food sector has decided to investigate the performance of certain of the stores currently in operation in order to compare their relative performance and has requested advice on how this can best be achieved. His objective is to determine which of the stores in the food sector are performing better or worse than average. Once this has been determined he will then be able to try to determine *why* such differences in performance exist.

Let us further assume that as a preliminary part of the project it has been decided to examine in detail the operations of two stores in different parts of the country, store A in the northern region and store B in the southern region have supplied details of their daily sales (measured in £s) for the last 100 days.

Table 4.1 shows gross daily sales for store A and Table 4.2 shows the equivalent data for store B. Put simply, what information that may be useful to management can be extracted from these data sets and what similarities and what differences can be determined from the data supplied?

TABLE 4.1   **Daily sales in £s for store A**

1298	1125	954	1582	1196	1066	1682	1167	1330	1296
1520	1752	1593	1677	943	1693	944	766	1123	1385
1898	1090	1173	1279	1451	751	1161	1018	842	1994
1390	955	1492	1285	1252	874	987	1350	875	1086
1446	1070	1286	866	1044	892	1475	1328	1377	1093
1085	902	974	807	1797	1289	1336	1452	1879	2088
1373	1193	1599	1177	1470	1492	1545	1106	1606	1064
1743	1541	854	1541	1265	1590	992	1394	1006	1186
1138	1294	1390	994	1035	1672	965	2094	1045	1078
908	1961	1296	1094	1176	1222	1066	1008	1484	1192

TABLE 4.2   **Daily sales in £s for store B**

1473	1653	1228	1378	1113	1530	1385	1330	1448	1158
1472	1288	1665	1025	1368	1210	1525	1208	1285	1153
1330	1333	1333	1155	1595	1125	1053	1310	1383	1648
1633	1308	1460	1533	1158	1398	1563	1105	1567	1365
1343	1263	1433	1438	1295	1310	1048	1518	1440	1385
1130	1405	1343	1463	1123	1305	1483	1448	1333	1515
1127	1213	1553	1325	1368	1275	1288	1608	1483	1475
1650	1078	1325	1423	1625	1035	1320	1303	1390	1240
1247	1263	1079	1180	1525	1343	1050	1250	1428	1325
1625	1405	1650	1378	1575	1258	1078	1225	1233	1425

It is apparent that the data in raw form are virtually useless. There is *too much* information in the tables to allow the key features to be readily identified or to allow any comparison between the performance of the two stores to be made. It must be reduced to a more manageable form and this can be achieved through appropriate statistical techniques. What is meant by 'statistics'? There are a variety of definitions, but for business decision-making an appropriate definition is *the analysis and interpretation of numerical information.*

There is thus a dual emphasis upon the *analysis* (the calculations themselves) and the *interpretation* of the results of the analysis. It is not sufficient simply to be able to work out the correct answer using a particular technique. It is also necessary to be able to assess and use the results produced in a way that is appropriate for the context of the problem under investigation, so the student must have an adequate understanding of the principles behind a particular calculation as well as the ability to perform the calculations themselves correctly. Without such an understanding the student will not be able to assess or determine the potential usefulness of such statistical calculations in business decision-making.

The first step in the process of identifying the key features of such a data set is to aggregate it: to present the raw data (like that in Tables 4.1 and 4.2) in a more compact form. This can be done by constructing a *frequency table*. The frequency table relating to the daily sales of Store A and Store B is shown in Table 4.3.

TABLE 4.3   **Daily sales for store A and store B**

Daily sales £s	Number of days	
	Store A	Store B
£700 < £800	2	0
£800 < £900	7	0
£900 < £1000	11	0
£1000 < £1100	16	8
£1100 < £1200	13	11
£1200 < £1300	11	17
£1300 < £1400	10	27
£1400 < £1500	8	17
£1500 < £1600	8	11
£1600 < £1700	5	9
£1700 < £1800	3	0
£1800 < £1900	2	0
£1900 < £2000	2	0
£2000 < £2100	2	0
Total frequency	100	100

The frequency table, which simply aggregates the original sales figures into broad groups or intervals, is both easy to construct and to interpret. A cursory examination of the table reveals that those daily sales which have similar values are grouped (or aggregated) together. So, for example, store A had daily sales of between £1000 and £1100 on a total of 16 days whilst Store B had only 8 days when sales fell into this particular interval.

This table allows us to begin the process of comparing and contrasting the two data sets. The key features that we can now determine from the frequency tables that were not apparent from the raw data are:

1   It is apparent that daily sales in store A are far more variable than in store B. The range of store B sales range only from (£1000<£1100) to (£1600<£1700) whilst store A's sales vary from between (£700<£800) and (£2000<£2100).

2   In both stores daily sales appear to cluster around certain values. In store A most of the frequencies are clustered around the £900 to £1300 range whilst in Store B around £1200 to £1500.

3   The clustering of observations in store B is around values that are generally higher than in store A.

In other words, a frequency table allows the identification of the key features of a data set. The construction of a frequency table is as straightforward as its interpretation:

STEP 1

From the raw data determine the range of values (minimum and maximum) with which we have to deal. This allows us to see the spread of data the table will have to deal with. Here, both the highest and lowest values are attributed to store A. The lowest sales figure is £751 and the highest £2094, so the table must allow for a range of approximately £1400.

STEP 2

Choose the number of intervals to be shown in the table. There is no hard and fast rule that can be applied here. We simply have to use whatever experience we have and, through trial and error, produce a table which looks most appropriate for the data. It is conventional to have between 5 and 15 intervals in such a table, with fewer intervals for small data sets than for large. If there are too few intervals then important details about the data set may be lost in the aggregation process. Conversely, with too many intervals the data will be insufficiently aggregated and because of the relatively small frequencies in most intervals no obvious patterns in the data will be apparent.

STEP 3

Decide how large each interval should be. In Table 4.3 our intervals are all £100. Obviously Steps 2 and 3 are related and we must choose interval sizes and the number of intervals together. This will often be a process of trial and error until a suitable table has been constructed. If possible, we should choose intervals which are all the same width as this makes the table easier to read and comparison of intervals is easier. It is not always possible, or desirable, to have equal classes and we shall see the effect of unequal classes later.

STEP 4

Ensure that the boundaries of the intervals are clear and unambiguous. In Table 4.3 the intervals are expressed so that there is no possible misunderstanding. A common mistake is to express intervals in the form:

£700 to £800
£800 to £900
£900 to £1000   and so on.

The problem is that when we come to aggregate the raw data we are uncertain whether to place an observation of, say, £800 in the first interval or the second. More importantly, other users of your analysis will be unclear as to how you have grouped the data and will have little confidence in the rest of your analysis.

STEP 5

Work through the data set, counting the frequency of data items in each interval.

As with any other sort of table we could show frequencies as a percentage of the total rather than as absolute figures. In this example there would be little purpose given that both data sets total 100 data items. In other instances, particularly when comparing data sets which may differ considerably in their totals, percentages are frequently more useful.

Frequency tables are useful in presenting an initial summary of the raw data. As with the general tables introduced in the last chapter a visual presentation can be more useful, however, as it allows us to identify trends and patterns in the data even more easily. Such a diagrammatic representation of a frequency table is known as a *histogram*.

4.2 HISTOGRAMS

Figure 4.1 shows the histogram for the data for store A in Table 4.3 and is obviously similar in construction to a bar chart. Here, each bar or rectangle represents a particular interval, and the height of each bar represents the frequency of that interval. As you can see, the histogram provides a clear and instant picture of the pattern of the variable.

FIGURE 4.1   **Daily sales (£s) store A**

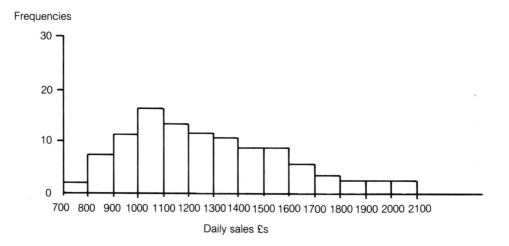

FIGURE 4.2 **Daily sales (£s) store B**

Frequencies

By comparing this with Figure 4.2, which is the histogram for the data relating to store B, we have a ready visual means of comparing data sets. The histogram for store A confirms that we have a considerable number of daily sales at the lower end of the scale, whilst that for store B indicates that sales are generally higher and more evenly-distributed than those in store A.

Drawing a histogram is as straightforward as drawing a bar chart and follows much the same procedure. The important point to remember is that we are aiming to present a quick, visual summary of the data that can be interpreted easily and accurately. The construction of histograms has no hard and fast rules and there are minor variations in terms of presentation.

One important difference is that data in a frequency table and histogram are usually regarded as being continuous so the individual bars in the histogram are joined together as opposed to being kept separate in a simple bar chart.

4.3 PROBLEMS OF CONSTRUCTING A HISTOGRAM

In general, there are only two aspects of histogram construction which may initially cause difficulties.

4.3.1 Open-ended intervals

These are intervals which have no upper (or lower) limit specified. In Table 4.3 assume that we had one interval where sales were defined as *less than* £800. Whilst this is not a problem in the frequency table, it does cause a problem when drawing the lower limit for the appropriate bar in the histogram.

Open-ended intervals are frequently encountered when using secondary data where a previous analyst has already grouped the data and the precise upper or lower limit of the range is not available. The simple solution is to choose an arbitrary, but realistic, limit. In this example, even if we did not already know the lowest daily sales figure was £751 it would be reasonable to assume a lower limit of £700 for this open-ended interval. This conveniently gives us an interval which has the same width (£100) as all the other intervals.

4.3.2 Unequal intervals

Earlier in the text it was stated that it was advisable to construct a frequency table with intervals that had the same width because intervals of unequal widths run the risk of giving a distorted view of the data distribution. In a bar chart all the bars have the same width so we are interested only in their height. In a histogram classes may also be of different, unequal widths so we need to compare not only the height of each bar but also its width. In other words, in a histogram we are comparing *area*.

A simple example will illustrate the problem that unequal intervals may cause. Table 4.4 shows a simple, illustrative frequency table and Figure 4.3 shows the associated histogram. There are four intervals of equal width and an obvious pattern in the data.

TABLE 4.4

Interval	Frequency
£100 < £200	40
£200 < £300	30
£300 < £400	20
£400 < £500	10
Total frequency	100

FIGURE 4.3

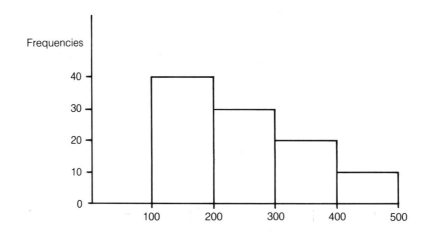

Let us now show the same data in different groupings. Table 4.5 shows the same frequencies, but the last two intervals have been grouped together into an interval which has twice the normal width.

TABLE 4.5

Interval	Frequency
£100 < £200	40
£200 < £300	30
£300 < £500	30
Total frequency	100

Figure 4.4 shows the histogram that we might, at first, construct for this frequency table.

FIGURE 4.4

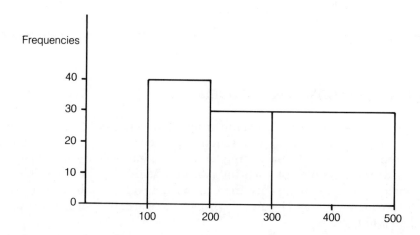

It is immediately apparent that Figure 4.4 gives a distorted picture with the last interval appearing more important than it actually is. This has occurred because no allowance has been made for the last interval which is now twice the usual width. What we are trying to show in a histogram is the relative frequency of each interval. If an interval is larger than usual we need to scale the frequency of that interval downward to bring it into line with our standard interval width and, conversely, if an interval were smaller than usual we would scale the frequency upwards. We do this by ensuring that the area of each of the bars in the histogram is proportional to the frequency and interval width. The area is calculated simply by the height × width.

So, in Table 4.5 the first interval has a frequency of 40 and a width of 100 and, therefore, an area of 4000 (40 × 100). The second interval has the same class width and a frequency of 30 so an area of 3000. The last interval has the same frequency as the second so must have the same area. But now the interval width is 200 we must adjust the height (frequency) to 15 to give an area of 3000 (15 × 20). Figure 4.5 shows the histogram with the last interval with an adjusted frequency of 15. As you can see, this produces a histogram which is somewhat fairer than Figure 4.4.

FIGURE 4.5

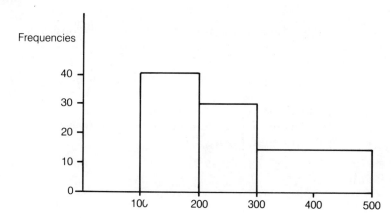

Effectively, we have scaled down the frequency of the unequal interval by a factor of *two* as the interval is *twice* the normal width. If the interval has been *three* times the normal width we would scale down the frequency by a factor of *three* and so on. Figure 4.5 is obviously still not as accurate a picture of the data as the original histogram, Figure 4.3, which reinforces the point that, even though they are easy to adjust, it is better not to use unequal intervals given the choice.

Histograms may also be constructed to show relative rather than absolute frequencies, that is, percentages or proportions. This may be more useful if we wish to compare two or more different histograms where the absolute frequencies may differ. We might have one set of data with, say, 500 observations and another with 5000. Relative frequencies allow us to compare the two distributions directly.

4.4   FREQUENCY POLYGONS AND FREQUENCY CURVES

A frequency table can also be shown diagrammatically using a frequency polygon rather than a histogram. Instead of drawing bars to represent the frequency of a particular interval a single point is used to represent the appropriate frequency. If the intervals are all the same width this point is plotted at the midpoint of each interval and at the height corresponding to the particular frequency. The midpoints are then connected with straight lines to produce the polygon. Such a frequency polygon frequently provides a clearer overall picture of the distribution of data than a histogram.

FIGURE 4.6   **Daily sales**

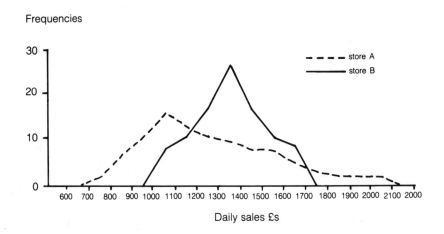

This is illustrated in Figure 4.6 which shows the frequency polygons for store A and store B. Note that the frequency polygon is connected to the horizontal axis. This is achieved by finding the midpoint for the interval preceding that in the frequency table and the midpoint for that following. So for store A the frequency polygon starts from the horizontal axis at 650 (the midpoint of the interval 600<700, which precedes the first actual interval in the table) and finishes at 2150 (the midpoint of the interval 2100<2200).

Occasionally, it may also be useful to convert the frequency *polygon* into a frequency *curve*. Such a frequency curve is illustrated in Figure 4.7.

FIGURE 4.7 **Daily sales**

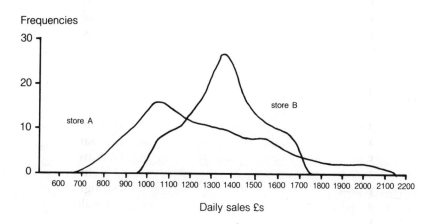

Daily sales £s

The frequency curve is drawn through the same midpoints as the frequency polygon but the lines joining the points are now smoothed rather than straight. The reason behind this is the fact that, frequently, the data in a frequency polygon represents *sample* data and smoothing the polygon may give a more realistic overall picture of the distribution of the statistical population from which the sample data have been taken.

4.5 CUMULATIVE FREQUENCIES AND OGIVES

It is also often useful to present the frequency table in a different way altogether, in the form of a diagram showing cumulative frequencies. This diagram is known as an *ogive*. Such a presentation is useful when we wish to ascertain the number of observations falling below (or above) a certain limit. For example, in our data set relating to store A's daily sales we might wish to ascertain the number of days when sales fell below, say, £1000. Whilst this is easy to identify directly from the frequency table there may be other values we are interested in, say, £1250 which cannot easily be identified from the table. The figure of £1250 may represent, for example, a sales target set by management who wish to determine how often the target is reached and how often it is not. Such information can easily be estimated from the ogive. Table 4.6 shows both the frequencies and the cumulative frequencies: that is, the number of observations up to and including that interval.

TABLE 4.6   **Daily sales for store A and store B**

Daily sales £s	Store A	Cumulative	Store B	Cumulative
£700 < £800	2	2	0	0
£800 < £900	7	9	0	0
£900 < £1000	11	20	0	0
£1000 < £1100	16	36	8	8
£1100 < £1200	13	49	11	19
£1200 < £1300	11	60	17	36
£1300 < £1400	10	70	27	63
£1400 < £1500	8	78	17	80
£1500 < £1600	8	86	11	91
£1600 < £1700	5	91	9	100
£1700 < £1800	3	94	0	100
£1800 < £1900	2	96	0	100
£1900 < £2000	2	98	0	100
£2000 < £2100	2	100	0	100
Total frequency	100		100	

Although we can see that, for store A, there are 20 days when sales were below £1000, the number of days when sales were less than £1250 is less obvious as this figure does not conveniently coincide with any of the interval groupings. But Figure 4.8 shows the cumulative frequencies used to construct the ogive.

FIGURE 4.8   **Daily sales (£s) store A**

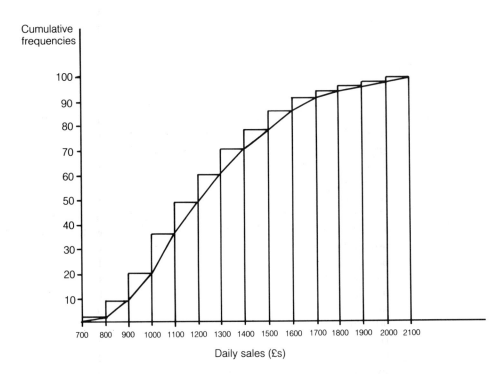

On the diagram the ogive is shown by joining the endpoints of the intervals together with straight lines. The more usual way of showing the ogive is, in fact, without the usual histogram bars and simply by joining the endpoints together as in Figure 4.9 which also shows the appropriate ogive for store B.

FIGURE 4.9   **Daily sales (£s) store A and store B**

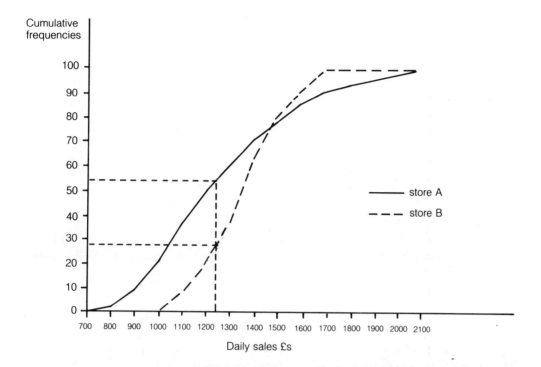

From the ogive we can estimate the number of observations falling below (or indeed above) a particular value. In this case, we can see that there are approximately 54 days when daily sales in store A were below £1250 (and obviously 46 days when sales were above this level). For store B it can be seen from the ogive that the comparable figures were 28 days when sales were below £1250 and 72 when they were above.

4.6   PERCENTILES, DECILES AND QUARTILES

Ogives may also be constructed to show relative or percentage frequencies in the same way as histograms. In such a case the ogive would show the percentage of observations falling *below* a specified value. Such ogives are frequently useful when comparing two or more data sets where the total frequencies differ. Again, in our example, there is no advantage in constructing such ogives as both data sets total to 100 in any case.

To illustrate the concept and use of percentiles, however, let us assume that Figure 4.9 shows the appropriate percentage ogives. Rather than find the frequency associated with a specific sales figure (as in the example in the last section) we may instead wish to determine the sales figure associated with a specific percentage value. For example, we have been asked to determine what sales figure represents the lowest 10% of observations. From the percentage ogive we would identify 10% on the vertical scale and determine that for store A the appropriate sales figure was approximately £915 and for store B approximately £1120. In other words, 10% of the time daily sales in store A are at or below £915 whereas in store B the equivalent sales figure is some £200 higher.

Such a figure (corresponding to 10%) is known as a *decile* and represents the division of the data into ten equal parts with the other deciles corresponding to 20%, 30%, 40% etc.

Frequently, we may wish to divide the data into four equal parts known as the quartiles which would correspond to 25%, 50%, 75%.

Less frequently we may wish to divide the data into 100 equal parts known as the percentiles.

All these values can be determined from the percentage ogive.

4.7   LORENZ CURVES

The final form of graphical presentation presented in this chapter is the Lorenz curve (some-times known as the Pareto curve). Such a curve is very similar to the ogive in that it uses a form of cumulative frequency (in this case it uses cumulative percentage frequencies) and is frequently used to examine the concentration of values in part of the data set. Typically, the Lorenz curve is used to examine income distribution where a relatively small number of individuals hold a large proportion of the income or wealth available. Conversely, the majority of the group will typically hold a disproportionately small part of the total income or wealth.

In business, however, Lorenz curves are potentially useful in a variety of applications including:

> stock control
> turnover/sales amongst individual outlets
> distribution of employees between departments
> distribution of wages and salaries

To illustrate the construction and use of Lorenz curves let us assume that MTG have collected data on the annual turnover last year for 200 of the stores in the group. The relevant data is shown in Table 4.7.

TABLE 4.7   **Annual turnover for 1987 for 200 stores in the group**
(Figures are in £000s)

Turnover	No of Stores
less than £320	52
£320 < £340	28
£340 < £360	22
£360 < £380	20
£380 < £400	18
£400 < £420	16
£420 < £440	14
£440 < £460	12
£460 < £480	10
£480 or more	8
Total	200

Source: *Accounts Department*

Typically, we may wish to examine the distribution of turnover amongst the 200 stores. It is apparent (and we could confirm this with the usual histogram or ogive) that the stores are not evenly distributed between the turnover intervals. It is apparent that a relatively small number of stores are of considerable importance to the group in terms of turnover as their turnover levels are particularly high. To identify the specific distribution of turnover amongst the 200 stores, however, it is necessary to construct a Lorenz curve. Such a curve will be drawn on the graph shown in Figure 4.10.

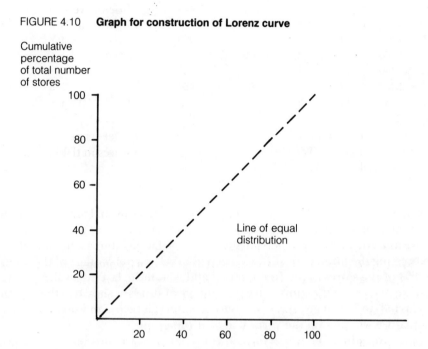

FIGURE 4.10   **Graph for construction of Lorenz curve**

On the vertical axis we shall show the cumulative percentage of the number of stores and on the horizontal axis the cumulative percentage of total turnover associated with those stores. The line that has been drawn on the graph is a reference line known as the *line of equal distribution*. It joins together all the points where the cumulative percentage of stores and turnover are equal. Thus, if 20% of the stores earned 20% of turnover, 40% of stores earned 40% of turnover, 60% of stores earned 60% of turnover and so on then all these points would fall on this line.

If the *actual* line that we are about to construct differs from the line of equal distribution this will indicate an unequal distribution of turnover amongst the 200 stores in the data set. Furthermore, the further away the actual line from this reference line the more unequal the distribution is.

The construction of the Lorenz curve is straightforward and the necessary calculations are shown in Table 4.8.

TABLE 4.8 **Construction of a Lorenz curve**

(Figures are in £000s)

Turnover	No of stores	%	Cumulative %	Interval midpoint	Frequency × midpoint	%	Cumulative %
£200 < £320	52	26	26	260	13,520	18.7	18.7
£320 < £340	28	14	40	330	9,240	12.7	31.4
£340 < £360	22	11	51	350	7,700	10.6	42.0
£360 < £380	20	10	61	370	7,400	10.2	52.2
£380 < £400	18	9	70	390	7,020	9.7	61.9
£400 < £420	16	8	78	410	6,560	9.1	71.0
£420 < £440	14	7	85	430	6,020	8.3	79.3
£440 < £460	12	6	91	450	5,400	7.5	86.8
£460 < £480	10	5	96	470	4,700	6.4	93.2
£480 < £750	8	4	100	615	4,920	6.8	100.0
Total	200	100			72,480	100	

To begin with we must close the two open-ended intervals in Table 4.7. We shall assume that the first interval is £200<£320 and the top interval is £480<£750.

Next we must determine the percentage of stores that fall into each interval. This is easily done by expressing the number of stores in each interval as a percentage of the total, 200. Thus there are 26% of the stores in the first interval and 4% in the last interval.

Third, we determine the cumulative percentage of stores as shown in the fourth column in the table. This tells us how many stores fall into the intervals below and up to that point. It is this set of data that we will plot on the vertical axis of the graph.

The same procedure is now performed for turnover—we must express turnover in each interval as a percentage of total turnover for the 200 stores. Because we are dealing with aggregated data we must use the midpoint of each interval as an approximation of the actual turnover for each group of stores. These midpoint values are shown in column 5. To estimate turnover in each group we then multiply the midpoint by the frequency. For the first group this will be £260×52, giving £13,520. The same calculation is performed on each interval. Adding these values together gives a total of £72,480 which is the estimate of total turnover of all 200 stores.

We can now express turnover in each interval as a percentage of the total turnover. This is shown in column 7.

Finally, we can calculate the cumulative percentage turnover shown in column 8.

The data in column 8 will be plotted on the horizontal axis of the graph.

Before we plot the Lorenz curve itself it will be worthwhile ensuring that the figures in the table are properly understood. To illustrate, we can see, for example, that 26% of the stores fall into the first interval (column 3). These stores, however, contribute only 18.7% of the total turnover (column 7). Conversely, the last interval contains only 4% of the stores but these contribute proportionately more to turnover, 6.8%. All the relevant information can be plotted on the graph, as shown in Figure 4.11.

FIGURE 4.11   **Lorenz curve for annual turnover**

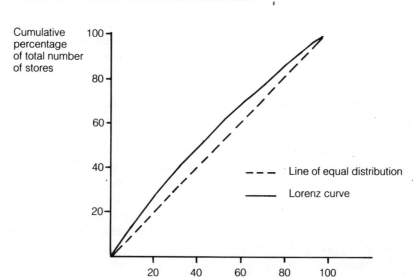

Cumulative percentage of total turnover

The diagram confirms the view that the distribution of turnover between the 200 stores is not equal. Effective use of the Lorenz curve could be made in a number of ways:

1   Having established that certain stores are more important contributors to total turnover future investment might be directed towards these stores rather than those which underperform.
2   The group may wish to bring in more effective managers into those stores which are under-performing.
3   By constructing a series of Lorenz curves over a period of years management can determine whether the gap between stores is getting larger or smaller.

SUMMARY

1   Frequency tables are a useful means of aggregating a mass of raw data. Such tables are relatively straightforward to construct and easy to interpret. Percentage frequency tables are particularly useful when dealing with data sets of unequal sizes
2   A histogram is a graphical representation of a frequency table and is constructed along the same lines as a simple bar chart. Care must be taken when dealing with unequal intervals to ensure the areas of intervals are comparable
3   An ogive shows cumulative frequencies graphically and is particularly useful for identifying specific percentile values of the distribution
4   Deciles, quartiles and percentiles break the distribution into equal parts
5   A frequency polygon is constructed from the histogram and may show more clearly the shape of the distribution
6   A frequency curve is a smoothed frequency polygon and the smoothing helps remove gaps in the data due to sampling
7   A Lorenz curve shows the distribution of a variable within the data set.

SELF-TEST QUESTIONS

1 Approximately how many intervals should a frequency table contain? (*Refer to page 31*)

2 What are the two main problems encountered when constructing frequency tables? (*Refer to page 33*)

3 What does the line of equal distribution show in a Lorenz curve? (*Refer to page 41*)

4 What is an ogive? (*Refer to page 37*)

5 Into how many parts do the quartiles divide the distribution? (*Refer to page 39*)

6 What is the difference between a histogram, a frequency polygon and a frequency curve? (*Refer to page 36*)

7 Under what circumstances would it be better to show a histogram in percentage terms rather than in absolute frequencies? (*Refer to page 36*)

8 Which diagram would use the midpoints: an ogive or a frequency polygon? (*Refer to page 36*)

9 What is the purpose of a Lorenz curve? (*Refer to page 40*)

10 How are unequal intervals treated when constructing a histogram? (*Refer to page 33*)

EXERCISES

1 MTG is currently undertaking negotiations with a trade union representing the sales staff who work in the group's stores throughout the country. The trade union is submitting a claim for increased wages for the sales staff and is basing part of its argument around the fact that clerical and administrative staff in the group are much better paid than the sales staff and that this differential should be reduced by giving the sales staff a pay increase.

   The head of the accounts department has taken two samples of data from the payroll file held on the computer at head office. In both cases the sample was of 50 employees and shows their typical weekly salary.

TABLE 1a **Weekly salary of 50 clerical/admin staff, measured in £s**

119.00	184.82	146.41	137.22	190.42
147.60	134.40	153.58	164.40	98.80
153.60	151.62	140.82	147.21	98.80
123.60	144.86	118.80	137.93	92.41
118.40	158.00	166.50	136.00	104.81
129.62	111.20	101.22	187.62	154.00
140.29	172.71	161.62	124.02	155.62
152.42	173.22	101.20	130.82	176.82
139.62	166.82	164.82	122.82	128.40
160.71	172.00	150.82	145.43	148.42

TABLE 1b **Weekly salary of 50 sales staff, measured in £s**

100.29	123.58	117.22	90.42	106.82
119.62	140.82	94.40	126.00	138.00
116.71	98.80	97.21	98.80	145.60
114.40	96.55	137.93	88.88	128.40
121.62	101.22	136.00	92.41	108.41
104.86	161.62	124.02	104.81	88.81
128.00	101.20	130.82	154.00	95.61
111.20	83.62	133.60	155.62	106.81
116.82	164.82	122.82	152.41	103.21
106.41	110.82	145.43	115.38	148.42

Required:

(a) Using the data in the above tables construct suitable frequency tables for the two sets of data

(b) Draw a histogram for each frequency table

(c) Construct a frequency polygon for each histogram

(d) Using the frequency tables, histograms and frequency polygons, as appropriate, compare the two distributions for similarities and differences.

(e) Do you think the trades union is correct to argue that sales staff are paid less than clerical/admin staff?

2 Using the data as in 1 above, construct suitable ogives for the two distributions.

(a) What proportion of sales staff earn less than £100 per week?

(b) What is the corresponding proportion of clerical/admin staff?

(c) What does a comparison of these two percentages reveal about the comparative pay levels of the two groups?

(d) What proportion of sales staff earn more than £175 per week?

(e) What is the corresponding figure for clerical/admin staff?

Answers on page 299.

Averages

In the previous two chapters we have seen how data can be summarised, presented and described in the form of simple tables or diagrams. In this chapter we introduce the first forms of **numerical** analysis that can be applied to such data. One of the first calculations we would normally wish to carry out is to determine a typical, or average, value for the data set. In the example of the last two chapters we may wish to determine and then compare, average daily sales in store A and store B. There are three common measures of average or 'central tendency' as statisticians refer to these statistics. These are the arithmetic mean, the median and the mode.

5.1   ARITHMETIC MEAN

The mean of the data set is simply the sum of all the values divided by the number of items in the data set. In the example of daily sales, to calculate the arithmetic mean of the raw data for store A we would simply add together all the observations we have for daily sales and divide through by 100, the number of observations in the set.

$$\frac{\text{Total of values}}{\text{Number of values}} = \frac{£127{,}630}{100} = £1{,}276.30$$

Thus, the mean daily sales for store A is £1276.30. In general, the formula for calculating the arithmetic mean is:

$$\frac{\Sigma x}{n}$$

where Σx refers to the sum of the values and n to the number of values. The formula simply states that the arithmetic mean is the sum of the x values divided by n. In the context of the application here, we have totalled all the individual sales figures (to get £127,630) and averaged these over the 100 days when they were collected.

5.1.1   Arithmetic mean for aggregated data

In the example above we used the *raw* data to calculate the mean. As has been indicated previously, we do not always have access to the individual values. Often we have only the aggregated data in the form of a frequency table but we are still able to calculate the mean value, although the method of calculation is different. The reason for this becomes apparent if we examine Table 5.1.

TABLE 5.1   **Daily sales for store A**

Daily sales £s	Number of days store A	Midpoint	Midpoint × Frequency
£700 < £800	2	750	1500
£800 < £900	7	850	5950
£900 < £1000	11	950	10450
£1000 < £1100	16	1050	16800
£1100 < £1200	13	1150	14950
£1200 < £1300	11	1250	13750
£1300 < £1400	10	1350	13500
£1400 < £1500	8	1450	11600
£1500 < £1600	8	1550	12400
£1600 < £1700	5	1650	8250
£1700 < £1800	3	1750	5250
£1800 < £1900	2	1850	3700
£1900 < £2000	2	1950	3900
£2000 < £2100	2	2050	4100
Total	100		126100

The table shows the frequency table for the data set we have been analysing. The difficulty in calculating the mean from this grouped data arises because we need to add the individual values (sales) together. The problem is that we no longer know what these individual values are because they have been grouped. We know, for example, that for store A there are 10 days when sales were between £1,300 and £1,400, but without the raw data we do not know precisely how much each day's sales were. To resolve the problem we make a simplifying assumption—that all items in a particular interval have the same value and that this value is in the middle of the interval (referred to as the midpoint). So, for this interval in the table we assume that all 10 days had sales of £1,350. The arithmetic mean can now be calculated, as before, by adding all the values together and dividing by the number of values. This can be simplified to the formula:

$$\frac{\Sigma fx}{\Sigma f}$$

where x refers to the midpoint of each individual and f to the frequency of each interval. The term Σfx is simply the total of the values in a particular interval, assuming they all have the midpoint value. Table 5.1 shows the appropriate calculations. The mean is calculated as:

$$\text{Mean} = \frac{£126100}{100} = £1261.00$$

As can be seen, the mean on the basis of the grouped data gives a slightly different value from that based on the raw data. This is hardly surprising as we had to make a simplifying assumption about values within each interval in order to be able to calculate this average. It is apparent that the mean calculated from the raw data will be more accurate than that calculated from grouped data and if only grouped data are available we should use the grouped mean with caution.

Two additional points about the grouped mean to note are:

1   It will be influenced by the intervals, and therefore the midpoints, that have been chosen. A different choice of intervals will tend to lead to a slightly different mean value.
2   It will be influenced by any assumptions made about any open-ended intervals in the frequency table. Different assumptions will lead to a different calculated value for the mean.

5.2   MEDIAN

The arithmetic mean is easy to calculate and interpret. In the context of the data set, it represents average sales in the sense that it would be the daily sales in store A if sales were the same each day. Unfortunately, the mean may not always give a realistic picture of the values in the data set. That is, the mean may not actually reflect the *typical* sales level.

A simple example will illustrate this important point. Suppose we have a smaller data set of 11 observations representing, say, the annual salaries of those employees working in store A. Table 5.2 shows the data values.

TABLE 5.2   **Annual salaries of employees in store A, in £s**

| 5000 | 5000 | 5000 | 5000 | 5000 | 8000 | 8500 | 8500 | 8500 | 8500 | 35000 |

It can be seen that there are effectively three groups of employees, perhaps junior staff with a salary of £5,000, senior staff with a salary of £8,000–8,500 and the store manager with a salary of £35,000.

The mean for this data set would be:

$$\frac{102000}{11} = £9,272.73 = £9,273 \text{ (rounded)}$$

However, as we can see, this average value is by no means typical or representative. No-one, in fact, actually earns a salary of £9,273. Indeed, only one salary lies above the mean, with the others falling below the average. It is obvious that the mean has been distorted by the one extremely high value. For this reason it is often useful to have an alternative statistic to the mean to represent the average where the mean may not be typical of the bulk of the data set. This alternative statistic is the *median*.

The median is another statistic which measures the average. It is the middle value in the ordered data set, that is, a value such that there is an equal number of values above the median as below. Unlike the mean, the median always splits the ordered set of data into two equal parts. In Table 5.2 the median *item* can be identified by:

$$\frac{\text{Total number of values} + 1}{2} = \frac{11 + 1}{2} = \frac{12}{2} = 6$$

The item in the middle of the data set is item 6. The data set is already ordered from low to high so we can simply count along until we get to item 6, which has a value of £8,000. This is the median *value* and its interpretation is straightforward: the median indicates that there are the same number of observations below the median as above. There are five people with a salary lower than the median and five people with a salary higher. The median *always* divides a data set into two equal parts in this way and this is a particularly useful feature.

In general, the steps for determining the median value in a raw data set are:

1   Order the data from lowest to highest
2   Determine which data item is the median item using the formula:

$$\frac{n+1}{2}$$

3   Count along the data set until this item number is reached. This number is then the median value.

We could calculate the median for our major data set relating to daily sales in store A in the same way. Given that there are 100 observations it would obviously take a little longer if we were to sort the data manually but if we were to do so we would find that the median for the raw data is £1,237. That is, half the time daily sales are below £1,237 and half the time they are above. We shall see shortly how the median and mean can be used together to reveal features of the data set.

One point to note at this stage is that when dealing with a data set containing an *even* number of items we must exercise a little more care in determining the median item. If we calculate (n + 1)/2 for store A this gives the result 50.5. Naturally there is no such item. Accordingly, to determine the median value we would take each item on either side (that is, item 50 and item 51) and average them. This would then represent the median value.

5.2.1 Calculating the median from aggregated data

We do not always have access to the raw data and we may need to calculate the median for grouped data. Again, we must remember that in such a case the value we obtain will only be an estimate of the true median value. Let us calculate the median for the data on daily sales for store A, shown in Table 5.3, together with the cumulative frequencies.

TABLE 5.3   **Daily sales for Store A**

Daily sales £s	Number of days store A	Cumulative Frequency
£700 < £800	2	2
£800 < £900	7	9
£900 < £1000	11	20
£1000 < £1100	16	36
£1100 < £1200	13	49
£1200 < £1300	11	60
£1300 < £1400	10	70
£1400 < £1500	8	78
£1500 < £1600	8	86
£1600 < £1700	5	91
£1700 < £1800	3	94
£1800 < £1900	2	96
£1900 < £2000	2	98
£2000 < £2100	2	100
Total	100	

First, we must identify the interval in which the median item falls.

Remembering that the median item will be item 50.5 we can see from the cumulative frequencies that this will fall in the interval £1,200<£1,300. (This can be easily determined from the cumulative frequency column. There are 49 observations up to £1,200 and 11 observations in the next interval £1,200<£1,300, so the median item must fall in this interval.) So, we know that the median item is one of the 11 values falling in this interval, but we do not know which one. Without the raw data we have no way of knowing and, as with the grouped mean, we must make a simplifying assumption as to how the data within this interval is distributed. We assume that the 11 values occurring in the interval are spread equally over the width of the interval, that is, they are spaced an equal distance apart over the £100 that the interval covers. Each value is £9.09 (ie 100/11) away from its neighbours within the interval. Since we are looking for item number 50.5 and since there are 49 items up to the start of this interval, item 50.5 will be 1.5 items from the start of the interval. Each value we assume to be £9.09 apart so the median item will have a value of £1213.64 (£1200 + (1.5 × £9.09)). This simplifies into the formula:

$$\text{Median value} = \text{LCV} + (\text{MI} - \text{CF}) \times \frac{\text{W}}{\text{F}}$$

where:
LCV is the lower class limit of the median interval
MI   is the median item
CF   is the cumulative frequency up to the median interval
W   is the width of the median interval
F   is the frequency of the median interval

For our data set we would have:

$$\text{Median} = 1200 + (50.5 - 49) \times \frac{1000}{11}$$

$$\text{giving } 1200 + (1.5 \times 9.09) = 1213.64$$

Note that as with the mean there is a slight arithmetic difference between the median for the grouped data and that for the raw data.

5.2.2 Estimating the median graphically

As well as calculating a value for the median of an aggregated data set it is also possible to estimate the median value from the appropriate ogive. Figure 5.1 shows the appropriate percentage ogive for store A.

FIGURE 5.1   **Estimating the median for daily sales of store A (£s)**

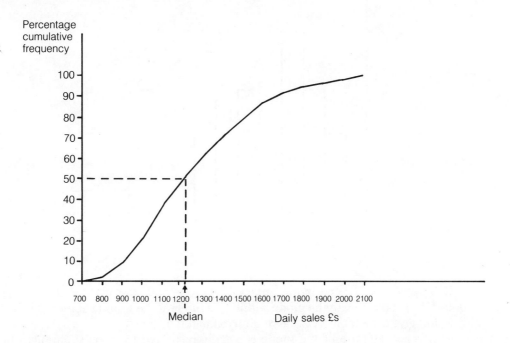

(Note that in this case there is no difference between the ogive of cumulative frequencies and the percentage ogive as the data set totals to 100. In practice, however, it is usually better to use the percentage ogive to estimate the median value.)

When estimating the median we know that the median is the middle item. This actually corresponds to the middle quartile (at the 50% position on the percentage cumulative frequency axis). A line from this point to the ogive curve and down to the sales value axis provides an estimate of the median at approximately £1,210. Again, it should be noted that estimating the median from the ogive graph will be inaccurate because of the limitations of the scales on the graph. It is preferable to calculate the median using the appropriate formula.

c

5.3   MODE

The third measure of average is the mode. Though employed relatively infrequently it is nevertheless a useful measure of central tendency in certain situations. The mode is simply the value that occurs most often in a data set. Returning to Table 5.2, the modal salary would be £5,000 and as such represents the salary value that occurs most frequently in the data set. In this context it would represent the salary that most people earn.

As an average the mode must be used with caution and in conjunction with other known features of the data set under examination. By itself, the mode provides no clear indication of other values in the data set. Although in this example there are five salaries of £5,000 there are almost as many salaries at £8,500 but the mode does not reveal this.

5.3.1   Estimating the mode graphically

For some data sets deriving the mode simply by counting the most common value in the data set may not be practical. Returning to daily sales in store A it is unlikely that any one sales figure will appear more than a small number of times. Instead we can estimate a mode from the histogram. The method is shown in Figure 5.2.

FIGURE 5.2   **Daily sales store A**

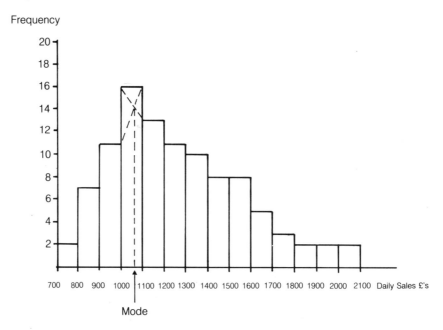

It is apparent that the modal interval (the one with the highest frequency) is that of £1,000–1,100. To estimate the mode within this interval the graphical method shown is used. This would give an estimated value of approximately £1,060.

In practice, the use of the mode is usually restricted to those situations where we are examining a discrete variable (that is, one which takes only certain fixed values). If, for example, we wished to determine the average number of children each married couple had it would be sensible to use the mode rather than to calculate the mean or median as the latter would be likely to give non-discrete results. Although the mode can be estimated for continuous data its use and meaning is limited.

5.4   CHOOSING A MEASURE OF AVERAGE

The obvious question which arises is, 'which measure of average should be used?' The answer, as always with statistics, is that it depends. All three have their particular uses and disadvantages, and the only effective answer is to consider carefully which characteristic of the data set you are interested in describing.

The *mean* is the most commonly used statistic, if only because it is the only one which uses all the data set in its calculation. This is essential if we are to undertake further numerical analysis on the full set of data. The mean, however, is easily distorted by relatively few extreme values.

The *median* is more representative in this context and provides more information about the spread of values in the data set, although it does not use a large part of the data set which can be a major disadvantage.

The *mode* tends to be useful in fairly limited circumstances, mostly when dealing with discrete data.

To illustrate the information that can be obtained from these averages let us turn to Table 5.4.

TABLE 5.4   **Comparison of averages for store A and store B**

	Store A	*Store B*
Mean	£1261.00	£1353.00
Median	£1213.64	£1353.70
Mode	£1060	£1350

Note:

1   The mean and median values have been calculated from the relevant frequency tables.
2   The mode values have been estimated from the relevant histograms.

The table shows the relevant averages for the two stores. What do these statistics reveal about differences and similarities between daily sales in the two stores?

First, *all* the averages for store B are higher than the corresponding figures for store A. Whichever statistic we wish to use we can say that, on average, sales in store B are higher than in store A. Such a statement must be interpreted with care, however. As we can confirm from the original data or from the histogram this does not mean that sales are higher in store B *every* day but simply over a period of time. We would also need to be cautious about using such information to project forward into the future. Just because average sales in store B have been higher in the past is not necessarily a guarantee that they will continue to be higher in the future.

Second, the median sales values can be used to compare relative performance in a more general way. In store A we can state that 50% of daily sales are above £1,213.64. In store B the equivalent median value is higher at £1,353.70. Not only does store B outperform store A in terms of mean sales but also in terms of the median sales.

Third, for store B the mean and median are virtually the same. For store A, however, there is a difference of some £50. Why should this be so and what are the statistical implications of such a difference? We have seen that the mean is easily distorted by a relatively small number of abnormally high (or low) values in a data set, whereas the median is concerned only with the middle of the data set and will thus be relatively unaffected by such extreme values. Given that the mean and median are virtually equal in store B this indicates that the distribution of the data is relatively symmetrical with few, if any, extreme values. In store A, however, the gap between the two statistics indicates that there are some extreme values pulling the mean away from the middle of the data set. Moreover, given that the mean is above the median, these extreme values must be at the high (rather than low) end of the scale. This, naturally, can be confirmed from the relevant histograms for the sales data.

SUMMARY

Statistics allow us to begin the process of describing a data set without having to resort to the raw data, the frequency table or the histogram. With these statistics alone we can identify many of the key features of a data set.

1   There are three common measures of average, the arithmetic mean, the median and the mode.
2   The statistics can be calculated from the raw data, the frequency table or histogram. Statistics based on the raw data are more accurate than those based on grouped data.
3   The mean is found by averaging the sum total of the numbers in the data set over the number of items.
4   The mean is easily distorted by a few extreme values in the data set which will make it unrepresentative of the majority of data items.
5   The mean has the advantage of using all the data items in the set.
6   The median is the item in the middle of the ordered data set. There is always an equal number of items above the median as below.
7   The median is particularly useful in data sets where the mean may not represent a typical value.
8   The mode represents the value occurring most frequently. It is typically used in data sets consisting of discrete values.

SELF-TEST QUESTIONS

1   Why are statistics based on the raw data more accurate than those based on aggregated data? (*Refer to page 48*)

2   Why will the calculation of the mean be affected by open-ended intervals whilst the median will not? (*Refer to pages 48 and 50*)

3   How would you determine the median from a percentage ogive? (*Refer to page 51*)

4   Under what conditions will the mean take a higher value than the median? (*Refer to page 53*)

5   When is it preferable to use the mode? (*Refer to page 53*)

6   Under what conditions would you prefer to use the median rather than the mean as the measure of average? (*Refer to page 53*)

7   Which quartile is the same as the median? (*Refer to page 51*)

8   What would you conclude about the distribution of data in a data set if the mean and median were the same? (*Refer to page 53*)

9   How would you estimate the mode from a histogram? (*Refer to page 52*)

10   Why will the choice of intervals in a frequency table affect both the mean and median if they are calculated from the table rather than from the raw data? (*Refer to page 48*)

EXERCISES

1   Confirm from your own calculations that the measures of average given in Table 5.4 for store B are correct.

2   Refer back to exercise 1, Chapter 4.

Required:
(a)   Calculate the mean wage level for each group of employees from the raw data
(b)   How do you interpret the fact that the mean value for clerical/admin staff is higher than that of sales staff?
(c)   Calculate the mean value for both groups of employees from the two frequency tables that you constructed
(d)   Why are there differences between these mean values and those based on the raw data? Which would you prefer to use?

(e)   Either from the frequency table or from the ogive determine the median value for both groups of employees

(f)   Compare the mean of each group with the median. Why are they different? Which measure of average would you prefer to use to represent 'typical' wages in each group?

(g)   Management are considering giving all sales staff a 10% pay increase. Estimate how much more per week this will cost the company

(h)   Refer back to Table 1b in the exercises in Chapter 4. You will see that one person in the sales group received a weekly wage of £123.58. It has been realised that this was a computer error and this person should have received a wage of £223.58. What effect would you expect this to have on the mean and median values for this data set?

(i)   Recalculate the mean and median values for this data set using this new wage value and determine whether your answer to part (h) was correct.

(j)   Why do you think the mode is of little use in this data set?

Answers on page 302.

Measures of variation

In the previous chapter we introduced the first group of statistics that can be used to describe certain features of the data set: the measures of average. We concluded that such averages do not always reflect a 'typical' value in the data set, because the actual data may vary considerably from the average.

In this chapter we shall introduce further statistics that allow us to describe and quantify such variation. In general, such statistics will measure variation around a specific measure of average:

the standard deviation measures variation of the data around the mean
the interquartile range measures variation of the data around the median

6.1 THE STANDARD DEVIATION

The standard deviation is the measure of dispersion most frequently used in statistics. It measures dispersion around the arithmetic mean. To see how it is calculated and how it can be interpreted we shall return to the data set in Table 5.2 which showed the salary of 11 employees. We saw in Chapter 5 that the mean value for the data set was £9,273 but that the mean was not really typical or representative of the bulk of the data. From the Table we were able to determine that this occurred because of one large value in the data set.

Frequently, however, we may not have access to the raw data. If we could not refer to the individual salaries but were simply told that the average salary was £9,272.73 how could we determine whether or not the mean was typical or representative of the data set?

The answer lies with the standard deviation. As we shall see it is a statistic which measures the variation of the individual data items from the mean value.

6.1.1 Calculating the standard deviation from raw data

We require a statistic which measures the variation of the data around the mean. The first logical step, therefore, would be to calculate the deviations from the mean—the amount by which each item in the data set differs from the average. Typically in statistics the mean is denoted with the symbol $\bar{X}$. So, using the symbol $\bar{X}$ to refer to the individual data items, the individual deviations from the mean can be expressed as $(X - \bar{X})$. These deviations are shown in Table 6.1.

The table shows the original data in Column 1, the arithmetic mean in Column 2, and the deviation of each data item from the mean in Column 3. The further away from the mean that an item in the data set lies, the larger the deviation.

The next step—as we are interested in measuring variability for the total data set—would appear to be to total these individual deviations to give a figure for the variation for the whole data set.

It can be seen from the table, however, that if we do this we arrive at a total figure of zero. In fact this will *always* happen and, on reflection, you should be able to see why: the positive deviations from above-average values will always be cancelled by the negative deviations of the *below*-average values.

In fact, we are not interested in whether a particular value is above or below the mean (that is, whether it is plus or minus) but rather *how far* away from the mean it is. Referring to Table 6.1 the important difference between the items £8,500 and £35,000 is not that one has a negative deviation and the other a positive but that one deviation is far larger than the other.

TABLE 6.1　**Calculation of the standard deviation**

X	$\overline{X}$ (Mean)	$(X - \overline{X})$	$(X - \overline{X})^2$
5000	9272.73	−4272.73	18256221
5000	9272.73	−4272.73	18256221
5000	9272.73	−4272.73	18256221
5000	9272.73	−4272.73	18256221
5000	9272.73	−4272.73	18256221
8000	9272.73	−1272.73	1619842
8500	9272.73	−772.73	597112
8500	9272.73	−772.73	597112
8500	9272.73	−772.73	597112
8500	9272.73	−772.73	597112
35000	9272.73	25727.27	661892422
Totals		0	757181817

Accordingly, we *square* the individual deviations (remembering that the square of a negative number will give a positive number as a result). These squared deviations are also shown in Table 6.1 in column 4 and total 757,181,817.

We now find the average of these squared deviations by dividing through by the number of items in the data set, 11 to give 68834710.64. This number is known as the *variance*. To derive the standard deviation we take the square root of the variance (the opposite of squaring the individual deviations) to give £8296.67. This is the standard deviation: a statistic measuring average dispersion of the data around the mean. The formula we have derived can be expressed as:

$$\text{Standard deviation} = \sqrt{\frac{\Sigma(X - \overline{X})^2}{n}}$$

All other things being equal, a larger value for the standard deviation implies more dispersion or a greater difference between the average and the individual items in the data set. It can be seen from the deviations column in Table 6.1 that the more the data varies from the mean the larger the squared deviation and the larger the total of these squared deviations. The lowest value that the standard deviation could ever take would be zero, implying that all values in the data set took the mean value (that is, there were no deviations from the mean).

In this case, the standard deviation at £8,297 is relatively large (particularly when compared to the mean of £9,273). We would conclude that there is considerable variation within the data set from the mean value, *even if* we had not seen the raw data first.

6.1.2　Calculation of the standard deviation from grouped data

As with the mean and median there are frequent occasions when we have to calculate the standard deviation for grouped rather than raw data. The formula to be used differs from the previous one in that it uses the *midpoint* values to estimate the individual values falling in a particular interval. The formula is:

$$\text{Standard deviation} = \sqrt{\frac{\Sigma fx^2}{\Sigma f} - \left(\frac{\Sigma fx}{\Sigma f}\right)^2}$$

where x refers to the midpoint of the interval.

To illustrate the relevant calculations we shall return to the example of the frequency table for daily sales in store A shown previously in Table 5.3.

TABLE 6.2   **Daily sales in store A**

Interval	Midpoint x	Frequency f	fx	x²	fx²
£700 < £800	750	2	1500	562500	1125000
£800 < £900	850	7	5950	722500	5057500
£900 < £1000	950	11	10450	902500	9927500
£1000 < £1100	1050	16	16800	1102500	17640000
£1100 < £1200	1150	13	14950	1322500	17192500
£1200 < £1300	1250	11	13750	1562500	17187500
£1300 < £1400	1350	10	13500	1822500	18225000
£1400 < £1500	1450	8	11600	2102500	16820000
£1500 < £1600	1550	8	12400	2402500	19220000
£1600 < £1700	1650	5	8250	2722500	13612500
£1700 < £1800	1750	3	5250	3062500	9187500
£1800 < £1900	1850	2	3700	3422500	6845000
£1900 < £2000	1950	2	3900	3802500	7605000
£2000 < £2100	2050	2	4100	4202500	8405000
Totals		100	126100		168050000

The first four columns in Table 6.2 are identical to Table 5.3 where the mean for grouped data was calculated. Column 6 shows the midpoint value squared and Column 7 shows the (frequency x midpoint value squared). The relevant totals are shown at the foot of the table and using these we can determine the standard deviation using the formula:

$$\sqrt{\frac{168050000}{100} - \left(\frac{126100}{100}\right)^2} = \sqrt{1680500 - 1590121} = £300.63$$

The standard deviation of daily sales in store A is, therefore, £300.63 based on the grouped data. This statistic can be used and interpreted in exactly the same way as the standard deviation for raw data.

As with the mean and median the calculation of the standard deviation for grouped data should be seen as an estimate of the true figure which would be obtained directly from the raw data. Manual calculation of the standard deviation for the raw data, however, is extremely time-consuming and tedious for anything more than a few numbers and the grouped calculation is usually used. Naturally, in computer based analysis this problem does not occur and the raw data calculation is readily available.

As a point of reference Table 6.3 shows the standard deviation calculated from both the raw data and the aggregated data for store A and store B:

TABLE 6.3   **Comparison of standard deviations: raw and aggregated data**

	store A	store B
Standard deviation—raw data	£307.37	£165.89
Standard deviation—aggregated data	£300.63	£165.80

It can be seen that there is a small difference between the statistic for each store, reinforcing the point made earlier that the statistic based on raw data is more accurate than that based on grouped data.

6.1.3   Standard deviation for populations and for samples

One important point to note about the calculation of the standard deviation is that, statistically, we ought to distinguish between a population and a sample. Strictly speaking, the formulae we have used to calculate the standard deviation is appropriate only if the data we are dealing with represents the **population**. However, the data that we have analysed should, strictly, be seen as a **sample**. For reasons that can only be explained in formal mathematical terms, we must use the term n–1 (or its equivalent f–1) rather than n when calculating the standard deviation either for raw or grouped data. Most computer packages will do this automatically.

In the case of reasonably large samples the arithmetic difference between the two calculations will be small.

The following formula shows the amended formula for the raw data.

$$\sqrt{\frac{\Sigma(X - \bar{X})^2}{n - 1}}$$

Table 6.4 shows the standard deviations for store A and B using the sample formula.

TABLE 6.4   **Comparison of standard deviations: raw and aggregated data**
Using the sample formula

	store A	store B
Standard deviation—raw data	£308.93	£166.73
Standard deviation—aggregated data	£302.15	£166.64

You will see that there is relatively little difference between the two methods of calculation. You should, however, use the sample formulae if the data you are analysing does not represent the total population.

6.1.4   Comparing two or more standard deviations

It is tempting to use the standard deviation from different data sets to compare dispersion. In our example, we might examine the standard deviation of store A and compare it with that of store B with the view to determining which store had more variability in its daily sales.

Such direct comparison is frequently misleading, however, as the two standard deviations are showing dispersion around different mean values. If we wish to compare two or more data sets in terms of their dispersion we must instead use another statistic, the *coefficient of variation*.

6.2   THE COEFFICIENT OF VARIATION

This is defined as:

$$\text{Coefficient of variation (\%)} = \frac{\text{Standard deviation}}{\text{Mean}} \times 100$$

Other things being equal, a higher CV implies more variability.

The statistic is easily calculated for stores A and B, as shown in Table 6.5.

TABLE 6.5   **Calculation of coefficient of variation stores A and B**

	store A	store B
Mean	£1276.30	£1349.27
Standard deviation—raw data	£308.93	£166.73
Coefficient of variation	$\dfrac{308.93}{1276.3} \times 100$	$\dfrac{166.73}{1349.27} \times 100$
	= 24.2%	= 12.4%

Comparing the two CVs we can see that variability in store A (at 24%) is, in relative terms, approximately twice that in store B (at 12%). In other words, daily sales in store B tend to be closer to the mean value than they do in store A. There is more variability in daily sales figures in store A.

(Note that we could equally have used the mean and standard deviation for the grouped data in the calculation.)

6.3   THE INTERQUARTILE RANGE

We saw in Chapter 5 that the mean is not always the most appropriate average: we may prefer to use the median as an alternative. In such a case the standard deviation would be of no use as it is based around the mean value. Instead we use the **interquartile range** to indicate variability around the median.

The interquartile range is defined as:

$$\text{Interquartile range} = Q3 - Q1$$

where Q3 represents the upper (75%) quartile and Q1 represents the lower (25%) quartile
(You will also remember from Chapter 5 that the median is the middle (or 50%) quartile.)
The upper and lower quartiles can be calculated in any one of three ways:

1   From the raw data set using the same method as for the median but looking for the 25% item and 75% item respectively for Q1 and Q3.
2   From the frequency table. The formula used to calculate the median can be used. Rather than looking for item (n+1)/2, however, we could calculate Q1 using (n+1)/4 and Q3 using 3(n+1)/4.
3   From the percentage ogive. Again, instead of finding the median at the 50% point we would find the lower quartile at the 25% point and the upper quartile from the 75% point.

Table 6.6 shows the appropriate quartiles for store A and B calculated from the relevant frequency tables:

TABLE 6.6   **Quartiles for stores A and B calculated from Table 4.6**

	store A	store B
Lower Quartile (Q1)	£1032.81	£1236.76
Median (Q2)	£1213.64	£1353.70
Upper Quartile (Q3)	£1471.87	£1475.00
Interquartile range (Q3–Q1)	£439.06	£238.24

Let us examine the quartiles first. The lower quartiles indicate that 25% of items in the data set fall below this value. Thus 25% of daily sales in store A fall below £1,032.81 whilst the corresponding figure for store B is £1,236.76. The fact that Q1 in store B is higher indicates that items in this part of the data set tend to be higher than the corresponding items in store A.

The upper quartiles indicate that 25% of daily sales lie *above* this value—£1,471.87 for store A and £1,475 for store B. In this case there is little difference between the two values.

Finally, the interquartile range is the difference between the upper and lower quartile. Simply, it represents the central 50% of the distribution. In both cases, 50% of daily sales fall in the interquartile range. In the case of store A the range is £439.06 whilst for store B it is £238.24. The fact that the interquartile range is smaller in store B indicates that the items in the middle of the data set are relatively closely clustered around the median. There is less of a difference between the top 25% sales figure and the bottom 25% sales figure than in store A. Thus, the smaller the interquartile range the less the data are dispersed in this part of the distribution.

6.4   QUARTILE DEVIATION

A further statistic frequently encountered is the quartile deviation (sometimes referred to as the semi-interquartile range). This is defined as:

$$\text{Quartile deviation} = \frac{\text{Interquartile range}}{2} = \frac{(Q3 - Q1)}{2}$$

In the case of store A the quartile deviation would be:

$$\frac{£439.06}{2} = £219.53$$

and for store B:

$$\frac{£238.24}{2} = £119.12$$

Interpretation of this statistic is similar to that for the interquartile range it indicates the average difference between the median and the quartiles. Other things being equal, a higher value implies more dispersion in the central part of the data set.

6.5   COEFFICIENT OF SKEWNESS

The final statistic introduced in this chapter relates to the measure of *skewness*. Such a statistic is concerned with measuring the general shape of the distribution, specifically whether the distribution tends to lean to the left, to the right or whether it is reasonably symmetrical.

$$\text{Pearson's coefficient of skewness} = \frac{3\,(\text{Mean} - \text{Median})}{\text{Standard deviation}}$$

The statistic allows us to identify the general shape of the distribution without resorting to histograms or frequency tables. As we have seen, the mean and median for a data set may well be different. The difference will be largely due to extreme values at one end of the distribution. Extremely high values included in the mean but not in the median will pull the mean higher than the median whilst extremely low values will pull the mean below the median. Three general cases are illustrated in Figure 6.1.

The top diagram illustrates where a relatively small number of high values will pull the mean *above* the median. Referring back to the formula, the skewness coefficient will be positive, hence this type of distribution is known as positive skew. The more extreme the higher values the larger the skewness coefficient will become.

The second diagram has a relatively small number of extremely *low* values which will pull the mean lower than the median, giving a negative skew.

Finally, a symmetrical distribution, as in the bottom diagram will have a zero skew, with the mean and median equal (or at least approximately so).

FIGURE 6.1 **Skewness**

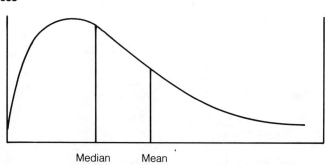

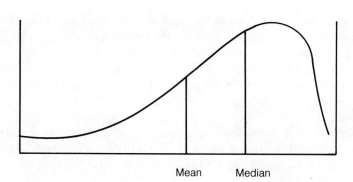

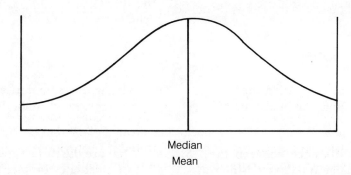

The skewness coefficients for stores A and B are readily calculated:

TABLE 6.7   **Skewness coefficients for stores A and B**
(Statistics based on raw data)

	store A	store B
Mean	£1276.30	£1349.27
Median	£1237.00	£1338.00
Standard Deviation	£308.93	£166.73
Coefficient of skewness	+ 0.38	+ 0.20

Both stores have distributions that are positively skewed although this skewness is more pronounced in store A.

SUMMARY

In this chapter, and in the previous chapter on averages, we have introduced a number of statistical measures that can be used to describe the main features of a data set. The important conclusion is that such a description can take place without reference to the original data, so, if we are provided with the key statistics of a data set (the mean, standard deviation, the three quartiles) we can easily provide a general and reasonably accurate description of the whole data set by comparing the different measures of average by using the measures of dispersion and by calculating the skewness.

It is frequently the case in business analysis that such descriptive statistics are all the information that is provided. Using what we have learned about the different measures provides us with a powerful means of describing the full set of data.

1   Measures of dispersion are based around the mean or around the median.
2   The coefficient of variation is a measure of relative dispersion expressing the standard deviation as a percentage of the arithmetic mean.
3   The interquartile range measures dispersion around the median value and is the difference between the upper and lower quartiles.
4   The quartile deviation (or semi-interquartile range) is half the interquartile range.
5   The coefficient of skewness is an indication of the general shape of the data distribution.
6   The standard deviation measures dispersion around the arithmetic mean.

SELF-TEST QUESTIONS

1   **Does the standard deviation measure dispersion around the mean or the median?** (*Refer to page 57*)

2   **What is the difference between the interquartile range and the semi-interquartile range?** (*Refer to page 62*)

3   **What statistic is used to compare two or more standard deviations?** (*Refer to page 60*)

4   **Does a positive skew distribution lean to the left or to the right?** (*Refer to page 62*)

5   **Why will dispersion statistics based on aggregated data be inaccurate?** (*Refer to page 59*)

6   **What are the three ways in which you can calculate the quartile deviation?** (*Refer to page 61*)

7   **What proportion of a distribution falls in the interquartile range** (*Refer to page 62*)

8   **What is the difference between the coefficient of variation and the coefficient of skewness?** (*Refer to pages 60 and 62*)

EXERCISES

The exercises for this chapter are based on the end-of-chapter exercises of Chapters 4 and 5.

1   Confirm from your own calculations that the measures of dispersion given in this chapter for store B are correct.

2   Refer back to the two data sets on salaries for the two groups of workers used in Chapters 4 and 5.
   Based on the two frequency tables you have constructed calculate the following statistics:
   (a)   The standard deviation
   (b)   The coefficient of variation
   (c)   The quartile deviation
   (d)   The coefficient of skewness
   Using these statistics compare the two distributions for similarities and differences.

3   For these same sets of data determine the upper and lower quartiles from the percentage ogives.
   Compare these with the equivalent figures calculated from the frequency tables in 2c. Which set of figures are more reliable and why?

4   For the data on incomes before and after tax answer the following questions:
   (a)   Determine the standard deviation before tax and after tax
   (b)   What conclusion do you come to about the effect of tax on incomes?
   (c)   Determine the quartile deviation before tax and after tax
   (d)   Which of the two measures of dispersion would you prefer to use in this case?

Answers on page 303.

Index numbers

In earlier chapters we saw the usefulness of being able to identify visually the trends in some variable over a period of time via the construction of some suitable diagram or graph. It is also useful to be able to identify equivalent trends using statistical rather than graphical means. This is frequently achieved by constructing a suitable **index** or a set of **index numbers**. Such an index is effectively a type of average, specifically a type of weighted arithmetic mean, and is frequently used in business.

You may well be familiar with some of the more well-known indices from the business literature: the Retail Price Index, the Financial Times All Share Index, the Index of Industrial Production, the Dow Jones Index, the Hang Seng Index and so on.

This chapter illustrates the construction of such statistics and their uses in business.

7.1   SIMPLE INDEX NUMBERS

We shall first introduce the concept and interpretation of a simple index number. In Chapter 3 we were examining the annual turnover of MTG over the last five year period. The relevant figures are duplicated below in Table 7.1.

TABLE 7.1   **MTG plc annual turnover 1983–87**

(Figures shown are in £m)

	1987	1986	1985	1984	1983
Total	161.6	146.1	134.0	122.4	109.9

Source: *Table 3.1*

Whilst such data shows a steady increase in the group's turnover over this period it is difficult to assess by how much turnover is increasing from one year to the next. The calculation of a simple index will help. The steps in constructing a simple index are straightforward:

STEP 1

Choose one period to represent the base period. This is frequently (but not always) the first period shown, here it is 1983.

STEP 2

Set the value of the variable in this year to an arbitrary level of 100.

STEP 3

Adjust the values in the other periods to represent a proportion of the initial base year value.

Thus, in this example we set turnover in 1983 to 100. 1984's turnover is £122.4m compared to £109.9m in the base year. As a proportion this is:

$$\frac{122.4}{109.9} = 1.114 \times 100 = 111.4 \text{ as an index}$$

What does this index mean? It shows that in 1984 turnover was 11.4% higher than in 1983, the base year.

If we perform the relevant calculations for the rest of the series we reach the results given in Table 7.2.

TABLE 7.2   **Index of MTG plc annual turnover 1983–87: 1983 = 100**

Year	Turnover £m	Index	Calculation
1983	109.9	100	$\frac{109.9}{109.9} \times 100$
1984	122.4	111.4	$\frac{122.4}{109.9} \times 100$
1985	134.0	121.9	$\frac{134.0}{109.9} \times 100$
1986	146.1	132.9	$\frac{146.1}{109.9} \times 100$
1987	161.6	147.0	$\frac{161.6}{109.9} \times 100$

The simple index allows a ready comparison of any year's turnover with the base year. Thus, we can see at a glance that turnover has risen over this period by 47% (from an index of 100 to an index of 147).

Note that in the table the base period must be explicitly shown. Here we have noted that 1983=100 which indicates that this was the chosen base period. The table title should always include this detail even if the base year itself is not in the body of the table.

7.1.1   Choice of base year

The choice of base year in the construction of an index is to a large extent arbitrary. However, you should try to choose a base period that is representative of the period and has not been affected by any extreme events such as strikes, takeovers, mergers etc which may distort the figures.

7.2   AGGREGATE OR COMPOSITE INDEX NUMBERS

In the previous section we examined the construction of a simple index which shows the relative change between two or more numbers. More typically, we may wish to calculate a composite index number. This is an index which represents an average value for a set of data. Although the interpretation of such index numbers is the same as before their method of calculation is somewhat different.

Let us examine Table 7.3.

TABLE 7.3   **Numbers employed and average annual salary: Eastern region**

Type of employee	1985		1987	
	Number employed	Average salary £s	Number employed	Average salary £s
Sales staff	120	5000	158	5500
Admin staff	41	8000	52	10000
Clerical staff	25	6000	30	8000
Managerial staff	21	15000	25	20000
Total	207		265	

Source: *Payroll department*

The table shows (for the Eastern region in the MTG group) the number of employees and their average annual salary for each of two years—1985 and 1987. Typically, we may wish to compare labour costs between the two years. Initially, we may consider simply determining the total wage bill in each of the two years and comparing these. The difficulty with this approach is that both elements making up the total wages bill have changed: average salaries have increased and so have the number of people employed in each category. It will, therefore, be impossible to distinguish the cause of any increase in the total wages bill. We shall not be able to distinguish whether total wages have increased because salaries have increased or because the number of people employed has increased.

Instead, we can construct a composite index where one of the two factors in the table is kept constant. This will enable us to see how the remaining factor has changed over these two years. Given that our interest is in total labour costs it would make sense to try to determine an average cost figure for 1985 and an equivalent average cost figure for 1987.

You should be able to see that if we simply averaged the annual salaries, say for 1985, this would not reflect the numbers of people in the different categories earning a particular salary. It is, therefore, necessary to calculate a weighted average where the weights represent the varying degrees of importance of the individual salary values.

In practice there are two common types of such a weighted average: the **Laspeyres** index and the **Paasche** index. We shall examine each in turn.

7.3   THE LASPEYRES INDEX

The Laspeyres (pronounced Lasspears) index is a weighted average where the weights used relate to some chosen base period. The general form of the Laspeyres index is given by the formula:

$$\frac{\Sigma\ P_n\ Q_o}{\Sigma\ P_o\ Q_o} \times 100$$

P refers to the cost or price figure we require an index for (here P would be annual salary)
Q refers to the weights or quantities to be used (here Q would refer to the number of people employed in each category)
the subscript $_o$ refers to the values of P and Q in the chosen base year
the subscript $_n$ refers to the values of P and Q in the year for which we are calculating an index.

The calculation method is straightforward. If we choose 1985 as the base year (so that all other values of the index are relative to the 1985 value) then the appropriate calculations are shown in Table 7.4.

TABLE 7.4   **Calculation of Laspeyres Index: Eastern region (1985)**

Type of employee	Q_o Number employed	P_o Average salary £s	$Q_o \times P_o$
Sales staff	120	5000	600000
Admin staff	41	8000	328000
Clerical staff	25	6000	150000
Managerial staff	21	15000	315000
Total	207		1393000

	1985 Q_o	1987 P_n	$Q_o \times P_n$
Sales staff	120	5500	660000
Admin staff	41	10000	410000
Clerical staff	25	8000	200000
Managerial staff	21	20000	420000
Total	207		1690000

First of all we calculate the relevant term for the base year 1985. This gives a total of 1,393,000. In this example, the interpretation of this number would be that it represents the total wage bill for 1985.

We then calculate the corresponding figure for 1987. In this case we use the same weights as before (those for 1985, the base year) and the 1987 average salary figures. This gives a total of 1,690,000. This figure can be interpreted as the total wage bill in 1987 *if* the same people were employed as in 1985.

The Laspeyres index is then the ratio of the two:

$$\text{Laspeyres index} = \frac{1690000}{1393000} \times 100 = 121.3$$

This index can be interpreted in exactly the same way as any other. Between the base year (1985) and the year the index relates to (1987) labour costs rose by 21.3%. It is important to realise, however, that the index shows the rise in labour costs *on the assumption that* the mixture of employees did not change. That is, we assume the employee structure as it existed in the base year.

The advantage of this assumption is that it allows us to focus on the variable of interest—the rate of change of labour costs.

If we now wished to calculate a comparable index for the next year, say 1988, this is easily achieved and the formula would now become:

$$\text{Laspeyres index for 1988} = \frac{\Sigma P_{1988} Q_{1985}}{\Sigma P_{1985} Q_{1985}} \times 100$$

It can be seen that the bottom half of the formula would still be 1,393,000. We would now be comparing labour costs in 1988 based on the employee structure in the base year, 1985.

7.4   THE PAASCHE INDEX

One of the problems with the Laspeyres index is that it uses weights from some base period. Inevitably these weights will have changed slightly by today so the Laspeyres index actually relates labour costs to 1985 rather than to 1987's employee structure. The Paasche (pronounced

Pash) index tries to resolve this shortcoming by using *current* weights rather than weights from some base period.

$$\text{The formula is: } \frac{\Sigma \; P_n \; Q_n}{\Sigma \; P_o \; Q_n} \times 100$$

In this case the weights used are for the year for which the index is to be calculated, 1987. Accordingly, the Paasche index is also known as the current date weighted index. The relevant calculations are shown in Table 7.5.

TABLE 7.5 **Calculation of Paasche Index: Eastern region (1987)**

Type of employee	Q_n Number employed	P_o Average salary £s	$Q_n \times P_o$
Sales staff	158	5000	790000
Admin staff	52	8000	416000
Clerical staff	30	6000	180000
Managerial staff	25	15000	375000
Total	265		1761000

	Q_n	P_n	$Q_n \times P_n$
Sales staff	158	5500	869000
Admin staff	52	10000	520000
Clerical staff	30	8000	240000
Managerial staff	25	20000	500000
Total	265		2129000

For the 1985 calculations we use the employee structure as it is *currently*, that is for 1987. This gives a total figure of 1,761,000. This is what the total wage bill in 1985 would have been if we had employed the same people as in 1987. The 1987 figure is calculated at 2,129,000. The Paasche index, therefore, is:

$$\text{Paasche index} = \frac{2129000}{1761000} \times 100 = 120.9$$

That is, based on current employee structure, labour costs have risen by 20.9% since 1985. Note that, as will usually happen, the two different methods produce differing results. If we now wished to calculate a Paasche index for 1988 the formula will be:

$$\frac{\Sigma \; P_{1988} \; Q_{1988}}{\Sigma \; P_{1985} \; Q_{1988}} \times 100$$

You should be able to see that, unlike the Laspeyres index, both parts of the formula will have to be recalculated as the new weights (for 1988) appear on both the top and bottom part of the expression.

Note also that whilst we could compare the value of this index against 1985 (the base year) we would not be able to compare it with 1987. This is because the index for 1987 and for 1988 use different weights (for their respective current years).

7.5 CHOOSING BETWEEN THE LASPEYRES AND PAASCHE INDEXES

Both methods of calculating an index have their advantages and disadvantages:

LASPEYRES INDEX

1   Easy to calculate for a series of years as it uses the same set of weights each time.
2   Allows a comparison of any one year with any other as all use the same weights.
3   The weights used will gradually become out of date and will no longer represent the contemporary situation.
4   Tends to over-estimate price increase because it uses out-of-date weights.
5   Requires little data in terms of weights.

PAASCHE INDEX

1   Involves more calculation for a series of years as the weights used are constantly changing.
2   Can only be compared against the base year as the weights for each year change.
3   Always uses the current weights and so reflects today's situation.
4   Will tend to under-estimate price increases.
5   Requires new weights each period which can be both costly and time consuming to collect.

In general, the Laspeyres index tends to be more popular and more frequent than the Paasche. Most officially produced index numbers are based on some form of the Laspeyres method with the base year periodically changed to bring the weights up to date.

7.6   QUANTITY INDEX NUMBERS

The aggregate index numbers calculated previously are examples of what are known as *price* indices because they relate to the rate of change in the price of some variable (here the price of labour). There are occasions where we wish to construct an index not for price changes but for *quantity* changes.

In our example, we kept the *quantity* of labour constant in order to calculate the price change. We could equally have reversed this and kept prices constant to see how the quantities had changed. In such a case we would use *price* as the weight in both the Laspeyres and Paasche formulae.

$$\text{Quantity Laspeyres index:} \quad \frac{\Sigma \; P_o \; Q_n}{\Sigma \; P_o \; Q_o}$$

$$\text{Quantity Paasche index:} \quad \frac{\Sigma \; P_n \; Q_n}{\Sigma \; P_n \; Q_o}$$

Otherwise the calculation and use of such indices is as before.

7.7   REBASING AN INDEX

Frequently when using a Laspeyres type index we find that, part way through a series, the index has been rebased: that is, the base year used (and the corresponding weights) has been changed.
Let us examine Table 7.6.

TABLE 7.6   **Index of labour costs for Eastern region: 1980–87**

Year	Index, base 1980	Index base 1985
1980	100	
1981	105	
1982	115	
1983	121	
1984	128	
1985	135	100
1986		110
1987		121.3

The Table shows two related sets of index numbers. The first series shows an index of labour costs with 1980 as the base year (and hence 1980 weights). The second series shows an equivalent index but with 1985 as the base (and hence 1985 weights used). The difficulty arises if we are asked to compare wage costs in 1987 with those, say in 1980. The two index numbers are not directly comparable because they relate to different base years. However, this problem can be resolved by a calculation known as 'chaining'.

First, we choose a year to act as the common base period. Here we shall use 1985 although any of the years could be chosen for which we had an index from both series. We then adjust the index for each preceding year to relate to the 1985 value of 100.

To illustrate this let us look at the index for 1984, currently taking a value of 128 (base 1980). The corresponding figure for 1985 is 135 (base 1980). However, the figure of 135 has effectively been converted into 100 so the 1985 figure must be adjusted proportionately:

$$\text{1984 index adjusted to 1985 value} = \frac{128}{135} \times 100 = 94.8$$

That is, the 1984 figure is 94.8% of the 1985 figure. This, therefore, becomes the 1984 index relative to 1985. The other figures in the series can be adjusted accordingly:

TABLE 7.7   **Index of labour costs for Eastern region: 1980–87**

Index year	Index, base 1980	Index base 1985	Revised base 1985
1980	100		74.1
1981	105		77.8
1982	115		85.2
1983	121		89.6
1984	128		94.8
1985	135	100	100
1986		110	110
1987		121.3	121.3

The chained index is shown in the final column. It is now possible to directly compare any two years in the series.

7.8   DEFLATING A SERIES USING AN INDEX

Apart from using an index number to show how prices (or quantities) have altered over some period one special use of indices is to **deflate** a series of some variable over time.

Let us return to Table 7.1 which showed MTG's total turnover for the period 1983–87. This is duplicated in Table 7.8 below.

TABLE 7.8 **MTG plc annual turnover 1983–87**

Year	Total turnover £m	Consumer price index (1983 = 100)	Total turnover £m, 1983 prices
1983	109.9	100	109.9
1984	122.4	110	111.3
1985	134.0	120	111.7
1986	146.1	125	116.9
1987	161.6	132	122.4

The problem with presenting such a series (particularly those relating to some financial variable) is that it may well give a distorted view of what is happening elsewhere. (Of course, this may be exactly what the statisticians who have prepared the table may want.) The turnover figures, for example, appear to indicate that MTG is improving its performance every year, as turnover gradually rises. What the table ignores, of course, is inflation—the general increase in prices in the economy as a whole. It may be that MTG is not increasing turnover in terms of the quantity of goods sold but merely in terms of prices which are rising throughout the economy anyway.

The only way in which we can reasonably assess the turnover figures is to deflate them, that is, to remove the effects of general inflation. This is achieved by adjusting the actual turnover figures with an appropriate price index to produce a set of turnover figures measured in real terms, without the effect of price changes.

Table 7.8 also shows a suitable index that we can use for such deflating. We can suppose that this is an index which shows the trend in consumer prices generally in the economy over the same period. Such an index is likely to be produced by the government and would be widely available for public use.

As we can see, although MTG's turnover has showed a large increase over this period so have prices generally with consumer prices rising by 32% over this period. What we really require is some means of comparing the change in turnover relative to the change in prices. If turnover is rising *faster* than prices it indicates the group is increasing the *volume* of sales. If turnover is rising *more slowly* than prices it indicates that the volume of turnover is falling. Obviously, if turnover is rising at the *same* rate as prices it means that the volume of turnover is constant.

The deflating of turnover is easily achieved using the price index.

$$\frac{\text{actual turnover}}{\text{index}} \times 100 = \text{real turnover}$$

The figure for 1984, for example, becomes:

$$\frac{122.4}{110} \times 100 = 111.3$$

That is, real turnover in 1984 was £111.3m as measured in 1983 prices. Effectively, this measures turnover in terms of what prices were in 1983 (the base year). In essence what the deflation calculation has done is to remove a proportion from the 1984 turnover figure equal to the general rise in price between 1983 and 1984.

Equivalent values are shown for the other years.

This deflated series shows rather a different picture than the original. In 1985, for example, actual turnover rose by some £12m. After allowing for inflation, however, the deflated turnover had risen by only £0.4 million. Almost all the extra turnover, in other words, was derived from increasing prices rather than through increasing volume.

SUMMARY

Index numbers are a particularly common business statistic.

1   An index number shows the percentage change in some variable over a period of time.
2   A simple index shows each item in a series relative to some chosen base period value.
3   A composite or aggregate index is constructed by calculating a weighted average of some set of values where the weights show the relative importance of each item in the data set.
4   A Laspeyres index is a base weighted index, where the weights used relate to some chosen base period.
5   A Paasche index is a current period weighted average where the weights used rebase to the current period.
6   Chaining an index is a method of joining series of index numbers together which have different base years.
7   Deflating a data series using an index is a method of removing inflation from the series to observe the underlying trend.

SELF-TEST QUESTIONS

1   **You are told an index currently has a value of 132.5. What does this mean?** (*Refer to page 68*)

2   **What is the difference between a simple and an aggregate index?** (*Refer to page 68*)

3   **Why is it necessary to use weights in the construction of an aggregate index?** (*Refer to page 69*)

4   **What is the difference between a Laspeyres index and a Paasche index?** (*Refer to page 72*)

5   **Why is it necessary to use a constant set of weights in an aggregate index?** (*Refer to page 69*)

6   **What advantages does the Paasche index have over the Laspeyres?** (*Refer to page 72*)

7   **What advantages does the Laspeyres index have over the Paasche?** (*Refer to page 72*)

8   **What factors would you take into consideration when choosing a base period for an index?** (*Refer to page 68*)

9   **How do you chain two index series together?** (*Refer to page 73*)

10   **Why is it necessary to deflate most time series data?** (*Refer to page 74*)

EXERCISES

1   In Table 3.1 data was given on turnover by sector for the MTG group for the period 1983–87. Using this data:
      (a)   Construct a simple index for each of the sectors
      (b)   Comment on which sectors have grown most and which least
      (c)   Construct a time series graph showing these indices (and the index for total turnover) over this period.

2   Following on from the data in Chapter 7 on employees and salaries the following data for 1988 has been collected:

Employee group	No employed	Average salary £s
Sales	160	6000
Admin	55	12000
Clerical	33	9000
Managerial	30	22000

(a)   Construct a Laspeyres index for 1988, base 1985

(b)   Construct a Paasche index for 1988, base 1985

(c)   Explain why your results for (a) and (b) are different

(d)   Management are considering using such an index in their monitoring of company financial targets. If they do so, the index will be needed every six months. Which type of index would you advise management to use?

Answers on page 304.

Data collection

The last few chapters have been analysing data in a number of ways designed to identify the key features of the data set. Before such a process can usually start, however, it is necessary to collect data. This chapter is concerned with the major methods of data collection, with particular reference to the various sampling methods which exist.

Such data collection exercises are of critical importance to every business organisation. We may wish to collect data on customer attitudes to a new product we are considering launching; we may wish to collect data on employee attitudes to some new type of productivity scheme we are thinking of introducing. We may require data to determine the stock levels in an organisation; an auditor may collect data on financial transactions listed in the company accounts and so on.

8.1   PRIMARY AND SECONDARY DATA

The distinction has already been made between primary and secondary data and this distinction is important not only for data collection but also for the reliability of any analysis undertaken on the data set. Primary data refers to data collected at first hand in order to meet the requirements of a specific statistical investigation.

Secondary data refers to data which was initially collected for some specific purpose but is now to be used as part of a different statistical investigation.

Let us assume—as we did in an earlier chapter—that MTG are considering opening a new store in a town where they do not currently operate. The group has decided to commission a survey of local residents to determine how many of them are likely to use the store for their shopping. If such a survey is undertaken and data on local residents collected then this data would be primary, because it will have been collected directly for the specific purpose under investigation.

If at a later date, however, the company is undertaking a different type of investigation— say investigating the provision of consumer credit to its customers—and decides to use the data previously collected on local residents, this would be secondary data as it will have been collected for purposes other than the current one.

The distinction between primary and secondary data is important because it affects the potential reliability and managerial usefulness of any statistical analysis undertaken. For secondary data we would need to ask a number of questions before using, analysing and reaching conclusions about the data:

1   What information was collected?
2   Who collected the information?
3   For what purposes was the information collected?
4   How was the information collected?
5   Where and when was the information collected?
6   Has any preliminary analysis been carried out on the data?

If we are dealing with primary data the reliability of the information is much higher.

8.2   SAMPLES AND POPULATIONS

Earlier in the text the distinction was drawn between a sample and a statistical population and this distinction is critical for data collection and for the statistical analysis based on the data collected.

Our interest, almost always, lies in analysing the statistical population, but we are usually forced to analyse instead only a sample part of the population. The reasons why we are usually forced to investigate a sample may be several:

1   There may be too many items in the population
2   It may take too long to collect data on the population
3   Even if we collected data on the population it might take too long to analyse
4   The costs of collecting population data may be prohibitive.

There may be other reasons for restricting our data collection to a sample. The important point is that our analysis of the sample will still reveal the key characteristics of the population provided that the sample is properly representative of the population from which it is taken.

This is a key assumption whenever we are analysing data collected from a sample. For the results of any statistical analysis to be valid we must be sure the sample is a fair cross-section of the statistical population.

Occasionally of course it is possible to undertake analysis of populations rather than samples. Governments regularly collect data relating to some statistical population, usually referred to as a census. Increasingly, with computer-based storage of data it becomes possible to access and analyse population data. A company may have all employee records stored on a computer database, for example, which permits statistical analysis of the entire employee population rather than restricting the analysis to only a sample of the workforce.

The discussion which follows, however, is equally relevant no matter whether we intended collecting population data or, as is more likely, sample data for our analysis.

8.3   STAGES IN DATA COLLECTION

We shall assume that the data to be collected is primary data.

There are a number of logical stages that can be identified in any data collection exercise:

1   Determine the purpose of the exercise
2   Determine the information to be collected
3   Determine the method of data collection
4   Determine the sampling method to be used to select the sample
5   Undertake a pilot survey
6   Undertake the main survey
7   Validate the data and the collection methods
8   Analyse the data collected.

We shall look at each of these stages in turn.

8.3.1   Stage 1—determine the purpose of the exercise

This is the first question to be raised and it must be adequately answered before proceeding with the subsequent stages of data collection. Any data collection exercise is both time-consuming and expensive and it is essential to know for what purpose the data are to be collected. The purpose will have a major effect on the subsequent stages of the exercise.

In general the purpose of the exercise could fall into one of two categories:

1   It could be part of a regular data collection program
2   It could be a one-off exercise.

We might also distinguish the ultimate uses to which the data collected could be put:

1   For general information
2   To assist in operational decision-making
3   To assist in strategic decision-making.

Depending on the circumstances, the information may simply be used by management in a general way as part of some overall information process. Equally, the information may be of use in operational decision-making on a day-to-day basis. We might, for example, collect data on employee absenteeism whereby the personnel department can, on a day-to-day basis, monitor absence from work of individual employees or a department. Again, the data may take on a far more important role if it is to be used to assist in strategic, or long-term, decisions. In our earlier example, a survey of local residents would clearly fall into the latter category as it will assist management in deciding whether the new store will be a feasible project or not.

8.3.2   Stage 2—determine the information to be collected

Following on from the first stage it then becomes necessary to determine precisely what information will be collected. At this stage it becomes necessary to balance two conflicting areas. On the one hand we wish to collect as much relevant data as possible. On the other, the more data we collect the more expensive and time-consuming the exercise will become. It is important, therefore, to know from Stage 1 what the ultimate purpose of the data collection is.

Again, returning to the example of a survey to determine potential customers for a new store we might identify the information we would require as: personal details (age, sex, occupation, income, family size etc); current shopping patterns; likely attitude to the new store; which features would attract the customer to the new store, and so on.

It is important to realise that, frequently, the data we may *wish* to obtain and the data we *actually* obtain may not be the same. For example, it may be considered especially useful to know the income of an individual to determine their likely spending power in the store. However, people may be very reluctant to reveal such details.

8.3.3   Stage 3—determine the method of data collection

Having decided on the data we wish to try to collect we must next determine *how* it is to be collected. Again, this will very much depend on the circumstances surrounding the exercise and the type of data we are trying to collect but we can generalise a number of alternative methods available.

PERSONAL INTERVIEW

This is where a person taking part in the survey is interviewed formally on a face-to-face basis. This method is probably one of the more expensive methods of data collection but with a high degree of accuracy (although this is very dependent on the skill and experience of the interviewer).

POSTAL QUESTIONNAIRE

This method is where some form of questionnaire is sent to those taking part in the exercise, completed by them and returned to the organisation collecting the data. This is generally less expensive than the first method but considerable effort is required in designing an appropriate questionnaire. Additionally, response rates to postal questionnaires can be quite low and the organisation has no way of knowing whether the person completing the questionnaire has properly understood the question and has given the correct response.

TELEPHONE INTERVIEW

This method tends to be restricted to certain types of survey. It tends to be inexpensive and easy to organise (you only require an interviewer and a telephone) but faces a number of potential problems. Only certain people may have access to a telephone which may introduce bias into your survey and it may be difficult to extract appropriate information over the phone.

DIRECT OBSERVATION

This method is appropriate where we do not require specific information about individuals in the survey. For example, if we are simply counting the number of customers going into a rival store this is easily achieved via direct observation. Similarly, if we wish to check the quality of output on some production line this also can be achieved by direct observation. The disadvantage of this method is that it does not provide information about the specific characteristics of the members of the sample selected.

USE OF COMPUTER DATABASES

Increasingly this method of data collection is used. More and more information is stored on computer databases and thereby provides a quick, inexpensive method of extracting data about some sample. Examples would be details of customer accounts, employee records, sales levels, credits and debits, stock levels and quantities ordered and so on. The disadvantage is that where such data exists it is of a secondary nature, with all the associated potential problems.

8.3.4   Determination of the sampling method to be used in the selection of a sample

The next stage is to choose an appropriate method for selecting those items in the population which are to form the basis for the sample. These methods are discussed in detail later in this chapter.

8.3.5   Pilot survey

No matter how well thought-out the previous stages it is virtually essential to undertake a pilot or trial survey before committing the organisation to the trouble and expense of the main survey. Such a pilot survey will allow you to determine whether there are any unforeseen problems in any of the previous stages, particularly relating to the data you are trying to collect, questionnaire design and the selection of sample members.

8.3.6   Main survey

Following the pilot survey any necessary amendments can be made to the data collection exercise and the main survey can then be undertaken. It is usually necessary to monitor the progress of the exercise periodically to ensure that it is conforming to the objectives and methods laid down.

8.3.7   Validation of data and collection methods

Having completed the data collection exercise it is then necessary to validate both the methods that have been used to collect the data and the data itself. This is particularly important if, as is likely, the data is to be analysed using computer-based methods.

8.3.8   Analysis of data collected

Finally, the process of analysing the data to provide the information that was originally required can begin using the techniques that we have already introduced.

8.4 SAMPLING TECHNIQUES

The process of choosing an appropriate technique for selecting a sample from a population is a particularly specialised and technical area.

In general, sampling techniques will fall into one of three broad categories:

1 Random sampling where each member of the population has an equal chance of being included in the sample.
2 Quasi-random sampling (semi-random) is a form of random sampling where the random selection only takes place within certain predefined (non-random) groups.
3 Non-random sampling refers to those techniques where the sample is specifically selected rather than chosen at random.

8.4.1 Simple random sampling

This is a method whereby each member of the population has an equal chance of being selected to form the sample. Assume, for illustration, that we had a population consisting of 100 people. The principle of simple random sampling is that we could, for example, write each person's name on a piece of paper, place all the pieces of paper in a box, and choose a piece of paper at random from the box. Each person in the population obviously has the same chance of being selected and the sample that would result would be a true random sample.

Selection of a sample under such conditions could easily be undertaken via a computer program.

The advantages and disadvantages of this method are:

1 The sample selection is obviously unbiased and can be seen to be representative.
2 It is necessary to know each item in the population which, obviously, will not always be the case.
3 Not all items in the population will be equally accessible once selected for the sample.
4 It is possible that certain parts of the population may by chance be under or over-represented.

8.4.2 Stratified sampling

This is also classed as a random method where we can identify certain groups—or strata—into which the population naturally falls. We can then undertake a random selection within each strata. For example, in the survey on potential customers for the new store we may classify potential customers by sex. If we know, for example, that 55% of the population are female and 45% male then we can ensure that these proportions are maintained within the sample. Each strata can then be randomly selected from the appropriate part of the population.

The advantages and disadvantages of this method are:

1 The sample will reflect the major groupings within the population
2 It is still necessary to know each item in the strata of the population
3 It may be more expensive to conduct.

8.4.3 Systematic sampling

This is a method of quasi-random sampling and can be used in certain structured populations. Returning to our survey of potential customers let us suppose that we have decided to interview those selected for the sample in their own homes. If we took a street of houses then simple random selection means that we could end up in any of the homes in any order. Systematic sampling, however, operates on the basis that the first item selected is chosen at random. From then on the population is systematically surveyed. If there were, say 1,000 houses and we wished to interview 100 people then we would select the first house at random. Subsequently, we would interview the person at every tenth house afterwards to give the total sample of 100.

The advantages and disadvantages of this method are:

1   It is particularly easy to conduct
2   Bias can easily occur if there is any pattern to the distribution of items
3   The method is not truly random.

8.4.4   Multi-stage sampling

This is a second method of quasi-random sampling and is convenient where the population may be spread over a large geographical area. Under such circumstances simple random sampling may require extensive travelling to the various parts of the area covered. Multi-stage sampling operates by splitting the population into geographically distinct areas, randomly selecting certain of these areas and then selecting a sample (either randomly or systematically or in a stratified way) within these areas only.

This means that certain members of the population have no opportunity of being selected for the sample.

The advantages and disadvantages of this method are:

1   The method should lead to unbiased results
2   The method saves time and expense
3   The method is not truly random
4   Great care must be taken in grouping areas to represent the population.

8.4.5   Quota sampling

This method is entirely non-random. The method is generally to stratify the population into groups using appropriate criteria and then to specify the exact number (or quota) required from each group for the sample.

Thus we may classify the population by sex, age group and by occupation. We would then specify, for example, that the sample must include a quota of 20 people who are females, aged between 20 and 30 and who are clerical workers.

The advantages and disadvantages of this method are:

1   The method can lead to highly accurate results
2   The method relies on an accurate identification of appropriate quotas
3   Much reliance is placed on the individual interviewer in selecting people to fill the quota.

8.4.6   Cluster sampling

This is also a method of non-random sampling and is prevalent where the population may be geographically separated.

The method involves selecting a certain number of areas and then sampling all members of the population found in that area. Other areas will not be sampled at all.

The advantages and disadvantages of this method are:

1   It is easy and inexpensive as the survey is undertaken in concentrated areas
2   Sampling is not random
3   The cluster areas must be properly representative of the population.

SUMMARY

1   A distinction must be carefully drawn between primary and secondary data in terms of its reliability.

2   It is usually necessary to base analysis upon some selected sample from the population.
3   The method of sample selection is critical and must be free from bias.
4   The stages in a data collection exercise must be clearly followed.
5   A variety of sample selection techniques exist, dependent upon the type of population to be dealt with and the types of information to be collected.

SELF-TEST QUESTIONS

1   **What is the main difference between primary and secondary data and why is this difference important?** (*Refer to page 77*)

2   **What is the difference between a sample and a population?** (*Refer to page 78*)

3   **Why is it necessary to analyse a sample rather than a population?** (*Refer to page 78*)

4   **Outline the main stages of a data collection exercise.** (*Refer to page 78*)

5   **What is meant by bias?** (*Refer to page 78*)

6   **What is the distinction between a random and quasi-random sampling method?** (*Refer to page 81*)

7   **What are the two main types of quasi-random sampling?** (*Refer to page 81*)

8   **What are the disadvantages of non-random sampling methods?** (*Refer to page 82*)

9   **What is the difference between simple random sampling and stratified sampling?** (*Refer to pages 81, and 82*)

10   **Why is it necessary for a sample to be properly representative of a population?** (*Refer to page 78*)

EXERCISES

1   In Chapter 4, sample data was presented showing daily sales for store A and store B.
     Suppose you had been in charge of collecting this data for this analysis.
     Determine the main stages you would have undertaken and discuss how you would have selected the sample data to be free of bias.

2   In this chapter we have discussed the survey into potential customers who may use a new store. You have been put in charge of the survey to collect this data.
     (a)   Draft a report to management outlining each of the main stages in the exercise, in relation to this survey.
     (b)   Determine which method of data collection you feel would be most appropriate.
     (c)   Draft a short questionnaire to be used in the pilot survey.
     (d)   Discuss the alternative sample selection methods that could be used and recommend which you feel would be most appropriate.

No answers are given. If you are in any doubt, refer again to the content of the chapter.

D

Probability

Typically, in business the circumstances surrounding a business problem and the related decisions we face are uncertain in terms of their outcome. Questions arise such as: Will the company win the contract against the competition? Will the new product be successful? Will the company increase profits next year? Will we need fewer workers next year? and so on.

Because decisions usually have to be taken under such conditions of uncertainty, it is frequently necessary to assess the **likelihood** of specific events occurring in the future. The analysis and quantification of such assessments is known as **probability theory** and forms the basis for this chapter.

It is particularly important that students have an adequate grasp of the underlying principles before we examine the wider potential uses of such theory in business decision-making.

9.1 INTRODUCTION

We shall illustrate most of the basic concepts with reference to a conveniently simple situation. Assume that we have placed 100 pieces of card in a box. The cards are in four different colours, yellow, blue, green and red and there are 25 cards of each colour. Additionally, on each card there has been written a symbol—either a cross or a circle. There are 40 cards with a cross and 60 with a circle and the different symbols are shared proportionately amongst the four colours. Table 9.1 summarises the cards in the box.

9.2 BASIC TERMINOLOGY

QUANTIFYING PROBABILITY

Conventionally, probability is expressed as a value between 0 and 1, either in fractions or as a decimal. A probability of zero implies the event has, literally, no chance of occurring whilst a probability of 1 indicates a guaranteed outcome. So the probability of choosing a card from the box which is white is zero. It can never occur.

Typically, most probability values will lie somewhere between the two extremes.

EXPERIMENTS AND EVENTS

Probabilities revolve around **events**, which are the possible outcomes from doing something. Choosing a card from the box and looking at the colour has four events associated with it: the event that the card chosen is yellow, is green, is red, is blue. The activity that produces an event is known as an **experiment**.

INDEPENDENT AND CONDITIONAL EVENTS

Some events are classed as **independent** whilst others are **conditional**. Independent events are those whose probability is not affected by other events. Some events, however, will be dependent, or conditional, on other events.

Consider the experiment of choosing a card from the box and noting its colour and its symbol. We define event 1 as the card being red and event 2 that the symbol is a circle. It is apparent that event 2 is in no way affected by event 1. The probability of the card showing a circle is independent of the colour of the card.

However, a different experiment may have events which are not independent. Assume we choose two cards at the same time at random from the box and we want to know the probability that the two cards chosen will both be red. The probability of the second event will depend on what happened with the first event as there is now one less card to choose from and there may also be one less red card to select. In this case the second event is said to be conditional on the first.

MUTUALLY EXCLUSIVE EVENTS

Two events are mutually exclusive when they cannot occur simultaneously. The events of choosing a card with a circle or a cross from the box are mutually exclusive, they cannot both happen at the same time. Some events, however, may happen simultaneously. Consider the example of choosing a card which was both red and had a circle symbol. It is obviously possible for **both** events to occur with the choice of card.

9.3   MEASURING PROBABILITY

The probability of an event occurring is expressed as:

$$P(Event) = \frac{\text{number of ways the event could occur}}{\text{total number of outcomes}}$$

For example, the probability of choosing a red card from the box:

$$P(red) = \frac{\text{number of red cards}}{\text{number of cards}} = \frac{25}{100} = 0.25$$

It is important to understand what the probability value represents. It does not mean that, if we were to repeat the experiment 100 times then exactly 25 red cards would be chosen. Rather, it is an indication of the average or long-run outcome. If we were to repeat the experiment a large number of times then, we would expect an average of 25% of cards to be red. The correct interpretation of a probability calculation is of considerable importance in decision making.

Similarly, if we were to choose one card and we wished to determine the probability that it was either red or green:

$$P(red\ or\ green) = \frac{\text{number of red or green cards}}{\text{total number of cards}} = \frac{25 + 25}{100} = 0.5$$

9.4   BASIC RULES OF PROBABILITY

The method of measuring probability can be formalised into a number of basic rules.

THE MULTIPLICATION RULE

The multiplication rule is concerned with situations where we are interested in a sequence of events occurring. For example, we choose a card and we wish to calculate the probability that the card is **both** red **and** shows a cross. To apply the multiplication rule correctly we need to distinguish those experiments where events are independent and those where they are conditional. If the events are independent—as in the example of red and a cross—the probability is calculated by multiplying (hence the name) the probabilities of the two events together:

Event A: card is red   P = 0.25
Event B: card shows a cross   P = 0.4

$$P(\text{card is red and a cross}) = P(A \text{ and } B) = P(A) \times P(B)$$

$$= 0.25 \times 0.4 = 0.10$$

That is, there is a probability of 0.10 of choosing a card from the box that is both red and showing a cross. Reference back to Table 9.1 confirms the rule: there are 10 cards which satisfy both criteria of being red and showing a cross.

The basic rule is easily extended to cover more than two events. If we had three events (A, B, C) then:

$$P(A \text{ and } B \text{ and } C) = P(A) \times P(B) \times P(C)$$

For events which are conditional, however, the basic multiplication rule must be amended. Assume we have an experiment to draw two cards and we wish to know the probability of drawing two red cards. We draw the first card and note whether we have drawn a red. Without replacing this card we draw a second and wish to know the probability that this card is also red. In this example the events are conditional as the probability of the second event is affected by the outcome of the first event.

Event A: the first card is red   P = 0.25
Event B: the second card is also red

To calculate the probability of event B is straightforward. Both events can only occur providing the first event is successful, ie a red card is chosen. Given that there are now only 99 cards left and only 24 of them are red P(B) will be 24/99 = 0.2424
Using the multiplication rule we have:

$$P(\text{both cards are red}) = P(A \text{ and } B) = 0.25 \times 0.2424 = 0.0606$$

That is, there is a chance of just over 6% of choosing two cards from the box that are both red.
Using standard probability notation we would express such a probability as:

$$P(\text{both cards are red}) = P(A) \times P(B|A)$$

where $P(B|A)$ refers to the probability of event B **given that** event A has occurred. For independent events it should be apparent that $P(B|A) = P(B)$.

THE ADDITION RULE

The addition rule is concerned with experiments where we are interested in **at least** one of two or more events occurring simultaneously. For example, we choose a card from the box and we wish to calculate the probability that the card is **either** red **or** blue.

The addition rule is easily applied to such event but again we must distinguish between two types of situation, those where events are mutually exclusive and those where they are not. With the example above, where the events are mutually exclusive, the probability is calculated by adding (hence the name of the rule) the probabilities together.

Event A: card is red   P = 0.25
Event B: card is blue   P = 0.25

$$P(\text{card is either red or blue}) = P(A \text{ or } B) = P(A) + P(B)$$

$$= 0.25 + 0.25 = 0.50$$

Obviously, the addition rule simply reflects that, in our example, 50 cards in the box are either red or blue.

For events which are not mutually exclusive, however, the rule as given will not work. Let us amend the problem so that we now wish to know the probability of choosing either a red card or a card with a cross symbol. If we apply the rule we have:

$$P(\text{card is either red or shows a cross}) = 0.25 + 0.4 = 0.65$$

which, on reflection, is incorrect. It is apparent that using the above rule we have double counted cards which are **both** red and show a cross. (You can see from Table 9.1 that there are a total of 10 cards in this category.) To resolve this we can amend the addition rule:

$$P(A \text{ or } B) = P(A) + P(B) - P(A \text{ and } B)$$

giving:

$$P(\text{red}) + P(\text{cross}) - P(\text{red and a cross})$$
$$0.25 + 0.4 - 0.10 = 0.55$$

The probability of 0.1 was obtained using the multiplication rule developed earlier. That is there are 55 **different** cards in the box which are either red or show a cross.

These two simple rules dealing with probability situations form the basis for complex problem solving and business decisions.

9.5   BAYES THEOREM

Earlier in the chapter the concept of **conditional** probability was introduced. The original probability of an event, A, has to be revised if A is conditional on event B and event B has occurred. This concept of revising probabilities in the light of additional information is an area of statistics referred to as **Bayesian** statistics. We shall introduce only the outline of the concept here.

Bayes theorem states that:

$$P(A|B) = \frac{P(B|A)P(A)}{P(B|A)P(A) + P(B|\bar{A})P(\bar{A})}$$

where A and B are some defined events and $(\bar{A})$ is the complement of A that is, the event that A does *not* occur.

Let us illustrate the theorem with a simple example.

MTG regularly purchase a particular product from two suppliers—supplier A and supplier B. The quality of the product supplied is varied and MTG has a policy of checking the products supplied and returning those items classed as 'faulty'.

Table 9.2 shows the results of this checking for the products supplied last month.

TABLE 9.2   **Items supplied last month**

	Faulty (F)	Not Faulty (NF)	Total items supplied
Supplier A	15	60	75
Supplier B	5	45	50
Total	20	105	125

Thus, a total of 20 out of 125 items were found to be faulty upon delivery.

This month another batch of items has been received from both suppliers. Unfortunately, the relevant invoices have been lost by the warehouse department and there is no way of knowing for certain which items were sent by which supplier. Upon checking the quality of the goods supplied the company has again found a faulty item. Naturally, we cannot determine for certain which supplier sent the faulty item but we can assess the relevant probability using Bayes theorem.

First, let us calculate the relevant probabilities from Table 9.2, shown in Table 9.3.

TABLE 9.3 **Items supplied last month: derived probabilities**

	Faulty (F)	Not Faulty (NF)
Supplier A	0.20	0.80
Supplier B	0.10	0.90

So, for example, supplier A sent 60 out of 75 items which were classed as not faulty giving a probability value of 0.8—that is 80% of A's supplies were not faulty.

Let us now define the following variables:

A —item came from supplier A
B —item came from supplier B
F —item supplied was faulty
NF—item supplied was not faulty

Given that we have found a faulty item we want to know the probability that it came from supplier A. This can be expressed as:

$$P(A|F)$$

ie the probability that it came from supplier A **given that** the item was faulty. Using Bayes theorem we have:

$$P(A|F) = \frac{P(F|A)P(A)}{P(F|A)P(A) + P(F|B)P(B)}$$

(Note that here B is the complement of A)

From Tables 9.2 and 9.3 we can determine the relevant probabilities:

P(A) = 0.6 (75/125)
P(B) = 0.4 (=1 − P(A))
P(F|A) = 0.2 (Given an item came from supplier A the probability that it is faulty) (15/75)
P(F|B) = 0.1 (Given an item came from supplier B the probability that it is faulty) (5/50)

Substituting these into the formula we have:

$$P(A|F) = \frac{0.2(0.6)}{0.2(0.6) + 0.1(0.4)} = \frac{0.12}{0.12 + 0.04} = \frac{0.12}{0.16} = 0.75$$

That is, if we have found a faulty item there is a probability of 0.75 that the item came from supplier A.

Similarly to find the probability that the item came from supplier B:

$$P(B|F) = \frac{P(F|B)P(B)}{P(F|B)P(B) + P(F|A)P(A)}$$

$$P(B|F) = \frac{0.1(0.4)}{0.1(0.4) + 0.2(0.6)} = \frac{0.04}{0.04 + 0.12} = \frac{0.04}{0.16} = 0.25$$

Note that the two probabilities sum to 1.0 as they must do (a faulty item **must** come either from supplier A or supplier B).

9.6 EXPECTED VALUE

Probability is of considerable importance in business decision-making. Decisions must be made on the basis of an assessment of their probable outcomes. The basic rules of probability are frequently used to calculate something referred to as the **expected value** or as the **expected monetary value**, given that many business decisions are finance-related. We can illustrate the concept with a simple example which shows the potential for using probability in decision making.

MTG are considering opening a new food store in a particular town where they do not currently operate. The accounts department has costed the potential investment and has estimated the likely daily revenue if the proposed store is opened. However, there is an area of uncertainty surrounding the project relating as to how popular (and hence profitable) the store will be with local customers.

The accounts department have undertaken some research into the popularity of MTG's store with local customers in terms of sales levels. Daily sales have been categorised as being either high, medium or low. If sales are high then daily revenue in the store will average £2,000. If sales are medium average daily sales will be £1,500 and only £1,000 if sales are low.

The chances of sales being high, medium or low is given in the table below:

TABLE 9.4   **Probability of sales levels**

Sales category	Probability
High	0.7
Medium	0.2
Low	0.1

We can use what we know about the problem and about probability to provide additional relevant information, such as the expected monetary value relating to the decision to open the store. The relevant details are shown in Table 9.5.

TABLE 9.5   **Expected monetary value associated with opening the store**

Sales	Daily revenue	Probability	Prob × revenue
High	£2000	0.7	£1400
Medium	£1500	0.2	£300
Low	£1000	0.1	£100
		Total	£1800

The table shows a total figure derived from multiplying the possible daily revenues by their respective probabilities. This figure (£1,800) is simply an average daily revenue weighted using the probabilities of a particular revenue figure being achieved. Such an average is known as the **expected value** and it is important to realise what such a figure represents. It does **not** represent the actual revenue earned (which will be either £2,000, £1,500 or £1,000 per day on average). It is an indication of likely profits in the sense that, if we were to repeat this problem with a large number of firms or over a long period of time daily revenue would average out at £1,800.

As such, this information could be used by the group to decide whether the likely revenue from opening the store is adequate given other aspects such as costs, interest rates, profit targets etc. Such an expected value allows a business to take into account not only the financial effects of a decision but also the likelihood of those financial effects.

In general the expected value can be found by:

$$\text{Expected value} = \Sigma \ Px$$

where x is a particular monetary value and P its associated probability.

Expected value is an easy method of incorporating uncertainty (and the respective probabilities) into decision-making.

SUMMARY

Probability allows a business organisation to choose between alternative decisions in terms of the likelihood that a decision will have a particular outcome. This is particularly useful when combined with financial information in the form of an expected value.

1 An event is a defined outcome of an experiment.
2 An experiment is a process which generates specified outcomes.
3 Independent events are events which have no influence on each other.
4 Conditional events are events which in some way affect each other's likelihood.
5 Mutually exclusive events are events which cannot occur together.
6 Probability indicates the likelihood that an event will occur.
7 The Addition Rule is used for situations where a probability in the form P(A *or* B) is required.
8 The Multiplication Rule is used for situations where a probability in the form P(A *and* B) is required.
9 Bayes theorem is used to determine conditional probabilities.
10 An expected value is the sum of a series of possible values and their associated probabilities.

SELF-TEST QUESTIONS

1 Give an example of each of the following:
   (a) an experiment
   (b) mutually exclusive events
   (c) independent events
   (*Refer to pages 85 and 86*)

2 How would you know that something was wrong if you were told that P(X) = 1.4? (*Refer to page 85*)

3 What is the general form of the addition rule? (*Refer to page 87*)

4 For what types of event is the addition rule used? (*Refer to page 87*)

5 What is the general form of the Multiplication Rule? (*Refer to page 87*)

6 For what types of event is the Multiplication Rule used? (*Refer to page 87*)

7 What is the general form of Bayes theorem? (*Refer to page 88*)

8 What is meant by expected value? (*Refer to page 90*)

9 What is meant by P(X) = 0.3? (*Refer to page 86*)

10 Explain what P(X|Y) means (*Refer to page 87*)

EXERCISES

1 Using the data in Table 9.1 and the appropriate rule determine the following probabilities if a card is selected at random:
   (a) the card is yellow
   (b) the card is blue
   (c) the card is yellow or blue
   (d) the card is not yellow
   (e) the card is blue with a circle
   (f) the card is blue and does not have a circle
   (g) the card has a cross
   (h) the card has a cross and is green
   (i) the card has a cross and is not green
   (j) the card does not have a cross and is not green
   (k) the card is either green or has a cross
   (l) why are the words 'at random' important?

2   Using Table 9.2 and Bayes theorem determine the following probabilities:
  (a)   an item is faulty given that it was supplied by supplier B
  (b)   an item was not faulty given that it came from supplier A

Answers on page 306.

Probability distributions

In the previous chapter we looked at the calculation and interpretation of the probability of individual events occurring. Equally useful is the **probability distribution**, which shows the probability of all outcomes occurring from some experiment. At this stage, perhaps the easiest way to visualise such a probability distribution is as a form of frequency polygon or frequency curve where the specific outcomes are measured on the horizontal axis and the probabilities on the vertical axis.

The importance of such probability distributions is that they extend the areas to which probability can be applied and provide a means of determining the probability of an event without having to resort to the probability rules introduced in the last chapter. There are three common probability distributions that we shall examine:

1   Binomial distribution
2   Poisson distribution
3   Normal distribution

10.1   THE BINOMIAL DISTRIBUTION

Let us assume that, as part of the group's operations, MTG have a small factory producing some particular item that is sold in the group's stores under its own brand name. In order to check the quality of the output produced an inspector is employed to regularly check the items. When checked they are classed either as faulty or as not faulty. On average 10% of items checked are found to be faulty.

The inspector chooses three items at random from the production line and he wants to calculate the relevant probability distribution. That is, he wants to calculate the following probabilities:

P(0 items are faulty)
P(1 item is faulty)
P(2 items are faulty)
P(3 items are faulty)

To work out the first of these involves a simple application of the Multiplication Rule.

P(0 items faulty) = P(Item 1 not faulty) × P(Item 2 not faulty) × P(Item 3 not faulty)

Given that P(item is not faulty) = 0.9 then:

P(0 items faulty) = 0.9 × 0.9 × 0.9 = 0.729

However, the next probability in the distribution—P(1 item faulty) is not as straight-forward, because there are a number of different ways, or *combinations*, in which we could have one item out of three faulty:

Item 1	Item 2	Item 3
F	NF	NF
NF	F	NF
NF	NF	F

Each of the three ways indicates one faulty item out of three and each will have the same probability:

$$0.9 \times 0.9 \times 0.1 = 0.081$$

The calculation of the probability for three ways is:

$$\text{P(1 Item faulty)} = 3(0.9 \times 0.9 \times 0.1) = 3 \times 0.081 = 0.243$$

We could now proceed in exactly the same way for P(2 faulty items) but a more general method of solution is required, using a formula to calculate the combination of ways a sequence can occur:

$$^nC_r = \frac{n!}{r!(n-r)!}$$

where n is the total number of items and r the specific number we require the value for. Thus in this example, n would be three and r would be one.

The term '!' is referred to as 'factorial' and represents a mathematical symbol indicating a specific piece of arithmetic—a series of multiplications.

For example, with n=3 then n! is the same as:

$$3 \times 2 \times 1 = 6$$

Similarly if n had been 10 then n! would be:

$$10 \times 9 \times 8 \times 7 \times 6 \times 5 \times 4 \times 3 \times 2 \times 1 = 3628800$$

It should be noted that 1! = 1 and 0! = 1.

So using the factorial expression we can confirm that there are three ways of having one item from three faulty:

$$\frac{3!}{1!(3-1)!} = \frac{3!}{1!(2)!} = \frac{3 \times 2 \times 1}{1(2 \times 1)} = \frac{6}{2} = 3$$

Returning to the calculations for the probability distributions we are trying to find P(2 faulty items).

Using the combinations formula we have n= 3 and r=2 so the formula gives:

$$\frac{3!}{2!(1!)} = \frac{3 \times 2 \times 1}{2 \times 1(1)} = \frac{6}{2} = 3$$

So, again, there are three ways in which we could get two faulty items from three. The probability of any one of the ways occurring is given by:

$$0.9 \times 0.1 \times 0.1 = 0.009$$

so P(2 faulty items) = 3(0.009) = 0.027

Finally, for three faulty items:

$$\frac{3!}{3!(3-3)!} = \frac{3 \times 2 \times 1}{3!(0!)} = \frac{6}{6 \times 1} = 1$$

that is, there is only one combination of having three faulty items out of three. The associated probability is given by:

$$(0.1 \times 0.1 \times 0.1) = 0.001$$

Collecting all these together we have:

No of faulty items	No of ways	Prob of one sequence	Probability
0	1	0.729	0.729
1	3	0.081	0.243
2	3	0.009	0.027
3	1	0.001	0.001
		Total	1.000

In fact we can generalise the probabilities of one sequence:

$$0 \text{ faulty items} \quad 0.9^3$$
$$1 \text{ faulty item} \quad 0.9^2 \times 0.1$$
$$2 \text{ faulty items} \quad 0.9 \times 0.1^2$$
$$3 \text{ faulty items} \quad 0.1^3$$

Thus combining the factorial expression with a general expression for calculating the probability of a specific sequence of events we have the general Binomial formula as:

$$^nC_r p^r q^{(n-r)}$$

where ^nC_r is the general term for determining the combination

p is the probability of a faulty item

$q = (1-p)$ the probability of a non-faulty item

n is the number of items

r the specified number of items we seek a probability for.

The general formula can be used for any Binomial application.

10.1.1   Recognising a binomial application

In order to use the Binomial probability distribution it is necessary to be able to recognise those problems where it is applicable. In general three conditions must be met:

1   The situation must involve some sort of experiment or trial of which there are a fixed number, n. In our example the experiment was defined as choosing an item from the production line. In total we undertook three such experiments

2   Each experiment must have two mutually exclusive outcomes, defined in general as success and failure. In our example we defined success as choosing a non-faulty item and failure as a faulty item. The definitions can be extensive—win/lose, profit/loss, high sales/low sales etc.

3   The probability of success must remain constant.

10.1.2   Mean and standard deviation of the binomial distribution

The probability distribution we have calculated for the Binomial situation above can be viewed like any other frequency distribution. The only difference is that we are measuring probability rather than frequencies. As with any distribution we could calculate the mean and the standard deviation. For a Binomial distribution the relevant formulae are:

Mean = np

Standard deviation $= \sqrt{np(1-p)}$

where n and p take the usual meaning.

In the example we have been using n=3 and p=0.1 so:

Mean $= 3 \times 0.1 = 0.3$

Standard deviation $= \sqrt{3(0.1)0.9} = 0.52$

The interpretation of these statistics is no different from that in any distribution. On average, we would expect 0.3 faulty items in any batch of three selected.

10.2 USING STATISTICAL TABLES TO DETERMINE A BINOMIAL PROBABILITY

Whilst it is possible to use the Binomial formula to determine the probability of a sequence of events it is also possible to derive selected probabilities from Statistical Tables which provide Binomial probabilities for certain combinations of p and n.

One such table is shown in Appendix A.

To illustrate the use of such tables let us assume we have carried out similar testing as before but this time we are selecting 10 items from the production line.

Let us define the following:

$$n = 10 \text{ (number of experiments)}$$
$$p = \text{probability of the item being faulty} = 0.1$$

Having selected 10 items we want to determine the probability that four of the items are faulty, in other words r=4. If we wish to use the Binomial formula we have:

$$^{10}C_4 \ 0.1^4 \times 0.9^6$$

$$\frac{10!}{4! \ 6!} \ 0.1^4 \times 0.9^6 = \frac{3628800}{24(720)} \times 0.0001 \times 0.531441 = 0.0112$$

However, the same result is more easily obtained from Appendix A. Looking for the combination of p=0.1 and n=10 we find that when r=4 the Appendix gives the value of 0.0112, exactly the same as was derived using the formula. As long as the combination of n and p that you require is in the table the probabilities are readily found.

10.3 PERMUTATIONS AND COMBINATIONS

In developing the Binomial formula we developed the idea of a combination. It is also worthwhile at this stage introducing the related idea of a permutation.

The concepts are similar and the formula for determining the number of permutations is given by:

$$\text{No of permutations} = \ ^nP_r = \frac{n!}{(n-r)!}$$

where n and r have the same meaning as in the combinations formula.

The difference between the two lies in the importance of ordering. Assume that we have three individuals currently on the Board of Directors and there are three vacant positions of Chairman, Treasurer and Secretary. All three people have been nominated for all three posts. We wish to determine the mixture of people to posts that we may end up with. If we denote the three people as A, B, C then the illustration below indicates the possible results:

Chairman	Treasurer	Secretary
A	B	C
A	C	B
B	A	C
B	C	A
C	A	B
C	B	A

Thus there are 6 different ways (or permutations) to this ordering. In this context the ordering is important so we would use the permutation expression:

n=3 r=3

$$\frac{3!}{(3-3)!} = \frac{3!}{0!} = 6$$

confirming that there are six distinct orderings of the three people between the three posts.

If ordering had not been important then we should have used the combination formula instead.

10.4   THE POISSON DISTRIBUTION

The second probability distribution is the Poisson (pronounced Pwasonn) distribution.

To illustrate this distribution let us assume that we are investigating the efficiency of a telephone switchboard at one of the stores. Customers and clients who wish to contact the store occasionally complain that it is difficult for them to get through. They frequently hear the line engaged tone when 'phoning. Investigation shows that the switchboard has the technical capacity for dealing with up to five calls at any one time. A preliminary investigation indicates that, on average, the switchboard receives two calls per minute. We need to determine whether the existing switchboard can deal with the existing demand by determining the probability that the switchboard will receive more than five calls per minute.

The immediate problem is that we cannot determine the specific probability of the defined event: a call being made. We have information only on the number of calls *received* not the total number of phone calls *made*.

The Poisson distribution is directly applicable to such situations where we have some average but cannot determine the probability of the defined event. The Poisson formula is given as:

$$P(\text{event X}) = \frac{e^{-\lambda}\lambda^x}{X!}$$

where e is a mathematical constant taking the value 2.718281828. . ., where λ is the average number of occurrences of the event, and where X refers to the specific value we are trying to calculate a probability for.

In this example, λ will take the value 2 and X the value 6, 7, 8 etc (given that we are looking for the probability that *more than* five calls will be received.) This will give:

$$P(\text{6 calls}) = \frac{e^{(-2)}\ 2^6}{6!} = .0120$$

$$P(\text{7 calls}) = \frac{e^{(-2)}\ 2^7}{7!} = .0034$$

$$P(\text{8 calls}) = \frac{e^{(-2)}\ 2^8}{8!} = .0009$$

$$P(\text{9 calls}) = \frac{e^{(-2)}\ 2^9}{9!} = .0002$$

There is obviously no need to work out P(10 calls) as it will be, effectively, zero. Collecting these together we have:

$$P(\text{more than 5 calls}) = 0.0120 + 0.0034 + 0.0009 + 0.0002 = 0.0165$$

That is, there is a probability of approximately 1.6% that the switchboard will receive more than 5 calls in any one minute. In other words, the chances of a customer calling the store and not being able to get through are very low.

In practice the Poisson probability is almost always found from the relevant statistical tables as illustrated in Appendix B. These are used in exactly the same way as the Binomial probability tables discussed earlier.

Confirming the probability we have just determined we look at the column headed $\lambda=2$ and search down until we get to X=6, 7 etc and the figures calculated above can be confirmed from the table.

As with the Binomial distribution, the Poisson distribution is applicable only under certain conditions:

1   Events occur at random.
2   A specific interval (either of time or space) is defined within which we focus our attention. Here we had an interval of a minute.

3 The average occurrence of the event remains constant within the interval and between intervals.

10.4.1 Mean and standard deviation of the Poisson distribution

As with the Binomial distribution the mean and standard deviation of any Poisson distribution can be calculated:

$$\text{Mean} = \lambda$$

$$\text{Standard deviation} = \sqrt{\lambda}$$

10.5 THE NORMAL DISTRIBUTION

The third of our probability distributions is the Normal distribution. This probability distribution is particularly important in statistics and underpins a large area of statistics referred to as **statistical inference**.

The Binomial and Poisson distributions deal with discrete variables. The Normal distribution deals with continuous variables. More importantly, the general shape of the Normal distribution always remains the same no matter what the variable is that we are examining. This general shape is illustrated in figure 10.1 and follows a symmetrical pattern often referred to as bell-shaped.

FIGURE 10.1 **Normal Distribution Curve**

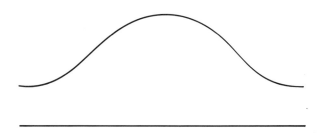

So, no matter what variable we are investigating, if we know that the variable is Normally distributed we automatically know it will follow the shape of the distribution in Figure 10.1. What will distinguish the different Normal distributions for different variables, however, will be the two key features of the distribution:

(a) its average, the mean value
(b) its dispersion, the standard deviation

The particularly useful feature of the Normal distribution is that for *any* normally distributed variable the same proportion of observations will occur in the same part of the distribution. For example, as we shall see later, for any normally distributed variable approximately 95% of observations will lie within two standard deviations of the mean of that data set.

Statisticians have taken advantage of the features of the Normal distribution to produce sets of statistical tables that show, for any normally distributed variable, the proportion of items that will occur within a certain distance of the mean. Such a table is shown in Appendix C and we shall illustrate its use shortly.

STANDARDISING THE NORMAL DISTRIBUTION

In order to use these tables we must first **standardise** the distribution for the specific variable we are dealing with. Such standardisation is necessary because although all Normal distributions take the same shape their means and standard deviations will tend to differ not only in size but also in the units of measurement.

Such standardisation allows us to relate any variable which is Normally distributed to the statistical tables and thereby to any other Normally distributed variable. We define a statistic, known as the Z statistic, as:

$$Z = \frac{X - \text{mean}}{\text{standard deviation}}$$

where mean is the arithmetic mean of the Normal distribution
standard deviation is the standard deviation of the Normal distribution
X is the value of the variable we are trying to find a probability for.

The Z statistic simply expresses the difference between the X value and the mean in multiples of the standard deviation of the distribution. The probability corresponding to this Z statistic can then be read directly from the table.

We shall illustrate with a simple example. MTG produces some of the foodstuffs it sells in its stores under its own label and brandname. One such item is a type of breakfast cereal. The group currently uses two machines which process and package the cereal. Machine X produces packs containing an average of 500 grams whilst machine Y produces packs containing on average 1,000 grams. The corresponding standard deviations have been calculated as 10g for machine X and 20g for machine Y. The weights of packs produced by each machine are normally distributed.

We are asked to evaluate the performance of each machine. We have decided, as an initial step, to calculate appropriate probabilities:

1   The probability that machine A will process a pack weighing less than 490g.
2   The probability that machine B will process a pack weighing less than 980g.

We know that the two distributions are identical (they are both Normal) except for their mean and standard deviation. Using the Z statistic we can transform the data from **absolute** to **relative** values.

Machine X

$$Z = \frac{X - \text{mean}}{\text{sd}} = \frac{490 - 500}{10} = -1$$

Machine Y

$$Z = \frac{X - \text{mean}}{\text{sd}} = \frac{980 - 1000}{20} = -1$$

We can see that both distributions have the same Z statistic which shows that for the values we have specified (490g and 980g respectively) each has a Z score of −1. In both cases, the X value is one standard deviation **below** the mean of its own distribution.

Effectively what the Z statistic formula does is to calculate **relative** values for a normal distribution in terms of the number of standard deviation above and below the mean. **Table 10.1** illustrates this for our example.

TABLE 10.1   **Calculation of Standard Scores**

Machine X							
Weight packed (g)	470	480	490	500	510	520	530
Machine Y							
Weight packed (g)	940	960	980	1000	1020	1040	1060
Z score (standard deviations from the mean)	−3	−2	−1	0	+1	+2	+3

Table 10.1 shows the comparable weights on the two machines, comparable in the sense that they are the same number of standard deviations away from their own mean. We can see that a pack weighing 510g on machine X is the equivalent of a pack weighing 1020g on machine Y.

This means that, as in both cases the Z score is the same, the same **proportion** of items lie below 490g and 980g respectively. In effect the probability is the same for each of our selections. The availability of a table showing the standardised Z scores means that such probabilities do not have to be calculated but can be read directly from the table in Appendix C. The first column in the Table relates to the Z score calculated. Note that only **positive** Z scores are shown. Given that the Normal distribution is symmetrical both halves of the distribution (around the mean) are identical. If the table shows the probability associated with a value a certain number of standard deviations **above** the mean, the value an equivalent number of standard deviations **below** the mean must have the same probability.

Thus, with our Z score of −1 we can follow this column down until we get to the appropriate row. We now read off a value opposite this Z score of 0.1587. This indicates that 15.87% of observations will occur to the **left** of a value 1 standard deviation below the mean. This is illustrated in Figure 10.2.

FIGURE 10.2   **P (Z < −1)**

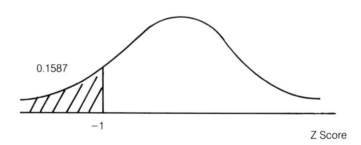

In the context of our problem, there is a probability of 0.1587 of machine X producing a pack weighing less than 490g or of machine Y producing a pack less than 980g. This is the equivalent of saying that 15.8% of packs produced by both machines will fall into this part of their respective distributions.

Note, that if our Z score calculation had given a value which included up to two decimal places we would use the rest of this row in the table. Thus, a Z score of 1.01 has an associated probability of 0.1563, a Z score of 1.02 a probability of 0.1539 etc. Note also that if you are using your own set of statistical tables the same information may be presented in a different format, sometimes showing the area to the **left** of the specified value not the right.

The important principle in this example is that this probability will apply to *all* Normal distributions. 15.87% of observations in any such distribution will occur in the area to the left of 1 standard deviation below the mean. What differs from problem to problem, of course, is not the probability but the mean and standard deviation values.

SUMMARY

Probability distributions allows us to calculate probabilities for groups of events as well as for individual events.

1 There are three commonly used probability distributions: the Binomial, the Poisson, the Normal.

2 The Binomial probability is applied where there are a number of identical experiments each of which has a constant probability of success or failure.

3 The Poisson probability is applied to situations where events occur randomly over some interval and the average occurrence is known.

4 The Binomial and Poisson probabilities can be calculated directly or determined from the appropriate Statistical Tables.

5 Normal distribution takes the familiar symmetrical or bell-shape and is characterised by the mean and standard deviation.

6 Normal probabilities relate to the probability that some value in the distribution has (or has not) been exceeded.

7 To use the Normal probability tables the variable under investigation must be standardised

SELF-TEST QUESTIONS

1 What is a Z score? *(Refer to page 99)*

2 Why can the Normal distribution not be used to find the probability that a specific value is obtained eg P(X=490)? *(Refer to page 98)*

3 What are the main features of the Normal distribution? *(Refer to page 98)*

4 What are the main features of situations where the Binomial distribution is applicable? *(Refer to page 95)*

5 What are the main features of situations where the Poisson distribution is applicable? *(Refer to page 97)*

6 What is the difference between a permutation and a combination? *(Refer to page 96)*

7 What is the formula for determining the Binomial probability? *(Refer to page 95)*

8 What is the formula for determining the Poisson probability? *(Refer to page 97)*

EXERCISES

1 Take the experiment of tossing a coin and noting whether it shows heads or tails. The coin is to be tossed a total of 5 times.
   (a) Using the Binomial formula determine the probability distribution of the coin showing heads (that is work out the probabilities that 0 heads will show, then 1, 2, 3, 4, 5).
   (b) Construct a simple bar chart of these probabilities
   (c) Confirm your answers to part (a) by using the Statistical Tables.

2 The Northern region of MTG have a fleet of 20 delivery trucks that they use to supply their various stores. On the payroll they currently have 25 truck drivers. From payroll records it has been estimated that 10% of drivers are not available for work at any one time (because of holiday, sickness etc.)
   Determine the probability that on any one day there will be sufficient drivers for the fleet of trucks.

3 Under Government regulations stores in the group have to regularly report any accidents involving staff. Over the last year such reported accidents averaged 20 per month.
  (a) Determine the following probabilities:
    (i) that there will be no accidents over the next month
    (ii) there will be more than 25 accidents over the next month
  (b) Do you think the conditions for the use of the Poisson distribution are being met in these circumstances?

4 An auditor is currently checking a batch of invoices for errors. Based on previous experience he anticipates that, in total, 6% of all invoices will contain some error.
    He takes a batch of 10 invoices. Determine the following probabilities:
  (a) None of the invoices contain errors
  (b) Exactly five of the invoices contain errors
  (c) No more than two invoices contain errors
  (d) At least nine invoices contain errors

5 Returning to machine Y in section 10.5, the machine packed an average of 1000g per box, standard deviation 20g. Determine the following:
  (a) The proportion of boxes weighing more than 1,020g
  (b) The proportion of boxes weighing more than 1,050g
  (c) The proportion of boxes weighing between 1,020 and 1,050g
  (d) The proportion of boxes weighing less than 950g.

6 One of the stores in the MTG group selling computer supplies is currently reviewing its policy of holding floppy disks in stock. On average the shop sells 30 floppy disks per day. The manager has decided that he wishes to minimise the risk of running out of supplies and having to turn potential customers away. Accordingly, he has decided that he wants a probability of 5% or less of running out of stock on any one day. What number of disks would you advise him to keep in stock in order to meet this target?

Answers on page 307.

Section B: Mathematical techniques

Mathematical techniques

In Section A we saw the necessity for analysing and presenting information using a variety of **statistical** techniques. In this section we introduce the corresponding **mathematical** techniques that are frequently used by business. As with statistical techniques it is necessary to develop not only an ability to find the answer to a mathematical problem but also to be able to understand the principles underlying the technique and the general areas of relevance for business applications.

Chapter 11 introduces basic mathematical concepts and notation and the use of linear functions to represent typical business problems.

Chapter 12 develops the use of linear relationships through the application of a specialised type of algebra, matrix algebra.

Chapter 13 covers the topic of linear programming which is concerned with the use of linear relationships to determine some optimum position.

Chapter 14 expands the use of mathematics to look at non-linear relationships, in particular the use of quadratic equations.

Chapter 15 introduces generalised methods of dealing with any type of mathematical function through the use of differential and integral calculus.

Chapter 16 introduces the technique of linear regression which is concerned with quantifying linear relationships between two variables.

Chapter 17 looks at the method of time series analysis, particularly in the context of business forecasting.

Chapter 18 examines the application of the mathematical techniques introduced in this section to an important business area—stock control.

Linear equations

Mathematics offers the business analyst a convenient method of representing and analysing business problems. Like the corresponding statistical techniques, mathematics has its own terminology which will be introduced and explained where appropriate.

Much of mathematical business analysis takes place through the use of *linear* equations. This chapter introduces such equations, their corresponding graphs and examines how sets of linear equations can be solved through the use of simultaneous equations.

11.1 FUNCTIONS

In applying mathematics to business we are normally interested in trying to relate two or more variables to each other, such as sales and profit, price and sales, productivity and profit and so on. This is initially achieved by expressing such a relationship in general **functional** form.

Assume that part of the MTG company which manufactures some product has been collecting and analysing data on two variables of particular importance to management:

1   The number of units of the product produced each week (measured in 000s of units)
2   The total cost of producing those units each week (measured in £000s)

If we denote the number of units produced as X and total costs as TC then we can express the relationship between the two as a simple function:

$$TC = f(X)$$

The term f( ) (a function of) is the mathematical way of expressing a generalised relationship between two or more variables. In business, such a function between variables implies some sort of dependency or **causal** relationship. Here, in expressing the relationship in this way we are suggesting that the level of output in some way determines or causes the level of Total Costs. In mathematical notation, TC is referred to as the dependent variable and X as the independent or explanatory variable. Whilst mathematically we could express the function the opposite way—output as a function of costs—it would make no sense to do so in a business context.

11.2 LINEAR EQUATIONS

The expression of such a functional relationship between two variables is typically the first step in mathematical analysis. However, for practical purposes we generally require more explicit information than that provided in a function. In this example, it is not sufficient to know that total costs are **in some way** dependent on output. We need to know *exactly* the precise relationship between the two variables.

Such a relationship may be expressed in the form of a **linear** equation:

$$TC = 8.0 + 1.2X$$

Such an equation is referred to as linear because it is represented graphically with a straight line.

The general form of a linear equation is given as:

$$Y = a + bX$$

where Y is the dependent variable, X is the independent variable and a and b are known as the parameters of the equation, ie, the numbers that give the equation its specific form. Here a would be +8.0 and b +1.2.

11.3 LINEAR EQUATIONS IN GRAPH FORM

Typically, we may wish to show the same information visually in the form of a graph. Most of the principles of graph construction were covered in Chapter 3, but there are a number of specific steps to follow in drawing the graph for a linear equation.

STEP 1

Choose an appropriate range for the X scale. Frequently it is apparent from the problem what the appropriate range of values for the X variable are. In other cases, we may simply have to make a reasonable assumption. In our example it is logical to set the lowest value of X to 0 (we cannot produce less than zero units after all). The highest value for X can be assumed to be 10.

STEP 2

Determine an appropriate range of values for the Y scale. This is readily done from Step 1.
  Using the equation determine the Y value when X takes its lower specified value. Here X=0:

$$TC = 8.0 + 1.2X$$

$$TC = 8.0 + 1.2(0) = 8.0$$

Again, determine the corresponding Y value when X takes its upper value, here set at X=10:

$$TC = 8.0 + 1.2X$$
$$TC = 8.0 + 1.2(10) = 8.0 + 12 = 20.0$$

STEP 3

Determine an appropriate scale for the Y variable. In our example it would be sensible to set Y from 0 to 20.

STEP 4

Draw a suitable scale for the X and Y variables on the graph. Conventionally, the Y variable is shown on the vertical axis and the X variable on the horizontal.

STEP 5

Taking the two pairs of X, Y values calculated in Step 2 plot each point on the graph—(X=0, Y=8) and (X=10, Y=20). These are shown in Figure 11.1 as point A and point B.

STEP 6

Join these two points together with a straight line. This is the line for the given equation.

STEP 7

Until you have had adequate practice it is always worth checking you have drawn the line properly.
  Take another X value (typically somewhere in the middle of the X range) and calculate the corresponding Y value from the equation. Plot this point on the graph. If it falls on the line you have drawn then the line is correct.

Here, we choose X=5.

$$TC = 8.0 + 1.2X$$
$$TC = 8.0 + 1.2(5) = 8.0 + 6.0 = 14.0$$

which is plotted as point C. This is on the line we have drawn confirming that the equation has been drawn correctly.

It is important to realise the relationship between the graph and the original equation. Both show exactly the same information. The graph shows the relationship between the two variable visually whilst the equation shows it mathematically.

11.4   PARAMETERS OF A LINEAR EQUATION

The two parameters of a linear equation, the a and b values, have particular importance both mathematically and in business. The a term is referred to as the *intercept* or *constant* whilst the b term as the *slope* or *gradient*.

11.4.1   The intercept or constant

The intercept is the point on the Y axis where the line crosses. In Figure 11.1 the intercept is at 8.0. It is evident that this intercept value is the same as the a term in the equation.

FIGURE 11.1   **Graph of TC = 8.00 + 1.2X**

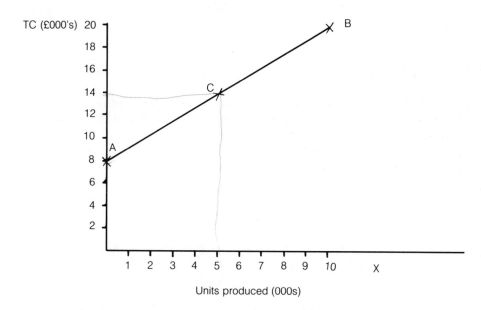

Units produced (000s)

The a parameter, it is clear, determines the general position of the line, in terms of where it crosses the vertical axis. Should the a term change its value for any reason, then the line will shift across the graph from one position to another as illustrated in Figure 11.2.

FIGURE 11.2   **Changes in the a term**

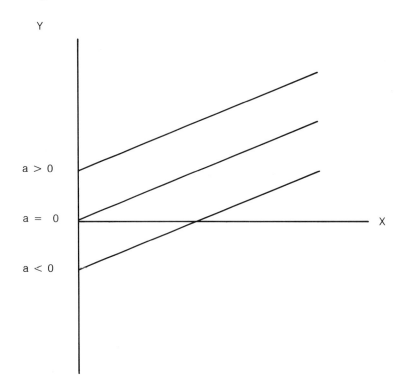

Apart from the mathematics, however, the a value frequently has a business interpretation. Naturally, this will vary depending on the problem. Here, TC=8.0 when X=0. That is, when output is zero total costs are £8.0(000). It is evident that in this example, the intercept term represents the **fixed cost** element of production.

11.4.2   The slope or gradient

The second parameter of the linear function is the b term which is referred to as the slope or gradient of the function and is particularly important in a business context. The b parameter in a linear equation shows the steepness of the line and the direction of its slope.

Mathematically, the slope shows the change in Y that will occur for each unit change in X.

Let us assume that output is currently 4 units. From the equation we know that total costs will be:

$$TC = 8.0 + 1.2X$$
$$TC = 8.0 + 1.2(4) = 12.8$$

Let us now assume that output is set to rise to 5 units. The new TC value will be given by:

$$TC = 8.0 + 1.2X$$
$$TC = 8.0 + 1.2(5) = 14.0$$

TC has increased, therefore, by 1.2 as a result of X increasing by 1. This is obviously the value of the b parameter in the equation. Simply, the b parameter shows the change that will occur in Y for a given change in X. Similarly, if X were to change by 2, Y would change by 2.4 (ie 2 × 1.2).

This is frequently expressed as:

$$slope = \frac{change\ in\ Y}{change\ in\ X}$$

The slope can also be identified from the graph of the equation as illustrated in Figure 11.3, which shows the X and Y axes for part of their range.

FIGURE 11.3   **Calculation of slope from the graph**

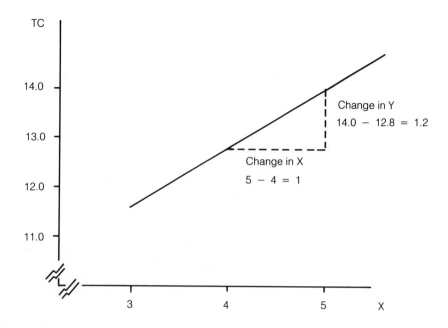

On the graph the change in Y and change in X can be established and their ratio confirms the slope at 1.2.

It is also evident from the graph and Figure 11.1 that it will not matter where on the line we measure the slope as we will always get the same result. The slope of a linear function, in other words, is constant.

As with the a parameter, the b term may take one of three general forms which are illustrated in Figure 11.4:

FIGURE 11.4   **Slope of a line**

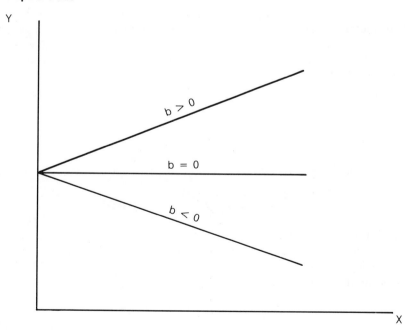

—a line with a **positive** b value slopes **upwards** from left to right, implying that an increase in X will lead to an increase in Y

—a line with a **negative** b value slopes **downward** from left to right, implying that an increase in X will lead to a decrease in Y

—a line with a **zero** b value is parallel to the X axis, and implies that as X changes there will be no change in Y. X and Y, in other words, are independent of each other

As with the a term the slope usually has an important business interpretation.

In our example, it shows how total costs change as output changes. Each unit extra of X leads to an increase in TC of 1.2. Remembering the units of measurement this implies that an extra 1,000 units add £1,200 to costs. It is evident that the b term shows **variable** costs in this example—that portion of costs which change with output.

11.5 SETS OF LINEAR EQUATIONS

Typically, in a business context, we deal not with just one equation but with two or more. Dealing with such sets of equations is straightforward. Let us assume that, in addition, to the information on costs and output used earlier we also have information on revenue and output: that is, on what we sell.

Assume that we have a linear revenue equation given by:

$$TR = 2.8X$$

where X is output (again measured in 000's of units) and TR is total revenue (measured in £000's).

It is apparent that TR is determined simply by the number of units sold multiplied by the price per unit. Using the concepts introduced earlier it is clear that the TR equation has an intercept of zero and a slope of 2.8.

You should be aware that the intercept will logically be zero because if X=0 (ie output is zero) the firm has no products to sell and therefore TR will be zero also.

Typically in such a situation we wish to use both equations to analyse some problem. For example, we have been asked to determine the company's breakeven point: the level of output where costs are just balanced by revenue.

11.6 GRAPHICAL SOLUTION

We can find such a point using a graphical method of solution. Figure 11.5 shows both the TC and the TR functions.

FIGURE 11.5 **Graphical solution**

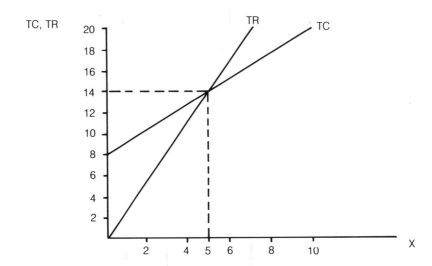

It is apparent that the point where the two lines cross will be the solution to the problem. From the graph it can be seen that this point will occur when X=5. At this point from the graph both TC and TR take a value =14.

This can be confirmed from the original equations.

Let X = 5

TC = 8.0 + 1.2(5) = 14.0
TR = 2.8(5) = 14.0

That is, when output is 5(000) units the company breaks even. It is evident that we are looking for a point where TC=TR. From the graph the two equations will take the same value for a given number for X only at one point and this is the point we have found.

11.7 SIMULTANEOUS EQUATIONS

Whilst such a graphical method of solution is straightforward it is not always practical: it may be difficult to read precise values from the graph and the problem we face may not be capable of being easily graphed. A more general method of algebraic solution is necessary. This method is known as the method of **simultaneous equations** because we are looking for a combination of X and Y values that will satisfy both equations simultaneously.

In order to be able to develop a general method of solution it is necessary to understand the general principles of algebraic manipulation. It is important to remember that an equation is simply a precise statement of some relationship between variables.

Suppose we have an equation such that $5X = 50$.

Obviously, $X = 10$. However, suppose we have an equation instead such that $10X = 100$. X still equals 10. Although the two equations **look** different they are in fact expressing the same relationship. We can generalise this to say that **we can manipulate an equation into a different form so long as we change both sides of the equation in the same way.**

It is apparent in the simple example above that this is what we have done. The original equation was $5X = 50$.

Suppose we multiply the left hand side (LHS) by two. The relationship will remain unchanged **as long as** we also change the right hand side (RHS) of the equation in the same way:

$$5X \times 2 = 50 \times 2$$
giving: $$10X = 100$$

So, we can make any arithmetic change to the LHS of an equation as long as exactly the same change is undertaken on the RHS. How does this help?

Let us return to the TR and TC equations. To provide a general solution method we shall transform each equation into a standard format:

$$cY + bX = a$$

where a, b, c are appropriate numbers.

Given that we have two equations we shall have two sets of values for a, b, c:

$$c_1Y + b_1X = a_1 \tag{11.1}$$
$$\text{and} \quad c_2Y + b_2X = a_2 \tag{11.2}$$

For the TC equation this would give:

$$1Y - 1.2X = 8.0$$

with $c_1 = 1$
$b_1 = -1.2$
$a_1 = 8.0$

and for the TR equation:

$$1Y - 2.8X = 0$$

with   with $c_2 = 1$
                                        $b_2 = -2.8$
                                        $a_2 = 0$

(You should confirm for yourself that these equations are identical to the original.)

The general solution method using simultaneous equations is then:

1   Multiply equation 11.1 by c_2
2   Multiply equation 11.2 by c_1
3   Subtract either of the resulting equations from the other. This will have the effect of removing the Y variable.
4   Rearrange this result to determine the X value
5   Substitute this X value back into 11.1 and 11.2 to determine the Y value.

This sounds far more complicated than it is.

(a)   We multiply $1Y - 1.2X = 8.0$ by c_2 (=1) to give:
                           $1Y - 1.2X = 8.0$ (11.3)

(b)   We multiply $1Y - 2.8X = 0$ by c_1 (=1) to give:
                           $1Y - 2.8X = 0$ (11.4)

(c)   We subtract one of the resulting equations from the other (it doesn't matter which). We shall subtract the second equation from the first

                           $1Y - 1.2X = 8.0$ (11.3)
            minus $1Y - 2.8X = 0$ (11.4)

to give $0 + 1.6X = 8.0$

(d)   Rearranging this gives:

                           $0 + 1.6X = 8.0$

divide by 1.6

$$\frac{1.6X}{1.6} = \frac{8.0}{1.6}$$

to give $1X = 5.0$

which is the result for X.

(e)   Returning to the original two equations and substituting X=5:

        Total cost $1Y - 1.2(5) = 8.0$
            giving $1Y = 8.0 + 6.0 = 14.0$

        Total revenue $1Y - 2.8(5) = 0$
            giving $1Y = 14.0$.

which confirms the graphical solution found earlier.

This solution method may seem trivial and long-winded given the nature of the problem. What we have developed however, is a general method of algebraic solution that can be applied to any problem. Although in this case we can find the solution easily in other ways, in other problems this will not be the case. The method outlined will always find the solution (providing there is one).

11.8 LARGER SETS OF EQUATIONS

The general method of solution developed can readily be applied to larger sets of equations, involving more than two variables and more than two equations. The solution to such larger equation sets is best approached through matrix algebra, which will be introduced in the next chapter.

SUMMARY

Linear functions, with relatively little practice, are easy to use and to interpret. However, they cannot always be reliably applied to all business problems. In particular, there are two aspects of linear functions which are inadequate.

The first is that the linear function we have introduced only allows for *one* independent (X) variable. Frequently in business analysis this may be a reasonable simplifying assumption. There will be other times when it is not. In our example, we have assumed that output is the only factor affecting costs. Whilst output may be the *major* factor there are likely to be other variables that will affect costs in some way.

The second is that not all relationships are linear: many business applications require the use of *non-linear* functions which are developed later.

1   A functional relationship expresses two, or more, variables in terms of their cause and effect pattern.
2   A linear equation is represented as a straight line on a graph, and consists of two parameters, a and b.
3   The constant or intercept value (the a term) indicates where on the vertical axis the line will cross.
4   The slope or gradient value indicates the steepness of the line and is represented by the b term. The slope measures the change in the Y value that will occur for a unit change in the X value.
5   Simultaneous equations are a general method of finding X and Y values that satisfy two or more equations. Such a solution is shown graphically where the lines representing the equations intersect.

SELF-TEST QUESTIONS

1   **What is the difference between the dependent and independent variable in a function?** (*Refer to page 107*)

2   **How would you calculate the slope of a linear function from the graph?** (*Refer to page 111*)

3   **You are told that a linear function has a negative intercept. What does this mean?** (*Refer to page 110*)

4   **What is meant by a functional relationship?** (*Refer to page 107*)

5   **What are the two parameters of a linear function?** (*Refer to page 107*)

6   **What are the two methods of finding the solution to a set of linear equations?** (*Refer to page 113*)

EXERCISES

1   Return to the TC and TR equations used in the chapter and shown in Figure 11.5.
    (a)   You are told that the company's overheads increase by £2,000. Determine the new TC and TR equations
    (b)   Draw these equations—together with the original TC equation—on one graph
    (c)   Find the new breakeven point graphically
    (d)   Confirm your answer to (c) by using simultaneous equations.
    (e)   You are now told that in addition to the change in overheads, the TR equation has changed to TR = 3X. Find the new breakeven point.

E

2   In one of the group's stores some data have been collected on the sales of one product and two equations derived.

$Qd = 100 - 10P$ (known as the demand function)

and

$Qs = -25 + 5P$ (known as the supply function)

where Qd is the quantity demanded of the product (000s units)
       Qs is the quantity supplied (ie offered for sale) (000s units)
and   P is the price charged per unit.

(a)   Why in both cases is Q expressed as a function of P?

(b)   Draw both equations on one graph

(c)   Why is it logical for the demand function to have a negative slope?

(d)   Why is it logical for the supply function to have a positive slope?

(e)   Why is it logical for the supply function to have a negative intercept?

(f)   At what price will Qd and Qs be the same?

(g)   What will happen if the store charges a higher or lower price than this?

3   The store now realises that the demand function has altered. The store manager has noted that when a price of £5 was charged customers bought 50 units whilst when a price of £3 was charged customers bought 90 units.

(a)   From this data determine the new demand function

(b)   Find the new point where Qd=Qs

(c)   Compare the new demand function with the previous one. What factors can you suggest that might have brought about such a change?

Answers on page 309.

Matrix algebra

In the previous chapter we saw the necessity for dealing with sets of linear equations in a typical business situation. In particular, it is necessary to be able to find the simultaneous solution to such a set of equations. The type of algebra that we have thus far introduced is perfectly adequate when dealing with one or two such equations but for larger scale problems an alternative method of presentation and analysis is required.

12.1 WHAT A MATRIX IS

Matrix algebra is such a method and is ideally suited for dealing with large sets of linear relationships. A matrix can be thought of simply as a rectangular array, or table, of numbers. For example, let us suppose that the Southern region of MTG have been reviewing their stock levels of certain products in a number of their stores:

Stock levels

	Store A	Store B	Store C
Product 1	100	50	40
Product 2	50	100	30
Product 3	30	10	20

Thus Store A currently has 100 items of product 1 in stock, 50 items of product 2 and 30 items of product 3. The corresponding matrix would be given by:

$$\text{Stock Matrix} = \begin{bmatrix} 100 & 50 & 40 \\ 50 & 100 & 30 \\ 30 & 10 & 20 \end{bmatrix}$$

The matrix is, therefore, a format for simply showing the data items or numbers relating to the problem. The matrix makes no reference to the labels or variables as such (stores and products here). It is up to us to remember what the rows and columns of the matrix represent.

Such a matrix is referred to as a 3×3 matrix because it has three rows and three columns. Not all matrices are symmetrical as we shall shortly see. By convention, when detailing the size, the first number indicates the number of rows and the second the number of columns.

In general, each element in the matrix can be uniquely identified by its row and column position. If we denote this matrix as Matrix X then we would denote the individual items as:

$$\text{Matrix X} \quad \begin{bmatrix} X_{11} & X_{12} & X_{13} \\ X_{21} & X_{22} & X_{23} \\ X_{31} & X_{32} & X_{33} \end{bmatrix}$$

Thus X_{32}, for example, refers to the item in row 3 column 2 (here = 10).

One particular type of matrix that we need to note is that consisting of only one row or one column. Such a matrix is more generally referred to as a *vector* and we shall see their use shortly.

Additionally, one more term must be introduced before we illustrate the use of matrices and matrix algebra. This is the term *scalar* which represents not an array or matrix of numbers but only a *single* number.

12.2 THE VERSATILITY OF MATRIX ALGEBRA

The potential use of matrices is not simply in their presentation of data but in their ability to allow us to carry out complex manipulations and algebra relatively easily. Just as we can carry out arithmetic on ordinary numbers so we can undertake the equivalent arithmetic on matrices. We shall focus upon a number of such types of matrix arithmetic:

Matrix addition
Matrix subtraction
Multiplication by a scalar
Matrix multiplication
Matrix division (known as determining a matrix **inverse**)

12.3 MATRIX ADDITION

Assume that, in addition to Matrix X above, we had a corresponding matrix which represents this week's deliveries of the three products to the three stores. Each store will receive a shipment of each product from the central warehouse. Matrix Y shows the relevant data:

$$\text{Matrix Y} \quad \begin{bmatrix} 10 & 25 & 15 \\ 20 & 0 & 30 \\ 30 & 20 & 40 \end{bmatrix}$$

You should ensure you understand the information in the Matrix before proceeding. Each column represents the deliveries to a particular store whilst each row represents the deliveries of each of the three products. Thus the number 40 represents a delivery of product 3 to store C.

We now wish to know the new stock levels of the three products in the three stores. This is easily achieved in matrix algebra by adding together the corresponding elements of the two matrices. Thus:

$$Z = X + Y = \begin{bmatrix} 100 & 50 & 40 \\ 50 & 100 & 30 \\ 30 & 10 & 20 \end{bmatrix} + \begin{bmatrix} 10 & 25 & 15 \\ 20 & 0 & 30 \\ 30 & 20 & 40 \end{bmatrix}$$

$$Z = \begin{bmatrix} 100+10 & 50+25 & 40+15 \\ 50+20 & 100+0 & 30+30 \\ 30+30 & 10+20 & 20+40 \end{bmatrix} = \begin{bmatrix} 110 & 75 & 55 \\ 70 & 100 & 60 \\ 60 & 30 & 60 \end{bmatrix}$$

So, at store B, for example, new stock levels will be 75 units of product 1, 100 units of product 2 and 30 units of product 3.

The only requirement for such matrix addition is that the matrices to be added together must be of the same size. That is, they must have the same number of rows and the same number of columns.

12.4 MATRIX SUBTRACTION

It will come as no surprise that matrix subtraction is as straightforward as matrix addition. Again, let us assume that after the deliveries detailed above each of the three stores sells certain quantities of the three products. The corresponding sales matrix is shown below:

$$S = \begin{bmatrix} 10 & 15 & 35 \\ 50 & 90 & 10 \\ 0 & 20 & 30 \end{bmatrix}$$

To find the new stock levels we have:

$$X = Z - S = \begin{bmatrix} 110 & 75 & 55 \\ 70 & 100 & 60 \\ 60 & 30 & 60 \end{bmatrix} - \begin{bmatrix} 10 & 15 & 35 \\ 50 & 90 & 10 \\ 0 & 15 & 30 \end{bmatrix} = \begin{bmatrix} 100 & 60 & 20 \\ 20 & 10 & 50 \\ 60 & 10 & 30 \end{bmatrix}$$

Again, as with addition the two matrices to be subtracted must be of the same size and you should ensure that you fully understand the numbers in the resulting matrix.

12.5   MULTIPLICATION BY A SCALAR

Frequently we may wish to multiply a matrix by a scalar or constant. Let us suppose that MTG wish to cut their stockholding costs. After all, stock held represents capital tied up in the business that is not being used. An order has been given that all stores must reduce their stock levels for each product by 10%. Effectively, this means that the new stock levels are to be 90% of the existing stock levels. The 90% figure (or 0.9) thus represents the constant or **scalar** value.

Multiplying a matrix by a scalar is simple. Each element in turn in the matrix is multiplied by the scalar value.

$$Y = X \times 0.9 = \begin{bmatrix} 100 & 60 & 20 \\ 20 & 10 & 60 \\ 60 & 10 & 30 \end{bmatrix} \times 0.9 = \begin{bmatrix} 90 & 54 & 18 \\ 18 & 9 & 54 \\ 54 & 9 & 27 \end{bmatrix}$$

So, if we look at X_{33}, for example, we have $30 \times 0.9 = 27$.

12.6   MATRIX MULTIPLICATION

Many of the advantages of using matrix algebra in business mathematics problems become apparent when we examine methods of multiplying matrices together. Let us examine the matrix that was derived in the previous section:

$$X = \begin{bmatrix} 90 & 54 & 18 \\ 18 & 9 & 54 \\ 54 & 9 & 27 \end{bmatrix}$$

You will remember that this relates to the existing stock levels in the three stores following the requirement from Head Office to cut back stock levels across the board by 10%. Management now want to know the amount of capital that is tied up in these stock levels. What is the value of the stock held?

Assume that the cost price of the three items is as follows:

Product 1   £1.00
Product 2   £1.50
Product 3   £2.00

We can represent this as a row matrix (often referred to as a row vector):

$$C = [1.00 \quad 1.50 \quad 2.00]$$

where the columns refer to each of the three products.

Thus, we require the product of $C \times X$, that is the cost of each product multiplied by the number of items of the product in stock at each store.

Let us denote the two matrices by their cell references:

$$C = [C_{11} \quad C_{12} \quad C_{13}]$$

$$X = \begin{bmatrix} X_{11} & X_{12} & X_{13} \\ X_{21} & X_{22} & X_{23} \\ X_{31} & X_{32} & X_{33} \end{bmatrix}$$

We now need to multiply each column in the X matrix by the row vector, C. Each column in X will represent the stock levels of the three products in a particular store whilst the row vector will show the cost price of each of the three products.

The product of the multiplication will be given by:

$$[(C_{11}X_{11}+C_{12}X_{21}+C_{13}X_{31}) \qquad (C_{11}X_{12}+C_{12}X_{22}+C_{13}X_{32}) \qquad (C_{11}X_{13}+C_{12}X_{23}+C_{13}X_{33})]$$

The arithmetic is as follows:

$$[1(90)+1.5(18)+2(54) \qquad 1(54)+1.5(9)+2(9) \qquad 1(18)+1.5(54)+2(27)]$$

$$CX = [225 \quad 85.5 \quad 153]$$

That is, the result of multiplying the cost price matrix by the stock matrix indicates that the value (at cost price) of stock is:

£225 at store A

£85.5 at store B

£153 at store C

You will be aware that what we have effectively done is to multiply each column in Matrix X by the row in matrix C. The result of each multiplication is a single value which represents the product of the multiplication.

In practice, multiplying any two matrices together is as straightforward as the example just shown. However, there are a number of basic rules to be aware of.

First, the two matrices to be multiplied must be compatible. This means that the number of **columns** in the first matrix must be the same as the number of **rows** in the second matrix. In this example, matrix C had three columns and matrix X had three rows so the two matrices were compatible for multiplication. Consider, however, the two matrices below:

$$A = \begin{bmatrix} 10 & 2 \\ 5 & 4 \end{bmatrix} \qquad B = \begin{bmatrix} 3 & 5 & 7 \\ 1 & 5 & 9 \\ 2 & 3 & 1 \end{bmatrix}$$

A is a 2×2 matrix and B a 3×3 matrix. The are *not* compatible for multiplication.

Second, the matrix resulting from multiplication will have the same number of rows as the first matrix and the same number of columns as the second. The result of our multiplying C by X was to produce the matrix of size 1×3 (C had one row and X had three columns).

Third, the process of multiplying larger matrices together follows the same structure as in the simple example used earlier. Each row in the first matrix is multiplied by each column in turn to produce a single value. The position of this value in the resulting matrix is given by the row/column combination of the first two matrices. This sounds far more complicated than it is. Let us illustrate with two matrices below:

$$A = \begin{bmatrix} 10 & 2 \\ 5 & 4 \end{bmatrix} \qquad B = \begin{bmatrix} 3 & 5 \\ 1 & 5 \end{bmatrix}$$

We wish to find A×B. The two matrices are compatible and will result in a 2×2 matrix. First we multiply each row of A by each column of B.

A row	B column	Product
1	1	10×3 + 2×1 = 32
1	2	10×5 + 2×5 = 60
2	1	5×3 + 4×1 = 19
2	2	5×5 + 4×5 = 45

To determine the resulting matrix values we use the row/column combinations:

$$AB = C = \begin{bmatrix} 1,1 & 1,2 \\ 2,1 & 2,2 \end{bmatrix} = \begin{bmatrix} 32 & 60 \\ 19 & 45 \end{bmatrix}$$

Thus each value produced from the multiplication takes its place according to the A row and B column used to produce it.

Fourth, it is important to note that, unlike ordinary algebra the *order* of matrix multiplication is critical. In ordinary algebra 3×2 is exactly the same as 2×3. In matrix algebra, however, this is not the case and a different result will be produced if the multiplication order is changed (assuming the matrices are compatible both ways). Let us illustrate with the two matrices used above.

We have already found the product of A×B:

$$AB = C = \begin{bmatrix} 32 & 60 \\ 19 & 45 \end{bmatrix}$$

If we now calculate the two matrices multiplied in the opposite way we have:

$$BA = D = \begin{bmatrix} 55 & 26 \\ 35 & 22 \end{bmatrix}$$

which is a totally different result from the first multiplication (you should confirm matrix D from your own calculations).

With practice, matrix multiplication is straightforward although you should initially take great care in ensuring you are multiplying the correct row/column combination and that the result is placed in its correct position in the derived matrix.

12.7 MATRIX INVERSION

Finally, we turn to the last form of matrix algebra, inversion. This can be viewed as the equivalent of algebraic division and is potentially the most important of the matrix algebra techniques.

The inverse matrix has much the same meaning as the inverse of a normal number. If, for example, we had:

$$7 \times \frac{1}{7} = 1 \quad \text{or} \quad 7 \times 7^{-1} = 1$$

you should have no difficulty recognising that the inverse of the number 7 is 1/7 (alternatively written as 7^{-1}) and that the original number multiplied by its inverse will give the result of 1. The same applies to matrix inversion. If we denote a matrix as A then:

$$[A \times A^{-1}] = I$$

where (A^{-1}) is the inverse of the A matrix and I represents what is known as an **identity** matrix—the matrix equivalent of the number 1. An identity matrix is easily recognised as it consists of the value 1 in the main diagonal of the matrix and 0 in each other cell. Thus if I were a 3×3 matrix it would take the form:

$$I = \begin{bmatrix} 1 & 0 & 0 \\ 0 & 1 & 0 \\ 0 & 0 & 1 \end{bmatrix}$$

To find the inverse is a matter of some straightforward arithmetic. There are, in fact, a number of alternative methods available. The one followed here is known as the **Gaussian elimination** method.

It is important to note that we can only determine an inverse where the matrix is **square**—that is, has the same number of rows as columns. Let us assume that we have a matrix A given by:

$$A = \begin{bmatrix} 1 & -1.2 \\ 1 & -2.8 \end{bmatrix} = \begin{bmatrix} a_{11} & a_{12} \\ a_{21} & a_{22} \end{bmatrix}$$

and we wish to find its inverse. First we create an augmented matrix consisting of matrix A and the identity matrix of the same size:

Row 1	1	−1.2	1	0
Row 2	1	−2.8	0	1

We now perform a series of arithmetic row operations at the end of which the original A matrix will have been transformed into an Identity matrix and what was the Identity matrix will now represent the inverse matrix.

To begin the transformation of A into I we take the first row and require $a_{11} = 1$ (the first diagonal element of the I matrix). This is generally achieved by dividing the entire row by the current a_{11} coefficient. In this example a_{11} is already 1 so no transformation is actually necessary. So Row 1 of the transformed matrix is still:

$$\text{Row 1} \qquad 1 \qquad -1.2 \qquad 1 \qquad 0$$

We now wish to transform a_{21} into 0 (to correspond to the I matrix). To do this we must use the new first row. If we take the new first row, multiply by -1 (the a_{21} coefficient) and add this to the current row 2 we have:

$$
\begin{array}{llrrrr}
& (-1 \times \text{row 1}) & -1 & 1.2 & -1 & 0 \\
+ & \text{Row 2} & 1 & -2.8 & 0 & 1 \\
\hline \\
& \text{New row 2} & 0 & -1.6 & -1 & 1
\end{array}
$$

to give a result at this stage of:

$$
\begin{array}{lrrrr}
\text{Row 1} & 1 & -1.2 & 1 & 0 \\
\text{Row 2} & 0 & -1.6 & -1 & 1
\end{array}
$$

We now wish to transform a_{22} (currently with a value -1.6) into 1 (to correspond to the I matrix diagonal). If we divide row 2 by the a_{22} coefficient (-1.6) we have:

$$\text{Row 2} \qquad 0 \qquad 1 \qquad 0.625 \quad -0.625$$

Again, we now wish to change a_{12} into 0 to correspond to the I matrix by using the new row 2. This can be achieved by multiplying row 2 by 1.2 (the current a12 coefficient) and adding to the current row 1.

$$
\begin{array}{llrrrr}
& (1.2 \times \text{row 2}) & 0 & 1.2 & .75 & -0.75 \\
+ & \text{Row 1} & 1 & -1.2 & 1 & 0 \\
\hline \\
& \text{New row 1} & 1 & 0 & 1.75 & -.075
\end{array}
$$

This gives a matrix as:

$$
\begin{array}{lrrrr}
\text{Row 1} & 1 & 0 & 1.75 & -.075 \\
\text{Row 2} & 0 & 1 & .625 & -.625
\end{array}
$$

As you can see the original A matrix has been transformed into an I matrix and the I matrix into what is the inverse of A. How can we check? Returning to the definition of the inverse we had:

$$A \times A^{-1} = I$$

so let us multiply A by its inverse:

$$
\begin{bmatrix} 1 & -1.2 \\ 1 & -2.8 \end{bmatrix} \times \begin{bmatrix} 1.75 & -0.75 \\ 0.625 & -.625 \end{bmatrix}
$$

You should confirm through your own calculations that this gives the matrix:

$$
\begin{bmatrix} 1 & 0 \\ 0 & 1 \end{bmatrix}
$$

thus confirming that our calculations have derived the inverse of the original A matrix.

The process adopted here to find the inverse of the 2×2 A matrix can be generalised into a series of stages that will allow us to determine the inverse of any sized matrix (although the manual derivation of a matrix greater than 3×3 is not to be recommended. A suitable computer program should be used for larger problems).

STEP 1

Derive the augmented matrix with the corresponding I matrix added to the A matrix.

STEP 2

Taking row 1, divide this row by the a_{11} coefficient to give the new row 1.

STEP 3

Using the new row 1, amend the second row in the matrix so that the coefficient in the first column is zero. This is generally achieved by multiplying the new row 1 by $(-a_{21})$ and then adding the result to the current row.

STEP 4

Repeat step 3 for each row in the matrix.

STEP 5

Return to step 2 for the next diagonal coefficient (ie a_{22}), then a_{33}, a_{44} etc) until the original A matrix has been transformed into an I matrix.

The original I matrix will now be the A inverse and should be checked by multiplying with the original A matrix to confirm that an Identity matrix results.

12.8 USING THE INVERSE TO SOLVE SIMULTANEOUS EQUATIONS

The prime use of matrix inversion is to allow us to solve sets of simultaneous equations. We saw in Chapter 11 that it is frequently necessary in business mathematics to find the solution to sets of simultaneous equations. Matrix inversion provides us with a ready method of finding such a solution for any sized problem.

You may remember from Chapter 11 that we examined such an equation system:

$$1Y - 1.2X = 8$$
$$1Y - 2.8X = 0$$

Such a system can be represented in matrix form:

$$AV = B$$

where:

$$A = \begin{bmatrix} 1 & -1.2 \\ 1 & -2.8 \end{bmatrix} \quad V = \begin{bmatrix} Y \\ X \end{bmatrix} \quad B = \begin{bmatrix} 8 \\ 0 \end{bmatrix}$$

That is, A is a matrix containing the Y,X coefficients, V is a column vector containing the variable labels and B is a column vector containing the right hand side values. We are looking for the value for Y and X that will satisfy both equations simultaneously. Let us perform some simple matrix algebra:

$$AV = B$$
$$A^{-1} AV = A^{-1}B$$
$$IV = A^{-1}B$$

That is, we multiply the original matrix expression by the A inverse. Given that A times its inverse will give an identity matrix, what this effectively means is that the solution to the system (ie the values for Y and X that satisfy both equations simultaneously) will be given by finding the result of the A inverse times the B vector.

You will now realise that in the previous section we have just derived the inverse of this A matrix. So if we find the product of A inverse times B we have:

$$\begin{bmatrix} 1.75 & -.75 \\ .625 & -.625 \end{bmatrix} \begin{bmatrix} 8 \\ 0 \end{bmatrix} = \begin{bmatrix} 14 \\ 5 \end{bmatrix}$$

Similarly, if we multiply the I matrix by V we have:

$$IV = \begin{bmatrix} 1 & 0 \\ 0 & 1 \end{bmatrix} \begin{bmatrix} Y \\ X \end{bmatrix} = \begin{bmatrix} Y \\ X \end{bmatrix}$$

So,

$$\begin{bmatrix} Y \\ X \end{bmatrix} = \begin{bmatrix} 14 \\ 5 \end{bmatrix}$$

That is, when Y=14 and X=5 we have the simultaneous solution of the two equations, confirming the solution derived in the previous chapter. Such a solution method is readily extended to any sized system of linear equations.

SUMMARY

1   Matrix algebra is a convenient way of dealing with large sets of linear relationships.
2   Algebra undertaken on matrices is similar in concept to ordinary arithmetic
3   A matrix is simply a table of values representing information
4   Each item in a matrix can be uniquely identified with its row/column position
5   Matrices can be added or subtracted provided they are the same size
6   Matrices can be multiplied provided they are of compatible size—where the number of columns in the first matrix is the same as the number of rows in the second
7   Matrix inversion is the equivalent of ordinary division. The inverse of a square matrix can be found using the Gaussian elimination method.
8   An Identity matrix consists of values of 1 in the main diagonal and values of 0 elsewhere.
9   Matrix inversion is particularly useful as a means of finding the solution to a set of simultaneous equations.

SELF-TEST QUESTIONS

1   **What is a matrix?** (*Refer to page 117*)

2   **What is a vector?** (*Refer to page 117*)

3   **How can each number in a matrix be uniquely identified?** (*Refer to page 117*)

4   **How are two matrices added together?** (*Refer to page 118*)

5   **What condition is necessary for two matrices to be added together?** (*Refer to page 118*)

6   **What condition is necessary for two matrices to be multiplied together?** (*Refer to page 120*)

7   **How are two matrices multiplied?** (*Refer to page 120*)

8   **What is the main use of an inverse?** (*Refer to page 123*)

9   **How do you recognise an Identity matrix?** (*Refer to page 121*)

10   **How can you check that you have found the correct inverse of a matrix?** (*Refer to page 122*)

EXERCISES

$$A \begin{bmatrix} 5 & 3 & 2 \\ 10 & 8 & 4 \\ -8 & 4 & 7 \end{bmatrix} \quad B = \begin{bmatrix} 4 & 3 & 1 \\ -1 & 5 & 4 \\ 2 & 7 & 9 \end{bmatrix} \quad C = \begin{bmatrix} 2 & 8 \\ & \\ 3 & 4 \end{bmatrix}$$

1   Determine which of the following are possible and which are not:

(a) A + B
(b) B − A
(c) C + B
(d) C − A
(e) AB
(f) BA
(g) AC
(h) CB

2 For the arithmetic in (a) that you have decided is possible calculate the result.

3 Find the inverse of each of the three matrices. Check your answer by multiplying the original matrix by the inverse.

4 MTG are investigating the value of stock held at the three stores.

	Store A	Store B	Store C
Product 1	100	50	40
Product 2	50	100	30
Product 3	30	10	20

For each product MTG have analysed the purchase cost, the selling price and the profit per item:

	Product 1	2	3
Purchase cost	1.0	1.5	2
Selling price	1.1	1.75	2.5
Profit	0.1	0.25	0.5

Find the value of stock held in each store, measured by cost, price and profit per unit.

5 In Chapter 7 (Index Numbers) Table 7.3 presented employees and salaries. Formulate this information into matrix form (one matrix for employees and a second for salaries). Using matrix algebra calculate the Laspeyres and Paasche index numbers.

6 For each of the problems at the end of the previous chapter formulate each problem in matrix terms and confirm the solution to the problem using matrix algebra.

Answers on page 311.

Linear programming

The last two chapters have focused upon the importance of sets of linear equations in business mathematics. Typically, we wish to find the unique solution to such a set of equations—the values of X and Y that satisfy all the equations simultaneously. The technique that forms the basis for this chapter takes a similar approach. The technique is concerned with finding some optimum combination of two variables, subject to a number of restrictions or constraints expressed mathematically in linear form.

13.1 THE PROBLEM

Let us assume that MTG produce their own brand of breakfast cereal for sale in their stores. The cereal comes in two varieties, Standard and De-Luxe. Both cereals are sold in 400g bags and are made from the same two basic components:

Ingredients	Standard	De-luxe
Oats/Fibre	300g	250g
Nuts/Fruit	100g	150g

On a weekly basis MTG has a contract with a wholesale supplier of these ingredients who will supply up to but no more than the following quantities:

	Maximum weekly supply
Oats/Fibre	1500kg
Nuts/Fruit	500kg

Additionally, the group knows that sales on a weekly basis have never exceeded 4,000 bags of both products, but that sales of the De-luxe cereal are at least 1,000 bags per week.

Currently, the Standard Mix sells at a profit of £0.25 per bag and the De-luxe at £0.35.

The basic problem the company faces is, how many bags of the two products should it manufacture each week?

At this stage there is no obvious means of determining the decision that must be taken, in terms of the mix of production. If we assume, reasonably, that the group wish to maximise profit it becomes apparent that on a weekly basis, there are a number of factors which will restrict the level of production and profit the company can achieve. Such factors are known as **constraints**.

13.2 CONSTRAINTS

The constraints to the problem are:

1 The maximum supply of oats/fibre
2 The maximum supply of nuts/fruit
3 Maximum sales of the two products
4 Minimum sales of the De-luxe

Let us focus upon the first of these constraints: supply of oats/fibre. The constraint the company faces is that the demand for this resource, generated by producing the two products, must not exceed the available supply. Let us denote the following variables:

A—the number of units of Standard cereal
B—the number of units of the De-luxe cereal

We know that we have up to 1,500kg of this resource available to us and that each unit of A requires 300g and each unit of B 250g. We can express this mathematically as:

$$0.3A + 0.25B \leq 1,500$$

The left-hand side of the constraint indicates the quantity of the resource that will be required for any combination of A and B whilst the right hand side shows available supply of the resource. So if, for example, we decided to produce 2,000 units of A and 1,000 units of B the total amount of oats required will be:

$$0.3(2000) + 0.25(1000) = 850 \text{ (kg)}$$

In the same way we can quantify each of the other constraints faced by the company:

$$0.1A + 0.15B \leq 500 \quad \text{(nuts/fruit)}$$
$$1A + 1B \leq 4000 \quad \text{(sales)}$$
$$1B \geq 1000 \quad \text{(minimum sales of De-luxe)}$$

13.3 GRAPHING THE CONSTRAINTS

To solve the problem we shall use a graphical method. It is evident that all the constraints and the objective function are **linear** in form. This means that each constraint can be represented by a straight line and, in order to graph these lines, we will require a minimum of two pairs of coordinates.

If we examine the first constraint, relating to the supply of oats:

$$0.3A + .25B \leq 1,500$$

Let us assume that we decide to produce zero output of A. That is, all of the available resource is used to produce B. Maximum production of B is:

$$\frac{\text{Units of B}}{\text{produced}} = \frac{1500}{0.25} = 6000 \text{ units}$$

This represents the maximum possible production of B when all of the available oats are allocated to B production. Similarly, we can calculate the maximum possible production of A, with respect to this constraint:

$$\frac{\text{Units of A}}{\text{produced}} = \frac{1500}{0.3} = 5000 \text{ units}$$

We now have two sets of coordinates for this constraint:

1 A=0 B=6000
2 A=5000 B=0

which allows us to draw the linear constraint, shown in Figure 13.1.

FIGURE 13.1   **Constraint 0.3A + 0.25B ≤ 1500**

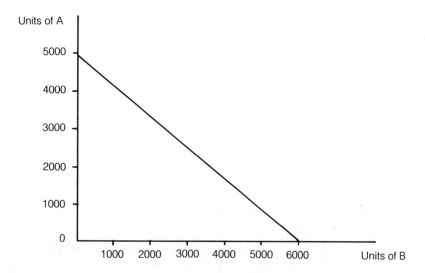

The line indicates all the combinations of A and B which require exactly 1,500 units of oats. More generally, the line divides the graph into three parts:

1   The area above the line. This represents those combinations of the two products that **cannot** be achieved, and is known as the 'infeasible' area.
2   The area below the line. This represents combinations of the two products which require less than the available supply of oats.
3   The line itself. Any point on the line represents a combination of the two products which requires **exactly** the amount of oats available.

The last two areas together represent the 'feasible' area.

The other constraints can be added to the graph in exactly the same way. The results are shown in Figure 13.2.

FIGURE 13.2   **Feasible area**

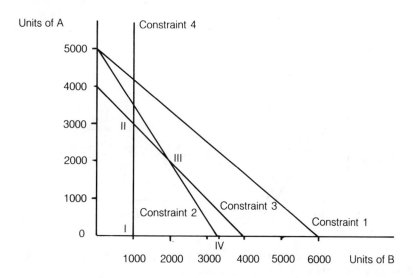

The feasible and infeasible areas for each constraint individually can be found from the figure. The area which is feasible for **all** constraints **simultaneously** can also be identified. This area runs from point I on the B axis to point II, point III and then point IV on the B axis and then back to point I.

13.4   FORMULATING THE OBJECTIVE FUNCTION

In the same way we can address the objective function:

$$\text{Profit} = 0.25A + 0.35B$$

where A and B again represent the units of the two products. For any combination of A and B we can, therefore, calculate the profit earned. If, for example, A=100 and B=200 then profit will be:

$$\text{Profit} = 0.25A + 0.35B = 0.25(100) + 0.35(200) = £95$$

13.5   GRAPHING THE OBJECTIVE FUNCTION

Figure 13.2 shows all the possible combinations of production which are feasible under the constraints we face. Into this we now need to introduce a line representing the objective function. This will allow us to determine which of the many feasible solutions will generate maximum profit and therefore meet the objective set.

In order to graph the objective function we have to determine appropriate coordinates as we did for the constraints. To do this we choose an arbitrary profit figure, say £700, and calculate the combinations of A and B which generate this particular profit level. For example, if A is arbitrarily set to 0 then we must produce 2000 units of B (700/0.35) to attain this profit level.

Similarly, if B is set to zero then we must produce 2,800 units of A to reach this profit of £700.

Figure 13.3 shows this £700 profit line: a line showing the same profit anywhere along its length. Any combination of A and B which occurs on this line generates a profit of £700 and the firm will be completely indifferent as to where on a particular profit line it is.

FIGURE 13.3   **Objective function**

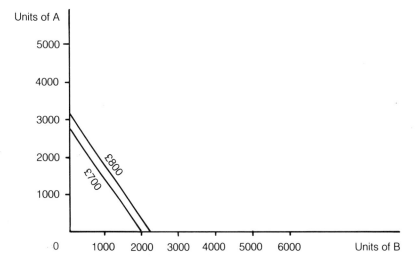

Similarly, we could draw the profit line representing, say £800 profit. This is also shown on Figure 13.3. The important points to note are that:

1   All such profit lines would be parallel. The slope is given by the ratio of A's profit to that of B, and this ratio stays the same no matter what we produce.
2   The further away the profit line is from the origin the higher the profit represented.

3 The firm will only be interested in which profit line can be attained, not where on a particular profit line the firm happens to be.

13.6 DETERMINING THE SOLUTION

It is now possible to determine the profit maximising solution to the problem. Figure 13.4 shows both the constraints and the profit line for £700 and £800. In terms of the objective function we seek maximum profit: that is, we wish the profit line to be as far **away** from the origin as possible.

It is evident that, as the profit line moves away from the origin, less and less of the line falls within the feasible area. There will eventually come a stage when, as the profit line moves away from the origin, it has only *one* point in common with the feasible area. In Figure 13.4 this will occur at point III.

FIGURE 13.4 **Optimum solution**

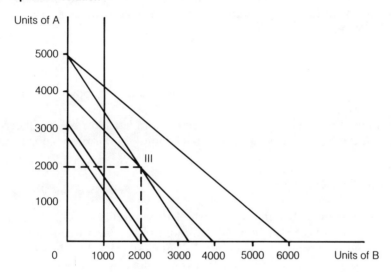

From the graph this point can be seen to represent:

$$A = 2,000$$
$$B = 2,000$$

which is our profit-maximising combination of the two products. Profit at this combination will be:

$$\text{Profit} = 0.25(2,000) + 0.35(2,000) = £1,200$$

The next higher profit line—£1,201—would have left the feasible area altogether and is therefore unattainable.

We can also confirm from the original problem that all the constraints are being satisfied:

$$0.3A + 0.25B \leq 1,500 \quad \text{(oats/fibre)}$$
$$0.1A + 0.15B \leq 500 \quad \text{(nuts/fruit)}$$
$$1A + 1B \leq 4,000 \quad \text{(sales)}$$
$$1B \geq 1,000 \quad \text{(minimum sales of de-luxe)}$$

Setting A to 2,000 and B to 2,000 this gives:

$0.3(2,000) + 0.25(2,000) = 1,100\text{kg}$ (less than the 1,500kg available)
$0.1(2,000) + 0.15(2,000) = 500\text{kg}$ (equal to the 500kg available)
$1(2,000) + 1(2,000) = 4,000 \text{ units}$ (equal to maximum production)
$1(2,000) = 2,000 \text{ units}$ (more than the minimum of 1,000 bags required)

So with this solution all the constraints are satisfied. Note that, in this case, two constraints (relating to nuts/fruit supply and to maximum sales) are satisfied exactly. That is both sides of the constraint are exactly equal. Such constraints are known as **binding** constraints. They represent critical factors in the problem. In this case, it is these two constraints which prevent profit from increasing further. We have exhausted the supply of nuts/fruit and we have reached the maximum production target of 4,000 bags.

The other two constraints (relating to oats/fibre and the minimum production of B) are **non-binding**, because they are not restricting profit as the current solution.

13.7 SIMULTANEOUS EQUATIONS SOLUTION

The graphical method of solution is, with practice, straightforward. Like all graphs, however, precise information is not always available from the graph. It is always advisable to confirm the graphical solution using simultaneous equations.

It can be seen from Figure 13.4 that the solution has occurred at point III, where the line representing the nuts/fruit constraint and the line representing maximum sales intersect. This is exactly the same as finding the solution to two linear functions. At this point the two constraints can be written as:

$$0.1A + 0.15B = 500$$
$$1A + 1B = 4000$$

Solving for A and B using normal simultaneous equation methods confirms the solution obtained from the graph.

It is worth noting that, typically, the solution to a simple LP problem will occur at one of the corner points of the feasible area, at the intersection of two or more constraints.

13.8 MINIMISATION PROBLEMS

In this problem we assumed that the firm wished to maximise profit. Problems involving minimisation, say in terms of costs, are equally common, and as easily formulated. In the case of a minimisation problem we would be seeking the smallest value for the objective function, trying to find the objective function that was as close to the origin as possible.

13.9 SUMMARY OF THE LP METHOD

To summarise the LP method:

1   Formulate the problem in terms of two variables.
2   For each constraint find two sets of coordinates: typically this is done by setting each variable in turn to zero and solving for the other. These coordinates indicate where the constraint line intercepts the X and Y axes.
3   Graph the constraints.
4   Identify the feasible area on the graph.
5   Draw the objective function on the graph using an arbitrary value to determine its slope.
6   For **maximisation** problems, determine the corner point the objective function will intersect last as it moves **away from** the origin.
7   For **minimisation** problems, determine the corner point the objective function will intersect last as it moves **toward** the origin.
8   From the graph determine the values for the two variables.
9   Confirm the graphical solution using simultaneous equations for the binding constraints.
10 Check your solution by substituting the values back into the original constraints to ensure none of them are violated.

SUMMARY

1 Linear Programming is a technique concerned with optimising some stated objective under various constraints. All the relationships are linear.

2 The objective function expresses, in mathematical terms, the objective to be attained. It may be expressed in **maximisation** or **minimisation** terms.

3 A constraint is an expression which rules out certain combinations of variables. Typically, it represents the availability of some resource. It may take the form of ($\geqslant$), ($=$) or ($\leqslant$).

4 A feasible solution is one which satisfies all the constraints.

5 An optimum solution is one which is both feasible and provides the optimum value for the objective function.

6 The optimum solution will generally occur at a corner point of the feasible area. For a maximisation problem this will be the last corner point intersected by the objective function as it moves away from the origin. For a minimisation problem it will be the last corner point as the objective function moves toward the origin.

7 Simultaneous equations can be used to confirm the graphical solution.

SELF-TEST QUESTIONS

1 **What is meant by the feasible area?** (*Refer to page 129*)

2 **What is a constraint?** (*Refer to page 127*)

3 **What is an objective function?** (*Refer to page 130*)

4 **What is the difference between a binding and a non-binding constraint?** (*Refer to page 132*)

5 **How is the graphical solution found?** (*Refer to page 131*)

6 **Why is it necessary to use simultaneous equations?** (*Refer to page 132*)

7 **How are simultaneous equations used?** (*Refer to page 132*)

EXERCISES

1 MTG have decided that at least 1,500 bags of the Standard cereal must be produced.
   (a) formulate an appropriate constraint
   (b) draw the constraint on one graph
   (c) determine the new solution

2 Instead of maximising profits MTG have decided to minimise the costs of producing the two cereals. A bag of Standard cereal costs £0.40 and a bag of De-luxe £0.50. Formulate a new objective function and determine the new solution.

   Check your solution using simultaneous equations. Which constraints are now binding? What is the cost of this combination?

Answers on page 313.

Quadratic and other non-linear functions

It is apparent that the type of mathematics introduced so far in the text, that relating to linear relationships, is inadequate in certain areas of business analysis. There are obvious relationships where it is unrealistic to assume the connection between two variables is linear. More typically, many relationships are **non-linear** and this chapter looks at non-linear equations in general and one particularly common non-linear function—the **quadratic**.

14.1 QUADRATIC FUNCTIONS

The general form of a quadratic equation is given as:

$$Y = a + bX + cX^2$$

where X and Y are the two variables and a, b and c are appropriate numbers or parameters. Such an equation will take one of two general shapes when drawn on a graph as illustrated in Figure 14.1.

A quadratic function will have what is known as a parabolic shape: it will follow a U-shape as in part (a) of the diagram with the Y value decreasing as X increases, reaching some minimum level and then increasing again. Alternatively, the function may follow an inverted U shape as in part (b) with the Y value climbing to a maximum then decreasing as X increases. The function may of course intercept either or both of the two axes, depending on the value of the parameters in the equation.

14.2 GRAPHING A QUADRATIC EQUATION

Drawing a graph of a quadratic equation is as straightforward as that for a linear equation. We shall illustrate by reference to the quadratic equation below:

$$Profit = -100 + 100X - 5X^2$$

We can assume that this represents a profit equation for some part of MTG's operations. X relates to the number of units of some product produced (in 000s) and Profit is measured in £000s.

You will remember that with a linear equation it was necessary only to determine two pairs of points to be able to draw the straight line. With quadratic equations it is necessary to obtain more pairs of points than this in order to accurately draw the parabola.

Before starting to draw a graph, however, it will be useful to know the general shape that the equation will take. We know that it will take one of the two general patterns illustrated in Figure 14.1. It is the c term in the quadratic expression which determines which of the two forms the quadratic function follows. If the c term is a positive number the function will take the standard U-shape whilst if the c term is a negative number the function will follow the inverted U shape pattern.

In this example the c term is -5, so we know that the function will follow the inverted U shape climbing up to some maximum Y value.

Knowing the general shape the graph will take we can now follow the same steps as with a linear function to draw a graph.

STEP 1

Choose an appropriate range for the X scale. Here X will range from 0 to 20 units.

FIGURE 14.1   **General form of a quadratic equation**

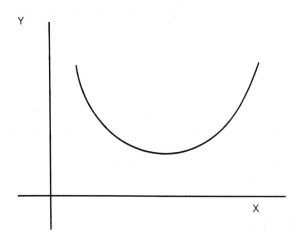

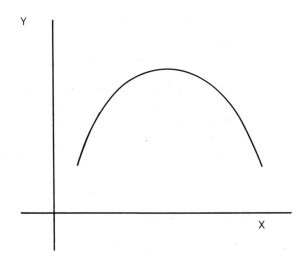

STEP 2

Determine an appropriate range of values for the Y scale.

It is necessary to use the equation to determine the Y values corresponding to specified X values. As a rule of thumb, approximately 10 pairs of values should be sufficient, spaced equally over the X range. These are calculated below:

X value	Y value	Equation
0	−100	$Y = -100 + 100(0) - 5(0)^2$
2	80	$Y = -100 + 100(2) - 5(2)^2$
4	220	$Y = -100 + 100(4) - 5(4)^2$
6	320	$Y = -100 + 100(6) - 5(6)^2$
8	380	$Y = -100 + 100(8) - 5(8)^2$
10	400	$Y = -100 + 100(10) - 5(10)^2$
12	380	$Y = -100 + 100(12) - 5(12)^2$
14	320	$Y = -100 + 100(14) - 5(14)^2$
16	220	$Y = -100 + 100(16) - 5(16)^2$
18	80	$Y = -100 + 100(18) - 5(18)^2$
20	−100	$Y = -100 + 100(20) - 5(20)^2$

STEP 3

Determine an appropriate scale for the Y variable. Here it would be sensible to set Y from −100 to 500.

STEP 4

Draw a suitable scale for the X and Y variables on the graph.

STEP 5

Taking the two pairs of X, Y values calculated in Step 2 plot each point on the graph.

STEP 6

Join these two points together as smoothly as you can with a curved line. This is the line for the given equation. Note that you should not join the points together with a straight line. The corresponding graph is shown in Figure 14.2.

FIGURE 14.2   **Profit = −100 + 100X − 5X²**

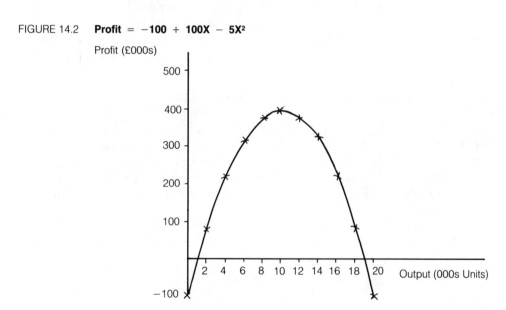

14.3   PARAMETERS OF A QUADRATIC EQUATION

With a linear equation we saw that there were two important parameters: the intercept and the slope. The same is true of the quadratic function.

The intercept, as with the linear function, is given by the a term in the equation, here at −100. This is the point where the quadratic equation crosses the Y axis. Note also that as with a linear equation the intercept frequently has a business meaning in the context of the problem. Here, this is the level of profit when output is zero. The equation (and graph) indicates that profit will be −£100(000) at zero level of output. (This means of course a loss of £100(000).) On reflection you will see the logic of this. If the firm is producing zero output its revenue will also be zero. However, it is still likely to incur overheads and fixed costs. Given that profit is simply the difference between revenue and costs, the company will be operating at a loss of £100(000) at such a level of output.

The slope of the equation also has an important meaning. However, unlike the linear function the slope of a quadratic equation is not constant but changes depending where we are on the X axis. You will see from Figure 14.2 that to begin with the slope is positive (upwards from left to right). The steepness of the slope gradually gets less and less until (in this example when X=10) the direction of the line changes and the slope becomes negative (downward from left to right). The calculation of the slope is not as straightforward as for a linear equation and we must wait for the techniques introduced in the next chapter before we can quantify the slope of a quadratic function.

The meaning of the slope, however, remains the same. In this case it refers to the change in profit as output changes. That is, the extra profit achieved as we increase output. This is of obvious importance to any organisation.

One specific feature of a quadratic equation that is usually of considerable importance is the point where the slope changes. In this example, we can observe from the graph that this will occur when X=10. Such a point is referred to as the **turning point**.

14.4 ROOTS OF A QUADRATIC FUNCTION

In fact, the turning point of a quadratic function is generally of significant importance in a business problem. If we refer back to the profit equation in Figure 14.2 it is clear that the turning point occurs at the **maximum** position of the function, that is where profit is highest. Similarly, if we had been dealing with a quadratic equation which took the opposite shape the turning point would represent a **minimum** Y value.

You will be aware that maximisation and minimisation are especially important in the study of business and economics. Apart from profit maximisation, such situations as maximising production, minimising costs, minimising the use of resources and so on are all common.

At this stage, we can find the turning point of the quadratic equation in two ways:

1   Directly from the graph
2   Using algebra to determine the roots of the equation.

As we have noted before extracting precise information from a graph is an inaccurate method and we shall concentrate on the algebraic method here. In mathematical terms the **roots** of a quadratic equation are simply the X values which generate a value for Y equal to zero. In other words, the roots represent the X values where the equation intercepts the X axis (for here Y=0).

Typically in most (but not all) quadratic equations there will be two such roots. In other cases there may be one or none.

In our profit example, it can be seen that the equation crosses the X axis at two points: these are the two roots of the equation and we require a general algebraic method of finding them. The equation below is generally used to determine the roots:

$$\text{The roots X1 and X2} = \frac{-b \pm \sqrt{b^2 - 4ac}}{2c}$$

where a, b, c are the appropriate parameters from the quadratic function. Thus in our example they would take the values:

$$a = -100 \qquad b = 100 \qquad c = -5$$

and substituting into the formula we have:

$$\frac{-100 \pm \sqrt{100^2 - 4(-100)(-5)}}{2(-5)}$$

$$\frac{-100 \pm \sqrt{10,000 - (2000)}}{-10}$$

$$\frac{-100 \pm 89.44}{-10}$$

To find the two X values we evaluate this expression by using the + and − signs in turn (it doesn't matter in what order). This gives:

Using + $\qquad$ $X1 = \dfrac{-100 + 89.44}{-10} = \dfrac{-10.56}{-10} = 1.056$

Using − $\qquad$ $X2 = \dfrac{-100 - 89.44}{-10} = \dfrac{-189.44}{-10} = 18.944$

That is, the quadratic function crosses the X axis when X=1.056 and again, when X=18.944. These two point can be confirmed from Figure 14.2 and from substitution into the original profit equation. From a business context these represent the two breakeven points: ie where profit=0.

One important point is that great care must be taken when using the formula to ensure the correct values for a, b, c are used and that the signs of these values are also used. A frequent (and careless) mistake seen on many exam answers is for a student to confuse the negative signs shown in the calculation.

14.5   THE TURNING POINT

Whilst we are frequently interested in the values of the roots of a quadratic function in their own right we are also usually interested in the turning point of the quadratic equation: that is, the X value which generates either the maximum or minimum Y value (depending on the type of function).

We can readily use the two roots to determine such a turning point. Without proof, we simply state that **the turning point of a quadratic function will be found midway between the two roots**.

In this example the two roots are 1.056 and 18.944. The point midway between them is found by:

$$\text{Lowest root} + \frac{(\text{Highest root} - \text{Lowest root})}{2}$$

In this example:

$$1.056 + \frac{(18.944 - 1.056)}{2} = 1.056 + 8.944 = 10$$

When X=10 the equation is at its maximum point. In a business context the group will achieve maximum profit for this product when output is 10(000) units. To determine profit at this level of output we return to the profit equation:

$$\text{Profit} = -100 + 100X - 5X^2$$

$$\text{Profit} = -100 + 100(10) - 5(10^2)$$

$$= -100 + 1000 - 500 = 400$$

So, profit is £400(000) at its highest point.

As with most mathematical calculations it is always worthwhile checking your answer wherever possible. We can make use of our knowledge of quadratic equations to confirm the result. If profit is maximised when X=10 then we know from the general shape of the function that when X is slightly less than 10 and X is slightly more than 10 profit should be less than the maximum of £400.

$$\text{Let us set } X=9.9$$
$$\text{and} \qquad X=10.1$$

Using the profit equation you should confirm that this will give profit at:

$$X=9.9 \qquad \text{Profit} = 399.95$$
$$X=10.1 \qquad \text{Profit} = 399.95$$

Both of these are slightly less than the maximum at £400. From Figure 14.2 you can see that such a combination of profit and X values can only occur at one point, at the top of the function, thus confirming that when X=10 profit is at the maximum point.

14.6   SETS OF QUADRATIC EQUATIONS

Just as with linear equations there are times when we may have two or more quadratic equations and wish to determine the point or points where the equations intersect. To find such points we can again use the concept of roots of quadratic equations. In this case, however, we are using the concept in a slightly different way.

Let us assume that the company is investigating two different aspects of its cost structure. It is examining average costs (defined as total costs divided by number of units of output produced) and marginal cost (defined as the extra cost involved in producing an extra unit).

A study of economics reveals that the two functions will intersect where average costs reaches its minimum point.

Assume the following equations:

$$AC = 500 - 20X + 2X^2$$

$$MC = 500 - 40X + 6X^2$$

For a range of output up to 10 units the two functions have been plotted on Figure 14.3.

FIGURE 14.3   **Average and marginal cost curves**

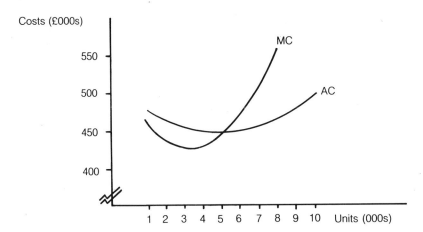

It is apparent that the point we are seeking (the point where the two functions cross) occurs when X=5. However, we need to be able to determine this algebraically.

In fact, we are not interested in the two equations as they stand, but rather in the **difference** between the two. The point we are seeking occurs when the difference between the two is zero.

Let us define a new equation:

$$Y = AC - MC$$

$$Y = (500 - 20X + 2X^2) - (500 - 40X + 6X^2)$$

Collecting terms together we have:

$$Y = 20X - 4X^2$$

where X still measures units of output but Y now measures the difference between the two functions. It is apparent that this equation is itself quadratic where:

$$a = 0$$
$$b = 20$$
$$c = -4$$

We now require the value for X which gives Y (the difference between the two) equal to zero. It should be apparent that this is exactly the same as saying we require the roots of this quadratic equation.

Solving for the roots using the general formula would give:

$$X1 = 0$$
$$X2 = 5$$

(You should confirm for yourself that these are the roots of the equation.)

As with most quadratic equations we find two roots. Here X=0 represents one point of intersection between the AC and MC equations which we can ignore, leaving the solution at X=5. This value for X gives Y=0 where Y is the difference between the AC and MC equations. As ever, we should check our solution. From the original equations we have:

$$AC = 500 - 20X + 2X^2$$
$$AC = 500 - 20(5) + 2(5^2) = 500 - 100 + 50 = 450$$

$$MC = 500 - 40X + 6X^2$$
$$MC = 500 - 40(5) + 6(5^2) = 500 - 200 + 150 = 450$$

thereby confirming the two equations are equal when X=5.

14.7 OTHER TYPES OF NON-LINEAR EQUATIONS

Occasionally, business problems may be represented by other types of non-linear equations. The solution of such equations is rarely required and, indeed, there is no common method of solution, the method depending entirely on the type of function used. A graph of the function is usually helpful, however, and you should be able to produce such graphs.

The method is the same as that for the quadratic function. It is necessary to determine a number of (X, Y) values in order to plot the function accurately.

For example suppose we have a total cost function given by:

$$TC = \frac{1000}{X} + 10 - 5X + X^2$$

where X is output (in 000s)
TC is Total Cost (in £000s)

Let us suppose that we wish to plot this function from X=0 to X=20. Following the standard steps for a non-linear graph we next determine the corresponding Y values over this range (note that we cannot determine a value when X=0 as we would be dividing 0 into 1000).

X	TC
1	1006
2	504
4	256
6	182.667
8	159
10	160
12	177.333
14	207.429
16	248.5
18	299.556
20	360

(You should confirm the values for TC for yourself from the equation.)

Note that if you are unsure of the general shape of the function you are plotting you should calculate the Y value for as many X values as is practical.

It would be sensible to use a Y scale from 0 to 1100 here, and Figure 14.4 shows the function plotted.

FIGURE 14.4 **Graph of TC equation**

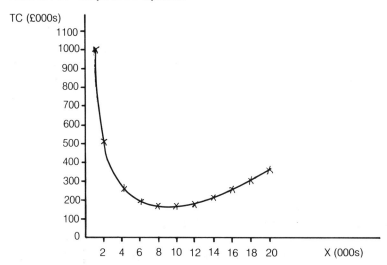

Virtually any non-linear function can be graphed in this way.

SUMMARY

1   Non-linear functions are common in business mathematics and can take almost any form (other than that given by Y=a + bX).

2   A quadratic function is a particular type of non-linear function typically used.
It is given in the general form: $Y = a + bX + cX^2$

3   Graphing a non-linear equation follows the same steps as for a linear function, with the exception that a reasonably large number of points need to be plotted to identify the specific shape of the function.

4   In a quadratic function the points where the function crosses the X axis are known as the roots and show the X values where Y=0. There may be two, one or no roots depending on the parameters of the quadratic.

5   The turning point of a quadratic represents the point where the slope of the function changes and gives a value for Y which is its maximum or minimum, depending on the type of function. The turning point is found midway between the two roots.

6   Sets of quadratic (or quadratic and linear) equations are frequently encountered. The solution to such sets in general is found by deriving an expression measuring the difference between equations in the set and finding where this equation equals zero.

14.8 SELF-TEST QUESTIONS

1 **What is the general form of a quadratic equation?** (*Refer to page 135*)

2 **Which part of the quadratic equation shows the intercept?** (*Refer to page 137*)

3 **Which part of the quadratic equation shows the slope?** (*Refer to page 137*)

4 **What does the c term in the quadratic tell us?** (*Refer to page 135*)

5 **What are the roots of a quadratic?** (*Refer to page 138*)

6 **How can the roots be found?** (*Refer to page 138*)

7 **What is the turning point and how is it found?** (*Refer to page 140*)

8 **What are the general steps involved in plotting a non-linear function?** (*Refer to page 135*)

9 **What does it mean if you know that a quadratic equation has no roots?** (*Refer to page 138*)

EXERCISES

1 Confirm by substituting back into the original profit equation that the two roots (at X= 1.056 and x= 18.944) are correct.

2 Plot the following quadratic equations and determine the roots and turning point:

(a) $Y = -50 - 5X + 2.5X^2$ (for X=0 to 20)
(b) $Y = 45 + 5X - 3X^2$ (for X=−5 to +5)
(c) $Y = -100 + 50X - 5X^2$ (for X=0 to 10)
(d $Y = -500 + 50X - 5X^2$ (for X=0 to 10)
(e) $Y = 100 + 50X - 5X^2$ (for X=0 to 10)

Why is it impossible to find roots for certain of these functions?

3 MTG have analysed the demand for one of their products and found it to be:

$$Qd = \frac{600}{P}$$

where Qd is the number of units demanded and P is the price charged.
(a)   Plot this function for a price up to 10.
(b)   Comment on the shape of the function in the context of consumer behaviour.

4 MTG have also analysed their employment of skilled computer programmers and found this to be linked to wage rates. On an hourly basis MTG pay their programmers between £10 and £25. The function linking number of programmers employed to wage rates is given by:

$$D_L = \frac{5000}{2W^2}$$

where D_L is the number employed and W is the hourly wage rate.
(a)   Plot this function.
(b)   Interpret the shape of the function and the implications for management.

Answers on page 314.

Differential and integral calculus

The importance of the **slope** of a function has been stressed in earlier chapters. The slope provides an easy method of determining the change in the Y value that is associated with a given change in the X value. In a business context, the slope is of fundamental importance. Businesses wish to know how profit, costs and revenue will change with output, how sales will change with the level of advertising, how productivity will change with the size of the labour force, how sales will change with price and so on.

When we were examining linear functions we saw that the slope was readily identifiable from the equation, with the b term indicating the value of the slope directly. With quadratics, and indeed with any type of non-linear function, the slope is not immediately obvious. In fact, as we saw with quadratics the slope of a non-linear equation changes depending where on the function we are and does not remain constant.

It is evident that we require some general method of determining the slope of any type of function.

15.1   DIFFERENTIAL CALCULUS

Let us return to the profit equation used in the previous chapter:

$$\text{Profit} = -100 + 100X - 5X^2$$

where X = output. We saw from the corresponding graph of this equation that the slope of the function changed with X. The slope started as very steep and positive, gradually became less steep and then reversed direction and became negative.

In a business context the slope of the profit function shows how profit will change as output changes: this is frequently referred to as a **marginal** concept—the extra (or marginal) profit achieved as an extra unit of output is produced. From the corresponding graph we can see that at low levels of output considerable extra profit can be achieved by increasing output. This extra profit gradually gets less and less as output increases and there finally comes a point where extra output has a **negative** effect on profit.

THE DERIVATIVE

In order to find the slope of such a function we must introduce the idea of a **derivative**. When we have a function which takes the general form:

$$Y = kX^n$$

then the derivative of that function can be expressed as:

$$\frac{dy}{dx} = nkX^{n-1}$$

where dy/dx (pronounced deeY by deeX) is the general symbol for the derivative. The derivative, as we shall see, is an expression which shows the slope of any function. We shall illustrate with a simple example. Suppose we have a linear function such that:

$$Y = 100X$$

Because it is a linear function we know that its slope will be 100 (=b). But we shall also use the derivative method. The linear function corresponds to the function form:

$$Y = kX^n = 100X^1$$

where k = 100 and n = 1.

Using the derivative rule we have:

$$\frac{dy}{dx} = nkX^{n-1} = 1(100)X^{(1-1)} = 100X^0 = 100$$

(You should remember that any variable raised to the power zero equals 1.)

The derivative expression shows the slope of the original (linear) function. That is, the derivative indicates that the slope of $Y=100X$ is 100, confirming what we already knew from the value of b.

If we have a quadratic function rather than a linear one the derivative rule is just as straightforward. Suppose we have:

$$Y = -5X^2$$

Here, $k=-5$ and $n=2$ so the derivative would be:

$$\frac{dy}{dx} = 2(-5)X^{(2-1)} = -10X^1 = -10X$$

What does this mean? Since the original expression ($Y=-5X^2$) was quadratic we know that its slope is not constant. The derivative is an equation which shows the slope of the original equation anywhere along its length. So if we wish to know the slope of $Y=-5X^2$ at the point when $X=10$ we would substitute $X=10$ into the derivative expression:

$$\frac{dy}{dx} = -10X = -10(10) = -100$$

When $X=10$ the slope of the original equation is -100. That is, at this point if X were to change by some amount Y would change by -100 times that amount. If we now wanted the slope when $X = 4$ we would again use the derivative expression and find the slope to be -40. That is, at this point on the original function there is a change in Y of -40 times the change in X. The derivative, therefore, provides a simple method of calculating the slope for any value of X.

Let us now return to the profit function:

$$\text{Profit} = -100 + 100X - 5X^2$$

We can represent each part of this function in turn in the standard format and find the derivative of each part. Then, reassembling the derivative components will give the derivative for the whole function. Thus,

$$-100 \text{ becomes } -100X^0$$

and its derivative $= 0(100)X^{(0-1)} = 0$

In other words, as $Y = -100$ represents a line parallel to the X axis the derivative confirms that such a function has a zero slope. Similarly, $100X$ has a derivative given (as we have already seen) by:

$$1(100)X^{1-1} = 100X^0 = 100$$

and finally $-5X^2$ has a derivative:

$$2(-5)X^{(2-1)} = -10X^1 = -10X$$

Reassembling gives:

$$\frac{d\text{profit}}{dX} = 0 + 100 - 10X = 100 - 10X$$

This derivative (itself a linear function) allows us to calculate the slope of the profit function at any level of output. So when $X=1$:

$$\frac{d\text{profit}}{dX} = 100 - 10X = 100 - 10(1) = 90$$

That is, at a level of output=1 a marginal change in this output will lead to a corresponding increase in total profit of 90 times the change in output.
Similarly, when X=20:

$$\frac{\text{dprofit}}{\text{dX}} = 100 - 10X = 100 - 10(20) = -100$$

That is when output is 20 a marginal increase will lead to a **decrease** in total profit of 100 times the change in output.

(It is important to realise from the mathematical theory supporting the derivative that these derivative values are applicable only for marginal changes in output, that is, for particularly small changes in X.)

The relationship between the original profit function and its derivative is shown in Figure 15.1. Up to an output level of 10 units the slope is positive, but less and less so. After an output of 10 units the slope is negative and becomes more and more so. At a level of output of 10 units it is apparent that the slope is zero.

FIGURE 15.1 **Profit (£000s)**

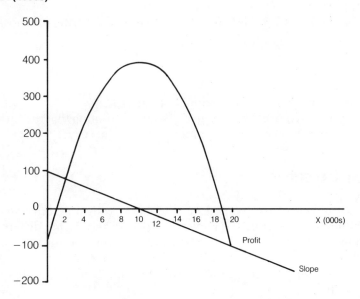

The derivative can, in fact, be applied to any type of mathematical function that is typically used in business and not simply to quadratics.

15.2 FINDING THE TURNING POINT USING DIFFERENTIAL CALCULUS

In fact Figure 15.1 leads us to one of the particularly important uses of the derivative. We saw in the previous chapter that it is frequently important to find the turning point of a quadratic equation: the X value which gives the maximum or minimum Y value for the function. Until now, we have used the two roots of the quadratic to determine the turning point. We can now find this point in a much easier way using the derivative.

The turning point for any quadratic will occur when the slope=0. Given that the derivative is an expression for calculating the slope at any point on the original function then we can use the derivative to find the turning point directly.

We wish to find the level of output when the slope of the profit function (that is the value of the derivative) is zero. Setting the derivative to zero and solving gives:

$$\frac{\text{dprofit}}{\text{dX}} = 100 - 10X = 0$$

$$100 = 10X \text{ hence } X = 10$$

F

When X is 10 units, therefore, we have reached a point on the profit function with a zero slope and this must represent the turning point for this quadratic function where Profit is maximised.

THE SECOND DERIVATIVE

In the example above we recognised that the turning point derived using calculus represented a maximum. In other situations, however, particularly if we develop business models using higher-power expressions, it is necessary to be able to check whether the turning point represents a maximum or a minimum position. This is achieved through the use of the '**second derivative**'.

A simple rule applies. Having determined the first derivative we can decide whether this represents a maximum or minimum value by taking its derivative in turn. If this second derivative is **negative** the zero-slope point found is a maximum. If the second derivative is **positive** we have a minimum point.

In this example, the (first) derivative was:

$$\frac{dprofit}{dX} = 100 - 10X$$

Applying the same rule of differentiation we can find the (second) derivative of this expression:

$$\frac{d^2profit}{dX^2} = -10$$

(The term ^{2} is used to indicate this is a second derivative.)

Here, the second derivative takes a negative value, indicating that the turning point found using the first derivative related to a maximum point on the curve.

15.3 INTEGRAL CALCULUS

The method of calculus we have focused on thus far is known as *differential* calculus as the process of determining the derivative is known as *differentiation*. Using differentiation we have found an equation which shows the slope of the original function for any value of X.

Occasionally, however, we may have the derivative and we wish to determine the original equation it represents. Suppose, for example, we were simply told that the slope of the profit equation was given by:

$$\frac{dprofit}{dX} = 100 - 10X$$

How can we determine the original equation from which this derivative was calculated? The answer lies in **integral** calculus which is the opposite of differential calculus. We can apply a simple rule (as we did to find the derivative). Given a derivative taken the general form:

$$\frac{dY}{dX} = aX^b$$

where a and b are appropriate parameters then the original function can be found by integrating the derivative using the rule:

$$\text{Integral} = \int aX^b \, dX = \frac{a}{b+1} X^{(b+1)} + c$$

where c is an arbitrary constant.

To apply the rule we integrate each part of the function:

$$\int 100 \ dX = \frac{100}{0+1} \ X^{(0+1)} = 100X$$

$$\int -10X \ dX = \frac{-10}{(1+1)} \ X^{(1+1)} = -5X^2$$

Reassembling gives:

$$Y = 100X - 5X^2 + c$$

We must include the c term, which is an unknown number, because we have no way of knowing what value this constant in the original function may have taken. You will remember from the section on differentiation that the derivative of a constant is zero, so we have no way of finding the integral value. Accordingly, we simply indicate, using the c term, that part of the original function is unknown from the information given in the derivative.

SUMMARY

The use of differential and integral calculus is extremely common in business mathematics. The derivative in particular is used extensively in marginal analysis and typical business applications include marginal revenue, marginal cost, profit maximisation, cost minimisation, and applications to demand and supply problems.

1   The derivative is simply an expression which shows the slope of the original function at any point along its length.
2   The derivative is frequently used to find the turning point of a function: when the slope = 0.
3   The second derivative results from differentiating the derivative of a function and is used to confirm whether the turning point identified is a maximum or minimum value.
4   The integral is the opposite of the derivative and is used to find the original function, given the derivative equation.

SELF-TEST QUESTIONS

1   **What is the difference between a derivative and an integral?** (*Refer to page 148*)

2   **What is the derivative rule?** (*Refer to page 145*)

3   **What does a derivative measure?** (*Refer to page 146*)

4   **What is the derivative of a constant?** (*Refer to page 146*)

5   **How is the derivative used to find the turning point?** (*Refer to page 147*)

6   **What is the second derivative?** (*Refer to page 148*)

7   **Why is the second derivative calculated?** (*Refer to page 148*)

8   **What is the integral rule?** (*Refer to page 148*)

9   **Why is it necessary to include a c term in the integral calculation?** (*Refer to page 149*)

EXERCISES

1   For each of the quadratic equations given in question 2 of the exercises in Chapter 14 find the corresponding derivative and turning point.

2   Using the derivatives from question 1 use the integral rule to determine the original equation.

3   For the demand equation given in question 3 of the exercises in Chapter 14 find the slope when P=2 and when P=8. (Remember $\frac{1}{P} = P^{-1}$.)

What use could management put this information to?

4   Refer back to the profit, TR and TC equations used in question 5 of the exercises in Chapter 14.
(a)   Find an expression for the derivative of each
(b)   Explain, in a business context, what each derivative means
(c)   Find the turning point of the TC function
(d)   Find the turning point of the TR function
(e)   Find the slope of the TR and TC function at the level of output which maximises profit. Comment on your results.

Answers on page 316.

Simple linear regression

In earlier chapters linear equations were introduced and discussed and their potential useful-ness in a variety of business applications evaluated. Up to now we have simply assumed that such equations have been provided without any concern for their source or derivation. This Chapter is concerned with **how** such linear relationships can be quantified from the raw data using the technique of simple linear regression.

16.1 SIMPLE LINEAR REGRESSION

Let us return to the linear equation introduced in Chapter 11 relating total costs to output:

$$TC = 8 + 1.25X$$

How would such an equation be derived in practice?

Let us assume that, over the past 12 months, the company has collected data on the two variables. The production department anticipates that next month's production will be 7.5 (000) units and wishes to estimate likely costs. The data collected are shown in Table 16.1.

TABLE 16.1   **Monthly costs and output levels for 1987**

Total costs (£000s)	Monthly output (000s units)
10.3	2.4
12	3.9
12	3.1
13.5	4.5
12.2	4.1
14.2	5.4
10.8	1.1
18.2	7.8
16.2	7.2
19.5	9.5
17.1	6.4
19.2	8.3

Source: *Production Department*

Figure 16.1 shows the two variables plotted on a graph. On the vertical axis we have total costs and on the horizontal axis the output levels. It should be apparent why TC has been placed on the vertical axis. In terms of convention the dependent variable is put on this axis and it is logical to suggest that TC is dependent on X. Thus, TC is denoted as the Y variable and output as the X variable.

FIGURE 16.1   **Scatter diagram**

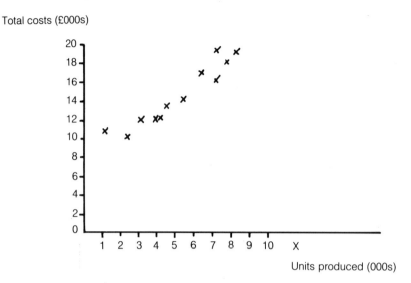

The figure shows what is known as a **scatter diagram**, so called because it shows the scatter of points of the two variables and is an essential first step in regression analysis. It allows us to see whether there is any linear relationship between the two variables in question.

We can see from the figure that there is indeed some connection between the two, with TC rising as X rises, although it is also evident that the relationship between the two variables is not perfectly constant as the points do not all fit on a single straight line. There is some variability in the linear relationship.

We require a **linear** equation that best represents the scatter of data that we have in the diagram, in the terminology of regression we are looking for **the line of best fit**. Such an equation will be the one that comes closes to the data set.

We could draw such a line ourselves, superimposing the straight line onto the scatter diagram. In doing this we would probably try to draw the line so that it came as close as possible to as many as possible of the various points on the graph. Such a method, however, is entirely subjective and unlikely to be perfectly accurate. We need a mathematical method of finding the equation.

You will remember that the general form of a linear equation is given as:

$$Y = a + bX$$

where a and b are the appropriate parameters for the equation. The two parameters of the line of best fit, a and b, can be calculated precisely using the following equations:

$$b = \frac{n\Sigma XY - \Sigma X \Sigma Y}{n\Sigma X^2 - (\Sigma X)^2}$$

$$a = \frac{\Sigma Y}{n} - b\left(\frac{\Sigma X}{n}\right)$$

where n is the number of pairs of data items
ΣX is the sum of the X values
ΣY is the sum of the Y values
ΣXY is the sum of X times Y

The appropriate calculations are shown in Table 16.2.

TABLE 16.2 **Calculations for linear regression**

Y	X	XY	X^2	Y^2
10.3	2.4	24.72	5.76	106.09
12	3.9	46.8	15.21	144
12	3.1	37.2	9.61	144
13.5	4.5	60.75	20.25	182.25
12.2	4.1	50.02	16.81	148.84
14.2	5.4	76.68	29.16	201.64
10.8	1.1	11.88	1.21	116.64
18.2	7.8	141.96	60.84	331.24
16.2	7.2	116.64	51.84	262.44
19.5	9.5	185.25	90.25	380.25
17.1	6.4	109.44	40.96	292.41
19.2	8.3	159.36	68.89	368.64
Totals 175.2	63.7	1020.7	410.79	2678.44

The calculation of the a and b parameters is then straightforward:

$$b = \frac{12(1020.7) - (63.7)(175.2)}{12(410.79) - (63.7)^2}$$

$$= \frac{12248.4 - 11160.24}{4929.48 - 4057.69} = \frac{1088.16}{871.97} = 1.248$$

$$a = \frac{175.2}{12} - (1.248)\left(\frac{63.7}{12}\right)$$

$$= 14.6 - 6.6248 = 7.9752$$

Thus, the equation representing the line of best fit is:

$$Y = 7.9752 + 1.248X$$

where Y is the total costs
and X is the output

For practical use we may wish to round this to:

$$Y = 8 + 1.25X$$

Interpretation of the line of best fit is the same as for any linear equation. The a term, at 8, denotes the intercept and the b term, at 1.25, denotes the slope of the line.

The line of best fit has been superimposed on the scatter diagram in Figure 16.2.

FIGURE 16.2   **Line of best fit**

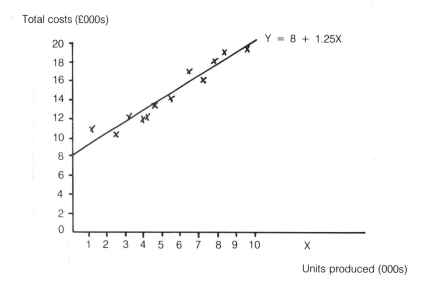

The line, as the name suggests, is that which comes closest to the set of data points that we have. As we can see from the diagram, however, there are differences between the observed points and the best fit line. That is, the line we have calculated is not a **perfect** fit to the scatter of data. Any line is likely to deviate, to a large or small extent, from the observed data. The regression equations used above find the line where this deviation is at a minimum. As with the standard deviation statistic introduced in Chapter 6, the deviations of the line from the data are not measured in absolute terms (given that some will be negative and some positive) but rather by squaring the deviations. The line of best fit is then the line where these squared deviations are minimised. Hence the alternative name for the method we have used, the **method of least squares**.

16.2   THE CORRELATION COEFFICIENT

Given that we are using regression to measure relationships between variables and that we wish to use such equations for forecasting it is essential that we have some measure of how accurate and reliable the equation we have obtained is. Obviously, we can obtain a visual assessment by superimposing the line of best fit onto the scatter diagram as we did in Figure 16.2. Visually, it appears that the regression line is reasonably close to the observed data and hence we would view predictions obtained from the equation with reasonable confidence. Such a visual impression, however, is insufficient. We also require some statistical measure of accuracy.

One such measure is to calculate a statistic known as the correlation coefficient or, more precisely, as **Pearson's product moment correlation coefficient** denoted as r. The formula is:

$$r = \frac{n\Sigma XY - \Sigma X\Sigma Y}{\sqrt{[n\Sigma X^2 - (\Sigma X)^2][n\Sigma Y^2 - (\Sigma Y)^2]}}$$

The calculations are straightforward and the appropriate totals can again be found from Table 16.2.

$$r = \frac{12(1020.7) - (63.7)(175.2)}{\sqrt{[12(410.79) - 63.7^2][12(2678.44) - 175.2^2]}}$$

$$= \frac{1088.16}{\sqrt{(871.97)(1446.24)}} = \frac{1088.16}{1122.98}$$

$$r = 0.969$$

The correlation coefficient measures the **strength** of the linear relationship between the X and Y variable: that is, how close the line of best fit comes to the scatter of XY points. Mathematically, the coefficient must take a value between 0 and 1. A value of zero implies that there is no correlation or connection between the two variables. Similarly, a coefficient of 1 implies a perfect connection between the two variables. In the latter case all the points would actually lie on the regression line.

The coefficient could also take either a positive or negative value. This indicates the slope of the regression line. So, here, we know from the correlation coefficient that the regression line would have a positive slope.

The correlation coefficient we have found at 0.969 is very close to the maximum value of 1, confirming our original view from the scatter diagram that the line of best fit is close to the data and, hence, predictions based on such a regression equation could be viewed as likely to be reasonably accurate.

The value of the correlation coefficient must be interpreted with care. Strictly, the coefficient measures the strength of the **linear** relationship between two variables. If the relationship (like many in business) is in fact **non-linear** the correlation coefficient is likely to take a low value. This may not mean that there is no connection between the two variables but rather that there appears to be no **linear** connection.

Suppose, for example, we were trying to obtain a regression equation for an average cost curve for a business. We know that such a curve is likely to be U-shaped rather than linear. If we performed a linear regression we would be likely to obtain a low correlation coefficient value. This would indicate, however, not that there was no connection between average costs and output but that the connection was a non-linear one. Obviously, the scatter diagram is essential as it allows us to visually confirm whether we had some non-linear pattern in our data.

16.3 FORECASTING FROM THE REGRESSION LINE

Apart from allowing us to quantify the relationship that exists between two variables the regression line provides us with a ready method for forecasting. We know that output next month is planned to be 7.5 (000) units. We wish to establish, perhaps for cash flow purposes, the likely costs associated with this output. Substituting X=7.5 into the regression equation we have:

$$TC = 8 + 1.25(7.5) = 17.375 \; (\pounds000)$$

This is the predicted level of costs based on a level of output of 7.5. Given that we have a value for the correlation coefficient of 0.969 we would tend to regard such a forecast as being reasonably accurate and it could be used with a high degree of confidence in its reliability, although we would expect some slight discrepancy between the forecast costs and the outturn costs. Apart from the value of the correlation coefficient (and obviously the scatter diagram) it is also important to distinguish between two general situations when using regression for forecasting purposes.

INTERPOLATION AND EXTRAPOLATION

From Table 16.1 and from the associated scatter diagram it is apparent that over the last 12 months output has varied between 1.1 and 9.5 units. Strictly speaking the line of best fit we have established (and the corresponding correlation coefficient) is appropriate only within this range of output. We actually have no information on what happens to total costs if output were to go outside this range.

In the example of forecasting above (with X=7.5) we would be confident about the validity of the forecast produced because the X value lies within the range used to determine the line of best fit. Such a forecast is based on **interpolation**, where we are basing the forecast on an X value within the observed range.

Suppose, however, we were required to forecast TC whcn X=12.1. Although we can use the same regression equation to produce a forecast value for TC of 23.125 we should regard the forecast with much greater suspicion. This is because we are now **extrapolating**, basing the forecast on a value for X outside the observed range. In effect we would have to say that we do not actually **know** what the relationship between X and TC is at such output levels. All we can do is assume it remains unchanged from that specified in the regression equation.

16.4 RANK CORRELATION COEFFICIENT

In the context of regression the measure of correlation that is used is the product moment correlation coefficient. However, other measures of correlation exist for use in more specialised applications.

One such is the **Rank** correlation coefficient, formally known as Spearman's Rank correlation.

To illustrate its use let us examine the information below in Table 16.3.

TABLE 16.3   **Performance of candidates in job selection procedures**

Applicant	Personal interview score (max 100)	Written test score (max 50)
A	78	43
B	62	34
C	85	42
D	68	39
E	65	30
F	71	44

Source: *Personnel Department*

Assume that the Personnel department have been undertaking a selection procedure for filling a vacant post in the Accounts department. There are a total of six applicants and each of them was interviewed by the selection panel and then asked to undertake a short written test.

The interview panel gave each applicant a score out of 100 and the written test was marked out of 50. The obvious question is, is there any correlation between an applicant's performance in the interview and his/her performance on the written test? Whilst we could calculate the product-moment correlation using the formula introduced earlier it is apparent on reflection that our interest lies not so much in the actual score of each applicant but in their **relative** performance when compared with the other candidates. Ideally, what we would like to know is: did the person who came top in the interview also come top in the written test, the second highest second and so on.

We can calculate an appropriate correlation statistic which measures the degree of relative rather than absolute association between two variables. This correlation coefficient is known as the Rank correlation. To do this we must rank the scores in Table 16.4.

TABLE 16.4   **Performance of candidates in job selection procedures ranked in order**

Applicant	Personal interview score (max 100)	Written test score (max 50)
A	2	2
B	6	5
C	1	3
D	4	4
E	5	6
F	3	1

The scores have now been ranked so that the applicant with the highest score is ranked 1, the second highest 2, and so on.

We now define the Spearman's Rank correlation coefficient as:

$$p = 1 - \frac{6\Sigma D^2}{n(n^2 - 1)}$$

where p denotes the coefficient
D is the difference between the two rankings for each applicant
n the number of pairs of items.

The relevant calculations are shown in Table 16.5.

TABLE 16.5 **Calculation of Spearman's Rank Correlation Coefficient**

Applicant	Interview Ranking	Written Test Ranking	D	D²
A	2	2	0	0
B	6	5	1	1
C	1	3	−2	4
D	4	4	0	0
E	5	6	−1	1
F	3	1	2	4
		Total	0	10

$$p = 1 - \frac{6(10)}{6(6^2 - 1)}$$

$$= 1 - \frac{60}{6(35)} = 1 - \frac{60}{210}$$

$$p = 1 - 0.286 = 0.714$$

The Rank correlation coefficient takes a value here of +0.714. Its interpretation and meaning are exactly the same as the product moment correlation. It takes a value between 0 and 1, and the closer to 1 the higher the correlation between the two variables. A positive value indicates a positive connection between the two variables and a negative value an inverse relationship.

Here, with p=+0.714 there is a reasonably strong positive correlation between the rankings of the applicants although perhaps not as strong as we might have expected given the two parts of the selection process should favour the same candidates.

One point to note in the calculation of the p value is that there are frequently tied values in the rankings. Assume, for example, that candidate C had achieved a written test score of 39 the same as candidate D. The two candidates would thus be ranked third and fourth together so would have a ranking in the table equal to 3.5 (half of 3+4).

SUMMARY

1   Regression is a technique for estimating the linear equation corresponding to a data set
2   The technique may be referred to as finding the line of best fit, or the method of least squares.
3   The technique finds the linear equation that comes closest to the scatter of data
4   Regression is particularly useful for forecasting a variable. A distinction must be made between forecasts based on interpolation and those on extrapolation.

5 The product moment (or Pearson's) correlation coefficient is used to measure the strength of association between two variables. It is typically used in regression as a general indication of how close the line is to the scatter of points.

6 Spearman's Rank correlation measures the strength of association between two variables where the order of the variables is of more importance than their specific values.

SELF-TEST QUESTIONS

1 What is meant by 'the line of best fit'? (*Refer to page 152*)

2 Why is a scatter diagram essential in regression? (*Refer to page 155*)

3 What does the Pearson correlation coefficient show? (*Refer to page 153*)

4 Why cannot the correlation coefficient be used to show cause and effect? (*Refer to page 155*)

5 When would you use the Rank correlation coefficient as opposed to the product-moment coefficient? (*Refer to page 156*)

6 What does a correlation of 0 mean in regression? (*Refer to page 155*)

7 What is the difference between inter-polation and extrapolation? (*Refer to page 155*)

8 What is the difference between a negative and a positive correlation? (*Refer to page 155*)

EXERCISES

1 Part of MTG's operations involve exporting to the United States. Over the last 10 years the value of the goods sold has steadily risen as shown below:
  (a) Determine the level of export sales in constant (1980) prices
  (b) Draw a scatter diagram of sales against the exchange rate
  (c) Comment on the scatter diagram
  (d) Determine the regression equation for the data
  (e) Interpret the two coefficients of the equation in the context of the problem
  (f) Calculate the correlation coefficient and interpret its value in the context of the problem.
  (g) How useful do you think the equation would be for forecasting future export sales?

	Export sales £000s	Retail Price Index 1980=100	Exchange rate ($US per pound sterling)
1978	102.8	85.7	2.50
1979	120.9	93.6	2.45
1980	163.2	100	2.34
1981	196.1	134.8	2.22
1982	253.8	157.1	1.81
1983	321.5	182	1.75
1984	358.3	197.1	1.92
1985	406.3	223.5	2.12
1986	476.3	263.7	2.33
1987	531.4	295.0	2.03

2   You have been asked to conduct an investigation into the productivity of the typing pool who use the latest wordprocessing systems at Head Office. For a sample of 10 typists you have collected data on the number of items typed during a day and the number of spoiled items which are those items which have to be completely retyped because of errors.

Typist	No of items typed	Spoiled items
A	94	4
B	98	5
C	106	6
D	114	7
E	107	6
F	93	5
G	98	6
H	87	4
I	95	5
J	103	7

(a)   Show the data on a scatter diagram
(b)   Determine the regression equation
(c)   Comment on the parameters of the equation in the context of the problem
(d)   Calculate the product moment correlation coefficient and interpret the result
(e)   Calculate the Rank correlation coefficient
(f)   Which of the two correlation coefficients do you think is more useful in this situation?

Answers on page 318.

Time series analysis

Much business analysis is concerned with investigating the movement of a variable over a period of time and trying to predict the future movement of that variable. We may be looking at sales, profits, costs, share prices or whatever and our interest initially is to determine the general movement in the variable. This chapter is largely concerned with a technique that is specifically employed in quantifying that movement.

The chapter also introduces a technique which provides a method of forecasting time series in the short-term: exponentially weighted moving averages.

17.1 SEASONAL VARIATION

Many business variables follow a regular and predictable pattern over a 12 month period. Such a pattern is referred to as the **seasonal variation**. Let us examine the data in Table 17.1 which shows sales of microcomputers for use in the home or small office at one of MTG's electrical outlets. The data relate to sales per quarter (3 month period).

TABLE 17.1 **Sales of small microcomputers in the Western region**
(Sales in 000 units per 3 month period)

Time	Sales	Time	Sales
1984 I	86.7	1986 III	113.5
1984 II	94.9	1986 IV	132.9
1984 III	94.2	1987 I	126.3
1984 IV	106.5	1987 II	119.4
1985 I	105.9	1987 III	128.9
1985 II	102.4	1987 IV	142.3
1985 III	103.1	1988 I	136.4
1985 IV	115.2	1988 II	124.6
1986 I	113.7	1988 III	127.9
1986 II	108.0		

Source: *Sales Department*

As usual such data is far better understood shown on a diagram and Figure 17.1 shows the corresponding time series graph.

FIGURE 17.1   **Sales: 1984 I–1988 III**

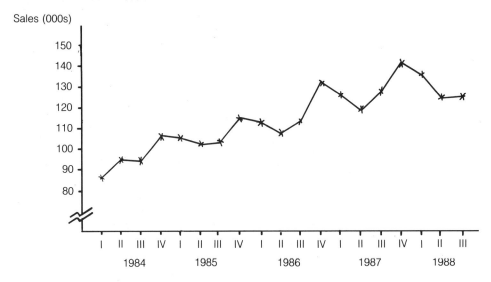

It can be seen from the diagram that there are two forces at work. One is a long-term movement in the variable. Over this five year period sales are seen to be steadily increasing. Such a movement is referred to as the *trend*. The second is a pattern which repeats itself at the same time each year. It can be seen that each year sales tend to rise dramatically in quarter IV and fall in quarter II.

It is obviously important to be able to distinguish between these two factors. We observe from the diagram that sales have fallen since 1987 IV. We need to know whether this is a **temporary** seasonal phenomenon which will correct itself at a later time in the year, or whether it represents a change in sales which requires some change in policy on the part of the company, say by cutting prices to stimulate sales to higher levels.

17.2   TIME SERIES MODELS

In general a time series such as that shown above can be broken into three major components (hence the alternative name for the technique, **time series decomposition**):

$$D = T + S + R$$

where:
D is the original data series
T the trend
S the seasonal variation
R the residual

Thus sales in a particular quarter will comprise both a trend element and an element of seasonal fluctuation. The residual component is a term for any random or unpredictable factors affecting sales in a particular period, such as a period of severe bad weather or the opening of a competitor's store, which have nothing to do with either seasonal variations or the underlying trend in sales.

Time series decomposition is concerned with quantifying the two major elements in the series, the trend and the seasonal factors, in order to calculate a derived series known as the **seasonally adjusted series**. This is defined as:

$$\text{Seasonally adjusted series} = D - S$$

that is, where the seasonal elements are removed from the original data.

Management can then focus their attention on this data series to determine whether any policy reaction is needed.

The first step is to calculate the trend for the series, using the method of moving averages. The trend can then be removed to find the seasonal deviation and, in turn, the seasonal variation removed from the original data to provide the seasonally adjusted series.

The method of moving averages was discussed in Chapter 3 when we looked at the construction of Z charts.

17.3 CALCULATION OF THE TREND

The trend is the underlying, long-term movement in the variable and the seasonal fluctuation is the temporary (and repetitive) variation that occurs over a 12 month period. Over any 12 month period, therefore, the seasonal fluctuations in a series should cancel out, given that in any one quarter or month such variation is, by definition, temporary. So if we were to take a set of four quarterly sales figures and calculate a simple arithmetic mean this average would contain no overall seasonal effects.

TABLE 17.2 **Calculation of a moving average trend**

Time	Sales	4 Period Total	8 Period Total	Trend
1984 I	86.7			
1984 II	94.9			
		382.3		
1984 III	94.2		783.8	98.0
		401.5		
1984 IV	106.5		810.5	101.3
		409.0		
1985 I	105.9		826.9	103.4
		417.9		
1985 II	102.4		844.5	105.6
		426.6		
1985 III	103.1		861.0	107.6
		434.4		
1985 IV	115.2		874.4	109.3
		440.4		
1986 I	113.7		890.4	111.3
		450.4		
1986 II	108.0		918.5	114.8
		468.1		
1986 III	113.5		948.8	118.6
		480.7		
1986 IV	132.9		972.8	121.6
		492.1		
1987 I	126.3		999.6	125.0
		507.5		
1987 II	119.4		1024.4	128.1
		516.9		
1987 III	128.9		1043.9	130.5
		527.0		
1987 IV	142.3		1059.2	132.4
		532.2		
1988 I	136.4		1063.4	132.9
		531.2		
1988 II	124.6			
1988 III	127.9			

Source: *Sales Department*

Referring back to Table 17.1 we could average sales over the first four quarters (1984 I to 1984 IV). We could then average sales over the next four quarters (1984 II to 1985 I) and so on for successive sets of four quarters through the series. The problem with this is that the resulting average would be the average for the *middle* of the period covered, in the case of the first calculation the average would refer to the moment in time between Q2 and Q3, rather than to a specific quarter as we require. Accordingly, we must undertake a process known as **centering** the averages calculated.

The appropriate calculations are shown in Table 17.2.

First of all we calculate the totals for each successive set of 4 quarters. These figures are shown in the column headed '4 Period Total'. So the first figure of 382.3 represents total sales over the first 4 quarters. If we were now to calculate an average directly from this it would represent an average for the middle of the period, which would actually fall midway between Quarter II and Quarter III.

Instead, we find the total of successive pairs of these values to give the 8 Period Total figures. So, for example, the first figure in this column, 783.8, is found by adding the first pair of values together in the 4 Period Total column—382.3 + 401.5. The next figure—810.5—is found by adding the next **successive** pair of a 4 period figures—401.5 + 409.0 and so on through the rest of the series. These totals now represent the sum of 8 quarters' sales and if we average these figures (dividing by 8) they will now correspond to a specific quarter.

This average is shown in the column headed 'Trend' and is known as a **centred moving average**.

The trend values calculated show the underlying or long term movement in the series as it is averaged over time. These trend values are shown in Figure 17.2 and the underlying trend in sales is readily visible.

FIGURE 17.2 **Trend sales**

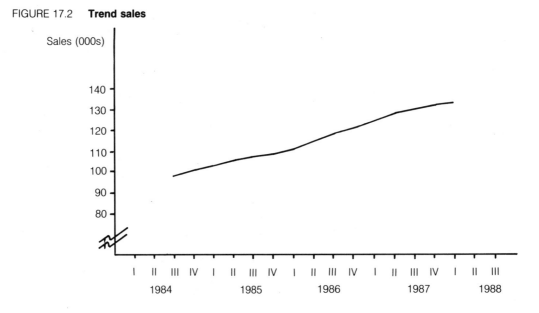

17.4 CALCULATION OF THE SEASONAL VARIATIONS

The trend values can now be used to determine the quarterly seasonal variations. If we ignore the residual terms (which are random and unpredictable by definition) we have:

$$D - T = S$$

that is, we can estimate the quarterly seasonal variations by removing the trend from the original series. These deviations are shown in Table 17.3.

TABLE 17.3 **Calculation of the seasonal deviations**

Time	Sales	Trend	Deviation from trend
1984 I	86.7		
1984 II	94.9		
1984 III	94.2	98.0	−3.8
1984 IV	106.5	101.3	5.2
1985 I	105.9	103.4	2.5
1985 II	102.4	105.6	−3.2
1985 III	103.1	107.6	−4.5
1985 IV	115.2	109.3	5.9
1986 I	113.7	111.3	2.4
1986 II	108.0	114.8	−6.8
1986 III	113.5	118.6	−5.1
1986 IV	132.9	121.6	11.3
1987 I	126.3	125.0	1.3
1987 II	119.4	128.1	−8.7
1987 III	128.9	130.5	−1.6
1987 IV	142.3	132.4	9.9
1988 I	136.4	132.9	3.5
1988 II	124.6		
1988 III	127.9		

Source: *Sales Department*

If we examine these deviations for the fourth quarter of each year, for example, we can see that there is a repetitive pattern each year in that in each quarter at this time of year there is a large positive deviation—sales are always above the trend. We can also see that these deviations in a particular quarter are not perfectly constant from year to year. The reason for this lies with the R term. The deviations in Table 17.3 include not only the seasonal variation but also any residual or random variation which will vary from year to year. It is reasonable to assume that over a number of years such residuals will tend to cancel each other. If, then, we were to take the individual deviations for a particular quarter and average them we can expect this to provide a reasonable estimate of the seasonal variation in this quarter.

If we collect the deviations together as in Table 17.4 the average seasonal fluctuation can be calculated.

TABLE 17.4 **Calculation of the seasonal variations**

	1	2	3	4
1984			−3.8	5.2
1985	2.5	−3.2	−4.5	5.9
1986	2.4	−6.8	−5.1	11.3
1987	1.3	−8.7	−1.6	9.9
1988	3.5			
Total	9.7	−18.7	−15.0	32.3
Average	2.425	−6.233	−3.75	8.075
Adjustment	−0.1293	−0.1293	−0.1293	−0.1293
Seasonal variation	2.296	−6.362	−3.879	7.946

Total of averages = (2.425 − 6.233 − 3.75 + 8.075) = +0.517

$$\text{Adjustment} = \frac{-(0.517)}{4} = -0.1293$$

STEP 1

We total the deviations for each quarter as shown in the table.

STEP 2

For each quarter we can find an average (mean) deviation because typically different quarters will have a different number of observations. Care must be taken to divide the total by the correct number of quarters. Thus for Quarter I we divide the Total of 9.7 by 4, whilst for Quarter II we divide the corresponding Total by 3.

STEP 3

The averages calculated **should** total to zero, given that over a 12 month period the seasonal effects will cancel each other out. In practice, this rarely happens because of arithmetic rounding. The averages need to be adjusted so that they do total to zero. We total the averages to determine how far from zero the sum is. In this case the four averages total to +0.517.

STEP 4

We now adjust each average by a quarter of this sum. Given that the averages total 0.517 **too much** we **subtract** a quarter of this (0.1293) from each average to give the final seasonal factor for each quarter as shown in the table.

The interpretation of these values is straightforward. Looking at QIII, for example, we see that, on average, sales fall by 3.879 at this time of year only to rise on average by 7.946 in the following quarter.

17.5 SEASONALLY ADJUSTED SERIES

It is more usual to use the seasonal factors to calculate the seasonally adjusted series. This is shown in Table 17.5 and Figure 17.3. The original series simply has the appropriate quarter's seasonal variation subtracted (remember that if the seasonal variation is negative this will have the effect of making the adjusted series larger than the original).

TABLE 17.5   **Calculation of the seasonally adjusted series**

Time	Sales	Seasonal factor	Seasonally adjusted sales (rounded to 1DP)
1984 I	86.7	−2.296	84.4
1984 II	94.9	−(−6.362)	101.3
1984 III	94.2	−(−3.879)	98.1
1984 IV	106.5	−7.946	98.6
1985 I	105.9	−2.296	103.6
1985 II	102.4	−(−6.362)	108.8
1985 III	103.1	−(−3.879)	107.0
1985 IV	115.2	−7.946	107.3
1986 I	113.7	−2.296	111.4
1986 II	108.0	−(−6.632)	114.6
1986 III	113.5	−(−3.879)	117.4
1986 IV	132.9	−7.946	125.0
1987 I	126.3	−2.296	124.0
1987 II	119.4	−(−6.632)	126.0
1987 III	128.9	−(−3.879)	132.8
1987 IV	142.3	−7.946	134.4
1988 I	136.4	−2.296	134.1
1988 II	124.6	−(−6.632)	131.2
1988 III	127.9	−(−3.879)	131.8

FIGURE 17.3   **Seasonally adjusted sales**

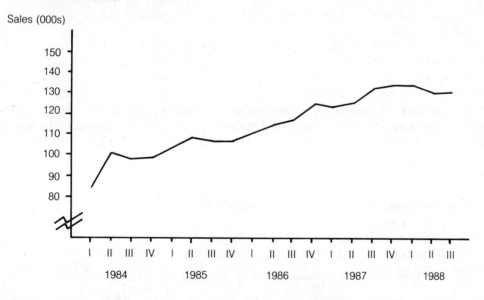

In general, for analysis purposes, it is this seasonally adjusted series that we should focus upon, for it allows us to examine the longer term movement in the data without being distracted by seasonal fluctuations. In the case of sales of microcomputers we can see a strong upward pattern in sales since 1984. The last three quarters sales since 1987 IV are beginning to show cause for concern. Seasonally adjusted sales (that is sales adjusted for the normal seasonal variation) have slowly been decreasing.

Management should be made aware of this movement and we would want to investigate further the recent sales of this product to identify the possible causes of such a movement.

17.6   USING MONTHLY DATA

Many series are available not only in quarterly but also in monthly form. Seasonally adjusting a monthly series follows exactly the same process except for the calculation of the trend. In this case we would first work out a 12 month total (instead of a four quarter total) and then add successive pairs of 12 month totals together to calculate a 24 month total which can then be divided by 24 (rather than 8) to provide the trend. The remaining calculations remain unchanged, although a considerable amount of data will be required in order to provide several deviations for each month of the year.

17.7   ADDITIVE AND MULTIPLICATIVE MODELS

The method we have used thus far is referred to as the **additive** model given that the components of the series are literally added together:

$$D = T + S + R$$

There is an alternative model available where the component terms are expressed in multiplication terms:

$$D = T \times S (+ R)$$

In such a case the seasonal factors would now be calculated as:

$$\frac{D}{T} = S$$

The seasonal factors for the **multiplicative** model will be ratios rather than differences. As ratios they will vary about the value 1.0 and will show the relative seasonal fluctuation. Thus a seasonal factor of, say, 1.08 for a data series using this type of model indicates that the data is 8% above the trend in this period. The sum of such ratios should be four for quarterly data, 12 for monthly data and the adjustment to the ratios so that they total to this value should be made accordingly.

The additive model implies that the seasonal variation around the trend maintains a constant **difference**. Thus, in our example no matter what the trend we are always adjusting the first quarter of the series by the same amount of seasonal variation. The multiplicative model assumes instead that the seasonal variation is a constant **proportion**. Accordingly, this model is often more useful in situations where the trend is undergoing considerable change. It may have been more appropriate in the example used in this chapter to use the multiplicative rather than additive model, although for short periods of time there will be little apparent difference in the results.

17.8   FORECASTING FROM A TIME SERIES MODEL

Management will be interested in the results of such analysis, not only in terms of identifying seasonal variations but also in terms of forecasting. To forecast such a series requires:

Forecast = forecast of trend + forecast of seasonal variation

It is generally assumed that the seasonal variation already identified will remain constant in the immediate future so all that is required is a forecast of the trend. Let us suppose that we wish to forecast sales for 1988 IV.

There are three general methods that can be adopted to forecast the trend.

REGRESSION

If the trend is relatively linear then regression can be applied. The Y variable consists of the trend values calculated using moving averages (in Table 17.2). The X variable is chosen to represent time. Typically, X will take a simple series of values starting at 1, 2, 3 . . . up to t where t is the number of period for which we have trend values.

So, in our example, X would take a value of 1 (corresponding to Y=98.0 and 1984 III) then 2 (Y=101.3, 1984 IV) and so on up to X=15 (Y=132.9, 1988 I).

From the resulting regression equation we would forecast Y (the trend value) for the appropriate X (or time) value. Given that X=15 represents 1988 I and we wish to forecast for 1988 IV then X would be given a value of 18 to produce the appropriate forecast.

The regression equation that can be derived for our problem is given as:

$$\text{Trend} = 94.87 + 2.645 \text{ Time}$$

Forecasting for period 18 (1988 IV) would give a value for the trend of 94.87 + 2.645(18) = 142.5.

BY EYE

If the trend is reasonably linear it may be possible to extrapolate visually on the graph. Naturally, such a method is very subjective and likely to be inaccurate but often serves as an approximation. Thus from Figure 17.2 we might suggest a trend forecast for 1988 IV of approximately 136.

SIMPLE EXTRAPOLATION

The third method is that of calculating the rate of change in the trend per period. From Figure 17.2 we observe that the trend has maintained a consistent movement over the whole period and over the period it covers has increased from 98.0 to 132.9. This represents an average (mean) rate of change per period of:

$$\frac{(132.9 - 98)}{15} = 2.33$$

So, if we assume that this rate of change continues (which may **not** be a valid assumption!) we wish to forecast the trend from its last calculated value (of 132.9) in 1988 I forward by three periods to 1988 IV. Thus the forecast would be:

$$1988 \text{ IV forecast} = 132.9 + (3 \times 2.33) = 139.9$$

Whichever method of forecasting the trend we use we can now obtain a forecast of the 1988 IV sales by adding the calculated seasonal component of 7.946 (remembering that on average in this quarter sales are this much above the trend).

If we had decided to use the simple extrapolation method of determining the trend, therefore, our forecast of sales would be:

$$139.9 + 7.946 = 147.8 \text{ (000) units}$$

17.9 FORECASTING USING EXPONENTIAL SMOOTHING

The method of time series analysis is a common technique in business where we require an analysis of some variable over a lengthy period of time and where, typically, we require a long-term forecast. Equally common, however, are situations where we require a forecast for a short-term situation. Consider the data below:

TABLE 17.6 **Sales of bread loaves in store A**

Day	Sales 00s' loaves
1	50
2	52
3	48
4	54
5	49

The table shows sales of a perishable food over the last five days. Typically, we wish to know how much to order for tomorrow. We need, in other words a forecast for tomorrow's sales. Whilst we could apply techniques such as regression, moving averages or time series analysis it is apparent that such techniques will be cumbersome to use. They require considerable data, lengthy calculations (even with access to computer facilities) and would have to be re-estimated every day as we had the last day's sales to add to our data set. Combine that with the fact that we would require such a forecast every day and it is clear that we require some alternative method.

Such an alternative is provided with the use of **exponential smoothing**. This is a technique commonly used in areas where reasonably accurate forecasts are required quickly, frequently and cheaply. Areas such as forecasting demand for individual items and stock control are typical areas of business application.

The derivation of the technique is beyond the scope of this introductory text. We shall simply state, therefore, that the method is:

New Forecast = Old Forecast + α (Actual Value − Old Forecast)

or in symbols:

$$F_t = F_{t-1} + \alpha(X_{t-1} - F_{t-1})$$

where t is used to refer to a specific time period, F to a forecast and X to an actual value. α is referred to as the 'smoothing' value and is typically around 0.1 to 0.3.

Let us illustrate with the use of the data in Table 17.6. Assume that we had forecast Day 5 sales to be 52 and we decide to use alpha at 0.2. The forecast of sales for Day 6 will be:

$$F_t = F_{t-1} + \alpha(X_{t-1} - F_{t-1})$$
$$= 52 + 0.2(49 - 52)$$
$$= 52 + 0.2(-3) = 51.4 \text{ (00 loaves)}$$

The logic of the method is straightforward. We base the new forecast on the previous one. But we also adjust the new forecast for any error in the previous forecast. For Day 5 the forecast (at 52) was too high compared with the actual sales so we adjust the new forecast downward (by 0.2 of the error) to 51.4.

Assume that actual sales for Day 6 are 48. The forecast for Day 7 thus becomes:

$$F_t = F_{t-1} + \alpha(X_{t-1} - F_{t-1})$$
$$= 51.4 + 0.2(48 - 51.4) = 50.7 \text{ (00 loaves)}$$

This simple forecasting system can progress indefinitely, forecasting one period ahead each time. Naturally, we would not expect a particularly high degree of reliability in such forecasts but they are easy to produce and to use. Picture the situation in a stock room where we are trying to forecast daily demand for several thousand stock items to determine when we need to reorder and you can imagine the usefulness of such a simple forecasting system.

The method is based on a number of assumptions:

(a) The simple method outlined here cannot be used if there is a strong upward or downward trend in the variable
(b) Fluctuations of the variable are assumed to be random

Additionally, the choice of α becomes a critical decision. In general, the lower the value then the less responsive the formula is to errors in the old forecast and the higher the value the more responsive.

SUMMARY

1   Time series analysis (sometimes known as time series decomposition) is a technique to quantify the component elements of a variable observed over some period of time.
2   The technique quantifies two major components: the trend and the seasonal variation. The third element of the time series is the residual or random component.
3   The trend is estimated using a method of centred moving averages.

4 The seasonally adjusted series has had the seasonal variation removed.

5 There are two basic approaches to time series analysis: the additive model and the multiplicative model.

6 Forecasting a time series requires a forecast of the trend and a forecast of the seasonal variation.

7 Forecasting the trend can be achieved by regression, by eye or by simple extrapolation.

8 Exponential smoothing is a short-term forecasting method that is simple and reasonably accurate under the appropriate circumstances.

SELF-TEST QUESTIONS

1 Why is it necessary to undertake time series analysis? (*Refer to page 162*)

2 What are the three main components of a time series? (*Refer to page 162*)

3 How is the trend estimated? (*Refer to page 164*)

4 Why is it necessary to centre the moving averages? (*Refer to page 164*)

5 How are the seasonal factors determined? (*Refer to page 166*)

6 What is meant by the seasonally adjusted series? (*Refer to page 167*)

7 How would you forecast a time series? (*Refer to page 168*)

8 What are the alternative methods of forecasting the trend? (*Refer to page 168*)

9 What is exponential smoothing? (*Refer to page 170*)

10 What effect does the value of α have? (*Refer to page 170*)

EXERCISES

1 The Computing Services Unit at HQ regularly has to use part-time programmers to supplement the full-time staff. The data below refer to the part-time hours required over the last few years:

			Quarter		
Year		I	II	III	IV
1985			805	912	830
1986		845	865	992	890
1987		902	915	1056	950
1988		960	965	1108	

(a) Draw a graph of the data

(b) Do you think the additive or multiplicative model would be more appropriate?

(c) Estimate the trend for the model you have chosen

(d) Identify the seasonal factors

(e) What reasons can you suggest for the seasonal pattern?

(f) Forecast the part-time hours required for 1989 I

2   The food department has continued monitoring daily sales of bread as detailed in the chapter.

Day 7	51
Day 8	53
Day 9	49
Day 10	47

Use an initial forecast for Day 1 of 50

(a)   Starting from Day 2, forecast daily sales to Day 10 using α at 0.3
(b)   Repeat (a) but using α at 0.9
(c)   What effect does the choice of α have?
(d)   Which of the two alternatives do you think is more reliable?

Answers on page 320.

Stock control

The chapters in this section of the text have introduced a variety of mathematical techniques and business applications. One area where such techniques are particularly useful is that of stock control. All organisations need to carry certain items in stock and need to determine an appropriate policy for controlling these stock levels. This chapter will introduce the key concepts involved in stock control and two of the basic models used in stock control decisions.

18.1   THE STOCK CONTROL PROBLEM

Most organisations face a dilemma over their stock control policy. Consider one of the stores in the MTG group. The store will carry hundreds, possibly thousands, of different items for sale to its customers. It needs to ensure that when customers enter the store wishing to purchase a particular product then that product is available. If it is not the store loses a potential sale and possibly discourages that customer from using the store again in the future. We have all, as consumers, experienced the frustration of entering a shop and being told that the item we wish to purchase is temporarily out of stock.

It may appear that the solution to this problem is simple: ensure that the store has adequate stocks of all items. The problem with this is that such stocks represent a cost to the store before they are sold. They have to be purchased and paid for by the store in anticipation of a future sale to a customer, they have to be transported, stored safely, looked after and so on. All this increases the firm's costs, so any organisation will face the dilemma of balancing the costs of holding large stocks against the possibility that customers will have to be turned away without purchasing because stocks were too small.

18.2   STOCK COSTS

Typically in stock control there are two broad categories of costs:

ORDER COSTS

The costs associated with ordering the product from the supplier. Typically they will include clerical and administrative costs involved in issuing the order, checking invoices, ensuring the goods are delivered and so on and transport costs involved in delivering the stock.

HOLDING COSTS

The costs associated with the actual holding or storage of the stock. They will include storage costs, insurance, loss through pilfering, obsolescence and deterioration, related staffing costs and the interest on the capital tied up in the value of the stock held.

Typically management are concerned with trying to minimise these costs. The problem arises that, taking each cost in isolation, the two sources of costs are affected by stock policy in opposite ways.

Let us examine order costs first. If management wish to minimise order costs then the obvious method is to place as few orders as possible. The logical outcome of this would be to place, say, one very large order for the item each year. The problem with this is that, although minimising order costs, it will drastically increase holding costs. With one very large order a large number of items will be held in stock for some considerable time before being sold. On the other hand, to minimise holding costs it would be sensible to have as few items as possible in stock but to place frequent and small orders to replenish the stock levels. Again, whilst this will minimise holding costs it will increase order costs.

Management's task is to balance this conflict and to find the policy that minimises **total** stock costs.

Let us use the following notation:

D = the demand for the item over, say, a year
O = the cost of placing an order
N = the number of orders placed per year
H = the holding cost of 1 item of stock for a year
Q = the number of items ordered

Typically, we wish to determine the value of Q in order to minimise costs and to determine the frequency of placing orders.

We shall illustrate with a simple example. Assume that MTG are investigating a suitable stock control policy for one of their products. Annual demand for the item is assumed to be 100,000 units. Order costs are £25 per order and holding costs are £0.20 per item per year. We shall make the following assumptions:

1   Demand for the item is known for certain and is constant through the year (ie, is linear).
2   Associated costs are constant.
3   Orders are supplied instantly with no time delay.

18.3   THE ECONOMIC ORDER QUANTITY (EOQ)

We wish to determine the quantity of items to be ordered, and the number of orders per year, in order to minimise costs. Total costs can be defined as:

$$TC = Order\ Costs + Holding\ Costs$$

ORDER COSTS

Order costs are £25 per order. Order costs will therefore be:

$$Order\ costs = ON$$

that is, £25 times the number of orders placed.
Further we can state that:

$$NQ = D$$

that is, the number of orders times the order size must match total demand. Rearranging this gives:

$$N = \frac{D}{Q}$$

giving:

$$Order\ costs = ON = \frac{OD}{Q}$$

HOLDING COSTS

Holding costs will be the number of items held in stock multiplied by the holding cost per unit. Ideally, we would want a situation where we start a particular period with stock level Q and at the end of the period stock levels have fallen to zero (as we meet customer demand from stock). Immediately at the start of the next period, we have another stock order delivered so stock levels immediately rise to Q again. This cycle repeats itself as shown in Figure 18.1.

FIGURE 18.1 **Stock Levels**

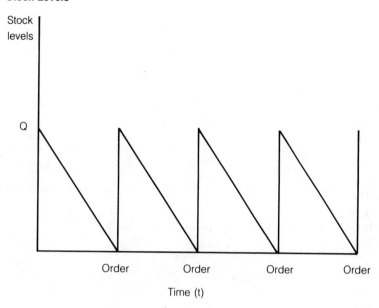

It is clear that, on average, stock levels will be given by:

$$\frac{Q}{2}$$

So, holding costs are:

$$\frac{QH}{2}$$

Total costs, therefore, are given by:

$$TC = \text{order costs} + \text{holding costs}$$

$$TC = \frac{OD}{Q} + \frac{QH}{2}$$

We wish to find the level of Q that minimises total costs. Using differentiation, we wish to find the turning point of the TC function, where the slope of the TC function=0.

Taking the derivative we have:

$$\frac{dTC}{dQ} = \frac{-OD}{Q^2} + \frac{H}{2}$$

Setting this to zero we have:

$$\frac{dTC}{dQ} = \frac{-OD}{Q^2} + \frac{H}{2} = 0$$

Rearranging gives:

$$\frac{-OD}{Q^2} + \frac{H}{2} = 0$$

$$\frac{H}{2} = \frac{OD}{Q^2}$$

$$\frac{Q^2(H)}{2} = OD$$

$$Q^2 = \frac{2OD}{H}$$

$$Q = \sqrt{\frac{2OD}{H}}$$

The optimum value for Q, therefore, is given by the derived formula. Let us apply it to our problem.

$$Q = \sqrt{\frac{2(25)(100000)}{0.20}}$$

$$Q = 5000$$

That is, to minimise total costs the optimum order size is 5,000 units each time. At this level order costs will be:

$$\text{Order costs} = \frac{OD}{Q} = \frac{25(100000)}{5000} = £500$$

and holding costs will be:

$$\text{Holding costs} = \frac{QH}{2} = \frac{5000(0.2)}{2} = £500$$

giving total costs of £1,000. It is no coincidence that Order Costs and Holding Costs are equal at this level for Q. Figure 18.2 shows the relationship between the three cost functions.

FIGURE 18.2   **Stock costs**

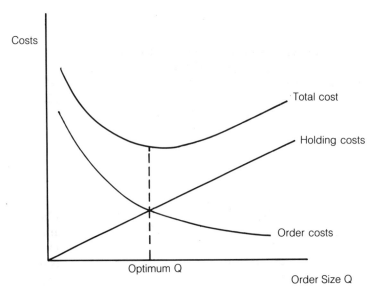

It can be seen that total costs are minimised at the intersection of holding costs and order costs.

NUMBER OF STOCK ORDERS PLACED

To determine how many orders are placed through the year is straightforward. We know the annual demand, D, for this item and we now know how much stock will be ordered each time, Q. So:

$$N = \frac{D}{Q} = \frac{100000}{5000} = 20 \text{ orders per year.}$$

TIMING OF ORDERS

Similarly we can determine the frequency or timing of the orders placed. If we assume, for example, that there are a total of 50 working weeks in the year (that is, excluding holidays) then an order for stock must be placed every 2.5 weeks (given that we know we must place a total of 20 orders over the year).

18.4   THE ECONOMIC BATCH QUANTITY (EBQ)

Not all stock control problems relate to situations like those outlined in the previous section. Frequently, organisations are engaged in the production of some item and as the item is produced it is added to stocks. The rate of stock arrivals, therefore, is continuous over some period of time. A different form of the stock control model developed earlier is needed. The relevant model is known as the Economic Batch Quantity (EBQ) as we determine the optimum production size to minimise total costs.

Assume the following situation. MTG manufacture their own breakfast cereal (as described in Chapter 14). Two varieties are produced: Standard and De-luxe. Only one variety can be produced at any one time. This means that, for example, the production line produces Standard cereal for a certain length of time and as it is produced it is added to stock to meet both current and future demand. At some pre-determined time, production of Standard cereal stops and the production line switches to De-luxe. Whilst this is being produced demand for the Standard cereal must be met from existing stocks. The situation is summarised in Figure 18.3.

FIGURE 18.3   **Stock levels of standard cereal**

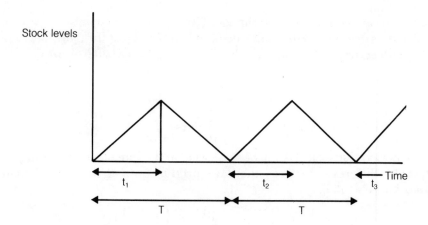

Period t_1 shows the time when Standard cereal is being produced. As can be seen, stock levels gradually increase through this production period and reach a maximum at the end of the production period. Production then switches to the other product so stock levels of Standard cereal gradually decline as stocks are used to meet demand. Ideally, stocks of this product will just reach zero at the time when production of Standard cereal starts again, period t_2, and the cycle repeats itself.

Period T covers the full production cycle, from the start of one production run at the beginning of period t_1 to the beginning of the next production run at t_2.

For this model the relevant variables are:

D = the demand for the product
P = the maximum possible production capacity of the product
H = holding cost per item per period
S = set-up costs
Q = the quantity to be produced each batch
N = the number of production batches per year

Only S requires further explanation at this stage. The set-up costs refer to those costs involved in switching from the production of one item to the production of another. Typically, there will be some wastage of materials, labour time will be required to clean machinery, check equipment and so on.

Note that it is necessary for P>D for the model to be appropriate (that is, the production rate must be greater than the rate of demand).

In our example, let us assume that the relevant values are:

D = 100,000 per year
P = 200,000 per year
H = £0.20 per item per year
S = £200 per batch

We wish to determine the value for Q that will minimise total costs. Total costs will be given by:

$$TC = \text{set-up costs} + \text{holding costs}$$

Set-up costs will, in turn, be given by:

$$\text{Set-up costs} = SN$$

But

$$N = \frac{D}{Q}$$

$$\text{so set-up costs} = \frac{SD}{Q}$$

Holding costs are also readily determined. First we need to establish the average amount of stock held. Let us denote d as the daily rate of demand and p as the daily rate of production, with t as the length of the production run. We will be producing a batch of size Q over the period t, so:

$$Q = pt$$

and

$$t = \frac{Q}{p} \text{ days}$$

Over the period t, stock levels will be increasing at the rate of (p−d) per day. That is, at a rate which is the difference between the day's production and the day's demand. So, the maximum stock levels will be:

$$(p - d)t = (p - d)\frac{Q}{p} = \left(1 - \frac{d}{p}\right)Q$$

However:

$$d = \frac{D}{n}$$

and

$$p = \frac{P}{n}$$

where n is the number of working days in the year so:

$$\frac{d}{p} = \frac{D/n}{P/n} = \frac{D}{P}$$

giving:

$$\text{maximum stock} = \left(1 - \frac{D}{P}\right) Q$$

The average stock held will be half this amount (given the constant rate of demand) giving:

$$\text{average stock held} = \left(1 - \frac{D}{P}\right) \frac{Q}{2}$$

and the associated holding costs as:

$$\left(1 - \frac{D}{P}\right) \frac{Q}{2} \times H$$

Total costs, therefore are:

$$TC = \frac{SD}{Q} + \left(1 - \frac{D}{P}\right) \frac{QH}{2}$$

Again, differentiating and setting the derivative equal to zero we obtain an equation:

$$Q = \sqrt{\frac{2SD}{\left(1 - \frac{D}{P}\right) H}}$$

which is the optimum production batch size. Substituting the appropriate values into the equation we have:

$$Q = \sqrt{\frac{2(200)(100000)}{\left(1 - \frac{100000}{200000}\right) 0.20}} = 20,000 \text{ units}$$

That is, in order to minimise the total relevant costs we should produce batches of 20,000 units of the standard cereal each time.

NUMBER OF BATCHES PRODUCED

As with the EOQ model, we can determine the frequency with which these batches are produced. Given that we require a total of 100,000 units through the year this implies that we shall produce five batches of this size (20,000 units each) through the year.

TIMING OF PRODUCTION BATCHES

Again as with the EOQ model it is frequently useful to know how often a production batch will be required. The annual rate of production is 200,000 units. Let us assume that there are a total of 250 working days available in the year (say, 50 weeks at 5 days per week). This implies a daily production rate of 800 units. Given that the batch size is 20,000 units, therefore, will require a production run of 25 working days (800×25 = 20,000).

18.5   DEVELOPMENT OF THE SIMPLE STOCK CONTROL MODEL

Both the models developed in this chapter operate under rigid assumptions, particularly relating to the rate of demand and the delivery/production of stock. Such assumptions are somewhat unrealistic but the models can be easily adapted to operate under less rigid assumptions. The operation of buffer or safety stock, the introduction of lead times for delivery, price discounts for large orders, non-constant demand can all be incorporated into the model. Such developments are beyond the scope of this text but can be built upon the basic stock control models developed in this chapter.

G

SUMMARY

1   The stock control problem arises from the need to balance stock costs with customer demand.
2   Stock costs consist of two elements: the holding cost and the order costs (or set up costs).
3   The Economic Order Quantity model determines the optimum size of stock orders to minimise costs.
4   The Economic Batch Quantity model determines the optimum production batch size to minimise costs.
5   Both models operate under rigid assumptions but are easily adapted to reflect more realistic applications.

SELF-TEST QUESTIONS

1   **What is meant by stock control?** (*Refer to page 173*)

2   **What are the conflicts in stock control?** (*Refer to page 173*)

3   **What is meant by the stock control problem?** (*Refer to page 173*)

4   **What are the relevant costs in the EOQ model?** (*Refer to page 174*)

5   **What are the relevant costs in the EBQ model?** (*Refer to page 178*)

6   **What is the formula for the optimum order size?** (*Refer to page 176*)

7   **What is the formula for the optimum production batch size?** (*Refer to page 179*)

EXERCISES

1   For the EOQ example given in the text draw a graph showing the TC function, the holding costs function and the order costs function for an order size ranging from 1,000 to 10,000 units.
     Confirm the optimum order size derived in the text.

2   The staff restaurant at one of MTG's stores is reviewing its current stock control policy. One item under investigation relates to cases of soft drinks. Last year a total of 4,000 cases were sold. Order costs are estimated at £25. Each case costs £5.00 and holding costs are estimated at 25% of the purchase price.
     (a)   Determine the economic order quantity
     (b)   Determine the number of orders to be placed each year
     (c)   If order costs rise to £30 determine the change in stock policy that will take place

Answers on page 322.

Section C: Financial mathematics

Financial mathematics

The previous section of the text introduced a variety of mathematical techniques relevant to business analysis. This Section extends the use of mathematics to cover the financial analysis typically undertaken in business organisation.

Chapter 19 introduces the concepts of simple and compound interest together with arithmetic and geometric series and presents a review of basic depreciation methods.

Chapter 20 looks at the calculation and use of present value and its role in investment appraisal. Discounted Cash Flow and Internal Rate of Return are also introduced.

Chapter 21 applies these financial mathematics techniques to a variety of typical business problems, including annuities and sinking funds.

The use of logarithms and antilogarithms is essential in this section.

Interest and depreciation

The necessity to be able to deal with and understand a variety of financial calculations in the business world is self-evident. Businesses and the people who manage them are primarily concerned with finance in one form or another. Businesses generate profits and have to determine where that profit should be invested for maximum return. Finance needs to be arranged to support investment plans and the cheapest sources of finance must be located. Underpinning most of the financial mathematics covered in the text is the concept of **interest** and this is the focus for much of this Chapter.

19.1 TIME PREFERENCE

The principles of financial mathematics and business finance are based on a simple and obvious feature of behaviour. If you were offered the choice of receiving £100 today or £100 in 12 months' time you would choose the £100 now. You would rationalise your decision on the grounds that even ignoring inflation £100 now has more value to you than £100 in 12 months' time. This preference for payment in the present rather than payment in the future is known as '**time preference**'.

Given that businesses and individuals frequently wish to borrow finance it follows that they have to find someone willing to lend. Following on from the time preference concept it is apparent that the person wishing to borrow money will have to offer the person lending the money some inducement or incentive for the sacrifice they are making.

This incentive is the **rate of interest**.

19.2 ARITHMETIC AND GEOMETRIC SERIES

To understand properly the principles and methods of calculation involved in financial mathematics it is necessary to examine two general mathematical principles: **an arithmetic series** and **a geometric series**.

19.2.1 Arithmetic series

Consider a sequence of numbers starting with the value a and progressing in the form:

$$a$$
$$a + d$$
$$a + 2d$$
$$a + 3d$$
$$a + 4d$$

and so on, where d is a fixed term added (or subtracted) to the previous value. Such a sequence is known as an **arithmetic series**. Without proof we state two general formulae for use with such a series:

1 to find the nth term in such a series we use

$$a + (n-1)d$$

2 to find the sum of the first n terms we use

$$\frac{n}{2} (2a + (n-1)d)$$

Let us illustrate with a simple problem. An individual is trying to plan for retirement. An investment broker has recommended a scheme whereby the individual pays a lump sum of money to the investment company and, in return, receives a guaranteed monthly income of £100. Moreover, the monthly income will increase by £10 per month.

The individual wants to know what monthly income he will be receiving in 5 years' time. Here a=100 and d=10. Using formula 1 we have:

$$a + (n-1)d$$

$$100 + (59)10 = £690$$

with n=60 (5 years × 12 months).

The individual also wants to know what his total income from the scheme would be over the first 5 years. Here we use formula 2.

$$\frac{n}{2} (2a + (n-1)d)$$

$$\frac{60}{2} (2(100) + (59)10) = 30(200 + 590) = £23,700$$

The only point of caution about such calculations is to ensure that you have the correct values for a, d and especially n.

19.2.2 Geometric series

Not all series we may be interested in will be arithmetic, however. Some will be geometric. This occurs where we have:

$$a$$
$$ar$$
$$ar^2$$
$$ar^3$$
$$ar^4$$

and so on where a is the initial sum and r is a common ratio (rather than difference as before).

Again, without proof, we state 3 formulae:

1   To find the nth term in such a series we use

$$ar^{(n-1)}$$

2   To find the sum of the first n terms we use

$$\frac{a(r^n - 1)}{r - 1}$$

3   To find the sum of all terms (to infinity) **provided** r<1 we use

$$\frac{a}{1 - r}$$

Note that in the case of formula 3 it is necessary to specify that r<1. In such a case as n increases the value of r^n approaches zero.

To illustrate the use of such a series, let us return to the individual contemplating his retirement. A second investment broker has found a scheme whereby, for the same lump sum investment, a guaranteed monthly income of £100 is provided, together with an increase in each month's income of 4 per cent.

Here a=£100 and r=1.04 (expressed as a decimal).

The individual again wishes to know his monthly income from the scheme in 5 years' time. Using formula 1 we have:

$$ar^{(n-1)}$$

$$100(1.04^{59}) = £1011.50$$

Similarly, the total income up to this time would be given using formula 2.

$$\frac{a(r^n - 1)}{r-1}$$

$$\frac{100(1.04^{60} - 1)}{1.04 - 1} = \frac{100(10.51962741 - 1)}{0.04} = £23799.07$$

It is clear that, in this example, we cannot apply the third formula as r>1.

19.3 SIMPLE AND COMPOUND INTEREST

Assume that you have the sum of £100 in a bank account, attracting an interest rate of 5 per cent per year (per annum). What does this mean and how is the interest determined?

The initial sum deposited, your £100, is known as the 'principal' and it is this amount on which interest will be paid at a rate of 5% pa. At the end of the first year your account would be credited with a further £5 representing the interest. Assume that you left the money (the principal plus first year interest) in the account for a further year. What interest would you be entitled to at the end of the second year?

You would not expect the interest to be £5 again. This amount would reflect interest paid on the principal. But you have had no reward for leaving your first year's interest untouched in the account. You would expect this sum to attract interest also. The appropriate interest credited at the end of year 2 should be:

£5 which is 5% of the principal
plus £0.25 which is 5% of the interest from Year 1

The interest paid should be £5.25. The same process can be applied to Year 3, 4, 5 and so on. Table 19.1 shows the relevant calculations.

TABLE 19.1 **Interest calculations**
(Principal of £100, interest rate of 5% pa.)

	Principal at start of year (£)	Interest on Principal at end of year (£)
Year 1	£100	£5
Year 2	£105	£5.25
Year 3	£110.25	£5.51
Year 4	£115.76	£5.79
Year 5	£121.55	£6.08
Year 6	£127.63	

The Table shows the initial principal sum and the interest earned at the end of each year which is then added to the account for the following year. You should ensure that you understand the timings implicit in the Table as they are critical for such interest calculations.

At the end of the five-year period (which is the same as the start of Year 6) the original sum of £100 will have increased to £127.63. This method of interest calculation, where the interest from one period itself earns interest, is known as **compound interest**.

If interest is based only on the original principal and not subsequent interest payments as well it is known as **simple interest**.

From such principles of compound interest we can determine a number of useful formulae.

We can express the calculation in Table 19.1 as a series:

$$\text{Value at end of period} = P(1 + i)^t$$

where

P = the original principal sum
i = the rate of interest expressed as a decimal per period
t = the appropriate number of periods.

(You will see the similarity here to the geometric series.)

Hence, for the example in Table 19.1 we could have calculated the value of our original sum (£100) at the end of the 5 year period as:

$$\text{Value} = 100(1 + 0.05)^5$$
$$= 100(1.05)^5 = 100(1.2763) = £127.63$$

This formula allows us to calculate easily the future value that a principal sum invested at a given rate of interest will have grown to by a specific period.

At the end of, say, a 10 year period the equivalent calculation would show that the original investment would increase to £259.37.

The basic formula can be presented in a different way to perform other related calculations. Let us suppose that we wish to invest a sum now, at a rate of interest of 5% pa, such that it will be worth £127.63 in 5 years' time. What sum should we invest (ie what principal amount)? Of course, we already know the answer from the example, but the formula would also confirm.

Rewriting the original formula we have:

$$P = \frac{V}{(1+i)^t}$$

Similarly the formula could be expressed as:

$$i = \sqrt[t]{\frac{V}{P}} - 1$$

to determine the rate of interest that will turn a given principal into a known value after a specified number of periods.

Thus the basic formula linking the variables (P, V, i) can be used to find any of these variables once we know the others.

19.4   NOMINAL AND EFFECTIVE INTEREST RATES

The formula derived earlier for compound interest can, as we have seen, be used for any combination of P, i and t. In the example used we assumed for simplicity that interest was added to the account at the end of each year. This will not necessarily be the case. Interest may be credited semi-annually, quarterly, monthly even daily. The same formula can still be used but in such cases we need to distinguish between the **nominal** and **effective** rate.

Assume that, instead of paying interest annually, an account credits the accrued interest to your account on a monthly basis. You decide to invest the principal of £100 and leave the principal and accruing interest untouched for 5 years. What would the final value of your account be if the annual rate of interest is 10%?

P = £100
i = 0.8333% per period (10%/12) (or 0.008333 as a decimal)
t = 60 (12 months for 5 years)

giving:

$$\text{Value} = 100(1.008333)^{60} = £164.53$$

If we had calculated the accrued amount in an account adding interest only once a year the amount would be £161.05 (you should confirm this yourself). The difference, understandably, is that interest in the first case is being added to the account more frequently and this interest will in turn attract interest for the rest of the 5 year period.

The quoted rate of 10% pa is known as the **nominal** rate. The rate actually earned is known as the **effective** rate or as the **annual** percentage rate (APR). You may well see the APR figure quoted in advertisements exhorting people to borrow money or take out credit to finance their consumer purchases. The APR can be calculated using the formula:

$$APR = \left(1 + \frac{i}{t}\right)t - 1$$

where

$$t = 12$$
$$i = 0.10 \text{ (10\% as a decimal)}$$
$$APR = \left(1 + \frac{0.1}{12}\right)^{12} - 1$$
$$APR = (1 + .00833)^{12} - 1$$
$$= 1.10471 - 1 = .10471 \text{ or } 10.471\%$$

The effective or actual rate of interest is, therefore, 10.47%.

19.5 DEPRECIATION

Depreciation can be regarded as the gradual reduction in the value of capital assets of an organisation. Typically, if a firm buys, say, a computer for use in the office, then over time the value of this item will get less and less. Allowance has to be made in the value for wear and tear, usage, obsolescence etc. It is standard accounting practice to allow for such depreciation in financial analysis and we shall examine two of the common methods of determining depreciation.

19.5.1 Straight line depreciation

This is the simplest method, where the value of the asset is averaged equally over the time period in which it is used. Let us suppose that MTG have purchased a new computer based desk-top publishing system for use within the accounts department. The system has cost £20,000 and is expected to have a useful life of 4 years after which it will be obsolete and will need to be replaced by an up-to-date, state of the art system. At that time the system will have a scrap value of £1,000.

Using this method the annual depreciation is simply calculated as:

$$\frac{\text{(Current value } - \text{ value at end of period)}}{\text{Number of periods}}$$

Here:
Current value is £20,000
value at end of period = £1,000
number of periods is 4

$$\text{Annual depreciation} = \frac{20000 - 1000}{4} = £4750$$

(You will be aware that it is referred to as the 'straight line' method because we are assuming a **linear** function for depreciation. A graph showing the current value and the final value would be joined by a straight line and the slope of the line would give the rate of depreciation.)

19.5.2 Reducing balance method

This second method assumes that the value of the asset is reducing not by a constant **amount** as in the Straight Line method but rather by a constant **percentage** or proportion.

The relevant formula is given by:

$$D = V(1-r)^t$$

where D is the depreciated value at the end of a particular time period

     V is the initial value of the asset

     r is the rate of depreciation

     t is the number of time periods.

By rearranging the formula (as with the compound interest formula) we can determine any of the variables in the set:

$$V = \frac{D}{(1-r)^t}$$

and

$$r = 1 - \sqrt[t]{\left(\frac{D}{V}\right)}$$

To illustrate let us assume, in the example above, that MTG decide to depreciate the computer at the rate of 40 per cent a year. At the end of the first year the depreciated value will be:

end Year 1   £20,000 − 0.40(20,000) = £12,000

That is, for Year 2, the asset is seen as having a value of £12,000. At the end of Year 2 the depreciated value will be:

end Year 2   £12,000 − 0.40(12,000) = £7,200

Subsequent calculations are shown below:

	Depreciated value (£)
end of Year 1	12000
end of Year 2	7200
end of Year 3	4320
end of Year 4	2592
end of Year 5	1555.2
and so on	

The depreciated values are, of course, easily found using the formula. With such a geometric series the value of the asset will technically never reach zero.

Assume instead that we wished to find the rate of depreciation to be used over a 4 year period. Here we would use the formula:

$$r = 1 - \sqrt[t]{\left(\frac{D}{V}\right)}$$

$$r = 1 - \sqrt[4]{\frac{1,000}{20,000}}$$

$$r = 1 - \sqrt[4]{0.05} = 1 - 0.4729 = 0.5271$$

ie r = 52.71%

SUMMARY

1   Interest arises from the time preference for money.

2   Simple interest is where a constant proportion of the principal is added each period.

3   Compound interest is where a proportion of the principal plus the sum of previous interest payments is added each period.

4   Interest rates are generally shown as nominal rates. Where the compounding period is not annual the effective rate of interest will be different.

5   An arithmetic series arises where a constant amount is added/subtracted from the initial value each period.

6   A geometric series is where a constant proportion is added/subtracted each period.

7 Depreciation can be viewed as the opposite of interest: a reduction in the value of some asset.

8 Two common methods of depreciation are the straight line method and the reducing balance method.

SELF-TEST QUESTIONS

1 **What is the difference between an arithmetic and a geometric series?** (*Refer to pages 185 and 186*)

2 **Why is interest paid?** (*Refer to page 185*)

3 **What are the two methods of depreciation?** (*Refer to page 189*)

4 **What is the difference between simple and compound interest?** (*Refer to page 187*)

5 **Is simple interest an example of an arithmetic series or a geometric series?** (*Refer to page 185*)

6 **How would you calculate the rate of interest being earned in an account if you knew V, t, P?** (*Refer to page 188*)

7 **Why is straight line depreciation so called?** (*Refer to page 189*)

8 **How would you work out the depreciated value of an asset using the reducing balance method?** (*Refer to page 190*)

9 **What is the difference between a nominal and an effective rate of interest?** (*Refer to page 188*)

EXERCISES

1 You decide to invest £100 in an account paying 7% interest pa, compounded annually. Determine the following:
   (a) The interest paid at the end of the first year
   (b) The interest paid at the end of the 5th year
   (c) The total interest paid for the first 5 years.

2 The same account now pays 7% pa compounded:
   (a) Quarterly
   (b) Monthly
   (c) Daily
   For each of these work out the effective annual rate of interest.

3 You are offered the following alternatives:
   (a) You can invest £2,500 in an account paying 10% pa compounded annually for 5 years.
   (b) You can invest £2,500 in an account paying 8% pa compounded quarterly for 5 years.
   (c) You can invest £2,500 in an account paying 6% pa compounded monthly for 5 years.
   Which would you choose?

4 A piece of equipment has been bought for £50,000, will last for 10 years and have a scrap value of £7,500.
   (a) Draw up an annual schedule showing the value of the machine and the annual depreciation using the straight line method.
   (b) Determine the annual rate of depreciation if the reducing balance method is used.
   (c) Draw up an annual schedule showing the annual depreciation and annual value of the asset using the reducing balance method.

Answers on page 323.

Present value and internal rate of return

In Chapter 19 the basics of interest rate calculations were presented. Such calculations lie at the heart of a particularly important area of financial appraisal: that of **present value**. Typically in an assessment of financial alternatives we wish to compare different projects or investments with a view to deciding which is 'best'. The problem frequently arises that such projects generate cash flows during different periods of time so direct comparison and evaluation is not possible. Accordingly we determine the present value of the cash flows—literally its current worth—in order to facilitate such comparisons. An extension to such present value is to examine the **Internal Rate of Return** on a project.

20.1 PRESENT VALUE

We have already established the principle of **time preference**. That is other things being equal, we would prefer a sum of money now (ie, in the present) to the same sum of money at some stage in the future. Given the choice of £100 now or £100 in a year's time we would choose the £100 now. But suppose, instead, the choice were £100 now or £110 in a year's time. Would we still choose the £100 now?

To answer such a question we need to assess the present value of the future sum of money. Literally, the present value is an indication of what some future sum is worth to us **now**.

Let us assume a rate of interest of 8%. The present value (PV) of £110 in one year's time is given by:

$$PV = \frac{V}{(1+i)^t}$$

where PV is the calculated present value
V is the value at some time in the future (here £110)
i is the rate of interest (here 0.08)
t is the number of periods into the future we are examining

so the PV is given as:

$$PV = \frac{110}{(1+0.08)^1} = \frac{110}{1.08} = £101.85$$

What does this mean?

It means that, for our purposes, the amount of £101.85 **now** and the amount of £110 in one year's time are identical and equal. Given a free choice between receiving £101.85 now and £110 in one year's time we would be indifferent. Effectively both are worth the same. It is apparent that from the compound interest formula introduced in the previous chapter, we could invest the principal of £101.85 at 8% pa interest and in one year's time it will have increased to £110.

Returning to the original alternatives we were offered £100 now or £110 in one year's time. Which should we take? The answer is evident. We should choose the £110 in one year's time because its present value (£101.85) is more than the alternative present value of £100 now.

Such a decision, naturally, is only based on the financial information available. Under normal business circumstances a number of other factors would also be considered before reaching a decision: the risk involved in the alternatives, the rate of interest to be used, whether the rate of interest will remain the same over the entire period, and so on.

The principles involved in present value remain the same, however.

20.2   SIMPLE INVESTMENT APPRAISAL

Let us illustrate the use of such present value calculations with a simple illustration. In their cereal production department MTG are considering investing in a new machine which will save on labour costs. The machine will cost £10,000 to purchase and install and will have a useful life of 5 years. It is estimated that the machine will reduce labour costs by £3,000 each year. The current cost of capital to the group is 10 per cent. What advice can we give on the viability of the investment? First, let us examine the relevant cash flows:

TABLE 20.1   **Project cash flows**

Year	Cash inflow (£)	Cash outflow (£)	Net cash flow (£)
0	0	10000	−10000
1	3000	0	3000
2	3000	0	3000
3	3000	0	3000
4	3000	0	3000
5	3000	0	3000
Total			5000

At first sight, the project looks viable, generating a net cash flow which is +£5000. However, this takes no account of the fact that the cash outflow takes place at the start of the project whilst the cash inflow (in the form of savings in labour costs) occurs throughout the life of the project. To determine whether the project is worthwhile we must determine its present value: the value of the future stream of cash flows now.

We can determine the PV of each year's cash flow using the PV formula:

TABLE 20.2   **Present value of cash flows**

Year	Net cash flow (£)	Discount Factor $1/(1+i)^t$	Present Value Cash flow × DF
0	−10000	1.000	−10000
1	3000	0.9091	2727.30
2	3000	0.8264	2479.20
3	3000	0.7513	2253.90
4	3000	0.6830	2049
5	3000	0.6209	1862.70
Total	5000		1372.10

The second column shows the Net Cash Flows, as in Table 20.1. The third column shows the Discount Factor $(1/(1+i)^t)$. This is taken from the PV formula and represents the rate at which we have to discount a future value to determine its present value. The final column shows the Present Value of each year's net cash flow determined by multiplying the Net cash flow by the Discount Factor.

So, for example, £3,000 in one year's time has a present value of £2,727.30.

There are two points to be noted about these present values. First, the present value for Year 0 is the same as the Net Cash Flow. This is not surprising as this cash flow is already taking place in the present. Second, the present value of £3,000 gets less and less the further into the future we go. Again, this is not surprising. The longer we have to wait to receive a given cash flow the less it is worth to us compared with the present.

The total Present Value (known as Net Present Value, or NPV, as it deals with net cash flows) is £1,372.10. What does this mean?

It means that the Present Value of the Net Cash Flows shown is equal to this amount. If you like, this is the present net worth of the cash flows generated by this project. If we were given the choice of a net cash flow **now** of £1,372.10 or a net cash flow spread over the next 5 years of £5,000 we would have no particular preference.

The NPV is positive and this indicates that, other things being equal, the project is worthwhile and that the NPV of the cash inflows is greater than the NPV of the cash outflows.

Had the NPV figure been **negative** it would indicate the reverse. The PV of the outflows was greater than that of the inflows. Similarly, an NPV=0 would indicate the PVs of the inflows and outflows was exactly the same.

Such NPVs all take account of the *timing* of the various flows.

USING DISCOUNTING TABLES

In the above example, the Discount Factors can be easily determined from the relevant formula. You will also find that Discount Tables are also published which show the results of the formula for different rates of interest over different periods of time.

The use of such tables is straightforward but they are not always available in examinations so it is better to ensure that you can determine the discount factors for yourself from the appropriate formula.

20.3 PROJECT COMPARISON

To illustrate the use and flexibility of NPV calculations let us examine a situation of project comparison where we use the method to compare two or more different projects. Let us return to the earlier example where MTG are considering acquiring a desk-top publishing system. There are currently two alternatives being considered. MTG can purchase the system outright for an initial sum of £10,000. This sum includes a maintenance contract from the supplier for the first twelve months. At the end of the first year (and at the end of each subsequent year) MTG can purchase an annual maintenance contract for £2,500. At the end of 5 years the system will be obsolete and will have a scrap value of £1,000.

Alternatively, MTG can lease the system from the computer supplier. MTG will pay £4,000 now and a further £4,000 per annum at the end of each subsequent year. So, the second lease payment will be due at the end of the first year (to pay for the system through year 2) and so on. At the end of 5 years the system will be scrapped but its scrap value will go to the supplier not to MTG. The leasing fee also includes maintenance.

Assume again, the group's current cost of capital is 10%.

A diagrammatic representation of the timing of the alternatives would be worthwhile as the correct timings are essential in this type of project appraisal.

TABLE 20.3   **Cash flows**

Year	Purchase			Leasing		
	Cash Inflows	Cash Outflows	Net Cash Flows	Cash Inflows	Cash Outflows	Net Cash Flows
0	0	−10000	−10000	0	−4000	−4000
1	0	−2500	−2500	0	−4000	−4000
2	0	−2500	−2500	0	−4000	−4000
3	0	−2500	−2500	0	−4000	−4000
4	0	−2500	−2500	0	−4000	−4000
5	1000	0	+1000	0	0	0
Total			−19000			−20000

You should ensure that you understand the flows shown in the table before proceeding. The timing of such flows is critical in NPV calculations. Note that in this case the 'year' refers to the end of the year shown.

In this case, both projects generate negative cash flows. On face value, the leasing option looks more expensive generating a larger negative cash flow than purchasing outright. However, these totals ignore the timings of these flows and it is apparent that we must determine the relevant NPVs.

TABLE 20.4   **Present values**

Year	Discount Factor	Purchase		Leasing	
		Net Cash Flows	Present Value	Net Cash Flows	Present Value
0	1.0000	−10000	−10000	−4000	−4000
1	0.9091	−2500	−2272.75	−4000	−3636.40
2	0.8264	−2500	−2066.00	−4000	−3305.60
3	0.7513	−2500	−1878.25	−4000	−3005.20
4	0.6830	−2500	−1707.50	−4000	−2732.00
5	0.6209	+1000	+620.90		
Total		−19000	−17303.60	−20000	−16679.20

In Table 20.4 the two series of Net Cash Flows have been discounted as shown. For the purchase option the NPV is −£17,303.60. Ensure that you understand properly the meaning of this figure. It indicates that the sum of £17,303.60 **now** is exactly the same as the cash flows shown over the next 5 years. Similarly, the figure for the Leasing option is −£16,679.20.

Comparison of the two NPV's reveals that the leasing option has the **least** negative value. This indicates that, other things being equal, the Leasing option is to be preferred. The present value of the cash outflows is smaller than that of the alternative—purchase.

Naturally, we would not recommend that the decision is taken purely on the basis of the

NPV calculations. We would need to assess other factors in reaching the decision: tax allowances, the likely rate of inflation and so on, as well as a view as to whether the rate of interest used to calculate the NPVs will remain constant at 10%.

This last point is critical for NPV calculations. Should the rate of interest/cost of capital change over this period then the present values will change also and possibly the recommendation we would make.

20.4 INTERNAL RATE OF RETURN

Partly because of the fact that the NPV will change if the rate of interest/cost of capital changes it is frequently useful to calculate the **Internal Rate of Return** (IRR). By definition the IRR is simply the discount rate which yields an NPV of zero for a project. That is, a discount factor that gives an NPV which is neither negative nor positive. This IRR can then be compared to the actual cost of capital to determine at what rate of interest/cost of capital the project would cease to be profitable.

By way of illustration let us return to the earlier example of MTG buying a labour-saving machine for £10,000. Earlier we used a discount rate of 10%. Let us use, instead, a rate of 15.24%. The relevant calculations are shown in Table 20.5.

TABLE 20.5 **Discount Rate 15.24 per cent**

Year	Net cash flow (£)	Discount Factor	Present Value
0	−10000	1.000	−10000
1	3000	.8678	2603.40
2	3000	.7530	2259.00
3	3000	.6534	1960.20
4	3000	.5670	1701.00
5	3000	.4920	1476.00
Total	5000		−£0.40

Allowing for arithmetic rounding (the Discount Factors are to only 4 decimal places) gives an NPV effectively equal to zero.

What does this mean?

It means that, at a rate of discount of 15.24%, this stream of cash flows has a zero present value: the present value of the inflows is exactly the same as that of the outflows. More usefully, however, is the following evaluation. At 10% the project had a positive NPV. At 15.24% a zero NPV. It is apparent that at a rate of above 15.25% the NPV will be negative (the present value of the outflows greater than that of the inflows).

Accordingly, if the cost of capital to fund this project is more than 15.24% the project is not worthwhile. At rates of interest/cost of capital less than this, however, the project is viable. At exactly 15.24% the project is at breakeven (in present value terms that is not in terms of costs and revenues). Similarly, the IRR of two or more projects can be compared to determine which is 'better'.

The question arises, however: how is the IRR determined? How did we know that the IRR of the project above was 15.24%. The brief answer is: use a computer package! It is possible, however, to estimate the IRR by manual methods. There are two such methods available. Both require the NPV of a project at **two different** discount rates.

TABLE 20.6   **Present value of cash flows with two discount rates**

Year	Net cash flow (£)	Present Value DF 10%	Present Value DF 16%
0	−10000	−10000	−10000
1	3000	2727.30	2586.21
2	3000	2479.20	2229.49
3	3000	2253.90	1921.97
4	3000	2049	1656.87
5	3000	1862.70	1428.34
Total	5000	1372.10	−177.12

In Table 20.6 the NPV for the project has been evaluated with a discount rate of 10% and again with a rate of 16%. The IRR can now be estimated using either of two approaches.

20.4.1   Graphical interpolation/extrapolation

This method requires the construction of a suitable graph with the NPV on the vertical axis and the Discount Rate on the horizontal. The graph for this problem is shown in Figure 20.1.

FIGURE 20.1   **Internal Rate of Return**

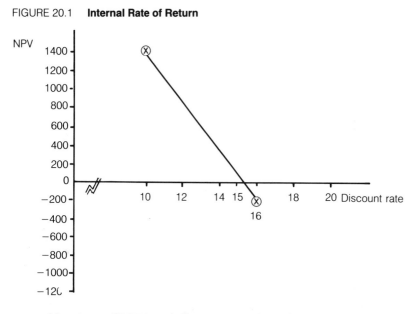

The two combinations of NPV and discount rate have been plotted and joined together with a straight line. The point where this line crosses the horizontal axis indicates the value for the IRR. This can be seen to be approximately 15.2%.

As with every graph it is frequently difficult to read off a precise value and such a method must be seen as an approximation only.

This example has involved **interpolating** the IRR between a positive NPV and a negative NPV. Occasionally we may choose a second discount rate which still gives a positive NPV. The same method can be followed but in such a case we are **extrapolating** from the two combinations and we would have to extend the straight line joining the two points until it crosses the horizontal axis.

20.4.2 Formula method

The IRR can also be found using an interpolation formula.

$$IRR = R1 + (R2-R1) \frac{|NPV1|}{(|NPV1| + |NPV2|)}$$

where R1 is the discount rate used for the first NPV

R2 is the discount rate used for the second NPV

$|NPV1|$ is the absolute value for the first NPV

$|NPV2|$ is the absolute value for the second NPV

Here:

$$IRR = 10\% + (16\%-10\%) \frac{1372.1}{(1372.1 + 177.12)}$$

$$= 10\% + 6(0.88567) = 15.3\%$$

Both these methods should be seen as linear approximations only. In fact the relationship between NPV and the discount rate is non-linear so the approximation methods used here are valid only over small parts of the function. Figure 20.2 illustrates a range of NPV and discount rate values for this problem and the non-linear pattern is clearly evident.

FIGURE 20.2 **IRR**

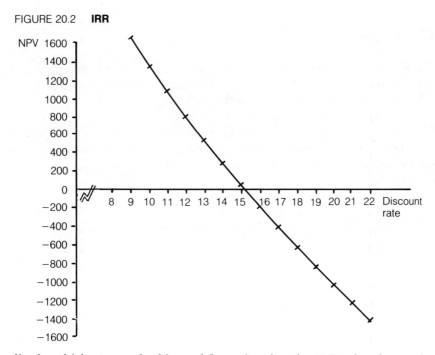

Accordingly, whichever method is used for estimating the IRR value the result should be treated as an approximation only and used with caution.

SUMMARY

1   Present Value is a method that enables a stream of future cash flows to be shown in terms of an equivalent sum of money today.
2   The Net Present Value (NPV) is the present value of both inflows and outflows.
3   The NPV shows whether the present value of inflows is greater than that of outflows. If NPV>0 inflows are larger, if NPV<0 outflows are larger. If NPV=0 the two are the same.
4   The discount rate used is critical in determining the NPV. Different rates will produce different NPVs.

5   The Internal Rate of Return is the discount rate that produces NPV=0. If the cost of capital is less than this the project is worthwhile.

6   The IRR can be estimated either from a graph or from an equation. In either case two combinations of NPV and discount rate are required.

SELF-TEST QUESTIONS

1   What is meant by a Present Value? (*Refer to page 193*)

2   What is meant by Net Present Value? (*Refer to page 195*)

3   Why is it necessary to use PV in project evaluations? (*Refer to page 193*)

4   How would you use NPV to choose between two alternative projects? (*Refer to page 196*)

5   What is the IRR? (*Refer to page 197*)

6   In what way is the IRR useful in project appraisal? (*Refer to page 197*)

7   What are the two methods of determining the IRR? (*Refer to page 198*)

8   Which of the two methods of determining IRR is preferable? (*Refer to page 199*)

EXERCISES

1   For the example used in the text on the alternatives of purchasing and leasing the computer compare the cash flows using a discount rate of 8% and then 12%.

How do you explain the fact that the NPV's have altered?

2   MTG are considering replacing part of their computer network with the latest equipment. Two suppliers have been asked to tender for the project. The relevant costs of the project and the corresponding savings (in terms of reduced labour costs, increased efficiency etc) are shown below:

| | Supplier A | | Supplier B | |
| Year | Cost | Savings | Cost | Savings |
	(£)		(£)	
Now	100000	0	75000	0
1	0	20000	25000	0
2	0	30000	0	60000
3	0	40000	0	40000
4	0	50000	0	35000
5	0	20000	0	25000

(a)   If the current rate of interest is 12% which supplier would you recommend should be given the contract?

(b)   What other factors would you wish to take into account before reaching a decision?

(c)   If the rate of interest were to fall how do you think this would affect your recommendation?

(d)   For both suppliers calculate the IRR.

(e)   How could you use this information?

Answers on page 325.

Annuities and sinking funds

The past two chapters have looked at the use of interest rates and present value techniques in the context of financial analysis. This chapter introduces a number of specialised, but common, applications of these techniques in the form of annuities and sinking funds.

21.1 ANNUITIES

An annuity is a term for a series of fixed equal payments or receipts made at specified periods of time. Such annuities (although they are rarely called this) occur frequently: payments of wages or salaries, repayments of loans, consumer credit repayments, repayments on mortgages, payments of insurance premiums and so on are all common examples.

Calculations involving annuities are based around formulae already introduced in Chapters 19 and 20.

1   Value of future amount $= P(1 + i)^t$

2   Sum of terms in a geometric progression $= \dfrac{a(r^n - 1)}{r-1}$

3   Present value $= \dfrac{V}{(1 + i)^t}$

We shall examine a number of typical applications of annuities.

Before doing so, however, it is necessary to be aware of a number of differing features of annuities.

1   The term of an annuity may be defined as:
    (a)   Certain. It starts and ends on given fixed dates
    (b)   Contingent. It depends on some event that cannot be fixed in time (eg insuring against a person's death)
2   The annuities may be paid/received
    (a)   On an ordinary basis. They are paid/received at the *end* of the payment intervals.
    (b)   On a due basis. They are paid/received at the *beginning* of payment periods.
3   An annuity may also carry on indefinitely: this is known as a perpetual annuity.

It is particularly important to establish exactly which type of annuity is applicable to a given problem. To begin with we shall concentrate on annuities which are due and certain.

21.2 VALUE OF AN ANNUITY

Let us suppose that MTG offer their employees the opportunity to invest part of their wages and salaries in an investment scheme. At the start of each year, for 5 years, an employee will pay the scheme £1,000. This will be invested on his behalf and is expected to earn 8% pa. The employee wishes to know what the investment is worth on an annual basis. You should see that, although this is similar to a compound interest problem, the difference is that the principal sum does not remain constant. However, the basic calculation is straightforward.

We are dealing here with an annuity which is certain and due. The first payment—invested at the start of Year 1—will attract interest for the first year at 8% pa. This gives:

$$£1000(1.08) = £1080.00$$

Similarly, the second premium of £1,000 will be added to this amount at the start of Year 2. All of this will now attract interest of 8% during Year 2 to give:

$$£2,080(1.08) = £2,246.40$$

We could progress in the same way through the remainder of the period to produce the results shown in Table 22.1.

TABLE 22.1

Year	Premium (£)	Total in fund at start of year (£)	Interest 8% (£)	Total in fund at end of year (£)
1	1000	1000	80	1080
2	1000	2080	166.4	2246.4
3	1000	3246.4	259.71	3506.11
4	1000	4506.11	360.49	4866.60
5	1000	5866.60	469.33	6335.93

At the end of 5 years, therefore, the fund contains £6,335.93.

In the same way we could use the geometric progression approach. The first payment will attract interest for the full 5 years:

$£1,000(1.08)^5$
whilst the second for 4 years: $£1,000 (1.08)^4$
the third for 3 years: $£1,000(1.08)^3$
the fourth for 2 years: $£1,000(1.08)^2$
and the last for one year: $£1,000(1.08)$

Collecting these together we have:

$$£1,000 [1.08 + 1.08^2 + 1.08^3 + 1.08^4 + 1.08^5]$$

where the term in the square brackets is evidently a geometric progression with a at 1.08 and r at 1.08. Using the formula to find the sum of a geometric series we have:

$$\text{Sum} = \frac{1.08(1.08^5 - 1)}{1.08 - 1} = 6.33593$$

giving £1000[6.33593] = £6335.93

SUM OF AN ORDINARY ANNUITY

The appropriate formula for the sum of an ordinary annuity can be derived in the same way. Remember that ordinary annuities are paid/received at the end of the period not at the beginning like the due annuity.

The relevant formula is:

$$\text{Sum} = \text{Payment} \frac{[(1+i)^t - 1]}{i}$$

For example, assume that you are investing in an annuity for 5 years of £1,000 at a rate of 10 per cent, the sum to be invested at the end of each year. The corresponding sum will be:

$$\text{Sum} = 1000 \frac{[(1.1)^5 - 1]}{0.1} = 1,000 [6.1051] = £6,105.10$$

21.3 NPV OF AN ANNUITY

Frequently we wish to determine the Present Value of an annuity (often in the form of income receipts). Assume that an employee who has retired from the MTG group has certain pension rights. These rights involve receipt of an annual income of £2,000 a year for the next 10 years. Assume that the employee receives the payments at the start of the periods.

We wish to determine the PV of this due, certain annuity. Let us assume a discount rate of 10 per cent. It is apparent that the series of income receipts could be discounted individually:

	Receipt (£)	PV (£)
Start	2000	2000
Year 2	2000	$\frac{2000}{1.10}$
Year 3	2000	$\frac{2000}{1.1^2}$
Year 4	2000	$\frac{2000}{1.1^3}$

and so on through the series. This could be presented as:

$$\text{Sum of PV} = £2000[1 + \frac{1}{1.1} + \frac{1}{1.1^2} + \frac{1}{1.1^3} \ldots]$$

It is also apparent that we have a geometric series in the PV calculations with a = 1 and r = 0.9091 (ie, 1/1.1).

To calculate the sum of such a series we have:

$$\text{Sum} = \frac{1(0.9091^{10} - 1)}{0.9091 - 1} = 6.759$$

Sum of PV = £2000(6.759) = £13518

The interpretation of this result is the same as for any present value calculation. This sum represents the value now of the stream of annuity income over the next 10 years.

PV OF AN ORDINARY ANNUITY

Similarly the formula for the PV of an ordinary annuity is given as:

$$PV = \frac{P[1 - \frac{1}{(1+i)^t}]}{i}$$

and the present value is interpreted in the same way as before.

21.4 REPAYMENT ANNUITY

Annuity calculations are often applied to repayment of debt. For a sum of money borrowed for a fixed period of time a certain and due annuity can be used to repay both capital and interest. Such a series of repayments is sometimes known as an amortisation annuity. Typically, the problem faced relates to determining the periodic payment in order to repay the sum borrowed plus related interest in a stated number of periods.

Assume that MTG offer their employees a mortgage facility whereby the employee can borrow money to purchase a house. One individual has borrowed £20,000. The rate of interest is 10 per cent and the loan (and interest) is to be repaid over the next 10 years. To calculate the annual payment needed to amortise the debt we can use the following approach.

If we denote the repayments as V, i as the rate of interest and the amount initially borrowed as P then we can relate P to the present value of the future stream of repayments:

$$P = \frac{V}{(1+i)} + \frac{V}{(1+i)^2} + \frac{V}{(1+i)^3} + \ldots + \frac{V}{(1+i)^t}$$

This can be rewritten as:

$$P = V\left[\frac{1}{(1+i)} + \frac{1}{(1+i)^2} + \frac{1}{(1+i)^3} + \ldots + \frac{1}{(1+i)^{10}}\right]$$

and the term in square brackets is seen to be a geometric series with a and r both equal to $1/(1+i)$.

So here, with rate of interest$=0.10$ we have $1/(1+i) = 0.9091$ to give:

$$\frac{0.9091\,(0.9091^{10} - 1)}{0.9091 - 1} = 6.144567105$$

$$\text{So with } P = V\left[\frac{1}{(1+i)} + \frac{1}{(1+i)^2} + \frac{1}{(1+i)^3} + \ldots + \frac{1}{(1+i)^{10}}\right]$$

we have £20,000 $=$ V[6.144567105] to give V $=$ £3,254.91. Note that we have used $1/(1 + i)$ to 9DP for accuracy.

That is, £3,254.91 must be paid each year for 10 years to repay both the principal sum borrowed and the interest on the amount outstanding.

Frequently, it is necessary and useful to draw up a period repayment schedule to confirm the detailed payments.

Year	Debt	Interest	Debt + Interest	Payment made	Amount owing	Principal repaid
1	20000.00	2000.00	22000.00	3254.91	18745.09	1254.91
2	18745.09	1874.51	20619.60	3254.91	17364.69	1380.40
3	17364.69	1736.47	19101.16	3254.91	15846.25	1518.44
4	15846.25	1584.63	17430.88	3254.91	14175.97	1670.28
5	14175.97	1417.60	15593.57	3254.91	12338.66	1837.31
6	12339.66	1233.97	13572.53	3254.91	10317.62	2020.94
7	10317.62	1031.76	11349.38	3254.91	8094.47	2223.15
8	8094.47	809.45	8903.92	3254.91	5649.01	2445.46
9	5649.01	564.90	6213.91	3254.91	2959.00	2690.01
10	2959.00	295.90	3254.90	3254.91	−0.01	2959.01
Total		12549.19		32549.10		19999.91

Allowing for arithmetic rounding it can be seen that the annual payment of £3,254.91 repays the principal sum and the interest charged on the loan.

21.5 SINKING FUNDS

A sinking fund is another common method of debt repayment. If a sum of money is borrowed at a given rate of interest for a fixed period then the total amount owing at the **end** of the period is easily calculated. An annuity can then be arranged with regular payments such that the value of the annuity at the end of the fixed time period is just sufficient to repay the debt. Such a scheme is known as a **sinking fund**.

For example, let us consider the example in the previous section. An employee of MTG takes out a mortgage of £20,000 over 10 years at a rate of interest of 10 per cent. He wishes to invest regularly in an investment scheme paying a rate of 12% pa in order to use the proceeds from the scheme to repay the mortgage loan with a lump sum at the end of the period. How much per year should he invest in the scheme?

At the end of 10 years the employee will owe the following amount in relation to his mortgage debt (principal plus interest):

$$20{,}000(1+0.10)^{10} = £51{,}874.85$$

The proceeds from the investment scheme must equal this sum.

It is clear that the investment scheme (the sinking fund) represents a geometric series. Using the appropriate formula to find the sum of such a series we have:

$$\text{Sum} = \frac{1.12(1.12^{10} - 1)}{1.12 - 1} = 19.65458328$$

Here:

$$V = P(19.65458328)$$

where V must equal £51,874.85 in 10 years' time. This gives a value for P of £2,639.33. This is the annual amount to be invested in the sinking fund to generate the amount needed to repay the loan in 10 years' time.

The corresponding schedule is shown below:

Year	Debt		Sinking Fund			
	Total Debt	Debt interest	Premium	Amount in fund (start of year)	Interest	Amount in fund (end of year)
1	20000	2000	2639.33	2639.33	316.72	2956.05
2	22000	2200	2639.33	5595.38	671.45	6266.83
3	24200	2420	2639.33	8906.16	1068.74	9974.89
4	26620	2662	2639.33	12614.20	1513.71	14127.90
5	29282	2928.20	2639.33	16767.30	2012.07	18779.30
6	32210.20	3221.02	2639.33	21418.70	2570.24	23988.90
7	35431.20	3543.12	2639.33	26628.20	3195.39	29823.60
8	38974.30	3897.43	2639.33	32462.90	3895.55	36358.50
9	42871.80	4287.18	2639.33	38997.80	4679.74	43677.60
10	47159	4715.9	2639.33	46316.90	5558.03	51874.90
	51874.8			51874.9		

Columns 2 and 3 show the amount of debt outstanding and the interest charged on the debt on an annual basis. At the end of 10 years (ie at the beginning of Year 11) a total of £51,874.8 is owed. Column 4 shows the regular sinking fund premium whilst column 5 shows the value of the fund at the start of the year. Column 6 shows the interest earned on the fund during the year and column 7 the value of the fund at the end of the year. This figure is then carried forward to Column 5 for the next year. It can be seen that the value of the fund rises to match the total debt by the end of the period.

SUMMARY

1   An annuity is a series of equal payments or receipts over a number of equal time periods.
2   Annuities may be ordinary if payment/receipts occur at the end of a period or due if payments/receipts occur at the start of a time period.
3   Annuities may be certain if it begins and ends on fixed dates or contingent if it depends on some event whose occurrence is not known for definite.

4 An amortised debt involves a series of equal repayments spread over a fixed number of periods sufficient to repay the principal and the interest.

5 A sinking fund is a series of regular payments sufficient to provide a fixed sum at some definite future time period.

SELF-TEST QUESTIONS

1 **What is an annuity?** *(Refer to page 201)*

2 **What is a sinking fund?** *(Refer to page 204)*

3 **What are the different types of annuity?** *(Refer to page 201)*

4 **What is the purpose of a sinking fund?** *(Refer to page 204)*

5 **What is an amortisation schedule?** *(Refer to page 203)*

6 **What is the difference between a due and an ordinary annuity?** *(Refer to page 201)*

7 **What is the difference between a certain and a contingent annuity?** *(Refer to page 201)*

EXERCISES

1 You invest in an annuity paying a rate of 5% pa. If you invest £500 per year determine:
(a) The value after 5 years if the annuity is due.
(b) The value after 5 years if the annuity is ordinary.
(c) The PV after 5 years if the annuity is due.
(d) The PV after 5 years if the annuity is ordinary.

2 You own an annuity which will pay you £1,000 a year for 10 years. How much would you want now to sell the annuity to someone else (assume a rate of interest of 8%):
(a) If it was due.
(b) If it was ordinary.

3 A loan of £25,000 is amortised over 8 years. If the current rate of interest is 6 per cent draw up an annual repayment schedule.
   Recalculate the schedule if the rate of interest rises to 9 per cent.

Answers on page 326.

Section D:
Information Technology

Section D:
Information Technology

The next five chapters are concerned with information technology and its application to business systems. The following is a brief introduction to each chapter.

Chapter 22 distinguishes between software and hardware, digital and analogue. It concentrates on the hardware components of digital computers, particularly the central processing unit (cpu) and secondary storage. It concludes with a review of the connection of hardware units, particularly in the context of local area networks (LANs). Topics covered are: Description of hardware; micro, mini and mainframe computer systems; Local Area Networks (LANs).

Chapter 23 examines the concept, evolution and implementation of computer programs. Three modelling tools for program definition are introduced—flow charts, decision tables and Structured English. These program definitions are then illustrated by the BASIC programming language. Topics covered are: Basic principles of system modelling, system procedures and problem specification, tools and techniques, decision tables; stored programs; recognising simple instructions in the computer language BASIC and being able to trace the action of a simple program; tracing the evolution of computer languages.

Chapter 24 shows that many questions are formulated in the framework of a business system and illustrates how answers should also be made in this context. This chapter introduces three financial and three non-financial business systems, illustrating each activity with a data flow diagram. This latter model will become the basis of subsequent design. Topics covered are: Basic principles of system modelling, system procedures and problem specification, tools and techniques; business systems and levels of systems, hierarchical structure of organisations and the alignment of data processing systems.

In *Chapter 25* the design of each facet of a business computer system is considered in the framework of the data flow diagram. Specific design issues considered are: input, output, interface, file, process and control design. Topics covered are: Design of simple business systems: (data capture and input, file creation, file processing, operation, output forms, documentation, security and integrity of data); software packages; use of computer bureaux; software construction of files on magnetic tape and disk; man–machine interface with input and output facilities.

Chapter 26 examines facets of the electronic office. The information activity of the office is split into verbal, textual, data and visual information and the opportunities for the automation of each activity and also the transmission of that activity are explored. Topics covered are: Functions and applications of the electronic office; Local Area Networks (LANs).

Many of the exercises are abstracted from past ACCA examinations. All illustrative prices are in UK Sterling (1988).

Elements of hardware

22.1 HARDWARE VERSUS SOFTWARE

It is important to make a distinction between hardware and software. The various electronic and electromechanical devices (such as terminals and printers) that make up the physical parts of a computer system are termed the **hardware**. In contrast the sets of instructions that form the operating systems and programs needed to allow these physical components to function correctly are collectively called **software**.

This chapter is concerned with examining elements of the former while software is considered in the following chapter.

The difference between hardware and software can be illustrated in a simple road transport example. The physical aspects of the system—cars, buses, roads, traffic lights—represent the hardware. The software encompasses drivers, routes, traffic light sequences (and their meaning) and driving regulations. A bus and a road are two hardware components. However, the feat of driving the bus along the road, picking up and discharging passengers, obeying laws and directions cannot be achieved without recourse to software. The same is true of the computer. Plugging in and switching on the machine will only generate a little light and a little heat. Software is needed for the computer to perform useful tasks.

The distinction between hardware and software is not always as clear cut as the above descriptions might suggest. For example the term firmware has been coined to describe software permanently stored by the hardware. A detailed discussion of whether a particular facet of a computer system should be classified as hardware or software is often not particularly profitable.

22.2 DIGITAL AND ANALOGUE

Another distinction which needs to be made is between analogue and digital. Some physical quantities, such as the temperature in an office, take values on a continuous range, whereas others, such as the number of people working in that office, take only specific, discrete values. In general terms analogue concerns continuous variations whereas digital refers to discrete values. A simple physical example is provided by the two ways of controlling an ordinary light bulb. A simple 'on/off' switch is a digital device whereas a dimmer switch, providing as it does all possible light intensities between off and full on, is an analogue device.

Since a computer requires data to be stored and manipulated electronically the choice of either a digital or analogue representation is clearly of some relevance. In an analogue computer the temperature of 16 degrees could be associated with a stored voltage level of 8 volts, the temperature of 10 degrees as a voltage level of 5 volts and so on with the different temperature values being represented by the physical differences in the voltage level. This means that the handling of data is done through the direct physical representation rather than via numeric representation and manipulation.

In a digital computer the numeric temperature would be stored as a combination of switches being set to on and off. Conventionally the 'on' and 'off' states are represented by the symbols 1 and 0 respectively. These are called binary digits or bits.

All digital computers use the binary system and so it is useful to briefly state its principle. The decimal numbering system uses a base of 10 whereby each number is worth ten times the number on its immediate right. For example:

Example:

$$112$$

1	1	2
1 × 100	1 × 10	2 × 1

The binary notation uses a base of 2, so that each number can only be 0 or 1 (just as a base of 10 only allows digits of 1–9) and each number is worth twice that of the number to its immediate right. For example:

Example:

1110000

1	1	1	0	0	0	0
1×64	1×32	1×16	0×8	0×4	0×2	0×1
			= 112			

The binary format may look bulky but, from a computer's point of view, it is an attractive way of holding data. It means that any number can be represented by an appropriate combination of switches (eg, the number 23 could be stored as 10111).

Furthermore, it is possible to adopt an appropriate code convention so that non-numeric characters such as A, ?, [, etc can also be represented.

Two such code conventions are commonly used: Extended Binary Coded Decimal Interchange Code (EBCDIC) and American Standard Code for Information Interchange (ASCII). EBCDIC is an 8 bit (binary digit) code (ie each character is uniquely represented by a combination of 8 switch settings) whereas ASCII is a 7 bit code. ASCII is commonly extended to encompass an eighth bit to allow for further characters such as graphic or foreign language symbols. A combination of 8 bits used to represent a symbol is called a **byte**.

Although some specialised applications of computing, such as process control where the physical change in one or more quantities can be directly related to the control of physical changes in others, are handled by analogue or hybrid (involving both analogue and digital elements) computers the majority of computers in use today are digital devices. The reasons for this are to be found in the advantages that digital computing holds over analogue.

1   Digital information is less prone to error. The electronic fluctuation necessary to cause a switch setting to change from 'on' to 'off' or vice versa is far greater than that which would cause an analogue variable to change value.
2   There is theoretically no limit to the precision of digital information. Adding extra 'switches' to the representation increases the accuracy of the stored information.
3   When transmitted over distances simple 'booster' devices designed to confirm an 'on' or an 'off' setting placed at regular intervals along the line of transmission ensure that digital information can be sent error free. Such 'boosting' of an analogue signal would have the effect of altering the value it represents.

Because of these advantages, even applications which are suited to analogue computing are handled using digital computers with the relevant analogue input being converted into digital form to allow for the necessary manipulation. The conversion of the analogue waveforms of speech into digital form provides an example of such a process.

The development of digital computer hardware has been classified into a number of generations corresponding to the technologies used. The details of the technologies need not concern us here. However, what must be appreciated is that the passage of these generations reflects the search for more reliable, cheaper and faster mechanisms of implementing digital principles.

1   **First generation.** This was based on a valve technology and typified the machines of the 50s and early 60s. The machines were physically extremely large, of limited application and very unreliable with work time measured in minutes rather than hours before a valve failure occurred.

H

2   **Second generation.** Transistor based technology replaced valves resulting in a much more compact, versatile and reliable system.

3   **Third generation.** This made use of integrated circuits. Silicon chip technology allowed large numbers of different electronic components to be incorporated on to a single chip. A further reduction in size resulted. The mass production techniques available for the production of this technology meant a reduction in price.

4   Fourth and fifth generations are also referred to involving **Large Scale Integration** (LSI) and **Very Large Scale Integration** (VLSI) of the silicon chip circuitry.

Overall the effect has been to reduce not only the physical size of the computer but also to greatly reduce the cost of the processing power available to the extent that even the humblest of home microcomputers is more flexible, powerful and of higher capacity than the very first mainframe machines. All this at a fraction of the cost.

22.3   HARDWARE FUNDAMENTALS

A computer is at its simplest a device which processes an input or combination of inputs to produce an output. Indeed the British Standard definition of a computer is 'any device capable of accepting data automatically, applying a sequence of processes to this data, and supplying the results of these processes'.

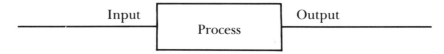

The main components of a computer are listed below and their inter-relationship illustrated in Figure 22.1.

(a)   Input device
(b)   Output device
(c)   Central Processing Unit (CPU)
          — Control Unit (CU)
          — Arithmetic and Logic Unit (ALU)
          — Primary Storage
(d)   Secondary or backup storage

FIGURE 22.1   **The component parts of a computer**

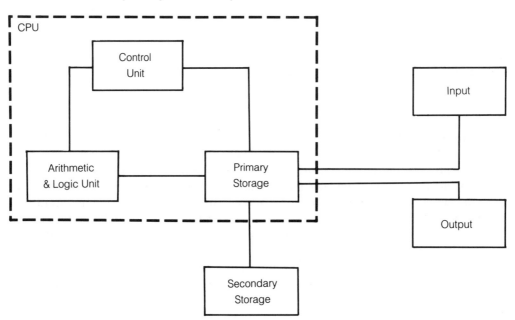

The inter-relationship can be further considered in the problem of adding three single digit numbers together.

The speed with which we can answer this simple question may lead us to believe that we have added the three numbers simultaneously. However, if the thought process is slowed down it reveals the real mechanism that has been used. The problem has been solved by adding the first two numbers together and adding this sum to the third to obtain the final answer.

This sequence of events has close parallels to the way a computer would process the same data. Both require:

1 Some way of finding out what the problem is.
2 Long term memory to recognise the symbols 4, 7, 5, + and = and their meaning.
3 The processing power necessary to perform the two additions accurately.
4 Short term memory to store the intermediate answer resulting from the first addition.
5 Some method of communicating the final answer either in written or verbal form.

Item 1 corresponds to the use of an INPUT device. Item 2 corresponds to INTERNAL MEMORY. Item 3 corresponds to the ALU. Item 4 corresponds again to INTERNAL MEMORY. Item 5 corresponds to the use of an OUTPUT device.

The whole operation is being controlled and co-ordinated by the *control unit* which ensures that the correct numbers are input, added, stored and output.

If a more complicated manipulation is required, such as a sophisticated statistical analysis of a set of numeric data, then it may prove necessary to look up the precise method together with an appropriate formula in a text book. This retrieval of information from an external source is equivalent to the backup or *secondary storage*. Indeed, it is likely that in this case the volume of data, 300 numbers say, would necessitate the use of secondary storage for the data itself.

Having used this simple example to illustrate the inter-relation and function of the various components their form within a computer will now be examined and discussed.

22.3.1 Central Processing Unit

The Central Processing Unit (CPU) comprises three main parts: control unit, arithmetic and logic unit (ALU), and primary storage. The **control unit** is in many respects best regarded as the 'brain' of the machine. The circuitry it contains controls and coordinates the functions of the other components of the computer system. In the three number addition problem the control unit would determine the operations to be performed and the location of the original data as well as determining where the intermediate and final answers are to be stored. The actual operation of addition is however performed in the **Arithmetic and Logic Unit**.

Thus the control unit is concerned with:

(a)   Obtaining and decoding the instructions to be used
(b)   Locating and obtaining the required data
(c)   Sequencing any competing instructions
(d)   Synchronising the various operations involved
(e)   Triggering the functions of the other components of the computer.

The **arithmetic and logic unit** (ALU) contains circuitry that enables additions (and other associated arithmetic operations) and comparisons to be made. Areas of storage, called registers, are incorporated into the ALU with the purpose of holding intermediate answers such as those needed to find the result of multiplying two numbers together using the principle of repeated addition.

Primary storage is dedicated to the storage of information in the form of both data and the sets of instructions (programs) required to manipulate that data. The process of accessing information is referred to as **reading** and that of storing is referred to as **writing**.

Primary storage can be divided into two categories: **Read Only Memory** (ROM) and **Random Access Memory** (RAM). There are two significant differences between these types of memory. Firstly, ROM only contains information that can be read. It is used to store data that the computer user has no need or right to alter. In contrast RAM is capable of being written to and read from. In some respects RAM can be thought of as the blank pieces of paper that the computer puts at the user's disposal to do whatever is required. Secondly, the RAM is often **volatile** and hence data held in it is lost when the machine is turned off. On the other hand a ROM has fixed data patterns established at manufacture which remain if there is any loss of power.

The capacity of storage is measured in bytes. The following multiples are commonly used:

1024 bytes = 1 kilobyte (1K or 1Kb)
1024 kilobytes = 1 megabyte (1Mb)
1024 megabytes = 1 gigabyte (1Gb)

Using the byte (or character) as a unit of storage is in many ways not a particularly useful one. For example 1 megabyte comprises 1,048,576 characters. Apart from the fact that this is a substantial number it is not very meaningful. A more useful measure is that a printed page of A4 contains on average 2–3 K. Consequently a megabyte can be equated to a 400 page book and the RAM size of a typical business microcomputer of 640K could be interpreted as about 250 pages worth.

22.3.2   Input devices

The commonest way of inputting information is via a keyboard. Computer keyboards are in many respects similar to a standard typewriter. However in addition to the usual 'QWERTY' keyboard layout (so called because of the sequence of keys in the top row of the layout) a number of extra features are usually included.

1   A numeric keypad with a calculator style format which duplicates the effect of the 0, 1, 2, ..., 9 keys in the 'QWERTY' layout.
2   A bank of 'function' keys. These are used to enable particular commands and functions to be executed by a single keystroke. The actual effect of any 'function' key will depend upon the context in which it is being used.
3   A bank of 'cursor control' keys. These are used to position the cursor on the screen for data entry.

Although the standard 'QWERTY' layout still predominates the market the context of its design (to support the functions of a mechanical typewriter) no longer applies. A number of ergonomically designed alternatives are available but are not in widespread use.

A variety of direct input devices into the computer are also available. These are examined in Chapter 25.

22.3.3 Output devices

The commonest form of output device is the **Visual Display Unit** (VDU), often simply termed a 'screen'. This is a video monitor (monochrome or colour) capable of displaying up to 25 lines of 80 characters. This is a relatively low **resolution** and gives a limited graphical capability. Specialist, high resolution monitors are commonly used in conjunction with applications with a high graphic content such as a Computer Aided Design (CAD) system.

The strength of the VDU as an output medium is its immediacy. On the other hand when the next output is required the previous one is lost. If a permanent record (**hard copy**) is required then use will need to be made of a printer or plotter. Again, these are considered in Chapter 25.

22.3.4 Secondary storage

The component parts described so far (input, processor and output) are in fact all that is required for a computer system. However in order to make full and most effective use of the processing power available a fourth component needs to be introduced. This is called **secondary storage** or **backup storage**. There are three main reasons for the inclusion of this extra facility.

1   Only data held in primary store is available for processing. However, it is unlikely that the RAM capacity of primary storage will be sufficiently large to hold all the required information. Consider a simple example of a customer mailing list holding information on 10,000 customers. The information that would be stored for each customer (contact name, position, company name, address, telephone number, product area, company size, turnover etc.) would typically require 500 characters (bytes). This requires a total of 5Mb. Take into account all the other functions that the computer would be needed for (accounts, payroll, personnel records, stock control and so on) and the total requirement is considerably in excess of this. There will simply not be enough room in the RAM to store all the organisation's data and the programs used to manipulate it.
2   RAM is the most expensive (per byte) form of storage available.
3   The volatility of RAM means that in order for all the data to be kept available the computer would need to be kept switched on at all times. A power loss would result in the loss of all the data which would then need to be re-input. This is clearly unsatisfactory. What is needed, therefore, is some means of making a copy of some or all of the contents of RAM in a form which does not need a power supply to sustain it. The information held in this **secondary storage** could subsequently be copied back into RAM thus removing the need to re-enter the data manually.

Secondary storage should demonstrate a number of properties. These include:

(a)   The ability to represent physically sequences of 1s and 0s
(b)   Physical compactness
(c)   Reliability, permanence and possibly the opportunity to re-use the media once its contents have become unwanted
(d)   Cheapness
(e)   Support for fast transfer rates of data to and from the RAM.

The earliest examples of secondary storage are provided by paper tape and punched cards. In both instances a combination of hole patterns provided the means of character storage. While both are still to be found in limited use the drawbacks associated with them (low capacity, not reusable—the physical holes cannot be removed—relative physical frailty, low speeds etc) make them an unattractive choice.

The current standard form of secondary storage is magnetic media. This makes use of the fact that a thin film of magnetisable material can be magnetised in one of two directions and so provides the means of representing 0s and 1s. Long strips of this surface can hold substantial quantities of information. This long strip can be presented in a variety of physical configurations—drums, tapes and disks.

However, before embarking on a more detailed discussion of these various configurations a distinction needs to be made between the two main types of access—sequential and direct. **Sequential access** demands that the data must be read in a particular order. To access the required pieces of data all preceding items of data have to be read. This would be equivalent to checking the spelling of zyxomma by having first to read through aardvark, aardwolf etc in a dictionary. **Direct access** on the other hand permits all items of data to be almost equally accessible. It is not necessary for the read device physically to go through all the preceding data; instead it can access the required item directly. This issue is raised again in Chapter 25 but it is worth a brief mention now because it distinguishes between the major magnetic media. Magnetic tape is an example of sequential access; magnetic disk one of direct access.

MAGNETIC TAPE

Magnetic tape comes in reels which are typically 2,400 feet or 3,600 ft long and 0.5 inches wide. The storage capacity of such a tape varies with the quality of the magnetic surface. The best quality will store 6,250 bits/inch giving a total capacity of 125 Mb for a 2,400 ft reel. The data is stored in magnetic bit patterns across the tape with one character represented by one row of bit patterns. The number of characters that can be stored in each inch of the tape is known as the packing density and is measured in bits/inch (bpi). This unit of measure is a little confusing as it actually refers to characters per inch.

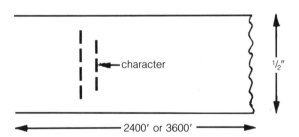

The tape is read by means of a tape drive which is very similar in principle to its musical equivalent. The high speeds of rotation involved necessitate the use of vacuum feeder tubes to take up the 'slack' from each reel. Without these the high accelerations and decelerations involved would cause the tape to stretch or even break. These high speeds also mean that the data is transferred in blocks rather than a record at a time with blank spaces (inter block gaps) on the tape used as separators. Whilst cheap, compact and reusable the time taken to locate and load the required tape together with that to find and transfer the required data make access times relatively slow. Other disadvantages include the relative fragility of tape and its susceptibility to magnetic interference.

However, the tape is a very cheap mechanism of storing data. It is possible to buy a 2,400 ft 6250 bpi tape giving 125Mb of storage for about £14. Tape is also particularly suitable for applications where all data records are sequentially accessed (see Chapter 25).

Magnetic disk has the long strip of magnetisable material laid out in a series of concentric circles or **tracks**. Disks can be used singly or, more commonly, as part of a stack of disks—a **diskpack**. Removable diskpacks are available which allow for a variety of sets of disks to be loaded and unloaded in much the same way as tapes.

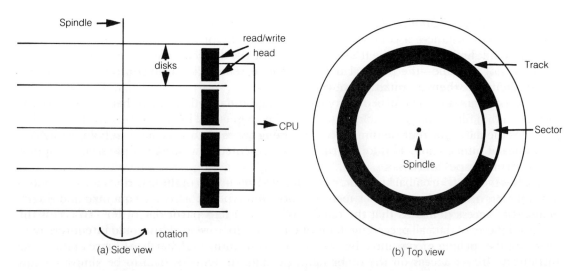

(a) Side view   (b) Top view

The disks rotate at high speed (c 3,000 rpm) and the read/write heads move in and out to access a stack of different tracks (a **cylinder**). Some technologies make use of multiple fixed read/write heads with one head per track. The total capacity of a disk pack would be in the region of 200–500Mb depending upon specification.

The time to access a particular piece of data held on a disk is made up from three components:

1   Head movement. The time taken to move the head to the correct track.
3   Rotational delay. Having located the correct track this is the time taken for the required data on that track to reach the read head. At most it constitutes 1 revolution of the disk.
3   Transfer. This is the time taken for the required data to pass the read head and to be read into the CPU.

Overall the average access time to a piece of data is likely to be measured in hundredths if not thousandths of a second.

Hard disks are faster but more expensive than tape. A typical 300Mb disk pack currently costs around £300.

Hard disks are available for use with all types of computer—mainframe, mini and micro. The size and hence capacity varies with a typical hard disk for a microcomputer having a capacity of 40Mb. The increasing popularity of microcomputers has also resulted in the development of the floppy disk. This is a plastic disk coated with iron oxide and enclosed within a reinforcing envelope. The 5.25 inch and 8 inch sizes are held in flexible plastic covers whilst the 3 inch 'micro floppy' has a rigid plastic cover.

Capacities of floppy disks vary according to machine type but are typically in the range 360Kb to 1.5Mb and cost about £2 each.

Floppy disks are more prone to damage than their rigid counterparts and so need to be treated with care. In addition, they can literally 'wear out' as the read/write heads actually touch the magnetic surface in contrast to hard disks where the heads skim the surface on a cushion of air.

Magnetic drum storage was the earliest form of magnetic surface used. It comprised a cylinder coated with magnetisable material (usually iron oxide). The cylinder rotated past a series of read/write heads which transferred the relevant data to and from the primary storage. The speed of rotation (1,000–3,000 rpm) ensured moderately fast access albeit with limited capacity. Although little used today the use of a drum as a form of secondary storage has left its mark in that the drum symbol is often used in computer flowcharts to indicate secondary storage.

22.4 TYPES OF COMPUTER

The terms **mainframe**, **mini** and **micro** are commonly used (elsewhere in this chapter for example) as descriptions of different types of computer. The distinction between them is becoming less concerned with the nature of the jobs they can undertake and more with the amount of data that can be stored and processed and the speed at which that processing takes place.

Historically a mainframe is so called because of the reference to the framework or cabinet in which the circuit boards of the CPU were housed. Although with VLSI this no longer applies the term remains. Mainframes are associated with handling large quantities of data with capacities measured in Gigabytes. They operate in a multi-user, multi-tasking environment (see Chapter 23) and usually require substantial operational support from data processing staff. The mainframe also usually demands a controlled environment for operation—air-conditioning, false flooring, temperature control—and it represents a significant corporate investment. It is difficult to give a typical configuration but mainframes tend to be used in applications where hundreds of terminals have to be supported from a centralised computer centre housing a large data processing department. Initial hardware costs are typically over £500,000.

Minicomputers were among the first to make use of the miniaturisation of electronic circuitry and so were able to perform a similar range of tasks to the mainframe but with reduced storage space and processing speed. Furthermore, they tended to adopt standard operating systems (see Chapter 23) such as UNIX rather than the vendor dependent facilities of the mainframe. A typical minicomputer configuration supports around sixty terminals and probably cost about £100,000. However, the need constantly to seek new markets means that such prices are falling and an entry level system (supporting four users) for one of the most successful minicomputers is now on offer at about £12,000.

When microcomputers first appeared in the mid-1970s they were very different in their characteristics. They had low storage capacities and were almost exclusively single user, single tasking machines. However the last decade has seen the rapid development of this market and the current generation of microcomputers is capable of operating in a multi-user, multi-tasking environment with access to a substantial amount of secondary storage. The ability to connect these machines together in a network has also opened up new opportunities. However, in general, microcomputers are still overwhelmingly used in single user applications or where only a few users (say 2–16) need to use the system. Typical prices range from £1,000–£5,000 per terminal.

FIGURE 22.2 **A typical microcomputer configuration**

640K RAM
20MB Disk drive
360K Diskette drive
£1,250

20 Mbyte Hard disk drive

Standard screen

360K 5" Floppy disk (diskette drive)

80 column printer
168cps dot matrix
56cps NLQ

£395

Function keys

Standard typewriter layout

Numeric keypad

Illustrative prices only (1988 rates)

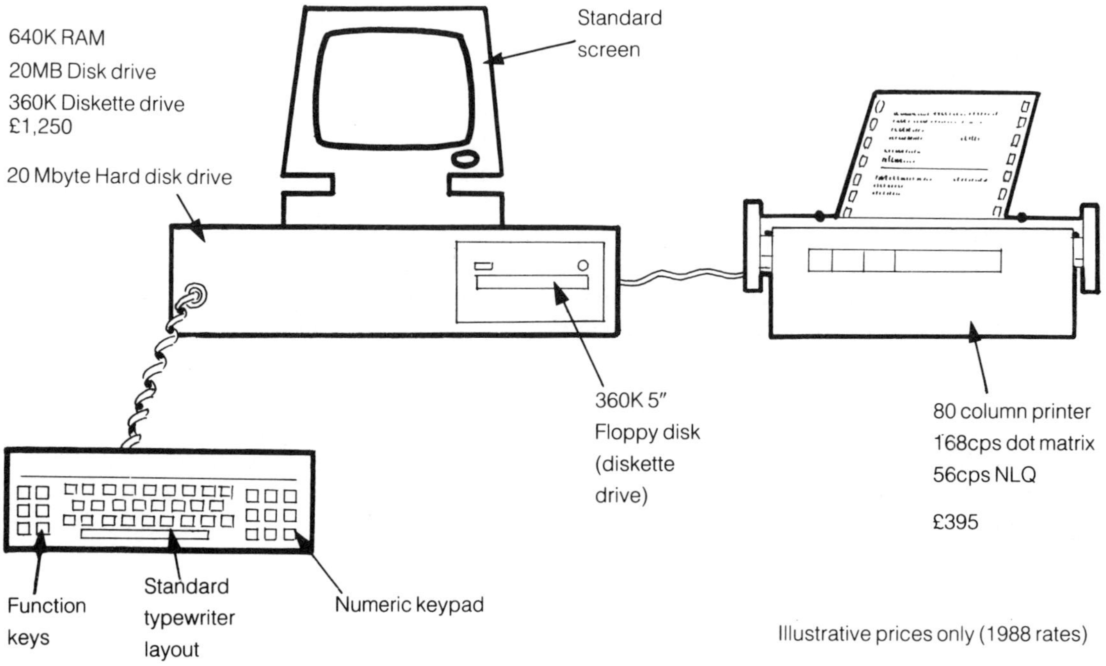

Mainframes still remain important in areas of large scale data processing or arithmetic manipulation. Minicomputers have extended their range of facilities in the last decade. Top specification minicomputers cannot be easily distinguished from mainframes, whilst 'entry-level' models threaten the domain of the microcomputer. These latter machines have also stretched themselves upwards and hence the middle ground of data processing (say 4–64 terminals) has become a bloody battleground with users offered different technological options that appear to offer the same specification. An important combatant in this battle is the network.

22.5   NETWORKING

This chapter concludes with a brief review of how computers can be connected to each other. Two cases will be considered: connection of a number of microcomputers in a local area network, and connection of a number of remote terminals to a mainframe.

22.5.1   Local Area Network

A network is the inter-connection of autonomous computers. A network can span many continents (a so-called Wide Area Network—WAN) or may be restricted to a relatively confined set of buildings—a campus, office block, office floor etc (a Local Area Network—LAN). The computers in a LAN are usually connected together by copper media or optical fibres.

A LAN offers the facility for users to:

(a)   Transmit data to and from each other
(b)   Share data
(c)   Share expensive items of hardware such as a laser printer.

There are three basic configurations: star, bus, and ring.

STAR CONFIGURATION

The **star** configuration has the network controller or file server at the hub with all other devices connected to this. All communications between devices is done via this central device.

Advantages
There is only one device or terminal per connection. The failure of one connection means that only one terminal is not functional and the rest of the network can carry on working normally.

Faults and problems can be easily diagnosed through the central server.

Disadvantages
A large amount of cabling is necessary because each node is connected to the centre.

If the central node fails then the whole network 'goes down'.

FIGURE 22.3 **Star configuration**

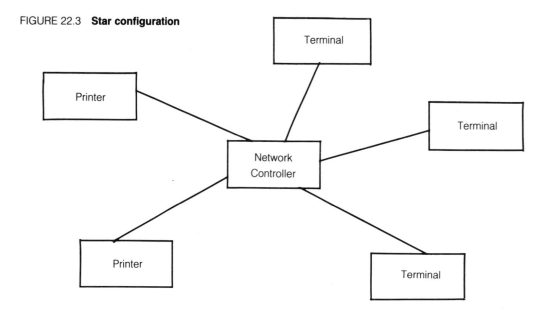

BUS CONFIGURATION

The **bus** configuration consists of a transmission line—often coaxial cable—to which are attached the required devices.

Advantages

Very simple to maintain and extend. Extra terminals can be connected to the existing bus at any point. More significant additions can be achieved by connecting extra cable and using a repeater to boost the signal.

It is simple architecture based on a single common data path.

Disadvantages

It may be difficult to diagnose and isolate faults. The absence of a central controller means that error detection will be more painstaking.

Each terminal must be relatively sophisticated. The absence of the central server means that the control of the network is vested in the nodes.

FIGURE 22.4 **Bus configuration**

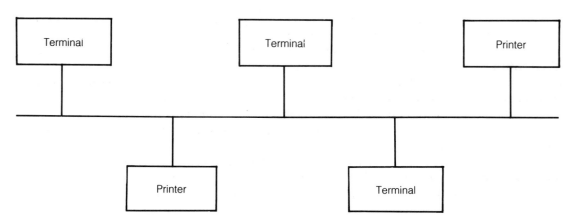

RING CONFIGURATION

The **ring** configuration has all the devices connected in a loop. Communication is usually one way only with data being passed from node to node.

Advantages

Less cabling is needed than for a comparative star network.

Data on the ring only passes in one direction. This makes it suitable for optical fibre transmission. This offers high speed transmission unaffected by interference.

Disadvantages

Network failure is caused by the loss of one terminal. If a node fails to pass data on then no transmission can take place until the faulty node is replaced.

Fault diagnosis may again be difficult. There is no central controller to show which node is causing the failure.

FIGURE 22.5 **Ring configuration**

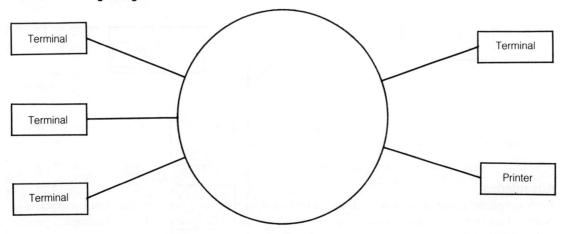

In practice these configurations will tend to be merged into hybrid systems that try to exploit the advantages of each type.

22.5.2 Remote terminals

Figure 22.6 shows a company having offices in Bristol, Liverpool and a Head Office in London where the mainframe computer is sited. Each office has a number of terminals. These terminals are linked to a device called a multiplexer. This has a two-fold function. Firstly it co-ordinates and controls the information being sent to and from each terminal. It ensures that two competing messages do not get 'scrambled' and that responses from the mainframe are directed to the correct terminal. Secondly it converts the digital output from the terminal into the analogue waveform necessary for transmission down the telephone line used in the long distance transmission. A similar reverse conversion has to be performed for all incoming messages. The telephone line used can either be a standard dial up line or a specially commissioned and exclusive leased line.

At the Head Office end of the communication lines similar functions have to be performed. However the greater volume and complexity of incoming and outgoing messages means that a good deal of communication processing needs to be done. To relieve the burden of this from the mainframe an auxiliary computer or **front end processor** is used. This frees the mainframe computer to get on with the main processing tasks of the enterprise.

FIGURE 22.6 **A remote terminal**

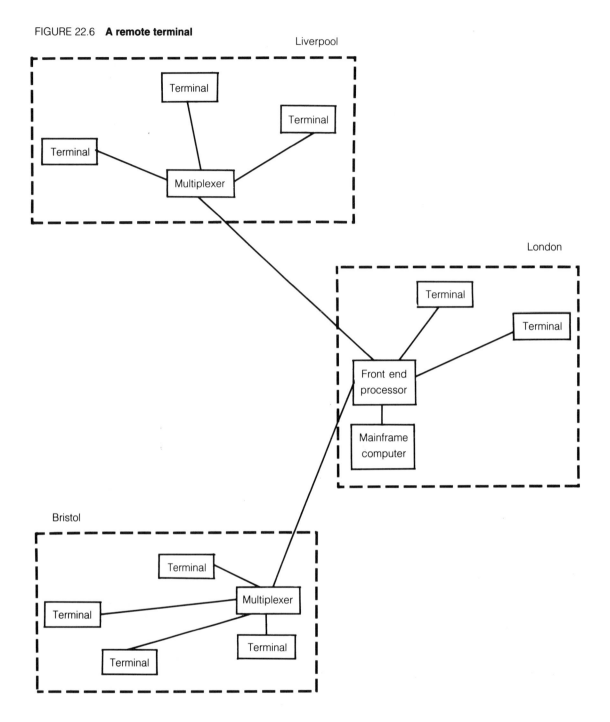

Summary

1 A distinction can be made between computer hardware and software. Most contemporary hardware is based upon digital principles.

2 Digital computers hold data in binary. EBCDIC and ASCII are two binary code conventions.

3 The physical representation of these binary conventions has led to computers passing through four successive generations.

4 A computer consists of an input device, output device, a central processing unit and secondary storage.

5 The CPU consists of three parts—the control unit to coordinate, the arithmetic and logic unit to calculate and the primary store to hold data and program instructions.

6   The primary store can be divided into two categories: RAM and ROM. The capacity of these is measured in bytes.
7   The standard device for input is a keyboard and for output, a VDU or screen.
8   Secondary storage is required to hold data not immediately required by the CPU. Two primary methods of storage—the magnetic disk and tape—were introduced.
9   A general distinction can be made between mainframe, mini and microcomputers, but this is open to blurring and redefinition.
10   The marketplace is also affected by the continued emergence of local area networks (LANs) which can be arranged as stars, rings or on buses.
11   Remote terminals may be attached to a central mainframe via the telephone lines. This will normally require both a multiplexor (to change signal type) and a front-end processor to deal with message handling.

SELF-TEST QUESTIONS

1   Are the various electronic and electromechanical devices that make up a computer system referred to as hardware or software?

2   What is the decimal equivalent of 10111?

3   What do the letters ASCII stand for?

4   How many bits are there in a byte?

5   List two advantages of digital over analogue representation.

6   What technology was used in second generation computers?

7   What are the three parts of a CPU?

8   Distinguish between RAM and ROM.

9   Approximately how many bytes would be required to store the text of a 40 page book?

10   Give two reasons why secondary storage is needed in a computer system.

11   What are two typical lengths of magnetic tape?

12   What is bpi and why is it potentially misleading?

13   What three factors affect the speed of access to data held on a magnetic disk?

14   Give one advantage and one disadvantage of a star network.

15   What is the purpose of a multiplexor?

Answers on page 327.

EXERCISES

1   Explain the difference between computer hardware and software.

ACCA December 1985

2   Explain the terms RAM and ROM.

ACCA June 1986

3   Distinguish the main difference between floppy disks and fixed disks.

ACCA June 1986

4   Describe, with suitable illustrations, what is meant by the cylinder concept as applied to magnetic disks.

   ACCA June 1986

5   Distinguish between mainframe, mini and microcomputers.
   (Refer to section 22.4)

6   (a)   What is meant by a LAN? *(Refer to section 22.5.1)*
     (b)   Describe a typical configuration of a LAN noting two advantages and two disadvantages of that configuration.
           (Refer to section 22.5.1)

Answers on page 327.

Fundamentals of software

The previous chapter made the important distinction between hardware and software. This chapter examines the creation of software—programming—in some detail.

It begins by reflecting on the task of the programmer and the evolution of the tools that he or she has at his or her disposal. The point is made that all four generations of languages are still in use and that, unlike hardware, succeeding generations can legitimately co-exist.

BASIC is then introduced as an example of high level language and some elementary commands are listed and demonstrated. These are then placed in the context of the programming craft and common program structures of sequence, selection and iteration are shown with their appropriate BASIC code. This section also demonstrates how such structures can be modelled using Structured English and flowcharts. A supplementary modelling technique, decision tables, is introduced for problems with particularly complex logic.

Two aspects of system software are also briefly considered in this chapter—compilers and operating systems, and it concludes with a short examination of how such processing can be both distributed and operated.

This chapter is designed to give an appreciation of the design and development of programs and some of the other software issues that might be significant to an organisation. It is not concerned with teaching programming!

23.1 PROGRAMMING AND THE PROGRAMMER

Computer programmers write sets of instructions, called programs, which direct the computer through the steps necessary to complete a given task. The programmer will address three main issues: **input**, **processing** and **output**. A parallel can be drawn with a non-computing example.

A manager will be away at a conference on Monday and must leave instructions for a new member of staff to complete a required job. He considers three main issues:

1   Input. Where are the materials which the new employee will need to complete the task? He writes, 'Get the blue file from the stock room. It contains last month's stock purchase forms'.
2   Processing. In what sequence must actions be performed? 'Starting with supplier A, add the total purchase price on each form to give monthly totals by supplier'.
3   Output. What will be produced by the task? 'Write down the supplier's names and monthly totals (one per line) and give a monthly grand total for all stock purchases at the bottom of the page'.

The instructions left by the manager are incomplete and ambiguous. The phrase, 'Starting with supplier A' implies that the task is to be performed in alphabetical order and it is assumed, rightly or wrongly, that the recipient of these instructions will interpret them satisfactorily. Computers do not make inferences. Programming languages have specific rules and are usually constructed in such a way as to avoid ambiguity. For example, the first of the following phrases is not as definitive as the second.

```
IF TITLE = 'MS' OR 'MRS' OR 'MISS'
IF TITLE = 'MS' OR TITLE = 'MRS' OR TITLE = 'MISS'
```

23.2   THE EVOLUTION OF PROGRAMMING LANGUAGES

Computer programming languages have, so far, passed through four distinct evolutionary stages. These four language generations are all in current use because each one has certain advantages.

MACHINE CODE

It is important to remember that computers can only execute programs written in machine code. Each type of machine has its own native language. These machine languages are all variations on a theme: Bit patterns represent hardware level operations, such as ADD, and the internal memory locations of the data to be operated upon.

Example:

1110 0011	The operation code
0000 0100	The address of the first data item
0000 0101	The address of the second data item
0000 0100	Store the result of the operation at this address

Writing machine code is a highly skilled task which requires knowledge of how the computer works internally. The programs are large and very difficult to decipher which makes it time consuming, and therefore expensive, to fix errors (bugs) or make changes. Furthermore, because machine language is specific to each computer a program written for one make or model of machine cannot be run on any other. This can have a disproportionate effect on the cost of upgrading hardware.

However, machine code programs use the computer very efficiently and are commonly used to solve extemely time critical problems such as fast response defence applications.

ASSEMBLER

In assembler programs machine code operations are represented by mnemonics or single words. This makes it easier for the programmer to write code and the programs are easier to read, debug and amend. In the following example two storage areas are loaded with values which are then added together.

Example:

LR	9, (PARTS)	Load register 9 with a value
LR	11, (LABOUR)	Load register 11 with a value.
AR	9, 11	Add the contents of registers 9 and 11.

The assembler programmer still requires knowledge of machine level operations but does not need to keep track of data storage locations. This task is fulfilled by a piece of software called an assembler. It must be remembered that assembler programs cannot be understood directly by the computer. The source code statements (as above) must be translated into their equivalent machine code instructions by the assembler. This assembled code is then run.

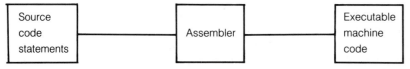

Like machine code, assembler is 'low level', computer specific and therefore not transportable.

HIGH LEVEL LANGUAGES

The high level languages, such as COBOL (Common Business Oriented Language) and BASIC (Beginners All purpose Symbolic Instruction Code), brought programming one more step towards human readable language. Programs are written in simple English-like phrases. This source code is then passed to a program called a compiler which, like the assembler, translates the statements into machine code instructions. However, the compiler will transform a single high level language statement into a number of machine code instructions. The following is an example of a COBOL statement. Its purpose is immediately apparent.

ADD PARTS TO LABOUR GIVING TOTAL_COST.

Because the machine code produced by compilers is 'general purpose', it does not achieve the levels of speed and efficiency attainable with low level programming. However, high level languages are relatively easy to learn so programmers, always much in demand, can be trained faster. The programs are simpler to write and to understand which reduces the costs of developing and maintaining computer applications.

In addition, high level languages are transportable from machine to machine. This is possible because the syntax, or rules of the languages have been standardised and so compilers have been written to translate the English-like source code into suitable machine code for most computer types.

FOURTH GENERATION LANGUAGES (4GLS)

It is very difficult to define the term Fourth Generation Language without fear of contradiction from one quarter or another. However, in some way all 4GLs bring the task of computer programming one stage higher. That is to say, one step nearer the human and one step further away from the machine.

Typically, a 4GL is actually a 'toolkit' of programs which allow the software developer to describe how he or she wishes a finished system to appear. The required data items are defined using one tool from the toolkit. Another tool aids the design of input and enquiry screens. Forms and report designs are produced with yet another. The 4GL then uses these definitions of requirements to produce the necessary programs.

Most 4GLs are built around a database (see section 26.2) and offer graphical output and, perhaps, spreadsheet features (see section 26.5.1).

High level languages are said to be 'procedural' because they list the steps needed to perform a given task. Fourth Generation Languages are non-procedural in so far as it is the problem or requirement that is defined. This can be illustrated by the following:

Example:

A routine is required to produce a list of customers residing in the North West sales area.

To satisfy this requirement in a procedural language the programmer must code statements to:

1   Open the customer file
2   Read a record from the file
3   Test for the end of the file
4   Test the area item on the record for a value of 'NW'
5   Display the record if appropriate
6   Repeat the sequence from 2.

However, using a non-procedural language the programmer is not concerned with the steps (procedure) necessary to accomplish the task. Only the requirement is defined. In this case two statements might be needed:

1   Use the customer file
2   List for area equal to 'NW'.

The early publicity for 4GLs described scenarios wherein end users of computer systems would design and produce their own applications and programmers would become obsolete. This has not yet been the case. Fourth generation language solutions require a great deal of design effort and a detailed knowledge of individual 4GL idiosyncrasies. Instead of dispensing with computer development staff 4GLs have simply created another area of expertise which is in short supply. However, where fourth generation languages are in use, the time required to produce computerised business solutions has often been dramatically reduced.

These four generations of computer languages reflect the evolving hardware technology and the accompanying shifts in computing costs. In the 1950s computer time was very expensive and programmer time was relatively cheap. Programs had to use the machine's resources as efficiently as possible. As the power of computers increased and the demand for automated business systems rose, the cost of computer time became very much less significant compared to that of developing and maintaining the applications. This trend continues. A modern desktop computer may cost around £3,000 and it can out-perform 1960s mainframes which cost hundreds of thousands of pounds and required expensive, controlled environments.

23.3 COMPILERS AND INTERPRETERS

All high level and fourth generation languages are either compiled or interpreted. The role of the compiler has been introduced in the previous section. It translates a source program written in a high level language into coded instructions.

These coded instructions are called object code and consist of bit patterns that are similar to machine code but are not directly executable by the CPU. This object code can be combined with other programs by a linker to produce a machine code program. It is this machine code program that is actually executed when a compiled program is run.

In contrast, an interpreter translates source programs directly into machine code. It takes an instruction from the source program, changes it into its machine code equivalent and then immediately executes it. These steps are then repeated for the subsequent instructions. Thus, there is an immediacy between the execution and error detection and consequently it is relatively easy to correct a statement and re-run the program. In a compiled system the errors need to be traced and corrected in the source program, the program is then re-compiled, linked and then executed. This can easily take 20–30 minutes.

However, because the product of compilation is a machine code program it will normally run faster than its interpreted equivalent. The interpreted version will have to access the interpreter (held in memory) each time it needs to execute a statement. Consequently, compiled programs are normally run faster but are more painstaking to develop and debug.

FIGURE 23.1 **The different stages involved in compiling and interpreting**

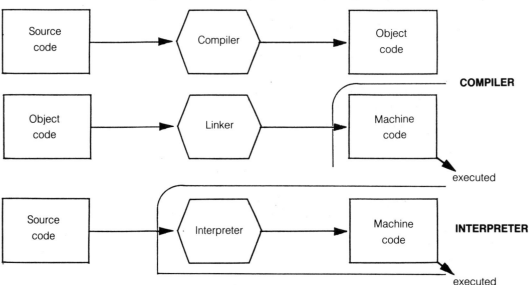

23.4 ELEMENTS OF BASIC

BASIC is an example of a high level language. This section examines some of the elementary constructs of BASIC, while the following section attempts to place these in the context of program structures.

The concept of the **variable** is central to all programming. Values should rarely be defined in a program because this provides unnecessary restrictions on the use and application of the software. Defining variables in a program allows different values to be passed through successive runnings and hence increases the usefulness of the software. For example, a stock item costs £50.00 and VAT is applied to it at 15% to give its gross price. The following program could be written but would be very restrictive.

$$50.00*(1+0.15)=57.5$$

Notice the use of * to represent multiplication and the use of brackets to enforce precedence.

This statement can be made more general by defining variables:

$$NET\_PRICE*(1+0.15)=GROSS\_PRICE$$

This is applicable to all values of NET_PRICE (of which 50.00 is just one example). A further enhancement is to permit changes in the VAT rate:

$$NET\_PRICE*(1+VAT\_RATE)=GROSS\_PRICE$$

The result is a general purpose statement which holds for all products and for which the values of the variables (NET_PRICE and VAT_RATE) are entered at the 'run-time' of the program.

The assignment of a value to a variable is performed in BASIC by the LET statement. Variables in BASIC are traditionally given names which can be a single letter or a letter followed by one digit. This restriction has been removed from many contemporary compilers.

```
10      LET A = 50.00
20      LET B =  0.15
30      LET C = A*(1+B)
```

The figures on the left hand side are the line numbers of the program. These line numbers give the order of which a program executes.

A SELECTION OF BASIC STATEMENTS

1   PRINT is used to output a value to a terminal:

```
40      PRINT C
```

Character strings can be included in the statement to permit annotation of the output. These are placed within double quotes in the print line and usually followed by a comma or semi-colon to ensure that the value appears on the same line as the explanatory text. For example:

```
40      PRINT 'Gross Price=';C
```

This will be output as:

```
Gross Price = 57.50
```

2 INPUT calls for values to be entered by the user from the terminal:

> 5   INPUT A,B

The variable names are separated by commas. When the program encounters this statement it will stop and request two values from the user for use in subsequent program execution.

3 REM allows the annotation of programs. It permits the definition of remarks which annotate and explain the purpose and activity of the program:

> 3   REM GROSS PRICE CALCULATION PROGRAM

REM statements are ignored by the program.

4 END denotes the termination of the program. Each program should have one (but only one) END statement and this should be given the highest line number:

> 60   END

5 STOP also permits the termination of the program. However, unlike END this does not need to have the highest line number in the program and so can appear anywhere.

6 IF . . THEN controls the direction of the program:

> 31   REM CHECK FOR DISCOUNT
> 32   REM IF GROSS PRICE LESS THAN OR EQUAL TO 1000
>   THEN SKIP TO LINE 40
> 32   IF C<=1000 THEN 40
> 33   REM ENTER DISCOUNT RATE
> 34   INPUT D
> 35   LET E=C*D
> 36   LET C=C–E

The control of programs is dealt with in more detail later.

7 GOTO also permits the execution of ascending lines to be overruled. A GOTO switches control directly to the line number specified in the GOTO statement. For example:

> 55   GOTO 5

routes the program back to the statement contained in line 5.

8 A similar facility is provided by the GOSUB command. Most programs are constructed from a set a modular sub-routines. Each sub-routine contains a set of self-contained instructions that perform a well-defined function—for example, calculating a discount, establishing a new customer record, updating the stock records, etc. These sub-routines are called by the main program, executed and terminated by returning control back to the calling program. The GOSUB command directs control to the first line of the sub-routine, which itself ends with a RETURN statement that will allow the main program to continue execution at where it left off. For example:

> 400   GOSUB 2000
> 410   PRINT A
> . . . .
> . . . .
> 2000   REM SUB-ROUTINE FOR DISCOUNT CALCULATION
>   . . . .
>   . . . .
> 2370   RETURN

9 INPUT is concerned with the interactive input of values for variables in that the program will stop and request entry from the screen. The input values are allocated to variables through the LET statement.

10 For a large number of predictable values BASIC uses the READ command to assign values contained in a DATA statement to specified variables. A DATA statement gives a list of values separated by commas, for example:

200   DATA 0.15,0.12,0.09,0

These are assigned to appropriate variables through the READ command which gives variable names separated by commas.

150   READ M,N,O,P

This will allocate M=0.15
N=0.12
O=0.09
P=0

During the execution of a program a READ variable will be allocated the next available DATA value.
So, for example, in the following program:

```
10    READ A
20    READ B
30    LET C = A +B
40    READ D
50    LET E = C/D
60    DATA 10,20,3
70    PRINT E
80    END
```

The variable A will be assigned 10
The variable B will be assigned 20
The variable D will be assigned 3
The output value E will be 10.

11 DATA statements are usually collected together at the end of the program immediately before the END statement. If all values have been assigned then the next attempted READ will lead to an OUT OF DATA message.

12 BASIC programs can also access external files, so importing data values for use in the program. Clearly, internally stored figures (in the DATA command) has limited scope and reduces the generality of the program.

23.5 THE CRAFT OF PROGRAMMING

Programming can be viewed as a three phase task.
1 **Problem definition**   A program is required to validate customer orders. Before any code is written, a detailed analysis of the requirements must be carried out. When are discounts applied? What happens when an item ordered is out of stock? How are customer credit limits checked? and so on.
2 **Problem description**   To aid understanding, a suitable way of documenting the findings of the analysis must be used. This documentation is best produced in a way that 'models' the proposed solution. The model must be validated by following the logical processes that

it describes using suitable test data. This validation will ensure that the program design is complete before any code is written. It is very time consuming, and expensive, to fix design faults during the program coding phase.

There are a number of modelling techniques available. Among those most commonly used are **Structured English, flowcharts** and **decision tables**. Examples of these techniques appear later in this text.

3 **Program Coding**   The programmer will now write the program statements to perform the steps defined in the program design. Once written, this source code is submitted for compilation. At this time the compiler may reject the program because of syntax (language rules) errors in which case the programmer will correct the code and recompile until no errors are found.

Compilers do not check that programs are logically correct, only that they obey the rules of the language. To verify that a program provides the required solution, data is designed to test each circumstance that the program will encounter. Predicted results are evaluated against the actual output of the program and any inconsistencies investigated and resolved.

The first two phases will overlap. As the analysis is conducted so the model will emerge. However, if the problem definition and description are not complete before phase three begins then any errors in the design may not become apparent until the program is tested. This is an expensive waste of time and effort and leads to badly structured programs which are difficult to maintain causing yet another increase in software costs.

Structured English assists program design by simplifying the task of describing logical processes. Structured programs consist of three basic construct types: sequence, selection and repetition and may, in addition, pass control to other programs or routines. Some languages directly support Structured English constructs. In those which do not, equivalents can be coded.

Flow charts aid program design by diagramatically representing the logical processes required to complete the application. In this text the following flowchart symbols are used.

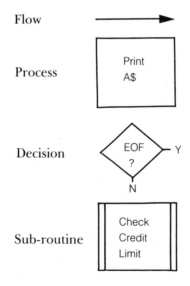

The following are examples of Structured English constructs with equivalent flowcharts and high level language statements. The chosen language is a form of BASIC which does not directly support Structured English constructs using REMarks. Note that indentation is used to help clarify the logic.

It is also worth noting that many modern BASIC compilers, such as Borland's TURBO BASIC, not only allow longer variable names, as shown in this text, but also fully support structured programming constructs such as IF/ENDIF and CASE/ENDCASE. Using such compilers makes structured programming both simpler and more efficient than it appears here.

SEQUENCE

Statements are executed in the order written.

Example 1

Structured English

Open order file
Get order
Print order number

Flowchart

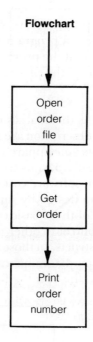

BASIC statements

```
100   REM Open order file
110       OPEN 'ORDERS' FOR INPUT AS #1
120   REM Get Order
130       INPUT #1, ORDNO$, CUST$, ITEM$, QTY, VAL
140   REM Print order number
150       PRINT 'Order Number: '; ORDNO$
```

PASSING CONTROL (DO)

Control is passed to another routine which could be within the program (as in Example 2) or may be another program. In either case, once the called routine has completed, control returns to the calling routine.

Example 2

Structured English

Read order
DO Look up stock item routine
IF . . .

Flowchart

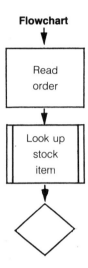

BASIC Statements

```
1180  REM Read Order
1190      INPUT #1, ORDNO$, CUST$, ITEM$, QTY, VAL
1200  REM DO Look up Stock Item Routine
1210      GOSUB 3000
1220  REM IF . . .
1230      IF . . .
. . . .


. . . .
3000  REM Look up Stock Item
3010  REM
3020  REM Read Stock Table
. . . .
3250  REM End Of Look up Stock Item
3260      RETURN
```

SELECTION

Selections are dependent upon conditions. That is, if a condition is true then one action is taken, if the condition false, another. Conditions are evaluated against current storage contents.

SELECTION—SINGLE BRANCH (IF, ENDIF)

In Example 3 the number ordered for a particular item is compared to the stock level for that item. If there is insufficient stock to fulfil the order then the condition is true (stock level *is* less than order quantity) and a reject flag is set to the value 1. However, if the condition is false no action takes place. In either case, control passes to the ENDIF and the following DO statement is executed.

Example 3   **Structured English**

IF Stock Level Is Less Than Order Quantity
      Set Reject Flag To 1
ENDIF
DO . . .

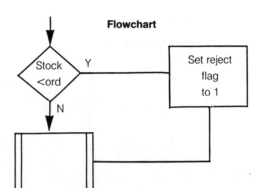

Flowchart

BASIC statements

```
1690   REM IF Insufficient Stock Set The Reject Flag To 1
1700        IF STKLVL < QTY THEN LET RJCT = 1
1710   REM DO . . .
1720        GOSUB . . .
```

SELECTION—DOUBLE BRANCH (IF, ELSE, ENDIF)

In Example 4, if the condition is true then one process must take place and control passes to the
ENDIF. If the condition is false control is passed to the ELSE statement and the second process
is actioned. In no case will both processes occur.

Example 4   **Structured English**

IF Order Value + Outstanding Balance Exceeds Credit Limit
      Set Reject Flag To 2
ELSE (Credit Limit Is Not Exceeded)
      Add Order Value to Outstanding Balance
ENDIF
IF . . .

Flowchart

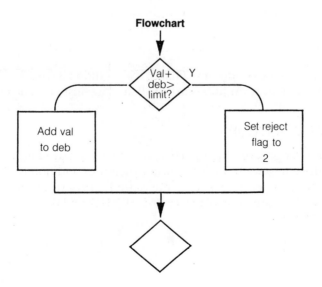

BASIC Statements

```
1840   REM Check Order Does Not Exceed Credit Limit
1850        IF VAL + DEB > LIMIT THEN 1860 ELSE 1890
1860          REM Credit Limit Exceeded – Set Reject Flag To 2
1870          LET RJCT = 2
1880          GOTO 1910
1890   REM ELSE (Credit Not Exceeded) Add Order Value To Debit
1900          DEB = DEB + VAL
1910   REM ENDIF
1960   REM IF . . .
```

SELECTION—MULTIPLE BRANCH (CASE, ENDCASE)

Where a number of possible conditions exist, each with an exclusive consequence, the multiple branch CASE constsruct will be used. Each condition is evaluated in turn. False conditions are not actioned. When a true condition is found the appropriate statements are executed after which, no other CASEs in the constraint are evaluated. Control passes directly to the ENDCASE.

Example 5

Structured English

```
CASE Reject Flag Is Set To 1
       Print 'Insufficient Stock'
       DO Send Advice Routine
CASE Reject Flag Is Set To 2
       Print 'Credit Level Exceeded'
       DO Send Statement Routine
CASE Reject Flag Is Set to 3
       Print 'Invalid Stock Code'
CASE Reject Flag Is Set To 4
       Print 'Invalid Customer Code'
ENDCASE
DO . . .
```

Flowchart

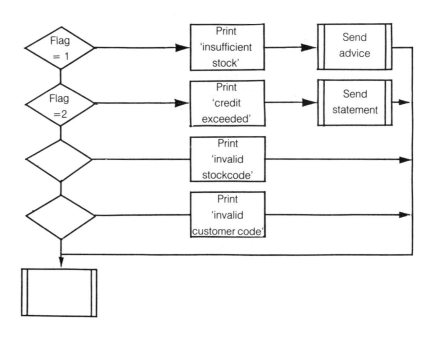

BASIC statements

```
2510   REM CASE
2520       IF RJCT = 1 THEN 2530 ELSE 2570
2530         REM Reject Flag Is Set To 1
2540         PRINT 'Insufficient Stock'
2550         GOSUB 4000
2560         GOTO 2720
2570   REM CASE
2580       IF RJCT = 2 THEN 2590 ELSE 2630
2590         REM Reject Flag Is Set To 2
2600         PRINT 'Credit Level Exceeded'
2610         GOSUB 5000
2620         GOTO 2720
2630   REM CASE
2640       IF RJCT = 3 THEN 2650 ELSE 2680
2650         REM Reject Flag Is Set To 3
2660         PRINT 'Invalid Stock Code'
2670         GOTO 2720
2680   REM CASE
2690       IF RJCT = 4 THEN 2700 ELSE 2720
2700         REM Reject Flag Is Set To 4
2710         PRINT 'Invalid Customer Code'
2720   REM ENDCASE
2730 REM DO . . .
. . . .


. . . .
4000   REM Send No Stock Advice Routine
. . . .
4780       RETURN
. . . .

. . . .
5000   REM Send Statement Routine
. . . .
5690       RETURN
```

REPETITION (DOWHILE, ENDWHILE)

This construct is termed a DOWHILE meaning 'DO these following statements WHILE this condition exists'. If the condition is true control passes to the next statement and all following statements are executed until the ENDWHILE is encountered. Control then loops back to the DOWHILE and the condition is evaluated again. If the DO WHILE condition is false, control passes to the statement following ENDWHILE.

Example 6

Structured English

```
DOWHILE There Are Orders To Be Processed
        IF Reject Flag Is Set
          DO Print Reject Reason
        ELSE (Order Not Rejected)
          Add Order Value To Daily Revenue Total
        ENDIF
ENDWHILE
DO . . .
```

Flowchart

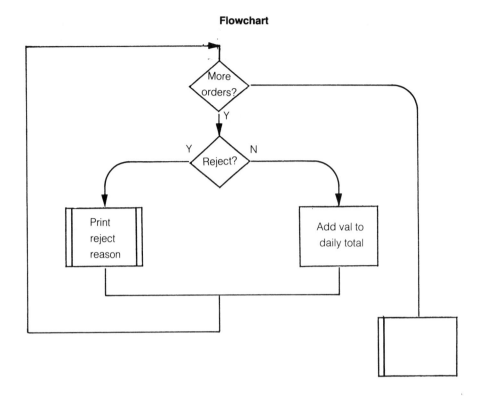

BASIC Statements

```
270   REM DO WHILE Not The End Of The Orders File
280       IF END #1 THEN 420
290        REM IF Reject Flag Set
300        IF RJCT > 0 THEN 310 ELSE 340
310          REM DO Print Reject Reason
320          GOSUB 2400
330          GOTO
340        REM ELSE (Not Rejected)
350          REM Add Order Value To Daily Revenue Total
360          LET TOTREV = TOTREV + VAL
370        REM ENDIF
380        REM Get Next Order
390        INPUT #1, ORDNO$, CUST$, ITEM$, QTY, VAL
400   REM ENDWHILE
410       GOTO 270
420   REM DO . . .
```

23.5.1 Decision tables

Complex logic can often be better summarised by using a limited entry decision table. For example, the following text describes the basis upon which discount is allocated to a customer's orders.

> If an order exceeds $5,000 then it automatically qualifies for a 5% discount. If this customer has, in the past year, totalled orders of over $30,000 then an extra 2.5% discount is given for orders over $5,000. In addition, there are a number of specifically targetted new customers who are also given 3.5% discount on orders below $5,000. No other discounts are currently in use.

The decision table shows the conditions that affect the discount decision and the actions associated with a condition or combination of conditions. The decision table is divided into four sections:

Condition stub	Condition entries
Action stub	Action entries

The table is constructed by:

1   Identifying all the conditions in the narrative and writing these down in the condition stub.

        c1:   Is Order > $5000?
        c2:   Is Total Orders > $30000?
        c3:   Is Order from a Special Target Customer?

        Care must be taken to not specify mutually exclusive conditions. Is Order >$5000? is simply the flip-side of condition 1 (c1).

2   Identifying all the actions possible and recording them in the action stub.

        a1:   7.5% discount (5 + 2.5)
        a2:   5.0% discount
        a3:   3.5% discount
        a4:   No discount

3   This gives the following layout:

```
c1:   Is Order > $5000?            |
c2:   Is Total Orders > $30000?    |
c3:   Is Order from a Special?     |
-----------------------------------+---------------------------
a1:   7.5% discount                |
a2:   5.0% discount                |
a3:   3.5% discount                |
a4:   No discount                  |
```

4   The number of rules, shown as columns, can be calculated by using the formula 2^c where c is the number of conditions in the table. In this example three rules generates $2^3 = 8$ rules. The rules express whether a condition holds or not and this is represented by a Y(es) or a N(o). A suggested format for entering these Ys and Ns is given below. For Z rules, the first row has Z/2 Ys and Z/2 Ns, reducing down to the last row which is always YNYNYN etc.

```
c1:   Is Order >$5000?           |  Y  Y  Y  Y  N  N  N  N
c2:   Is Total Orders > $30000 ? |  Y  Y  N  N  Y  Y  N  N
c3:   Is Order from a Special?   |  Y  N  Y  N  Y  N  Y  N
---------------------------------+---------------------------
a1:   7.5% discount              |
a2:   5.0% discount              |
a3:   3.5% discount              |
a4:   No discount                |
```

5 Action entries are now made. These are derived by applying each rule or combination of conditions to the narrative.

c1:	Is Order>$5000?	Y	Y	Y	Y	N	N	N	N
c2:	Is Total Orders > $30000?	Y	Y	N	N	Y	Y	N	N
c3:	Is Order from a Special?	Y	N	Y	N	Y	N	Y	N
a1:	7.5% discount	X	X						
a2:	5.0% discount			X	X				
a3:	3.5% discount					X	X	X	
a4:	No discount								X

6 Check the table for redundancy. This is present if a condition is irrelevant in the definition of an action. This happens in the above example where a targetted new customer cannot have a cumulative order of over $30000.

This is removed from the final table and a dash substituted. This effectively means that this condition is irrelevant to the action outcome and so can either be Y or N.

c1:	Is Order>$5000?	Y	Y	Y	N	N	N
c2:	Is Total Orders > $3000?	Y	N	N	Y	N	N
c3:	Is Order from a Special?	–	Y	N	–	Y	N
a1:	7.5% discount	X					
a2:	5.0% discount		X	X			
a3:	3.5% discount				X	X	
a4:	No discount						X

23.6 OPERATING SYSTEMS

A type of system software—the compiler—has already been introduced. However, there is an even more fundamental layer of software between the hardware and application programs and packages. This is the operating system.

Operating systems try to achieve two major objectives:

1 To provide a friendly and useful interface between the user and the computer hardware. The operating system takes care of file storage and file location, ensuring that each file can be reliably retrieved when the appropriate command is given by the user. It will also give error messages (file does not exist) and perhaps suggest remedial action (replace disk and re-try).

2 To manage the computer resources efficiently so that fast devices (such as the CPU) are not slowed down by slow devices such as printers and human beings sitting at terminals. This is particularly critical in multi-user systems where the processor needs to be acting on several tasks at once. The operating system swaps jobs in and out of the processor so that while one task is waiting for further input the processor can be working on other jobs. It should be clear that this complicates the work of the operating system, because, for example, it must record exactly where a task has been interrupted so that it may be resumed correctly when the CPU is free.

The operating system also has a number of subsidiary tasks:

(a) **Memory management** The processor can only work on data and programs resident in the primary storage. Most operating systems have a memory management facility which allocates primary store to those programs or part of programs that need it whilst everything else is written out on disk. This leads to continual swapping between memory and disk and appears to give more memory than is actually available.

(b) **Input and output control** An example of this is spooling whereby print requests are placed in a queue of files waiting to be printed. Each file is then printed in turn and the user can return to other tasks as the processor is not tied up with the relatively simple job of file printing.

(c) **Accounting information** An operating system will record how long it spends on tasks so that charges can be levied against the appropriate departments. It will also record information about file accesses (such as sources, time, date, etc) and has been instrumental in the detection of most computer fraud.

(d) **Housekeeping commands** The operating system will have a number of commands which permit the deletion and renaming of files, the display of disk and memory space, the transfer of files, etc.

Most mainframe computer manufacturers have developed their own proprietary operating systems designed around their particular hardware. In contrast, the microcomputer market has standardised around MS-DOS (PC-DOS) and, previously, CP/M. Microcomputers are normally single user machines with the processor dedicated to the tasks required by that user. However, this means that only one task can be performed at a time. This can be overcome by making the operating system **multi-tasking** where the user can undertake a number of simultaneous tasks. These **concurrent** operating systems are still restricted to one user but that one user may undertake a number of simultaneous tasks.

This multi-tasking facility must be distinguished from **multi-user** systems where many users may simultaneously execute different tasks. One of the most popular of these multi-user operating systems is UNIX. In making the leap from single to multiple users the operating systems begin to encounter some of the processor and memory management problems that have always faced mainframe systems. Further complications are caused by the need to ensure an adequate response time for users at every terminal whilst minimising the size of the operating system itself so that it does not take up a disproportionate amount of memory and disk space.

23.7 PROCESSING OPTIONS

This chapter has concentrated on the processes of an information system. The context of these within the business system will become clearer when the data flow diagram model and its associated design concepts are introduced in the next two chapters. The programming of processes has provided the focus of this chapter, supplemented by descriptions of system software such as compilers and operating systems.

This chapter concludes with a brief examination of the options that are available for organising the processing. These are concerned with distribution and operation.

DISTRIBUTION

There is a distinction between centralised and distributed processing. A centralised processing policy is typically implemented with a large corporate mainframe which undertakes all significant processing in the organisation. It may be connected to remote sites for data input but the terminals at those sites have little processing power. They are essentially means of data entry.

There is a tendency to move away from these monolithic mainframes to a more distributed policy which places processing power at local sites. These sites are then connected to allow data transfer and organisation-wide processing. Two distinct types of distribution are worth mentioning:

1   **Hierarchy of processors** This uses a large central mainframe at the top of the hierarchy connected to regional minicomputers which are linked, in turn, to departmental microcomputers.

2   **Networks** Workstations all cooperating without a clear hierarchy. Topologies of such networks were examined in the previous chapter.

The growth of distributed processing is due to a number of factors, including:

(a)   Reaction against the lack of control and access to large central mainframes. The tendency for enterprises to re-group themselves on de-centralised lines and establish cost and profit centres works against centralised systems. These groups need to have control over the scheduling, cost and delivery of their information systems.

(b)   Avoidance of catastrophic effects of losing a data centre due to natural hazards or industrial strife. Distributed systems should provide higher availability and reliability than centralised systems.

(c)   Pacing the growth of development more carefully. Upgrading centralised mainframe systems often required massive investments which taxed the financial resources of the company. Distributed systems offer a more modular approach, upgrading in planned increments throughout the organisation.

OPERATION

1   **Batch processing** refers to systems where documents are collected together and entered into the system as a complete batch. Most of these batches contain related documents— sales invoices received today, this week's time-sheets, all notifications of absences this month, etc. Certain batch controls can be applied in an attempt to ensure correct data entry (see Chapter 25).

2   **On-line applications** enter individual data transactions into the system. Consequently, data is entered as it occurs (an order is received, a resignation is accepted). This makes the transaction available for processing much sooner than its batch counterpart and this may provide significant organisational advantages. However, this is likely to be a more expensive option as well as giving less opportunity for data control.

3   **Real-time** is a term often associated with fast response on-line systems. Perhaps a more appropriate definition of a real-time system is that it is an application where each transaction must be dealt with immediately and the resulting output is returned to the system sufficiently quickly to affect the state of the system. Thus a lift control system must respond to a transaction (a request from a floor) and this radically changes the state of the system (the position of the lift) and its response to the next transaction. A similar transaction (a request from Floor 2) could be dealt with in completely different ways depending upon the previous transaction (the lift may be on Floor 3, Floor 8, out-of-service, ascending, descending, etc). Contrast this with an on-line entry of employee resignations where the processing of the transaction will be unaffected by previous transactions and will have no immediate effect on the physical employment system.

In general, applications are moving away from centralised batch systems towards distributed on-line applications. However, there are still instances where batching input documents is appropriate and the large central mainframe fits the organisational style and nature of the company's processing.

SUMMARY

1   Computer programmers write sets of instructions, called programs, which direct the computer through the steps necessary to complete a given task.

2   Programming is concerned with problem definition, modelling and coding.

3 Computer programming languages have passed through four generations—machine code, assembler, high level languages and fourth generation language. All are still currently in use.

4 High level and fourth generation languages use compilers which turn the source code of the language into machine code instructions.

5 Elementary syntactical constructs of BASIC were introduced as an example of a high level language.

6 BASIC statements were then examined within common program structures—sequence, selection and repetition. Three models for problem definition were introduced—Structured English, flowcharts and decision tables.

7 A further element of system software was introduced—the operating system.

8 The chapter concluded with a review of modes of processing operation and distribution.

SELF-TEST QUESTIONS

1 Name the four generations of programming languages

2 What is an important distinction between an assembler and a compiler?

3 Distinguish between a procedural and a non-procedural statement

4 What does BASIC stand for?

5 What instruction would you give in BASIC to:

(a) end a program
(b) output a value to a terminal
(c) make comments about the function of the program
(d) jump to line 120

6 What symbol is used on a flowchart to show a decision?

7 If a decision table has 6 conditions, how many rules would it have?

8 List four functions of an operating system

9 Give two reasons why processing might be distributed throughout an organisation

10 List three ways of organising the operation of processing

Answers on page 329.

EXERCISES

1 The following computer program has been written in BASIC and is used to smooth a set of data relating to the quarterly expense account of your company.

```
10    REM EXPONENTIAL SMOOTHING PROGRAM
20    REM READ SMOOTHING FACTOR
30    READ S
40    REM READ PERIOD REFERENCE
50    READ P
60    IF P=99 THEN STOP
80    READ E
90    IF P=1 THEN LET F1=E
100   LETF2=F1+S*(E–F1)
110   PRINT "EXPENSE VALUE=£";E
120   PRINT "OLD FORECAST=£";INT(F1+0.5),
130   PRINT "NEW FORECAST=£";INT(F2+0.5)
```

```
140   LET F1=F2
150   GOTO 40
160   DATA 0.2
170   DATA 1,743,2,782,3,827
180   DATA 4,876,5,805,6,842
190   DATA 7,876,99
200   END
```

Required:

The command RUN is entered into the computer. What is the action at the following statement lines the first time each statement is executed?

> line 30
> line 50
> line 60
> line 80
> line 90
> line 100
> line 130

ACCA June 1986

2   In clearing the papers of a colleague who recently left your company you come across the computer program listed below together with its test data and its associated results.

```
10    LET A=0
20    LET B=0
30    LET C=0
40    INPUT D
50    IF D=999 THEN 200
60    INPUT E
70    LET A=A+D*E
80    LET B=B+E
90    LET C=C+D*D*E
100   GOTO 40
200   PRINT A/B
210   PRINT(C/B)–(A/B)*(A/B)
220   STOP
230   END
```

Test Data 30,4,35,7,40,9,45,6,50,2,999
Test results (to the nearest integer) 39,32

Required:

(a)   i   Accepting that your colleague was not an expert programmer but he was able to produce accurate results, trace the action of the program, by tabulating the contents of the registers A,B,C,D and E when it is run using test data.

        ii   Using the analysis in (i) describe the purpose of the program.

        iii List with a brief explanation those items which you would consider should be included in the documentation of a computer program so that a proper company standard can be achieved.

(b)   i   Distinguish between a low level language and a high level language.

        ii   Distinguish between a compiler and an interpreter.
           (Refer to section 23.3)

ACCA June 1987

3   Your company has recently installed a new mainframe computer system. The company's own programming team has been given the task of producing a new program suite to enable the company payroll to be computerised. You have been asked by management to produce an article for the staff newsletter explaining the steps involved in producing the payroll programs.

Required:
(a)   Explain what is meant by a source program and describe how it might be coded. *(Refer to section 23.3)*
(b)   Explain what is meant by testing and debugging.
(c)   Outline the likely details to be found in the program documentation.

ACCA December 1985

4   Explain the difference between machine code, assembly language and a high level language. *(Refer to section 23.2)*

5   Construct flowcharts for the programs given in Exercises 1 and 2 of this chapter.

Answers on page 329.

Business systems

It is important to appreciate something of the activity of business before the computer's contribution to the enterprise can be properly understood. Consequently, most examinations require a background understanding of common business systems and the way that they interact. These usually provide the context for examination questions rather than forming a question in their own right. The significance of this must be appreciated. Questions cast in the framework of an order processing system must be answered within that context. Answers that fail to respond to the business issues concerned are likely to be penalised.

This chapter explores common business systems using the data flow diagram model. It does not prescribe 'ideal' or complete ways of organising the activity but rather explores some of the issues involved. It must be stressed that these diagrams are simply being used as a mechanism for:

(a)   Showing how enterprises work and how their systems interact.
(b)   A basis for system design. The diagrams highlight four important design facets: inputs, outputs, processes and files. These design areas are examined in detail in the following chapter.

24.1   BUSINESS ACTIVITIES—THREE LEVELS OF SYSTEM

A business system operates at three levels:

1   **Physical** The provision and passage of goods and services. Goods are assembled and sent to customers.
2   **Information** Each physical activity is normally recorded in an information flow. For example: The despatch of goods is shown in a despatch note, the purchase of services in a purchase note or requisition.
3   **Accounting** Financial expenditure and income is normally associated with every activity. Each action has a cost (labour, materials, stationery, insurance, heating, lighting, etc) and these all have to be accounted for and built into the price of a product.

Many of the information and accounting systems are suitable for computerisation. This chapter examines three information systems (sales, purchasing and stock control) and three accounting systems (sales, purchase and nominal ledgers). It concludes with a brief review of other business systems.

24.2   A MODEL FOR SHOWING BUSINESS SYSTEMS: THE DATA FLOW DIAGRAM

The data flow diagram is a simple model for showing the activities of a business system. It is introduced here as:

(a)   A mechanism for exploring the content of business systems. This is based on the principle that 'a picture is worth a thousand words'.
(b)   A basis for the computerisation of those business systems. The diagram highlights the design requirements of a business computer system. Each design feature is picked up in the next chapter from the data flow diagrams introduced here.

The data flow diagram shows the passage of data through a system with four basic symbols.

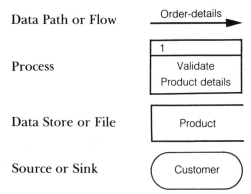

Data Path or Flow

Process

Data Store or File

Source or Sink

DATA PATH OR FLOW

A data path or flow can be viewed as a route which enables packets of data to travel from one point to another. The path can be viewed as a road with busloads of data passing along it at certain intervals. Data may flow from a source to a process, or vice versa, or to and from a data store or process. The flow is shown as an arrowed line with the arrowhead showing the direction of flow.

Data flows must be named, preferably with titles which clearly describe the flows, and no two data flow should have the same name. The data flows moving in and out of stores do not require names, the store name being sufficient to describe them.

PROCESSES

Processes represent transformations, changing incoming data flows into outgoing data flows. Processes must also be named using descriptions which convey an impression of what happens to the data as it passes through the process. An ideal naming convention is an active verb (extract, compute, verify) followed by an object or object clause. For example, verify that customer is credit-worthy.

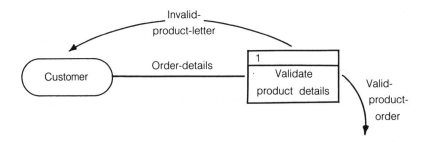

DATA STORES OR FILES

The store is a repository of data. It may be a card index, a database file or a wastepaper basket. Stores should also be given convenient descriptive names. Data stores may be included more than once to simplify the presentation of the data flow diagram. This is indicated by the use of an additional stripe on the repeating store.

A flow to a store may be single headed with the arrow head pointing towards the process. This is to signify that the process does not alter the contents of the store, it only uses the data available. However, if the contents of the store are altered by the process, as well as being read, then the diagram uses a double-headed arrow.

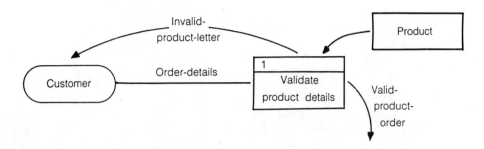

In this way a single-headed arrow shows READ (looking at the data only) or WRITE (changing data only) operations. In circumstances where the data is both examined and changed (READ and WRITE) then a double headed arrow is used.

SOURCES OR SINKS

A source or sink is a person or organisation which enters or receives data from the system but is considered to be outside the context of the data flow model. Stores may again be duplicated in a completed data flow diagram to permit simpler presentation. An additional vertical stripe is again used to show this duplication.

A duplicated source   A duplicated store

24.3 BUSINESS SYSTEMS

This brief review of business systems begins by examining the procedures required to deal with customer orders.

24.3.1 Customer order entry

An order entry system is concerned with controlling the passage of a customer order through from receipt to notification of despatch. The main objective of the system is to minimise the time taken for this process. Fast order turnaround is a key factor in customer service.

Order handling also places particular emphasis on validation. It might check whether:

(a)   the products requested are actually sold by the company
(b)   the customer has paid the correct amount for the products ordered
(c)   the customer requesting credit has a satisfactory credit rating
(d)   the products ordered are in stock.

Speed of processing can be a major company objective. If an enterprise offers 'same day delivery' then the order entry system must effectively support this.

Figure 24.1 is primarily concerned with order processing for a cash with sale system, such as a mail-order company requiring payment with order. Other systems, particularly those concerned with business to business transactions, usually adopt an 'on account' arrangement where goods are supplied on credit with the understanding that the account will be settled within a certain time—usually 30 days.

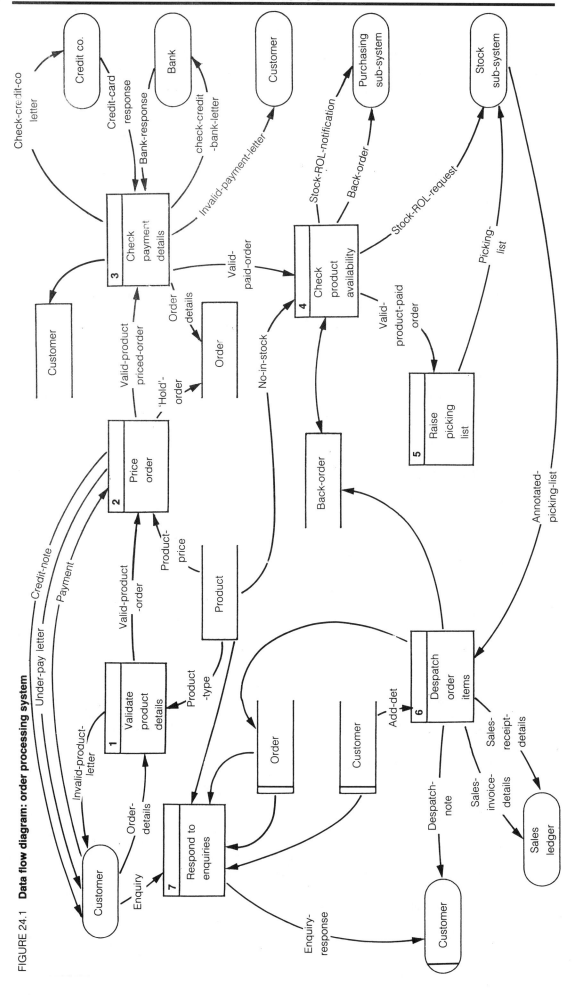

FIGURE 24.1 **Data flow diagram: order processing system**

Seven major processes are shown in Figure 24.1

1 **Validate product details** The customer order details are checked to ensure that they refer to products actually stocked by the company. These product types are maintained on a product file. Invalid products are notified to the customer in a standard letter.

2 **Price the order** The price for each order is calculated by multiplying the cost of each product (from the product file) by the quantity ordered. This value is validated against the payment submitted by the customer. Over payment results in a credit note, under payments are notified to the customer and 'held' on the order file until the balance is submitted.

3 **Check payment details** The payment method in this example can either be cash, cheque or credit card. Cheques are cleared with the appropriate bank and the order is held until the cheque is cleared. Credit card payments are checked with the appropriate credit card company.

4 **Check product availability** The ordered goods are checked for availability (from the product file). If an order cannot be completely fulfilled then a back order is raised for the outstanding goods. Products that have now reached their Reorder Level (ROL) are notified to both the purchasing and stock re-ordering systems.

5 **Raise picking list** The picking list is a summary of all the product line quantities for a batch of orders. This is passed to the stock sub-system where the goods are physically 'picked'.

6 **Despatch order items** The annotated picking list gives the items that have been picked and packed ready for despatch. The list should be the same as in process 5 (with a tick confirming picking) but in practice the two may be different. Products that are theoretically in stock may have disappeared due to carelessness, decay or theft.

   The order file can now be updated to record delivery and the despatch note is raised and sent directly to the customer. Sales receipt and invoice details are sent to the stock ledger system. It is likely that a confirming invoice will be optional and will only be provided when the customer specifically requests it.

7 **Order enquiries** It is common for an organisation to receive many queries concerning particular orders, products and accounts. Good customer relations dictates that these are answered quickly and accurately.

   If the system uses an 'on account' facility then processes 2 and 3 are replaced by:

(a) Check customer credit. A customer order is checked against the credit information stored on a customer file. If the credit limit is not exceeded then the order is passed for subsequent processing. However, if the amount on credit now exceeds the agreed credit limit then the order is placed on hold whilst the account is investigated. Management may request the payment of outstanding invoices and make it clear that no further goods will be supplied until that payment is received and cleared. Alternatively, management may simply sanction an extension of the credit limit—so freeing the order for processing.

(b) New customers will have a credit limit given to them after appropriate checks with the bank and other professional references.

(c) Sales invoice details are sent to the sales ledger for the raising of an appropriate invoice. This will itemise the goods and services provided and specifies when payment is due. An invoice must be prepared whenever credit is extended to a customer.

The order entry system is fairly straightforward. It benefits from:

1 Integration with the financial ledgers. Raised invoice details are passed directly to the accounts receivable system (The sales ledger).

2 Integration with inventory control. Sales orders from customers is one of the major inputs required by the stock control system.

3 Order data is very important to an organisation because it reflects the fruit of its activities. Thus, the ability to request information about the pattern of orders may aid marketing and product strategy. Similarly, order volumes may be used to evaluate sales promotions and marketing initiatives.

24.3.2   Purchasing

Purchasing is primarily concerned with identifying and agreeing requests for products and materials, ensuring efficient and correct delivery of goods and reviewing suppliers so that they continue to offer the enterprise the best possible combination of price and service.

The importance of management information is shown on the data flow diagram (Figure 24.2). The management reports should aid the control, selection and evaluation of the company's supplies as well as contributing to the company's cash flow analysis.

The data flow diagram gives six main processes:

1 **Price stock request** The example system shows purchase requests coming from three main sources:
(a) A purchase request from the stock system identifying items that have reached their Reorder Level (ROL).
(b) Back orders from the order sub-system.
(c) Back orders already pending in the purchasing sub-system.
The stock-ROL-notification is used as a fourth source when it differs from the purchase request.
The products on these requests are priced (using the price on the product file) and passed to the second process.

2 **Establish order list** The cost of the requested order items is compared with the likely incoming funds derived from custsomer sales. Other costs (such as administrative overheads, salaries, etc) are also contained in the cash flow analysis. An established order list is agreed that reflects what can safely be afforded. This may contain all purchase requests (in the good times) or only the most urgent (in times of financial difficulty). Requests which cannot be fulfilled are raised as back orders.

3 **Check supplier data** The cost and availability of products are checked in a supplier file.

4 **Place order** Purchase orders are placed with selected suppliers.

5 **Check received details** The company receives three things back from the supplier:
(a) A purchase invoice showing the amount owing for the goods and services.
(b) A goods despatched note giving the items physically picked and dispatched.
(c) The physical goods themselves.
Each of these is checked against each other before the purchase invoice is passed for payment.

6 **Produce management reports** A number of reports are required. For example:
(a) A list of current suppliers and their terms of supply.
(b) Back orders currently in the system and their value and creation date.
(c) Order listings for cash flow analysis.
(d) Analysis of notional price and price paid so that purchasing policies can be evaluated and adjusted.

Thus, the purchasing system is mainly concerned with determining and monitoring the supply of goods and services. It also needs to ensure that purchases are made in the light of the projected cash flow analysis. It is usually unacceptable to place orders for goods which are unlikely to be paid for.

FIGURE 24.2 **Data flow diagram: purchasing sub-system**

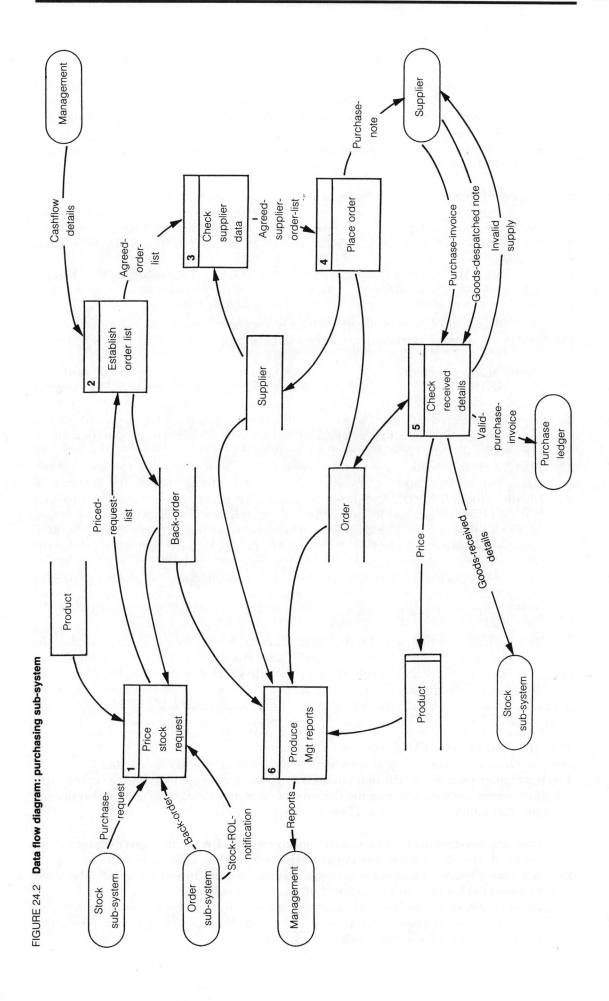

24.3.3 Stock (inventory system)

The previous two sub-systems have been concerned with selling and purchasing goods and services. The stock control system reflects the balance between the two. Its main purpose is to establish the product records and maintain these against orders placed with suppliers and sales orders from customers.

Stock systems are particularly concerned with the production of management reports. These might include:

1 Stock out report: reporting all items where the stock level has reached zero.
2 Reorder level report: showing all items which have reached their recommended reorder levels. The suggested reorder quantities may also be printed if required.
3 Stock quantity and value: the stock balances on each item and the financial value of these balances.
4 Slow moving stock: it may be useful to identify slow moving goods which may then become the subject of a 'special offer'.

Stock adjustments should be allowed after a physical stock check. Six main processes are identified in the appropriate data flow diagram (Figure 24.3).

1 **Check product quantities** The picking list received from the order sub-system is re-checked for quantity available for supply. A checked picking list is agreed. A picking list states the quantity of each product required to make up the orders.
2 **Decrease product quantities** The values on the checked picking list are physically picked and an annotated picking list is sent back to the order sub-system. The product quantity in stock on the product file is decremented.
3 **Produce stock reports** Various stock reports will be made available for management action. Possible contents have already been described in the introduction to this section.
4 **Identify products < ROL** A particularly significant report is the notification of products that have fallen below their Re-order Level (ROL). These will require purchasing action.
5 **Raise purchase note** A purchase request note is raised for all goods below the ROL (whether identified by the order sub-system or by the stock sub-system). This is sent to the purchasing sub-system.
6 **Increase product quantities** The goods received details give the goods ordered by purchasing and confirmed as delivered from an appropriate supplier. This data increments the product quantities on the product file.

The discussion of supply and ordering has been simplified by the assumption that the product is not manufactured by the enterprise under consideration. The description has essentially been of a distributor. Stock is held by the firm which is replenished by ordering the same stock items from a supplier—who may indeed be the original manufacturer. The items held in stock have been balanced against the cost of not holding that stock. 'Stock out' costs are incurred when important customers cannot be supplied and significant business is lost.

24.4 FINANCIAL SYSTEMS

The financial stewardship of an organisation is maintained through basic book-keeping functions and systems. These systems deal with transactions in an agreed formalised way reflecting established accounting conventions. There are three main parts:

1 **Accounts receivable** Money owed to the organisation for goods or services that it has provided. Details are maintained on the **sales ledger**.
2 **Accounts payable** Money owed to other organisations for goods and services they have provided to us. Details are maintained on the **purchase ledger**.
3 **Nominal ledger** Summarising the financial position of the organisation and presenting the results in an agreed convention so that they may be inspected and interpreted. This may also be called the **general ledger**.

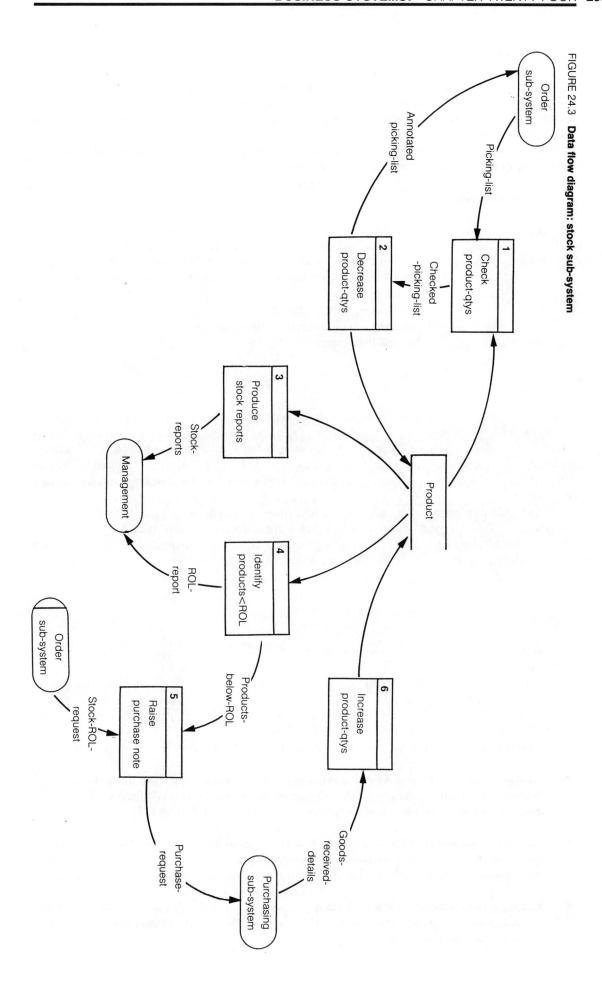

FIGURE 24.3 **Data flow diagram: stock sub-system**

24.4.1 Sales ledger

Most organisations allow their customers to purchase goods 'on account'. Goods and services are usually supplied on an understanding that they will be paid for within a specified period, for example, 30 days. The sales ledger or accounts receivable system is designed to record all amounts of money owed to the organisation by its customers. An efficient accounts receivable system is required to ensure that the firm's generosity is not stretched too far and that slow payers are identified and chased for payment. In this way the accounts receivable system should aid the reduction of amounts owing to an organisation, hence improving its cash flow.

There are three types of accounts receivable system:

BALANCE ONLY

This only maintains a record of the debtor's balance, not of individual invoices, remittances and credits. The statement produced for the debtor at the end of the month may only show:

> Previous month's balance
> Amount due for current purchases
> Net balance owing

BALANCE FORWARD

This has an opening balance—the amount owed at the start of the month; a record of transactions in that month—showing the date, type and amount of each transaction; a closing balance; this closing balance becomes the opening balance of the following month and subsequent statements do not show transactions prior to the current month, whether they have been settled or not. Thus, queries on old invoices usually requires the manual searching of filed statements.

The balances are aged in a balance forward system. Thus the total closing balance is analysed, for example, into balances which are three months or more overdue, two months overdue and one month overdue. Remittances and credits issued during the month are usually applied against the oldest invoices. The age analysis of the balances are usually included on the debtor's statement.

OPEN ITEM

This is a more complicated system where details of each invoice are maintained and all remittances and credits relating to that invoice are recorded against it until it is paid off.

It is easier to maintain an open item system when customers specify which transactions a certain remittance is supposed to cover. This is particularly crucial when one of the invoices is part-paid. If debtors fail to specify which invoices are covered by a remittance then the payment is usually credited against the oldest invoices.

The data flow diagram for the sales ledger (Figure 24.4) shows five main processes:

1 **Update sales ledger** Sales receipt and invoice details are received from the order processing sub-system and these are used to create transactions on the accounts receivable file.
2 **Sales invoices are raised** for appropriate transactions and despatched to the company's customers.
3 **Check payment details** Payments received from customers are credited against accounts or specific invoices and a valid payment list is produced which updates the details stored in the accounts receivable file. Invalid payments (under and over paid amounts) are passed to:
4 **Raise payment details** Credit notes (for over-payment) and balance requests (for under-payment) are raised and sent to the appropriate customers. Details are also recorded on the accounts receivable file.

FIGURE 24.4 **Data flow diagram: sales ledger**

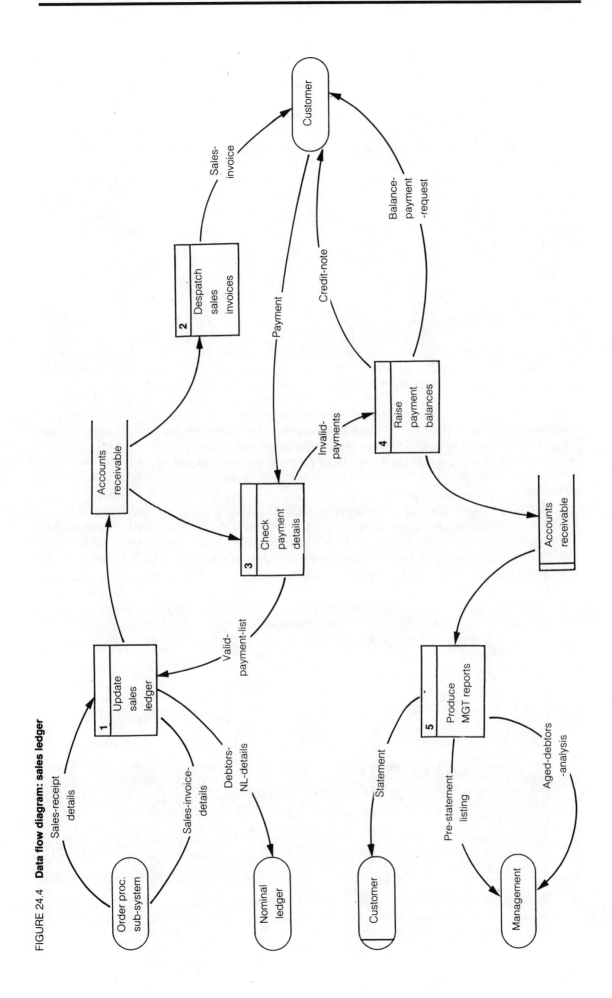

5   **Produce management reports** Typical reports include:
   (a)   The aged debtors report.
   (b)   The identification of dormant accounts.
   (c)   A listing of customers who have exceeded certain values of trading. These may be accorded special offers or terms of payment.
   (d)   Statements.
   (e)   A pre-statement listing for management action.

There may be a requirement for periodic processing of certain transactions where, for example, a given amount is paid in a 'standing order' on the same day of every month. It may also be desirable to extend the accounts receivable function to include sales handling and sales commissions. This permits the generation of sales analysis and salesman performance and commission reports.

24.4.2 The purchase ledger

The purchase ledger or accounts payable system monitors the money the organisation owes other companies for goods and services they have supplied on credit. The accounts payable requires just as much management as the accounts receivable if the most effective use is to be made of the organisation's cash. In general, it is desirable to settle all accounts within the agreed credit terms, particularly if there are penalties for late settlement. However, balanced against this, bills should be paid no sooner than is necessary so that cash needed for payment may be released for as long as possible to earn interest through investment.
   The data flow diagram (Figure 24.5) highlights five processes.

1   **Update purchase ledger** Valid purchase invoices are received from the purchasing sub-system and these are used to create transactions on the accounts payable file.
2   **Determine outstanding invoices** A list of outstanding invoices is sent to management together with an aged analysis showing the age profile of these invoices.
3   **Determine invoices to pay** Certain invoices are selected for payment. The selection of which invoices to pay will normally be made by a senior member of the accounts staff and will be based upon a number of factors. Some of these will be intangible, for example: promptly paying large companies whose credit limits are tight and highly regulated at the expense of one-off purchases from small firms who can safely be made to 'wait for their money'. However, judgments about which accounts to settle will also be supplemented by factual information about the firm's projected cash flow.
4   **Raise cheque details** Cheques are raised for the invoices selected for payment and the cheque detail list is used to update the accounts payable file. The cheque and a remittance advice note is sent to the supplier.
5   **Check statement details** Statements received from suppliers are checked for their accuracy. Discrepancies are taken up with the supplier.

The system may also produce reports similar to those available from the accounts receivable system. Furthermore, there may again be a need to support 'standing order' transactions.
   It may also be necessary to hold budget information in the system and to allocate invoices or parts of invoices against specific cost centres. So, for example, every department manager could be given a budget for the year and information regarding this is stored on the system. Every item purchased by the employees in that department is then recorded against that budget. This permits the manager to monitor the department's expenditure and to make adjustments as necessary. It also permits corporate managers to request a cost centre report showing the cost structure of the whole company.

FIGURE 24.5 **Data flow diagram: purchase ledger**

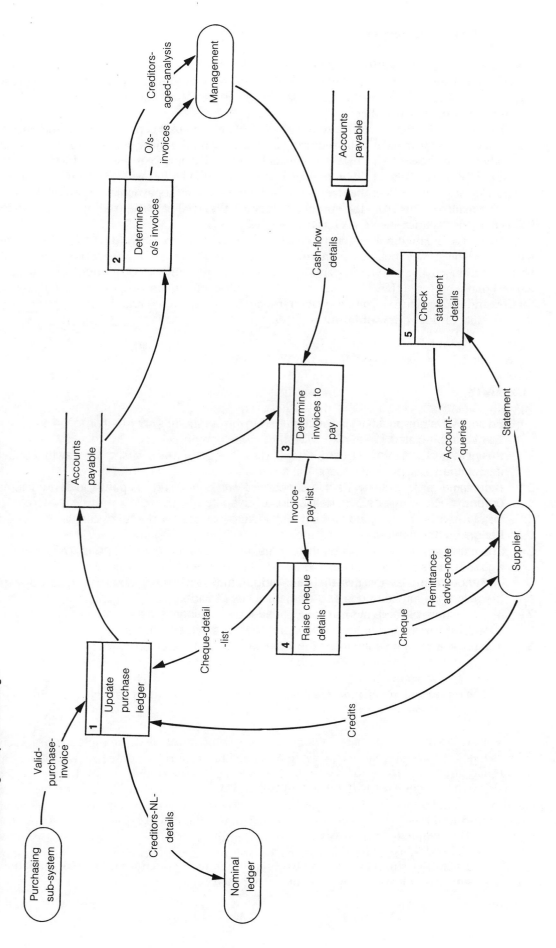

24.4.3 The nominal ledger

The nominal ledger (sometimes called general ledger) summarises the financial activity of an organisation in an accounting period. It is used to produce two important reports that communicate the financial status of an organisation. These are the trading and profit and loss statement and the balance sheet.

The nominal ledger uses the standard double entry book-keeping practice and ensures that the accounts are in balance by requiring each transaction to cause both a debit and a credit.

The correctness of the balance is usually verified prior to report production by the generation of a 'trial balance'. The structure of the nominal ledger will vary from company to company and should reflect the size, needs and operations of a particular organisation.

The main outputs from the nominal ledger are the: trial balance; trading and profit and loss statement; balance sheet; VAT return analysis.

In a sense the nominal ledger summarises the money received (from postings on the sales ledger) and the money spent. Elements of the latter have already been considered in the section which introduced the purchasing sub-system and the accounting convention (the purchase ledger) that monitored this. However, a further significant expenditure for most companies is salaries and wages. The payroll sub-system has not been considered and this serves to illustrate the partiality of this review of business systems.

SUMMARY

1   Business systems must be understood before the computer's contribution to the enterprise can be appreciated.
2   Business systems can be illustrated with data flow diagrams showing the way that data is transformed as it passes through the organisation.
3   A customer order entry system is concerned with controlling the passage of a customer order through from receipt to notification of despatch.
4   Purchasing is primarily concerned with controlling the products, materials and goods bought by the enterprise.
5   The main purpose of stock control is to establish product records and to maintain these against orders placed with suppliers and sales orders from customers.
6   The accounts receivable system (sales ledger) maintains details about the money owed to the enterprise for the goods and services it has provided.
7   The accounts payable system (purchase ledger) maintains details about the money the enterprise owes other organisations for goods or services it has used.
8   The nominal ledger summarises the financial status of the enterprise.

There are no self-test questions for this chapter.

EXERCISE

1   A payroll system has the following outputs:

> A payslip
> Pay cheques/credit transfers
> Coin analysis
> An annual summary of employee's earnings and deductions in the year-to-date for employees leaving employment during the year

and the following inputs:

Time sheets
Downtime reports
Holiday and sickness notifications
Deduction rate tables
Joiners and leavers

Using this information investigate payroll procedures and produce a suitable data flow diagram.

This is a reader based exercise requiring research into a representative business system. It is not thought appropriate to give an answer to this exercise because it will not reflect the variety of circumstances that are likely to be recorded.

Business Computer Systems

The data flow diagram introduced in the previous chapter explicitly identifies four areas of business computer system design.

1 Inputs. Data flows moving from a source to a process.
2 Outputs. Data flows moving from a process to a sink.
3 Processes inputs into outputs.
4 Files. Stores of data created and used by processes in their transforming of inputs into outputs.

Two further areas of design also have to be considered:

1 Interfaces between the user and the inputs and outputs of the system.
2 Controls required to ensure accurate data entry, manipulation and presentation.

25.1   INPUT DESIGN

Input design is concerned with collecting accurate and appropriate data for the system. There are five main tasks in data capture.

1   Data describing significant events is recorded by the data provider. An order is despatched to a customer and the details are recorded on a despatch note.
2   The collected data is conveyed to a place of processing. The despatch notes are batched together at the end of the day and sent to the computer centre in the internal mail.
3   The data is scrutinised for obvious omissions and errors. This is the task of data control.
4   Data is transcribed from 'human readable' to 'machine readable' form. In doing so transcription errors may occur and so, in some instances, the data is transcribed again and differences between first and second transcriptions are investigated. This is the process of verification.
5   Data items are entered into the main computer system and checked for logical correctness by a data validation program. Detected errors are listed out for appropriate action.

Thus input design is concerned with:
(a)   methods of recording data
(b)   methods of communicating data
(c)   locating errors in data.

The general objective of data capture is to collect and convert the data into machine readable form with the minimum delay, minimum introduction of errors and at minimum cost.

The contents of the input are defined by the data elements in the data flow. Input design is concerned with selecting an appropriate technology to capture these elements and, if necessary, to design an effective data capture document.

25.1.1 Input technologies

KEYBOARD TRANSCRIPTION

In this instance the data is converted from 'human readable' to 'computer readable' form by intermediate keyboard transcription. This is the traditional task of data preparation where the operator takes clerical documents and enters their values onto a suitable computer media. This media is usually some kind of secondary storage—tape, disk or cards.

Data entered in this way must be subjected to some kind of verification and validation. Verification is usually achieved by transcribing the data twice and investigating any discrepancies. Validation will be performed by a data validation program that examines incoming data and rejects entries that do not conform to an expected value range or format. These checks will be examined in more detail in the section on controls.

DIRECT INPUT INTO THE COMPUTER

Data transcription incurs cost, delay and error. The designer should attempt to minimise the number of times the data is transcribed and look for opportunities to capture data as close as possible to the form in which it is originally generated. Devices and technologies that permit direct entry of data into the computer eliminate transcription errors completely.
Possible technologies include:

Optical Character Recognition (OCR)
OCR readers interpret printed characters and automatically convert them into their digital equivalents. The technique is widely used in insurance premium notices, public utility billing and hire purchase agreements where much of the input data can be predicted and hence is pre-printed in an appropriate OCR font. The tolerances of contemporary OCR readers allow the input of handwritten characters particularly where the characters are likely to be from a limited set (say 1–9) and are confined within a physical box. Many systems have an associated screen and keyboard where unrecognised characters may be displayed and re-entered by the operator.

Magnetic Ink Character Recognition (MICR)
This is a more specialised form of character recognition. MICR readers magnetise, recognise and interpret the ferrite impregnated ink and this use of magnetic qualities makes it less vulnerable than OCR to damaged or folded documents. However, its high cost makes it little used outside the banking world where its characteristic font can be seen on the bottom of every cheque. Few other applications have to guard so rigorously against fraudulent data entry and hence justify the cost of MICR equipment.

Optical Mark Recognition (OMR)
OMR readers recognise hand or machine printed marks on forms. Current devices are not limited to soft lead pencil marks but can interpret any dense mark; biro, typewriter, etc. OMR forms give the operator a number of optional lozenges which are filled in as required. Common examples are multiple-choice tests, order forms and survey documents. Difficulties occur with OMR where a large amount of data has to be collected or where the details of the system change quickly (eg, fashion stores, record shops) demanding uneconomic alterations of the OMR form. Optical Mark Recognition is probably best used in a stable environment where there is a large number of short numeric records.

Bar Codes

A unique bar code can be attached to all items in the system and transactions that involve this item are then recorded via a bar code reader. For example, every member of a library may be issued with a membership card which includes a photograph and a bar code. Each copy of a text held in the library also has a bar code. When a book is taken out the librarian runs a light pen over the bar code on the membership card and over the bar code in each book. This effectively ties together the borrower and the book. Simple and efficient data capture.

Kimball Tags

These are small tags used primarily in the garment trade on which details about size, colour, style and price of goods are recorded. The label is attached to the garment and on sale of the item the tag is detached and details read by a kimball tag reader. This provides automatic capture of sales data, updating of stock records, sales statistics and product planning information.

The relative expense and specialist nature of the direct entry technologies and the problems of keyboard dexterity has led to other possible options designed to ease interaction with the computer. These include touch screens where operators select the required option by touching it with their fingers and mice where a small control unit (a mouse) may be used to 'draw' input directly onto the screen as well as being used as a selection pointer.

25.1.2 Input design—other considerations

Thus input design is concerned with:

(a) Determining the data elements required in input documents and displays. These will be taken from the data flows of the logical data flow model.
(b) Selecting an appropriate technology to perform data entry.
(c) Undertaking detailed design work on input methods. This will include form and dialogue design.

The input designer will wish to observe two important guidelines:

1 Seek to minimise transcription. It has already been noted that every transcription incurs cost, delay and error.
2 Strive to minimise the amount of data recorded. Many of the inputs of the system can be predicted in advance. For example, a request for payment of water rates can preprint or code data about the user's name, address, postal code, property reference and payment required. The data provider's only action is to pay the bill! In such circumstances the input forms may be printed in an appropriate OCR font ready for direct input on its return to the processing centre. The opportunity to code or print known data items varies from system to system but the designer should seek such opportunities because every additional data item required from the data provider increases the chance of error in the collected data.

25.2 OUTPUT DESIGN

Output design is a particularly significant element of business computer systems because it is the reason for the existence of the system itself. Information systems are established in organisations because they provide output information which is required by management (eg, an aged debtors report), by customers (eg, an invoice) or by law (a profit and loss account).

The content of the output is again derived from the output flows of the data flow diagram. These will give the data elements that must be presented on the output screen or document. These logical requirements may be supplemented by other needs, eg, legal requirements—VAT number; standard contents—company name, terms of business; controls—totals and sub-totals.

25.2.1 Output technologies

Some of the devices used to enter data may also be used to display output. The most popular methods of presenting results are Visual Display Units (VDU) and a variety of printers which produce printed paper copies of the data (so called 'hardcopy' to distinguish it from the transitory images presented on the VDU).

A distinction can be made between impact printers which operate in a similar way to the conventional typewriter where the character strikes an inked ribbon to leave the image on the paper, and non-impact printers which use a variety of techniques to produce an image without physically contacting the paper. Laser printers are typical examples of the latter category where the text is created by light and not direct contact. Such printers have become much cheaper in the last five years and are now a viable option for many users. Laser printers working at 8 ppm (pages per minute) are currently (1988) available for £2,000.

Impact printers vary in the way that they create the image on the paper. Dot matrix printers form their letters by printing an appropriate pattern of dots and this tends to produce an image of less clarity than those of the fully formed embossed character set of daisywheel printers. However, daisywheel printers are generally slower and more expensive than their dot matrix competitors. For example, it is possible to buy a matrix printer working at 480 cps (characters per second) for about £1,800. A daisywheel printer at the equivalent cost will operate at about 80 cps.

A compromise solution is offered by Near Letter Quality (NLQ) printers which offer a denser matrix, but at a slower speed. Many contemporary matrix printers offer this alternative speed and quality. For example, the matrix printer used above to illustrate speed and price also gives NLQ print at 180 cps.

In other circumstances the output may be used as subsequent input into another system. In this instance the data may be produced in a format suitable for direct entry. This may be in a human readable form (OCR font, kimball tag) or in a medium only suitable for machine reading (magnetic tape, paper tape). Organisations which need to store a considerable amount of data (libraries, hospitals, etc) may use Computer Output onto Microfilm (COM) devices which convert computer output into characters on rolls of microfilm. A sheet of microfilm, microfiche, can be selected as required and viewed through a microfiche viewer. COM devices are best used in applications with a large number of records where each record is accessed relatively infrequently.

25.2.2 Output design—other considerations

Thus output design is concerned with:

1   Determining the data items required on the output screens and documents. This will be provided by the output data flows given on the data flow diagram.
2   Selecting a technology to display or communicate these data items.
3   Performing detailed design of output screen and documents.

In the selection of an output technology the designer should again be guided by the demands of the system. A computer used mainly for word processing may dictate the purchase of a relatively sophisticated daisywheel printer. In other circumstances—printing out laboratory figures, drafting reports, etc a matrix printer may suffice.

25.3   INTERFACE DESIGN

The interface marks the boundary between the human and computer systems. The data flows that traverse this interface are the inputs and outputs of the system. The location of this boundary is a design decision. It will be guided by a consideration of the processes shown in the system. Some processes are extremely repetitive and predictable and consequently can almost certainly be carried out more successfully by using a computer. This is because of the rule-following nature of the machine that will cause it to consistently and tirelessly carry out the specified tasks. In contrast some processes are unpredictable and discretionary. These are unlikely to be suitable to computerisation and will be allocated to a more adaptable decision-making mechanism—the human being.

The interface can be shown on the data flow diagram as a bold thick line. Possible interfaces for two of the data flow diagrams introduced in the previous chapter are shown in Figures 25.1 and 25.2. The order processing system, which is mainly rule-following, has most of its processes inside the boundary line indicating that the majority of this sub-system can be computerised. In contrast the purchase ledger system has only three of its five processes within the boundary line. Determine invoices to pay, for example, is a management task affected by all kinds of pressure, politics, and priority. A computer system can support the task—by providing the outstanding invoice details—but is unlikely to replace it entirely.

The drawing of the boundary line can be used to explore different interfaces with the user. Once determined, the technology of the interface can be decided: for example, a direct input method might be used for entering order details. Many of the interfaces will demand a direct dialogue between a user and the system. The design of the dialogue, or conversation, between the computer and its operator has increased in significance in the last few years. This is mainly due to an increase in the direct use of computers by system users, so by-passing traditional intermediaries such as the data processing and data preparation departments. This has led to an increasing demand for 'user-friendly' interfaces.

There are three main ways of structuring the conversation between computer and user.

MENUS

The actions open to a user are displayed on the screen together with the user responses required for each action. Letter or numerical responses may be used. The former tends to be easier to use particularly if the response can be made to be the first letter of the action, for example:

E—Edit a record

Menus are usually organised in a hierarchical form with an option in a higher menu, say:

R—Reports

leading to a further menu giving the different type of reports available:

D—Daily value report
M—Monthly analysis
A—Audit report

Links between menus must be maintained. For example, by a

R—Return to main menu

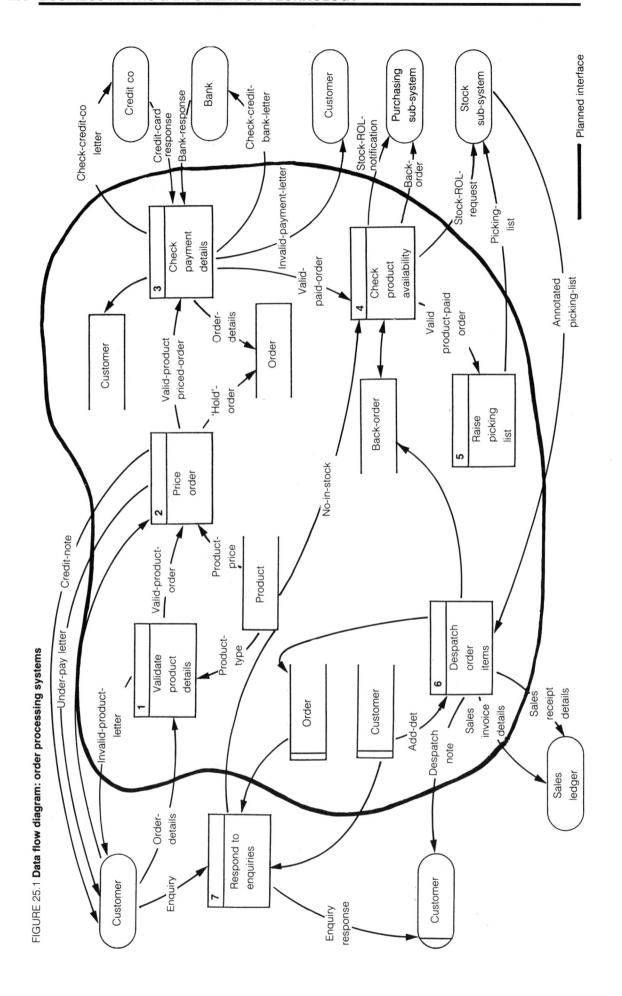

FIGURE 25.1 **Data flow diagram: order processing systems**

FIGURE 25.2 **Data flow diagram: purchase ledger**

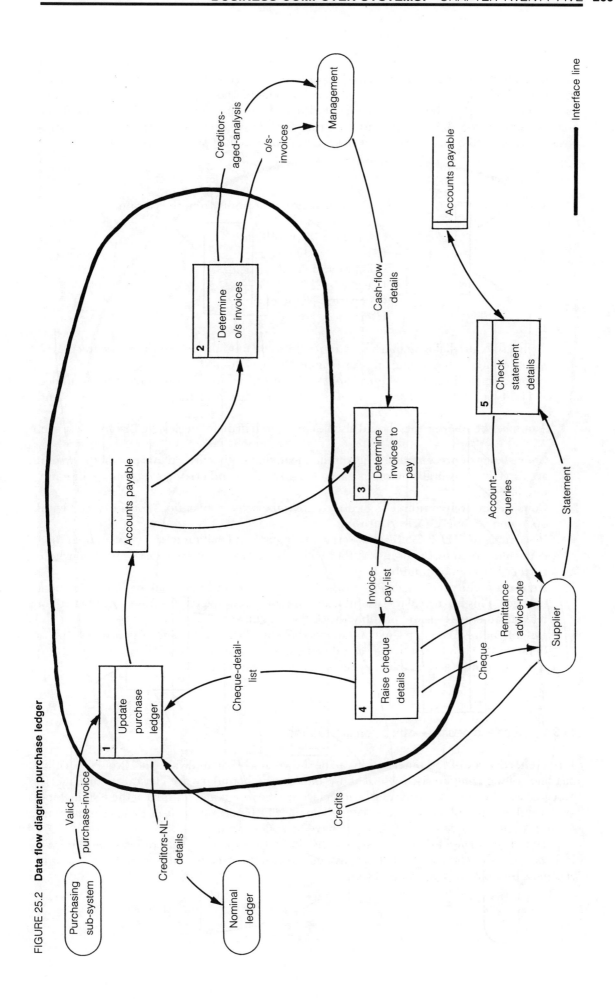

FORM FILL

In this method the designer lays the screen out as if it were a form and the operator makes entries in a similar way to a hand compiled example. This method is particularly suitable for fast data entry, although it should be remembered that the completion of a field entry should be unambiguous. It may be wise to insist on a carriage return after each entry so demanding a positive action to skip to a subsequent field. Error correction should be easy to perform.

QUESTION AND ANSWER

This is a sequence of actions where the user reacts to prompts from the computer.

    Computer: Type of field?
    User: Character
    Computer: Length of field?
    User: 15
    Computer: Name of field?
    User: Forename

Such a staccato dialogue quickly becomes tiresome but may be useful in certain circumstances, for example, suggesting and confirming the backup of discs.

In practice the designer will probably make use of all three of the structures outlined above. The type and level used will reflect both the task and the user's experience and expectations.

A number of other factors should also be considered in dialogue design. Briefly, these are:

1   **Consistency of presentation** This should mean that skills learnt in one part of the system are directly transferable to other parts. Format, entry and error correction are instantly familiar.
2   **Consistency of operation** Use of different symbols and conventions for the same logical operation is unnecessarily confusing.
3   **Provisions of HELP facilities** A screen giving an explanation of the current operation being attempted by the user, together with a reference to an appropriate manual where further help can be found.
4   **An abort facility** The facility to escape from the system without making any permanent changes. This is particularly useful when the user is completely confused and fearful of making an entry that will possibly wreck the system.
5   **Default values** Data entry may be speeded up by placing values in certain fields. If this default value is relevant to the record being entered then no direct entry is required and the value can be accepted by keying, say, a carriage return.

25.3.1 Interface design—other considerations

The intended scope of computerisation can be shown by a broad interface line. Processes within this line will be computerised whilst those outside the boundary are clerical or managerial procedures. The flows that traverse the interface are the inputs and outputs of the system. Most inputs and outputs will have an associated dialogue which permits the user to make inputs and request outputs. Three types of dialogue have been described.

It must be stressed that the designer should adopt a dialogue that reflects the expertise and vocabulary of the users. Furthermore, its effort to be user-friendly should not lead it to become either patronising or bewildering.

25.4 DESIGN OF OPERATIONAL CONTROLS

Most documented errors in systems are caused by accident; the wrong input of data, incorrectly defined processing, misinterpreted output. These are due to genuine mistakes, miskeying and misunderstandings. It is the task of the system developer to design systems that minimise the chance of such errors reaching processing or system outputs. Controls will be required on data at all stages of its collection, processing, storage and retrieval. Data should be accurate and complete at all times, and its manipulation both authorised and legitimate. It is important to recognise that the necessary controls will be implemented in the clerical procedures of the system as well as in the software itself.

CLERICAL CONTROLS

It may be possible to implement control totals that are summed both manually and automatically. These totals are compared and if they agree then the data is assumed to have been entered correctly and the batch can be posted for processing. Such totals are particularly common in accounting systems where the accuracy of data is paramount. Addition may be on inappropriate fields such as account numbers and the nominal codes entered on the batch. These are useful accuracy checks but clearly they have no particular significance. These meaningless sums are often termed **hash totals**.

Clerical controls are also of importance where source documents are posted around sections or buildings. It is very easy for forms or returns to be 'lost in transit' with the result that certain transactions, such as employee payments, do not take place. Movement control is usually enforced by the completion of batch control documents that give sufficient information for the recipient to check for the completeness of contents. Typical data on a control sheet will be:

(a) Serial number of the batch. To check whether this follows the last received batch of documents. Has a whole batch gone missing in the post?
(b) Count of batch contents. The number of forms that should be in the batch.
(c) Serial numbers of forms. The serial numbers or number range(s) of the enclosed forms.

A large data processing centre will have a section dedicated to data control, responsible for checking input data, enforcing input schedules, locating errors, organising and validating output etc. They will also wish to impose standards of good house-keeping so that disks are properly and clearly labelled, unused files deleted, proper control documentation established and maintained.

Software controls are used extensively in the data validation programs to trap input errors. Typical checks will include:

1 **Format checks** That data always conforms to the specified format. Thus a product code designated as two letters followed by four numbers is always entered this way. Invalid entries such as A2341 or AS231 are rejected.
2 **Range checks** The data has to lie within certain values. These may be set globally (eg, property reference code must be between 100 and 200) or may be more selective to identify uncommon occurrences. Thus, if 90% of all property reference codes are between 100 and 110, then legitimate, but infrequent codes may trigger a request for operator checking.
    'You have entered code 121. This is a warehouse. Please confirm that this code is correct . . .'
3 **Sequence checks** Used to test that transactions that are supposed to be in a certain order are actually arranged this way.
4 **Consistency checks** Two data items may be related in some way. Thus 'maternity leave' is always associated with sex='female'. Many such relationships exist and should be exploited to the full.

5   **Record and item counts** Counting the items (how many invoices have been entered) represents a simpler but less reliable alternative to control and hash totals.

6   **Flag fields** The inclusion of flag fields that record whether a certain state or process has taken place. These are essentially included in the file definition for control purposes only. Thus, if a salary field has been up-dated the flag is set to a value which traps all subsequent attempts to access the salary information. It can be viewed as a switch that is set once and prevents any subsequent activity until it is re-set.

7   **Code design** It may be feasible to implement a code design which has elements of self-checking. Thus the first facet of the code (say the first three numbers) may be split off and certain checks performed. Included amongst these might be consistency checks against other parts of the code.

'If the first three numbers of the code are less than 100 check that the fourth number is not greater than 7.'

This code was part of one used for supply requisitioning. The first three numbers were employee codes. Those with a code beginning with less than 100 could not order more than £7(000) worth of goods.

A code is helped by the addition of a check digit. This represents a number added to the end of the code which permits the rest of the code to be checked for transcription, transposition and random errors. One of the most common methods of allocating a check digit is the modulus 11 algorithm. This is best illustrated by an example.

Example:

A company uses product numbers of six digits. 345213 is a typical example. It wishes to incorporate a check digit into the code in an attempt to reduce the number of clerical input errors. This will thus make a new seven digit code.

The method of calculation is as follows:

Number	3	4	5	2	1	3
Multiplier	6	5	4	3	2	1
Product	18	20	20	6	2	3
Sum of Products			69			
Divide by Modulus 11	6 remainder 3					

The remainder is added to the code to make the new one:

3452133

Everytime that this code is entered by the operator the software undertakes a modulus 11 check to validate the check digit. If the last entered figure is 3 and the rest of the code is correct then the input is permitted. The value of this can be demonstrated by the effect of a simple transposition error.

Number	3	5	4	2	1	3	3
Multiplier	6	5	4	3	2	1	
Product	18	25	16	6	2	3	
Sum of products			70				
Divide by modulus 11	6 remainder 4						

The check digit is incorrect and so an error has been made in the entry.

It should be recognised that all these checks should be applied together. The erroneous input 3542133 may have survived format and range checks only to be tripped up by the check digit.

Controls are also required to protect the data from loss due to hardware failure or erroneous procedures. It is usual to specify the regular **'dumping'** of files to allow the data to be recreated from these back-up files after a catastrophic system failure. The frequency of dumping varies with the nature of the system. Real-time systems may dump several times a day whilst other applications might dump daily or weekly. Retaining **file generations** is another basic method of securing files. In this instance, successive generations of the file are retained together with the intermediate updating transactions. The grandfather method of file security keeps the son file, its father and its grandfather as well as the transactions between each generation. The son file can be re-created by running the father file against the appropriate transactions. The grandfather file is held in reserve should the father file be lost during the recreation procedure. This method is typically used in tape based sequential filing systems (discussed later).

25.5   FILE DESIGN

The implementation of files demands the consideration of three inter-related features.

1   The content of files. These can be based upon the data elements held in the data stores of the data flow diagram. These logical stores provide a reasonable basis for determining file contents although they are likely to encourage unnecessary and potentially harmful duplication of data values. The content of the files may also reflect implementation issues. For example, two logical files, customer and prospect, may be integrated into one large physical mailshot file which includes potential as well as actual customers.

Similarly, a logical file might be split on the basis of the activity on the file. For example, there may be a case for splitting off active customers from inactive ones (ie, those who have not placed an order for one year) on the assumption that most orders and queries will take place on the active customers. Organising the file in such a way utilises the concept of a **'hit group'**. A hit group are those records which are accessed the most often— for example, in a product catalogue 80% of the orders may be for only 20% of the products. These popular products constitute a hit group and are perhaps stored in a file split away from the more slow moving goods. A related concept is the 'hit ratio' which measures the activity on a file in a particular run or period of time.

$$\frac{\text{Number of records accessed}}{\text{Number of records on file}}$$

This is usually expressed as a percentage, for example, customer orders in one day hit 15% of the product file.

2   The order of the files refers to the physical sequence of the records in the file.

Four broad alternatives exist:

(a)   **Serial** The records are in no particular order. This is usually only relevant to temporary transaction files which are then sorted into an appropriate sequence prior to processing.

(b)   **Sequential** The records are stored in key field order. Hence the record for customer no 345 is stored before that of 346 in a sequential file held in ascending order.

(c)   **Indexed sequential** A file index only contains the key field values of the records together with a pointer to where the rest of that record may be found. This index may be used by the processing program to skip all the records that do not require processing. In small files it may be possible to index all records individually but as the file becomes larger the storage overhead of the index becomes increasingly significant. Consequently, it is usual to establish an index for a group of records where the index refers to a range of records. The address of this group is accessed and consecutive records are searched sequentially until the requested record is located.

(d)   **Random** The records are stored in an order dictated by the result of applying a mathematical transformation to the value of the key field.

It may be necessary to organise the sequence of the records to fit some characteristic of the system. For example, the output may be required in a certain sequence. The payslips of an organisation need producing in department/section order to save on time consuming manual sorting. Consequently, the file could benefit from being organised in this sequence. The file sequence may also be determined by the activity of the data. A customer file may be ordered in sequence of number of orders so that the most regular customers are placed together at the beginning of the file. Most of the activity, ie, processing of orders and customer queries, will take place on those customers and so seeks between customer accesses should be reduced.

3   The files can be processed in three different ways.
   (a) **Search** The records are processed in their physical sequence. A search compares successive records until it finds the key field of the requested record.
   (b) **Index** The process consults the index to the file before searching consecutive records of the addressed track for the required record.
   (c) **Directly** A mathematical transformation is applied to the key field which automatically results in the physical position of the record on the storage device.

The random file organisation with its associated direct access method is suited to enquiry systems where the records are not accessed in any particular order. The main problem is the definition of a suitable mathematical transformation (or algorithm) that efficiently uses the secondary storage space as well as minimising potential synonyms.

Serially searched sequential files are particularly appliable to processes that need to access every record in a run or where the hit rate is sufficiently high for the designer to accept accesses to unwanted records.

Indexed sequential files provide a compromise organisation that is very widely used. It is in this application that the significance of distinguishing the order and processing of the files becomes particularly relevant. For example, a personnel system may be stored in sequential order. It is processed using a serial search by the payroll programs that need to access every record on the file. At the same time a suite of enquiry programs have been written that use an index for the quick location of individual employee records.

25.5.1   File design—other considerations

The file must be supported by an appropriate secondary storage device. A file which is accessed via indexes or algorithms must be allocated to a random access or direct access device (such as magnetic disk). Files which are searched serially can also be allocated to serial access devices such as magnetic tape. The nature of most data processing makes the disk supported index sequential the most popular file organisation.

It is also helpful to make a distinction between **master files** holding basic data which changes little over time, such as customer name, address, etc, and **transaction files** which hold temporary data. Many systems have such characteristics. For example, in a personnel records system there will be a master file holding basic information about employees and a number of transaction files such as leavers and joiners, absences, holidays, etc, holding such transactions over a period of time. These will be run against the master file to update the details of the employees.

25.6   DESIGN OF PROCESSES

The processes of the data flow model use data items from flows (inputs) and stores (files) to produce further flows (outputs). The processes are only defined in a logical way and so it is up to the designer to decide how these activities will be carried out in the implemented system. This was considered in the definition of the interface.

Processes allocated to the computer will need refining into program specifications to allow the development of a suite of programs. Processes allocated to a human being will often demand clerical procedure documents which specify the actions that should be carried out under different circumstances.

25.7 RESPONSIBILITY FOR DESIGN

The tasks of system design are usually performed by staff in a **data processing** department. The location of this department in the organisation may reflect historical chance rather than corporate strategy. It is often determined by the first implementation within the company and hence certain departments show their accounting tutelage by still reporting to the Financial Director whilst others show their stock control roots by remaining in the operations department. This may cause unnecessary restrictions and retard the subsequent spread of computing through the company. Some organisations have relocated their data processing department into a wider management services section which also consists of operational research, statistical support and organisation and methods. In certain instances this group of activities has been established as a separate trading company.

A data processing department usually consists of at least three well defined groups of staff.

1   Systems analysts concerned with investigating and defining business computer systems and then designing software solutions to support them. The tasks of this and the previous chapter are typically performed by an analyst.
2   Programmers implement the designed software solution in an appropriate programming language adhering to defined programming and documentation standards. The tasks defined in Chapter 23 are indicative of the programmer's work.
3   Operations staff are concerned with the day to day running of the computer system. This will include data control, data preparation and the loading of machines—disk loading, printer control, paper changing, output despatch, etc.

The department will be under the control of a data processing manager who may be assisted by a data base administrator. The development of all bespoke solutions will be the responsibility of this section, as will the location, investigation and purchase of software packages.

25.8 SOFTWARE PACKAGES

This chapter has identified and discussed six areas of design: inputs, outputs, files, processes, interfaces and controls. It has assumed that the system being considered will be a bespoke software system tailored to the needs of this particular organisation. Thus, programs will be written in conventional high level languages to a specification specially developed for this enterprise. Files, interfaces and controls will also be tailored to the company's requirements and inputs and outputs will exactly reflect the needs of the system. A **'bespoke solution'** will be delivered which reflects the enterprise's exact specification.

However, the bespoke or **turnkey** solution will take time and money to develop. The similarity of many applications has inspired software developers to offer generalised software packages for common application areas. The operational systems outlined in the previous chapter are candidates for software packages because they describe activities that are likely to take place in all organisations, whether they are concerned with education, services or manufacturing. Software packages offer the general functions that are usually required in the application area and only require the input of the user's data to give an up and running system. A package usually consists of a disk or tape—which contains the packaged programs—a user manual and some element of training and support. Users of the package are licensed to use the software and seldom have access to the source code.

There must be an element of compromise in package selection. It is unlikely that a product will be found that will match the implementation exactly. A reluctance to waive any requirements is likely to lead to a bespoke solution.

Package solutions are much cheaper. One package known to the author consists of about 60,000 lines of COBOL and its authors conservatively estimate the development cost at £300,000. The package sells for about £2,500. The buyer is getting a high quality, tested product for a fraction of its production cost. In a bespoke development virtually all of the development costs are borne by the user.

Packages are supposed to be generalised answers to specific problems. Vendors will make changes with varying degrees of reluctance. There are many examples where software changes made for specific clients have led to operational difficulties with the package, particularly when upgrades, changes and enhancements have been issued.

The design issues raised earlier in this chapter are not made redundant by the use of a software package. However, the balance of the tasks is shifted away from program and file design (established in the package and hence unalterable by the user) to the design of inputs, outputs, interfaces and controls. The definition of these will guide the selection between competing products and so give a basis for further evaluation.

This step is particularly significant in the selection of microcomputer software where there are many competing packages in a defined market segment. It seems both wasteful and unwise to develop, say, a bespoke payroll application, until a number of the marketed products have been examined, evaluated and, if found to be inappropriate, discarded. The very variety of products now means that there are many circumstances where the ability to perform a competent evaluation of packages is more important than specific programming skills. General issues in package selection are covered in the next section but it must be recalled that the most significant criterion for evaluation is how well the package fits the target requirements.

25.8.1 General issues in package selection

It must again be stressed that evaluation against need is the most significant issue in package selection. However, there are a number of general points which are worth looking for in all packages.

Seven issues repay careful consideration in the evaluation of competing package products.

1   **Facilities**
    Calculations performed. Can the VAT amount be calculated from either gross or net input values? Can the VAT rate be varied if legislation alters it from its current 15% rate?
    Print options. Are certain reports 'screen only'? Can printer modes (such as condensed print, underscoring, etc) be controlled from within the package? How easy is it to enter these codes?
2   **Sizes**
    File sizes. There may be a restriction on how many customer records may be created. In other instances the number of records may be unrealistic given the constraints of the rest of the package.
    Number of transactions. In some circumstances the combination of the file structures and sizes affects how many transactions can be held on the system. This is particularly significant in an accounting system and as a result all such software should be accompanied by a sizing algorithm.
3   **Speed**
    Demonstration of packages are usually given on a limited number of records and as a result most of the features appear to work very quickly. This speed is unlikely to be maintained as the number of records approaches realistic operational volumes.
    Report production. Purchase of a slow printer can compound the slow production of reports. Can the machine be used for other tasks during the printing out or is the operator effectively 'locked out'?
4   **Security**
    Investigation of facilities to permit recovery from catastrophic failures.
    Time taken to produce back up copies of data and the implication of this for administrative arrangements.
5   **Privacy and control**
    Passwords. Existence and levels of passwords.
    Audit. The package should satisfy both internal and external auditors.

Privacy. The package should allow the purchaser to comply with the requirements of the Data Protection Act.

6   Accuracy

Calculations. How does the package deal with rounding errors?

Errors and warning messages. Does the package trap all user errors or does it permit arithmetical operations which are logically correct but are likely to be administratively meaningless? For example, the calculation of negative stock levels. What error messages are given and how easy is it to recover from various types of error?

7   Interface

Type and consistency of the software interface.

Flexibility of the interface. Can the package produce a variety of interfaces to suit different user types and skill levels?

Clarity of the documentation.

Arrangements for installation, training and software upgrades.

Finally, there will be a need to assess the software vendor on the same grounds as selecting suppliers of other goods and services. This will include financial viability, experience, geographical location and terms of payment. All suppliers will also supply reference sites. These must be visited and the operations of the package and the support of the supplier discussed in detail. Such visits give the potential purchaser an opportunity to see the package working under operational conditions and volumes. Discussions can be held about the type of support given by the supplier and learn about problems and difficulties, as well as opportunities, that had not been envisaged.

25.9 COMPUTER BUREAU

The enterprise may also elect not to develop computer systems within the company but to use the services of a computer bureau. Bureaus are essentially organisations with substantial computing facilities that sell part of these resources to client organisations. Thus, it is possible for a relatively small company to have access to a large amount of processing power without the overheads that this would normally incur. A number of processing alternatives may be available.

1   **Simple batch** Raw or pre-coded data is delivered to the bureau with regular and *ad hoc* print-outs provided in return.

2   **Remote batch** Data is keyed into a terminal at the client's office and transmitted to the bureau's computer. Print-outs are returned by courier or results are returned down the line for outputting on a printer in the client's office. The use of an in-house terminal may be logically extended to interactive processing where the client can access the machine as required, producing reports and analyses on demand.

3   **Time sharing** The bureau operates the computer but sells or leases rights to a certain proportion of the facility to various clients. This gives a fixed cost which may be budgeted for by the client organisation. This is conceptually different to the other two arrangements where there is a large amount of variable costs associated with the actual use of the bureau's machine. These variable costs are usually on top of a fixed annual charge.

A bureau may be a sensible approach to computing for certain organisations because the sub-contracting avoids all the operational tasks and problems of running a computer system. However, this may become an expensive solution if heavy use is made of the bureau's computer and there must clearly be a cut-off point where investment in the company's own facilities becomes worthwhile. It has also been argued that use of a bureau retards the 'computer-literacy' of the client company who are consequently less able to take initiatives in information system development.

SUMMARY

1   The data flow diagram has explicitly identified four areas of business systems design—inputs, outputs, processes and stores (files).
2   Two further areas of design are interfaces and controls.
3   Input design is concerned with collecting and converting appropriate data into machine readable form with minimum delay, minimum introduction of errors and at minimum cost.
4   The contents of an input is defined by the data flow of the data flow diagram. This has to be assigned on appropriate technology. Input technologies can be divided between direct input and keyboard transcription.
5   Output design is concerned with presenting appropriate data to management, customers and external agencies.
6   The contents of an output is defined in the data flow of the data flow diagram. This has to be assigned an appropriate technology. A distinction can be made between transient images and hard copy.
7   An interface marks the boundary between the human and the computer systems and hence defines the inputs and outputs of the system. The interface may require the selection and development of an appropriate dialogue.
8   Operational controls will be required to ensure that incorrect data is not entered into the system, that internal processing is defined correctly and that output is not misinterpreted.
9   Both clerical and software controls will be important in the definition of operational security.
10   File design is concerned with the content of files, the order of records in that file and how these records are accessed by different processes.
11   Processes will be distinguished between machine supported (rule-following) and clerical and managerial activities (discretionary).
12   Certain systems may be implemented using a software package. This changes the balance of design as well as introducing some general issues of product selection.
13   Part or all of the enterprise's computer requirements may be sub-contracted to a computer bureau.
14   In many organisations the responsibility for design is vested in the data processing department.

SELF-TEST QUESTIONS

1   Which two areas of design are not explicitly addressed by the data flow diagram?

2   Distinguish between data verification and data validation.

3   List four technologies which support the direct input of data into the computer.

4   What is meant by the term 'hardcopy'?

5   Is a dot matrix printer an impact or a non-impact printer?

6   What do the letters NLQ stand for?

7   What is a hash total?

8   List four typical checks that can be used in a data validation program.

9   Distinguish between file dumping and file generation.

10   What is a hit group?

11   Explain the concept of a file index.

12   What is the purpose of an algorithm in files that can be directly accessed?

13   List four features that should be evaluated in the selection of an appropriate software package.

14   What is the most important aspect in the selection of a software package?

Answers on page 333.

EXERCISES

1   Describe, with examples, the three main ways of structuring a dialogue between the computer and a user in an order entry system. (*Refer to section 25.3*)

2   Distinguish between sequential and index sequential files. (*Refer to section 25.5*)

3   (a)   Distinguish between the use of kimball tags and Point Of Sale terminals used in the retailing sector.
     (b)   Distinguish between indexed sequential files and random access files as used with magnetic disk filing systems. (*Refer to section 25.5*)
     (c)   Describe, with suitable illustrations, the file generation technique and how it is applied to file security when using magnetic tape filing systems. (*Refer to section 25.4*)

ACCA December 1986

4   (a)   Distinguish between data validation and data verification when applied to batch processing.
     (b)   Distinguish between a systems analyst and a computer programmer.

ACCA June 1986

5   Outline some of the advantages a small concern could gain by using the services of a computer bureau.

6   Outline the configuration of a microcomputer system which could be used to control stock in a warehouse.

ACCA December 1985

7   Describe how bar codes are used in the retailing sector.

ACCA December 1985

8   Your company operating as a wholesaler uses a batch processing system to process orders from customers and control its own stock position.
     The customers are allowed to submit their orders on their own forms. This data is input to the computer through operators working at visual display units to set up the corresponding transaction file.
     A new junior member of staff has just joined your department. It is your responsibility to train him and, in particular, to explain the procedures involved in processing a customer order and updating the stock file of the company.

Required:
Write notes on the following aspects as preparation for the training programme:
(a)   Suggest some batch controls that could be applied to the data entries being given to each operator. (*Refer to section 25.4*)
(b)   The validation of data prior to the updating of the master file is important. Suggest some of the checks that will be performed at validation. (*Refer to section 25.4*)
(c)   Explain the difference between the updating of a master file and the maintenance of a master file.
(d)   Explain the likely detail of the report generated as a result of updating the master file. (*Refer to section 24.3.3*)

ACCA June 1985

9   You have been called upon to act as a consultant on the application of computing to the business of a client company.

Required:

Explain what is meant by THREE of the following terms, giving an example which may be applied to a business situation: Real-time processing, time sharing, on-line processing, distributed processing.

Answers on page 333.

Office automation

Until recently the office has been little touched by automation. A stereotyped office might produce handwritten documents which are then typed and often re-typed by secretaries. A copy of the document is made and filed before the original is sent through a conventional mail system to the intended receiver. Queries are dealt with on the telephone but the lines are often busy and most intended calls are never connected or called back. Managers spend a lot of their time holding or travelling to meetings and have sleepless nights recalculating budgets and cash flow predictions. Presentations are usually marred by inferior documents and poor overhead projection slides.

This chapter examines five inter-related types of activity which take place in most offices. Briefly, these are:

1   **The manipulation of text**. Writing memos, letters, reports, briefings, technical manuals, etc.
2   **The manipulation of data** Storing and retrieving information about customers, clients, employees, competitors, etc.
3   **Talking** Giving instructions and information through directly talking with people.
4   **Image processing** Constructing and presenting graphs, diagrams and models.
5   **Manipulating data** Performing calculations, constructing mathematical models, experimenting with different data values.

The 'social' aspect of the office is not discussed. Much office talk is not directly about business, but concerns personal matters, climatic changes and observations about life in general. The unofficial office life is very important and generates the atmosphere of the day to day running of the company. However, it is not directly relevant to our immediate purpose. The role of gossip, rumour and grapevine is acknowledged but this chapter must concentrate upon the technologies of office automation.

26.1   MANIPULATING TEXT

Writing is an important way of communicating instructions, information and ideas. The resulting document may range from a short instructive memo to a technical report complete with supporting diagrams and references. The use of a typewriter to improve the clarity and uniformity of text dates from the 1870s.

Word processing is concerned with text manipulation, editing and printing. It permits documents to be stored on a secondary storage medium—usually floppy disk—and then recalled for editing and re-printing. Its main advantage over the traditional typewriter is that there is no need to re-type the complete document. Simple editing—correction of mistyped characters, insertion and deletion of words and sentences, is all that is required.

A distinction can be made between dedicated word processors and a business computer that offers word processing as a standard software package. The dedicated word processor performs only word processing. Their features are designed to support their sole function—the creation and manipulation of text. Consequently, they may have large, full page display screens, a larger keyboard, special function keys to perform common operations and the facility to support complex text requirements such as mathematical symbols, Greek letters and foreign letter sets.

The business computer gains word processing facilities when an appropriate software package is loaded into its memory. These machines are capable of handling other applications in addition to word processing. Typical word processing software packages are Wordstar, Multimate and Displaywrite IV.

It is probably true to say that dedicated machines perform word processing functions more efficiently than general purpose business computers. However, the non-dedicated machine does make up for this relative clumsiness by being able to do other tasks such as financial planning, stock control and database management. This increased flexibility is often of greater importance in the choice of machine than its ability to handle any particular application.

26.1.1 Word processing facilities

The list below indicates some of the features that a typical word processor or word processing package might possess. The list is not in any particular order—indeed different circumstances will determine different priorities.

1 **Scrolling** This enables any part of the document to be displayed and is essential for efficient editing.
2 **Deletion** This permits the erasing of unwanted letters, words, lines and paragraphs.
3 **Insertion** The insertion of letters, words, lines and paragraphs.
4 **Formatting** The re-formatting of text to restore the appearance of the text after editing, deletion and insertion.
5 **Substitution** Permitting the global replacement of an individual word by another.
6 **Movement** Blocks or columns of text may be moved or copied to other parts of the document.
7 **Reading** Standard paragraphs or other blocks of text can be 'read' from one file to another.
8 **Writing** Marked blocks of text can be written out onto a new file.
9 **Directory** This enables a check to be kept on files present on a disc and, more importantly, the amount of space left on a disc.
10 **Presentation** This includes features such as: right and left hand margin justification, the centering of headings, alternative line spacing, automatic page numbering, top and bottom margins, headings and footings.
11 **Tabulation** Permits columnar alignment of both text and figures. The latter benefits from decimal tabbing.
12 **Glossary** The user may predefine a number of long or complicated words and phrases which can be subsequently entered into the text at the touch of a single key.
13 **Enhancements** Printing features such as boldface, double strike, underlining and strike out.
14 **Spelling** All the words are checked against an extendable dictionary.

Word processing eradicates the need for repetitive copy typing of the same article, report or letter. Required amendments may be made and the contents re-formatted and printed. Powerful word processing software is currently available on computers costing less than £400.

26.1.2 Merge printing

One of the most useful features of word processing is merge printing facilities whereby different files may be merged at the time of printing. An obvious example is that of inserting an individual's name and address from one file (a name and address list) into another file (a standard letter). This gives the ability to quickly produce personalised letters.

26.1.3 Advantages of word processing

A word processing facility does not solve the problems associated with text and document production but facilitates the implementation of solutions when they are found. A word processor aids efficiency, not creativity.

The fundamental advantages of a word processor over even the most efficient typewriter are:

(a) The ease with which text can be edited and formatted speeds the production of documents and improves the quality of the final product.

(b) Once text has been entered it may be printed out in a variety of formats and at a variety of times. The updating of documents and lists becomes a simple matter as only the amendments and additions have to be entered, not the whole document. For example, a list of customer names and addresses once entered could be printed out in a number of ways: as a straightforward list of names and addresses; as a record card for sales calls; as part of a personalised mail-shot; as a printed address label for the mail-shot.

At least three issues require consideration in the implementation of word processing:

1 If full benefit is to be gained from the introduction of word processing then the manner in which the organisation generates and uses text has to be re-thought. Text production is probably one of the most wasteful of all management operations. Documents, memos, reports and quotations are all produced by a variety of personnel in an organisation using words and phrases which differ only marginally from user to user. If a level of agreement and rationalisation on the response to certain recurring circumstances can be reached then much correspondence can be handled quickly and accurately.

2 Although word processing embodies a filing system a computer is required to read the files. An efficient manual filing system is required to ensure that time is not wasted trying to trace the file from disk to disk. This means that disks must be properly documented, labelled and stored. This is particularly necessary if documents are to be accessed and updated by a number of managers and operators.

3 Without proper training of both operators and managers it is unlikely that full benefit will be gained from having a word processing system, even in the long-term. This leads to the under-utilisation of both equipment and staff which can incur substantial hidden costs. The misconception that a word processor is merely a 'super-typewriter' causes particular problems in the planning of training. Management frequently under-estimate the time and guidance needed to pick up these new skills and consequently do not reap the benefits. They also impose an unfair burden on typists and secretaries who are often left confused and ill-equipped. Furthermore, because the word processor is seen to be 'something to do with the typists', management do not undergo any training themselves and so are left in a position where they are unsure how to use and exploit the new opportunities.

26.1.4 The transmission of text—electronic mail

Documents are traditionally transmitted by internal mail, courier and external carriers such as the UK Post Office. Electronic mail allows the transmission of text from one place to another using a computer-based system to capture, transmit and deliver the information electronically.

An electronic mail system consists of:

(a) Users with terminals (these might be microcomputers) who need to communicate with each other.

(b) Hardware and software for controlling the receipt, routing and storage of electronic mail.

(c) Communication links between the terminals on the system and the host controlling machine.

Each user is allocated a mailbox into which messages are received. This mailbox can be 'opened' at any time to show the title and sender of new messages. This is similar to receiving a stack of envelopes with a return address printed on the back. The priority of the message will also be displayed, like letters, some will be marked 'Urgent!'

Each message (ie, envelope) can now be opened and the contents displayed on the screen. There is usually a facility to print off a hard copy of the message if this is required. Information recording the receipt of messages while the user is logged on to the system are often flashed on to the bottom of the screen, perhaps accompanied by a distracting noise (a keyboard beep). These messages can be examined when the user is ready. Communications which have taken place during a period of logging off (overnight, out of the office) are brought to the attention of the user when he or she next uses the system. The message 'new mail received' may be included in the logging on procedure.

A user prepares a message by creating the text on the screen using the normal editing facilities associated with word processing. The designated recipients are then specified. These may be individual names, departments or distribution lists maintained by the mailing system. Messages can be allocated priority as well as being arranged to arrive at or before a specified time. Once messages have been read and dealt with they may be stored for future reference and use. Periodic archiving will be required to copy these communications to secondary storage so freeing space on the electronic mail system.

Electronic mail systems must establish standards for security—ensuring that messages do not go astray and are not unlawfully intercepted—and logging. Traditional media have well understood costing systems (postage stamp, courier invoice, etc). An electronic mail system needs a logging device that will track and cost messages and bill departments accordingly.

26.2 DATA RETRIEVAL

The storage and retrieval of data is traditionally achieved through conventional drawer filing systems, card indexes, personal memory or some combination of all three. The development of many data processing systems was a response to the sheer problems of volume in storing and retrieving data in increasingly complex organisations.

The specification of conventional computer files was introduced in the previous chapter. These store records on magnetic media and individual records are retrieved by specifying the value of the identifying key field, eg,

'—give me Benyon's record—customer number 1078'

becomes relatively straightforward.

However, these file systems are essentially application centred and give little opportunity to share data across the organisation. Each application (personnel, payroll, training) develops its own private files with an organisation and content to suit the application. Similarly, difficulties occur in trying to exploit the data held in different application files, particularly when trying to access data across two or more application areas. Furthermore, inconsistencies may begin to appear in data duplicated in different files.

A data base can be formally defined as a shared, centrally controlled collection of data used in an organisation. The sharing of the data permits the elimination of inconsistencies because each application accesses the same data set. The control of the data base is usually vested in a data base administrator who decides the content of the data base, the storage structure and the security controls that are required.

26.2.1   A Data Base Management System

A Data Base Management System (DBMS) is a software package that organises the data in the data base and provides access to the data for different programs and users. Each DBMS will structure the data, provide a language for accessing and manipulating that data and a set of utilities to maintain, monitor and tune the performance of the data base.

It must provide a flexible filling system so that it can answer such queries as:

> '—Which customers have not placed an order for over £1000 for six months?'
> '—Who worked on the County Council project and left before completion?'
> '—What stock items exceed their maximum levels and for which purchase notes are still outstanding?'

26.2.2   Facilities of a DBMS

The flexible filing system concept introduced above remains the heart of any DBMS. The following features may also be present.

1   **File structure** Easy creation of files and, more importantly, the maintenance of those files. It should be easy to add, delete and amend field structures.
2   **Editing** Change, amend and deleting entries. The deletion facility might include a recall option, so permitting the retrieval of wrongly deleted data.
3   **Speed** Facility to sort and index files. Fast retrieval will require indexes.
4   **Reports** Flexible reporting facilities permitting the creation of user defined reports. Control over presentation of screen layouts.
5   **Programming** The provision of programming constructs to extend control over the file structures. This, again, is a mixed blessing. The inclusion of a programming language gives the package great flexibility but it does so at the cost of difficulty for non-programming users.
6   **External** Facility to transfer data to other software packages. For example the DBMS could be used to retrieve names which fulfill certain criteria. This can then be transferred to a merge-print package for the insertion of details into a standard letter.
7   **Query support** The provision of a simple query language accessible to all end-users.

The physical file organisation and retrieval methods employed by each DBMS is likely to include all of the conventional methods introduced in the previous chapter. These will be supplemented by other standard methods as well as proprietary techniques developed for that particular product. However, these will be transparent to the end-user and probably only accessible to the data administrator who might change certain parameters to improve the performance of the DBMS.

26.3   TALKING

Talking is particularly suitable for giving short instructions, small amounts of technical information and for giving immediate help and receiving instant reaction to ideas and events. For many years it was the main form of communication in societies and organisations. Quite complex narratives and procedures were passed from one generation to another without any formal written documentation.

Talking in contemporary organisations is primarily concerned with problem discussion, planning and other team activities usually undertaken in business meetings. 'Social' talking in the office has already been considered.

Meetings take up a large part of management time. In a widely quoted office activity study (Engel, 1979) top management spent over one-fifth of their time in scheduled or unscheduled meetings.

Two conventional support technologies for talking are dictation (allowing the production of written material) and, most importantly, the telephone.

26.3.1   Telephone systems

The original impact of the telephone on business must not be overlooked. It permitted managers to instantly give instructions to, and receive information from, geographically remote sites. Contemporary managers spend a considerable amount of time on the telephone (13.8%, Engel 1979) but are likely to be frustrated by:

(a)   Unsuccessful connections. The receiver is unavailable or engaged. The call may be placed on 'hold' but becomes 'lost' by the switchboard.

(b)   The nature of the call does not require a discussion with the intended receiver, it is merely a confirmation, request or instruction. However, this information cannot be given because the media demands an interaction.

(c)   Requests for the receiver to 'call back' are often unsuccessful because the caller is now busy. A tag game of frustrating phone calls begins.

There are a number of ways of tackling this problem.

(a)   A voice store and forward system where unconnected incoming messages are stored in a digital format on floppy disk and are accesssed in a similar way to the text mailbox messages of electronic mail. When the intended receiver next uses the telephone he or she is told that a message awaits them.

(b)   Use of a PABX (Private Automatic Branch Exchange) that permits calls: to be re-routed to a different extension if the telephone is unanswered after a specified number of rings; to dial extensions directly, hence cutting out switchboard bottlenecks and errors; to hold a busy number until it is free and to store calls awaiting that number in order of receipt.

26.3.2   Tele and audio conferencing

PABX systems often support audio conferencing whereby several remote personnel can effectively hold a meeting over the telephone. Tele-conferencing is similar in concept but radically different in technology. The participants sit in a television studio being filmed by cameras for transmission to the studios of other conference participants. The images are displayed on a large screen in each studio. Tele-conferencing is often used by television companies to hold a multi-national discussion on a world event. This is both cheaper and more spontaneous than flying all the participants to one convenient studio. The savings of delay and cost are also important advantages to a general business enterprise. Senior managers spend a lot of time travelling (13.1%, Engel 1979) and this time is generally unproductive. Tele-conferencing frees time for the manager to concentrate at activities at his or her base yet gives the opportunity to take place in urgent business deals and decisions.

26.4   IMAGE PROCESSING

Graphs, diagrams, pictures and photographs have a role to play in the contemporary office. It is often easier to present or supplement an idea using a diagram, graph or model—based upon the principle that a 'picture is worth a thousand words'. This method was used in the chapter on business systems where the data flow diagram was only partly reinforced by the accompanying text.

Presentation is particularly central to enterprises concerned with construction and design. Computer Aided Design (CAD) can be used in applications ranging from the construction of billion pound office complexes to the design of a kitchen. It is roughly analogous to word processing. In this instance the 'text' is shapes, images and artefacts. There should be productivity gains in design production alone. Alterations and extensions to the original drawing can be executed by re-calling the file and making the changes on the screen. The file is saved before re-printing. The levelling of diagrams can also be important. Many CAD programs have a 'zoom' facility which allows the model to be viewed at different levels and to ripple changes through those levels. For example, a screen might be used to show the overall plan of a house. The plan of an individual room is selected by moving the screen pointer (usually controlled by a mouse) to that room and selecting the zoom option. A screen plan of the room is then presented on the screen.

An improvement in the physical presentation of graphs can be achieved by using a dedicated software package (such as Harvard Graphics). The graphs produced by general packages such as Lotus 1–2–3 tend to be more restricted and less impressive, but they have still made a considerable contribution to improving the graphical display of data. Colour can also improve the graph's chance of successfully communicating its message and the reducing cost of colour plotters and printers has made this feature more accessible.

26.4.1 Transmission of images

Most documents are duplicated (using a photocopier) and despatched to their intended receiver through conventional text transmission systems—mail and couriers. Colour copying and automatic document collation enhance the image and speed of photocopying.

Facsimile (fax) transmission permits the fast transmission of images using a machine that converts the graphical data into signal waves and transmits them over the telephone network to a receiver where the signals are re-coded into the original image. A contemporary fax machine is both transmitter and receiver, having the technology to both code and de-code messages. Transmission is not restricted to images in the sense that text is just another image. Consequently faxs can be used for the fast despatch and receipt of documents such as orders, urgent memos and examination papers!

26.5 MANIPULATING DATA

Another common office task is the manipulation or modelling of data to respond to 'what-if' demands for information. For example, 'what would our profit have been last year if inflation had been 4% not 5% and salary settlements had been 2% lower than we agreed?' This manipulation of information often produced a time-consuming recalculation and reworking of data. Furthermore, the length and complexity of the task often ensured that the result was incorrect!

The use of dedicated mathematical modelling languages (such as SIMULA) and purpose built programs (often in FORTRAN or BASIC) provided possible solutions to this problem. However, these were not extensively used in most administrative offices.

26.5.1 Spreadsheets

Spreadsheets are a response to this need to construct elementary models that reduce time consuming recalculations. They use the memory of a computer as if it were a large piece of paper divided up into a matrix of cells. Into these cells may be entered numbers, text and formulae. The power of these systems is that the data held in any one cell can be made dependent on that held in other cells and changing a value in one cell can set (if wanted) a chain reaction of changes in other related cells. Thus, models can be built where cells are related through formula. Different values (inflation at 2%, 4%, 5%) merely become variables used in the model and the results are automatically generated for each of these values.

In addition the 'paper' can be 'cut' and 'stuck' together in different ways as appropriate. Some, or all, of the spreadsheet can be printed out directly or saved on disc for insertion into reports using a word processing package.

26.5.2 Spreadsheet facilities

A spreadsheet may offer:

1 **Presentation** Right and left justification. Facility to draw lines.
2 **Formats** A range of formats to display the text and numbers; scientific, fixed decimal etc.
3 **Copying** Powerful copying facilities. This means that the logic of, say a column addition, only has to be entered once and then it is copied to other columns.
4 **Functions** Functional commands such as SUM and NPV greatly cut down the time needed to develop models. The scope of such commands will vary from product to product. However, the inclusion of such commands as future value (FV) does aid the construction of certain financial models.
5 **Programming** The inclusion of programming constructs such as IF . . . THEN . . . ELSE greatly extends the control that may be built into the model. In some respects this may be something of a mixed blessing. On the one hand it provides an effective system development tool, whilst on the other it provides problems of program and system maintenance. Spreadsheet programming constructs are usually terse and unfriendly.
6 **Consolidation** The facility to bring several spreadsheets together into a summary sheet. This is a facility often required by users and which is provided for in a variety of ways by competing products. Indeed, a comparison of consolidation methods gives a good insight into the philosophy behind the package construction.
7 **Graphs** Graphs may be available as an integral part of the spreadsheet software (as in Lotus 1–2–3) or as output which has to be used in a specific graph package. The range and scope of graphs will also vary enormously.
8 **Others** Windows to permit the simultaneous viewing of dispersed areas of the spreadsheet. The provision of data tables to permit sensitivity analyses may also be a useful facility. Some spreadsheets also offer statistical regression and matrix manipulation.

26.5.3 Preparing a spreadsheet model

The user of a spreadsheet has two distinct problems.

LEARNING THE BASIC COMMANDS OF THE SPREADSHEET

The 'learning curve' gets longer as spreadsheets become more sophisticated and offer more facilities.

PREPARING AND SPECIFYING THE MODEL

This is often a difficult and time consuming task. The logic of the model has to be carefully specified so that it works properly when entered into the computer. This is not only concerned with the logic of the application, ie: that the standard cost labour unit is calculated correctly, but also with the requirements for 'what if?' experiments. Values cannot be increased by 5%, only formulas. Thus if you wish to see the effect of different inflation rates on a certain set of figures then these figures must be set up so that they reference an inflation multiplier. This may be set to 1.00 to start with, but may then be changed as required.

It is also important to recognise that most spreadsheets are constructed in RAM. Therefore, a memory status check is very helpful so that worksheets can be saved to disk before the memory runs out. Memory size also provides a restriction on the size of the model that can be built. It is likely that this restriction will be met before the theoretical limit of the software. This problem has been recognised by, amongst others, the Lotus Development Corporation who have sponsored and encouraged the development of expanded memory boards giving up to an extra 4MB of extra memory on top of the 640K RAM limit of IBM PC hardware.

26.6 ENABLING TECHNOLOGY

This review of office technologies has introduced five areas of application and examined some of the opportunities in those areas. Space does not allow a complete review of office automation technologies and so other key terms are included in the summary diagram (Figure 26.1). These can be the basis of further research (see exercises at the end of the chapter) for readers who wish to further pursue this topic.

A Local Area Network (LAN) is probably the predominant method of linking the new office technologies. It permits the linking of personal microcomputers, workstations, printers, facsimile devices and storage medium. It is particularly suited to word processing, spreadsheets, data management, electronic mail and voice transmission and storage.

FIGURE 26.1 **Office technology: a summary**

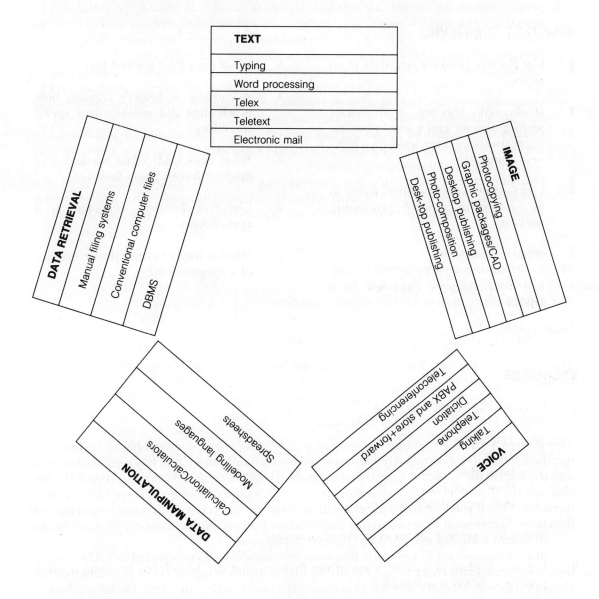

TEXT
Typing
Word processing
Telex
Teletext
Electronic mail

DATA RETRIEVAL
Manual filing systems
Conventional computer files
DBMS

IMAGE
Photocopying
Graphic packages/CAD
Desktop publishing
Photo-composition
Desk-top publishing

DATA MANIPULATION
Calculation/Calculators
Modelling languages
Spreadsheets

VOICE
Talking
Telephone
Dictation
PABX and store + forward
Teleconferencing

SUMMARY

1   There are five main ways of exchanging information in the office: text manipulation, data retrieval, talking, image processing and data manipulation.
2   Writing is an important way of communicating information. Word processing offers significant productivity and quality gains and electronic mail is emerging as an important method of transmitting the finished document.
3   Increasingly complex data retrieval requirements has led to the development of a shared data base controlled by a DBMS.
4   Talking remains an important way of sharing information. Improved telephone technologies should reduce the amount of time wasted in making unconnected calls and remote conferencing can improve the use of management time.
5   The quality of graphs, diagrams and images is improved by using dedicated presentation and design software. Fax is becoming the dominant way of communicating these images.
6   The time-consuming manipulation of data has been addressed by the development and widespread use of spreadsheets.
7   A LAN is a popular way of integrating these new office technologies.

SELF-TEST QUESTIONS

1   List the five primary activities of an office.

2   Distinguish between a dedicated word processor and a word processing software package used on a business computer.

3   List four different facilities likely to be offered in a word processing package.

4   What is a DBMS?

5   List four features expected in a DBMS.

6   What does PABX stand for?

7   According to Engel's figures, how much time did management spend travelling?

8   What does CAD stand for and why might it have a zoom facility?

9   List five features expected in a spreadsheet.

10   What is likely to limit the actual size of a spreadsheet?

Answers on page 335.

EXERCISES

1   Research two of the following:

>   Teletext
>   Telex
>   Intelligent copiers
>   Photo-composition
>   Desk-top publishing

No answer is supplied for this as it is 'research activity'.

2   List and explain to a client some of the facilities that can be offered by using a word processor. (*Refer to section 26.2.1*)

ACCA June 1987

3   Explain the purpose of a database and give an example of its use. (*Refer to section 26.2*)

ACCA June 1987

4   Explain the purpose of a spreadsheet and give an example of its use. (*Refer to section 26.5*)

ACCA June 1987

Solutions to questions

Solutions to Chapter 2 questions

ANSWERS TO EXERCISES

1 (a) Variable is discrete

   (b) Discrete   — no of children, shoe size
        Continuous   — height, weight
        Attribute   — male/female, married/single, pass/fail exam

   (c) i $\Sigma\,Q$ = 70 (This represents total sales in the store)
        ii $\Sigma\,P$ = £8.40
        iii $\Sigma\,(QP)$ = £103.71 (This represents total revenue in the store)

   (d) 5

   (e) i   £103.70
        ii   £104
        iii £100
        iv   £100

   (f) Raw

   (g) Secondary

2 (a) 7
       (b) 10
       (c) 2.601
       (d) 2.09

3 (a) 2.093421685 + 1.294466226 + 3.408983567
           = 6.796871478
           Antilog = 6264284.56

   (b) (2.120573931 × 2) + (−0.116338564) + 3.297432205
        = 7.422241502
        Antilog = 26438785.55

   (c) 2.127752516 − 1.376576957
        = 0.751175558
        Antilog = 5.63866

   (d) (1.991669007 − (−0.124938736)) + 1.100370545 + 2.965483924
        = 6.182462213
        Antilog = 1522166.687

Solutions to Chapter 3 questions

ANSWERS TO EXERCISES

1   (a) and (c)

MTG plc annual profit 1983–87 by market sector

	1987		1986		1985		1984		1983	
Sector	£m	%	£m	%	£m	%	£m	%	£m	%
Food	1.07	5.5	1.19	6.6	1.01	6.6	0.99	7.0	1.02	8.5
Clothing	10.51	53.6	10.05	55.8	8.19	53.4	7.98	56.2	6.73	56.2
Footwear	0.29	1.5	0.24	1.3	0.19	1.2	0.21	1.5	0.20	1.7
Furniture	2.12	10.8	2.04	11.3	1.81	11.8	1.72	12.1	1.63	13.6
Electrical goods	5.62	28.7	4.49	24.9	4.14	27.0	3.29	23.2	2.39	20.0
Total	19.61		18.01		15.34		14.19		11.97	

(b)   Total profit has steadily increased
Clothing is the largest contributor to total profit
Profit in all sectors has increased

(d)   Electrical goods are becoming increasingly important to total profit with all other sectors showing a decrease in the percentage contribution to the total

(e)   **MTG profit (£ millions) 1983–87**

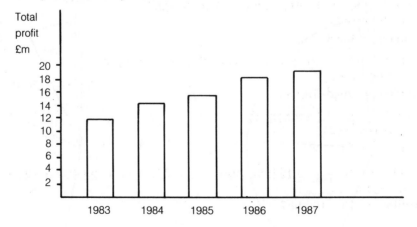

(f) **MTG profit per sector as a percentage of the total 1983–87**

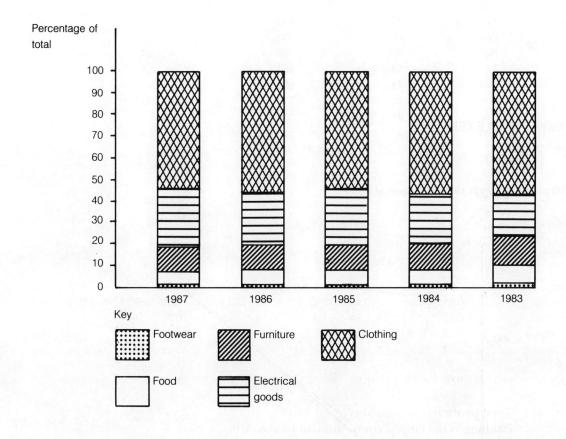

(g)

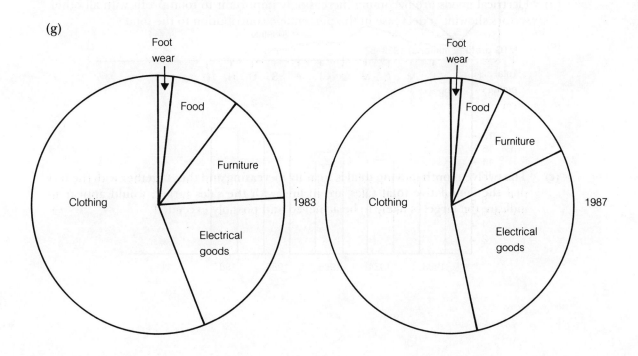

2 The following figures can be derived:

	Sales	Moving Total	Cumulative Total
Jan	27	493	27
Feb	29	494	56
Mar	35	498	91
Apr	59	503	150
May	73	508	223
Jun	36	510	259
July	37	513	296
Aug	33	516	329

(a), (b)

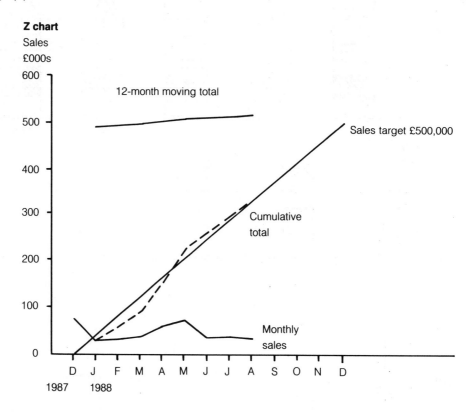

(c) The twelve-month moving total is steadily increasing and this, together with the fact that the cumulative total sales are in line with the sales target, would appear to indicate the target is likely to be achieved and possibly exceeded

Solutions to Chapter 4 questions

ANSWERS TO EXERCISES

1 (a)

	Frequency	
Weekly Salary	Clerical/Admin	Sales Staff
£80 < £100	3	11
£100 < £120	7	18
£120 < £140	11	12
£140 < £160	16	7
£160 < £180	10	2
£180 < £200	3	0
	50	50

(b)

Histogram and frequency polygon for weekly salary of clerical/admin staff

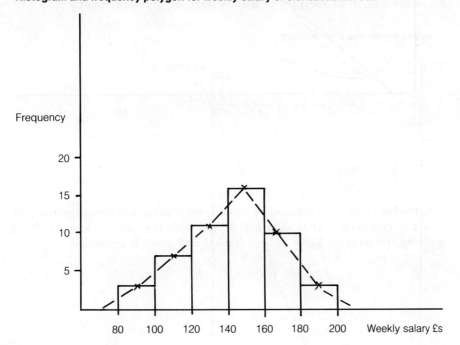

(c) **Histogram and frequency polygon for weekly salary of sales staff**

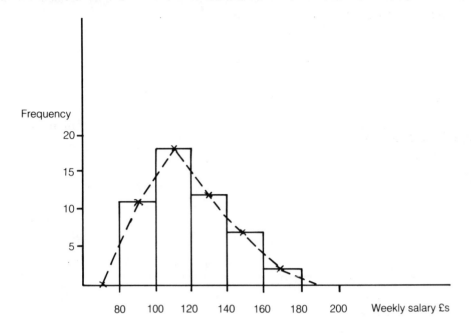

(d) The two distributions are similar in that one interval has a large frequency—£140 < £160 for clerical/admin and £100 < £120 for sales staff

They differ in that the bulk of frequencies for sales staff occur to the left of the bulk of frequencies of the clerical/admin staff

(e) From the data it does appear as if sales staff are generally paid less

2   **Ogives for the two distributions**

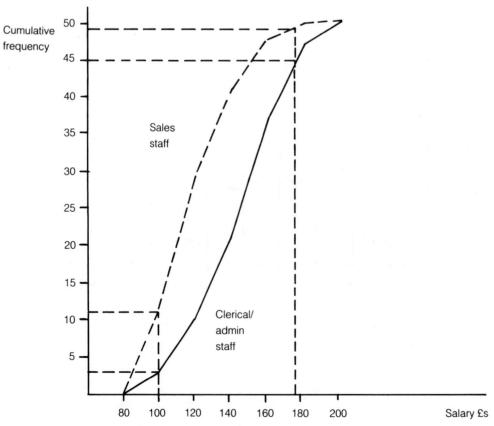

Note: Answers to this question are derived from the ogive—this yields slightly different results than using the new data supplied in the question

(a) $\frac{11}{50} = 22\%$

(b) $\frac{3}{50} = 6\%$

(c) The comparison reveals that a larger percentage of sales staff fall into this category

(d) $\frac{1}{50} = 2\%$

(e) $\frac{5}{50} = 10\%$

Solutions to Chapter 5 questions

ANSWERS TO EXERCISES

1   Refer to the text

2   (a)   Clerical/admin = £142.85
            Sales   = £118.22

      (b)   Using the mean we can say that, on average, clerical/admin staff are better paid

      (c)   Clerical/admin = £142.80
            Sales   = £118.40

      (d)   The differences arise because of using the midpoints to calculate the mean from grouped data. It is better to use the raw data although in this case there is little difference

      (e)   Clerical/admin = £145.62
            Sales   = £116.11

      (f)   In the case of clerical/admin staff the mean is *below* the median indicating that employees at the bottom of the salary scale are pulling the mean down. In the case of sales staff it is a small number of employees at the top end of the salary scale who are pulling the mean *above* the median. Unless the distribution is symmetrical it is better to use the median as the measure of average

      (g)   For this calculation we use the mean as it includes all the data.
               For sales staff the total salary paid will be £118.22 × 50 = £5,911 and for clerical/admin staff will be £142.85 × 50 = £7,142.50. Total salaries at present are £5,911 + £7,142.50 = £13,053.50
               If an increase of 10% occurs this will be £1,305.35 extra

      (h)   It will increase the mean (which includes all the data) but will not affect the median (as this person was above the median value in any case)

      (i)   Based on the raw data:
            mean   = £120.22
            median is unchanged

            The data set is continuous and the mode is more suitable for use with discrete data

Solutions to Chapter 6 questions

ANSWERS TO EXERCISES

1   Refer to text

2   (a)   Clerical/admin   =   £25.80
        Sales   =   £22.16

   (b)   Clerical/admin   =   £18.06
         Sales   =   £18.72

   (c)   Clerical/admin   =   £18.75
         Sales   =   £16.74

   (d)   Clerical/admin   =   −0.33
         Sales   =   +0.31

From the standard deviations the clerical/admin data have a larger *absolute* variation. Looking at the coefficient of variation the *relative* dispersion around the mean is very similar.

   The quartile deviation indicates that, for the middle group of data, there is more dispersion in the clerical/admin data set.

   Finally, the coefficient of skewness highlights the very different shapes of the two distributions, with the sales group positively skewed but the clerical/admin group negatively skewed

3   Lower and upper quartiles from the frequency tables are:

	Clerical/admin	Sales
Lower	£125.00	£101.94
Upper	£162.50	£135.42

The figures estimated from the ogive are less reliable because they are estimated from the graph rather than calculated from the statistics.

4   (a)   Before tax   =   £6445.51
        After tax   =   £4539.95

   (b)   Tax has had the effect of reducing the absolute dispersion around the mean income

   (c)   Before tax   =   £3335.21
         After tax   =   £2586.11

   (d)   The quartile deviation would probably be preferred given the skewness of the distribution

Solutions to Chapter 7 questions

ANSWERS TO EXERCISES

1   (a)   Index of turnover by sector 1983–87 (1983 = 100)

	1987	*1986*	*1985*	*1984*	*1983*
Food	131	122	113	110	100
Clothing	156	141	127	113	100
Footwear	176	124	109	109	100
Furniture	116	112	105	104	100
Electrical	157	139	130	117	100
Total	147	133	122	111	100

(b)   The clothing and electrical sectors have grown most on a consistent basis although the footwear sector index increased dramatically in 1987. The furniture sector has performed badly consistently.

(c)

Index of turnover by sector 1983–87
(1983 = 100)

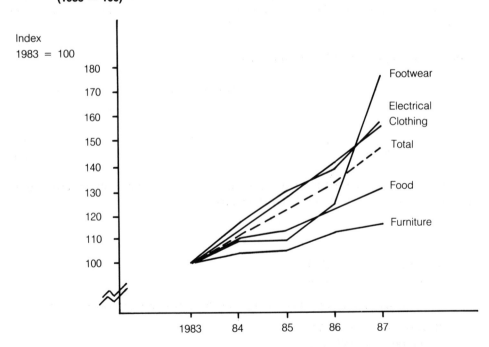

2 (a) $\dfrac{1899000}{1393000} \times 100 = 136.3$

(b) $\dfrac{2577000}{1888000} \times 100 = 136.5$

(c) The results differ because the Laspeyres index uses weights for 1985 and the Paasche uses weights for 1988. The weights are the numbers employed in each category which has changed over this 3 year period

(d) The Laspeyres index would probably be preferred given that the index is required every 6 months. The Paasche index would require new weights twice a year

No answers are given for Chapter 8 questions as reference to the text will reveal whether the correct approach has been suggested

Solutions to Chapter 9 questions

ANSWERS TO EXERCISES

1   (a)   25/100 = 0.25
    (b)   25/100 = 0.25
    (c)   0.25 + 0.25 = 0.50
    (d)   75/100 = 0.75
    (e)   0.25 × 0.6 = 0.15
    (f)   0.25 × 0.4 = 0.10
    (g)   40/100 = 0.4
    (h)   0.4 × 0.25 = 0.10
    (i)   0.4 × 0.75 = 0.30
    (j)   0.6 × 0.75 = 0.45
    (k)   0.25 + 0.40 − (0.25 × 0.4) = 0.65 − 0.10 = 0.55
    (l)   The significance of the rows is that if cards were not chosen at random the probability would not be correct

2   (a)   Using the same notation:

$$P(F|B) = \frac{P(B|F)P(F)}{P(B|F)P(F) + P(B|NF)P(NF)}$$

$P(B|F) = 5/20 = 0.25$

$P(B|NF) = 45/105 = 0.43$

therefore: $P(F|B) = \dfrac{0.25(0.16)}{0.25(0.16) + 0.43(0.84)} = \dfrac{0.04}{0.4012} = 0.10$

    (b)

$$P(NF|A) = \frac{P(A|NF)P(NF)}{P(A|NF)P(NF) + P(A|F)P(F)}$$

$P(A|NF) = 60/105 = 0.57$

$P(A|F) = 15/20 = 0.75$

$P(NF|A) = \dfrac{0.57(0.84)}{0.57(0.84) + 0.75(0.16)} = \dfrac{0.4788}{0.5988} = 0.80$

Solutions to Chapter 10 questions

ANSWERS TO EXERCISES

1 (a)

No of heads	Probability
0	0.03125
1	0.15625
2	0.3125
3	0.3125
4	0.15625
5	0.03125
	———
	1.0

(b)

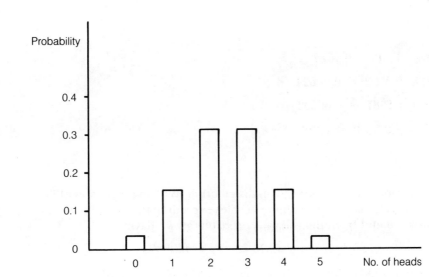

(c) Refer to the relevant tables in the chapter

2 P(driver not available) = 0.10

Required:

therefore P(no more than 5 drivers not available)

No drivers not available	Probability
0	0.07179
1	0.19942
2	0.26589
3	0.22650
4	0.13842
5	0.06459
	———
	0.96660

L

therefore P(no more than 5 drivers not available) = 0.9666
therefore P(more than 5 drivers not available)   = 1 − 0.9666
                                                   = 0.0334

There is a probability of 3.34% that there will be insufficient drivers and 96.66% that there will be sufficient

3   (a) $\lambda = 20$
          (i)   P(0 accidents) = 0
          (ii)   P(> 25 accidents) = 0.11

    (b)   Without further information it is impossible to tell. However, we may suspect that accidents may occur more frequently at certain times of the day, at certain days of the week, or at certain times of the year

4   (a)   0.53862

    (b)   0.00014

    (c)   0.98116

    (d)   0

5   (a) $Z = 1 : P = 0.1587$

    (b) $Z = 2.5 : P = 0.00621$

    (c) $P = (.1587 − 0.00621) = 0.15249$

    (d) $Z = −2.5 : P = 0.00621$

6   This is an application of the Poisson distribution. With average sales of 30 we must have a stock level such that the probability of sales exceeding the available stock is less than 5%. Here $\lambda = 30$ and from the relevant probabilities we have:

$$P(X \leqslant 39) = 0.95375$$

    That is, a probability of 95% that sales will be no more than 39 disks. If we keep a stock of 39 disks, therefore, the chance of running out of stock (ie, having more than 39 customers) is less than 5%

Solutions to Chapter 11 questions

ANSWERS TO EXERCISES

1   (a)   TC = 10 + 1.2X
            TR = 2.8X

     (b) and (c)

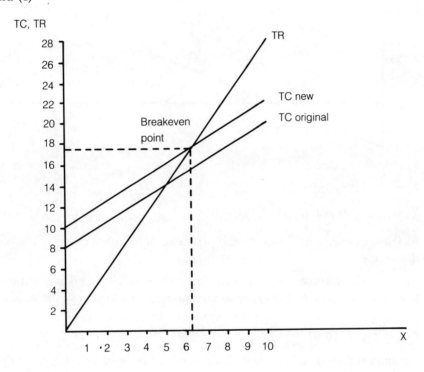

     (d)   X = 6.25
           TC = TR = 17.5

     (e)   X = 5.56
           TC = TR = 16.67

2 (a) Q is dependent on P

(b)

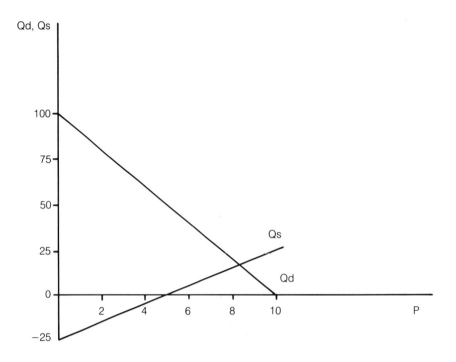

(c) As P increases Qd decreases. As the price rises people will buy less

(d) As P increases Qs increases. As the price rises it becomes more profitable to supply this item

(e) The negative intercept indicates the line will cross the P axis above the origin. The price must be greater than zero to encourage firms to supply the product

(f) P = 8.33
Qd = Qs = 16.67

(g) Quantity supplied and demanded will not balance. With a higher price Qs > Qd and the firm will not be able to sell all the items. At a lower price Qd > Qs and the firm will realise it can raise the price and hence make more profit

3 (a) Qd = 150 − 20P

(b) P = 7
Qd = Qs = 10

(c) Both the intercept and slope have changed. The intercept has increased implying that people wish to buy more of the product at the same price. The slope has also increased implying that people will react more to a change in price

Solutions to Chapter 12 questions

ANSWERS TO EXERCISES

1 and **2**

(a)
$$\begin{bmatrix} 9 & 6 & 3 \\ 9 & 13 & 8 \\ -6 & 11 & 16 \end{bmatrix}$$

(b)
$$\begin{bmatrix} -1 & 0 & -1 \\ -11 & -1 & 0 \\ 10 & 3 & 2 \end{bmatrix}$$

(c) Not possible

(d) Not possible

(e)
$$\begin{bmatrix} 21 & 44 & 35 \\ 40 & 98 & 78 \\ -22 & 45 & 71 \end{bmatrix}$$

(f)
$$\begin{bmatrix} 42 & 40 & 27 \\ 13 & 53 & 46 \\ 8 & 98 & 95 \end{bmatrix}$$

(g) Not possible

(h) Not possible

3 $A^{-1} = \begin{bmatrix} 0.3922 & -.1275 & -0.0392 \\ -1 & 0.5 & 0 \\ 1.0196 & -.4314 & 0.0980 \end{bmatrix}$

$B^{-1} = \begin{bmatrix} 0.1667 & -0.1961 & 0.0686 \\ 0.1667 & 0.3333 & -0.1667 \\ -0.1667 & -0.2157 & 0.2255 \end{bmatrix}$

$C^{-1} = \begin{bmatrix} -0.25 & 0.5 \\ 0.1875 & -0.1250 \end{bmatrix}$

4 $P = \begin{bmatrix} 1.0 & 1.5 & 2 \\ 1.1 & 1.75 & 2.5 \\ 0.1 & 0.25 & 0.5 \end{bmatrix}$

$Q = \begin{bmatrix} 100 & 50 & 40 \\ 50 & 100 & 30 \\ 30 & 10 & 20 \end{bmatrix}$

$P \times Q$ will give the required result. The product will be the stocks in each store multiplied by cost, price and profit.

$PQ = \begin{bmatrix} 235 & 220 & 125 \\ 272 & 255 & 146 \\ 37.5 & 35 & 21.5 \end{bmatrix}$

Thus, for example, for the stock in Store A the cost is £235, price is £272 and profit is £37.50

5   Let

$$P = \begin{bmatrix} 5000 & 5500 \\ 8000 & 10000 \\ 6000 & 8000 \\ 15000 & 20000 \end{bmatrix}$$

$Q_o = [120 \quad 41 \quad 25 \quad 21]$

$Q_n = [158 \quad 52 \quad 30 \quad 25]$

$Q_oP = [1393000 \quad 1690000]$

$Q_nP = [1761000 \quad 2129000]$

$\text{Laspeyres} = \dfrac{1690000}{1393000} \times 100 = 121.3$

$\text{Paasche} = \dfrac{2129000}{1761000} \times 100 = 120.9$

6   Refer to solutions given for the previous chapter

Solutions to Chapter 13 questions

ANSWERS TO EXERCISES

1   (a) $1A \geqslant 1500$

       (b)

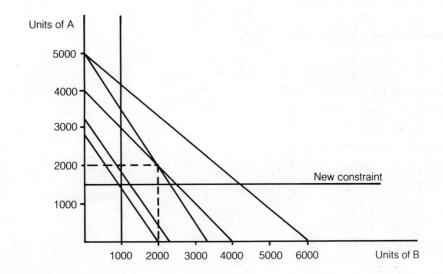

       (c)   A = 2,000
            B = 2,000
            Profit = 1,200

2   A = 1,500
      B = 1,000
      Cost = 1,100
      The two minimum production constraints are binding

Solutions to Chapter 14 questions

ANSWERS TO EXERCISES

1   Refer to text

2   (a) $X_1 = -3.58$
$X_2 = 5.58$
Turning point when $X = 1$

(b) $X_1 = -3.13$
$X_2 = 4.79$
Turning point when $X = 0.83$

(c) $X_1 = 2.76$
$X_2 = 7.24$
Turning point when $X = 5$

(d)   There are no roots
The equation does not intercept the X axis

(e) $X_1 = -1.71$
$X_2 = 11.71$
Turning point when $X = 5$

3   (a)

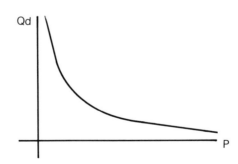

(b)   At a sufficiently low price demand for this product will be infinite, and even when the price is extremely high there will still be some demand for the product

4 (a)

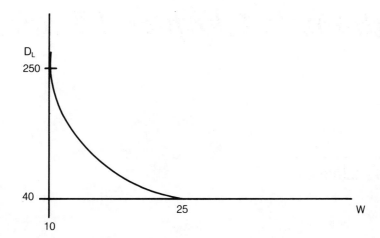

(b) As the wage rate increases D_L falls with MTG cutting back their employment of programmers at higher wage rates. It is also likely that, if W exceeded £25, D_L would continue to decline but would not reach zero, implying a need for some minimum number of programmers

Solutions to Chapter 15 questions

ANSWERS TO EXERCISES

1   (a) $\dfrac{dy}{dx} = -5 + 5X : X = 1$

             $\dfrac{d^2y}{dx^2} = 5$ giving a minimum

     b $\dfrac{dy}{dx} = 5 - 6X : X = 0.833$

             $\dfrac{d^2y}{dx^2} = -6$ giving a maximum

     c $\dfrac{dy}{dx} = 50 - 10X : X = 5$

             $\dfrac{d^2y}{dx^2} = -10$ giving a maximum

     d $\dfrac{dy}{dx} = 50 - 10X : X = 5$

             $\dfrac{d^2y}{dx^2} = -10$ giving a maximum

     e $\dfrac{dy}{dx} = 50 - 10X : X = 5$

             $\dfrac{d^2y}{dx^2} = -10$ giving a maximum

2   Refer to original equations

3    $Q_D = \dfrac{600}{P}$

    $\dfrac{dQ}{dP} = \dfrac{-600}{P^2}$

    When $P = 2$ $\dfrac{dQ}{dP} = -150$

            $P = 8$ $\dfrac{dQ}{dP} = -9.375$

In this case the slope indicates the rate of change in Q_D as P changes. Management are easily able to predict how the demand for the product will change for a given change in price

4   (a) $TR = 100X - 3X^2$ $\dfrac{dTR}{dX} = 100 - 6X$

          $TC = 100 + 2X^2$ $\dfrac{dTC}{dX} = 4X$

          $Profit = -100 + 100X - 5X^2$ $\dfrac{dprofit}{dX} = 100 - 10X$

   (b)   In each case the derivative shows the rate of change in the function for a given change in X. Thus, for a given change in output, X, we know the corresponding change in TR, TC and profit.

   (c)   Setting $\dfrac{dTC}{dX} = 0$ gives X = 0

          Minimum cost occurs when output is zero

   (d)   Setting $\dfrac{dTR}{dX} = 0$ gives X = 16.67

   (e)   Setting $\dfrac{dprofit}{dX} = 0$ gives X = 10

          When X = 10 $\dfrac{dTR}{dX} = 40$

                      $\dfrac{dTC}{dX} = 40$

          That is, the slope of TR and TC are equal when profit is maximised. At this point the addition to total revenue is matched by the addition to the total cost

Solutions to Chapter 16 questions

ANSWERS TO EXERCISES

1 (a)
1978	119.95
1979	129.17
1980	163.20
1981	145.47
1982	161.55
1983	176.65
1984	181.79
1985	181.79
1986	180.62
1987	180.14

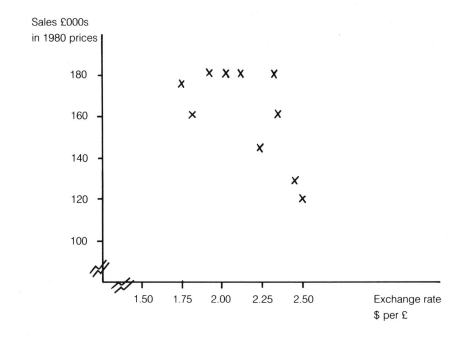

(b) and (c) The scatter diagram reveals a wide scatter of points but with an overall negative slope

(d) Y = 281.97 − 55.86X
Where Y = deflated export sales
X = exchange rate

(e) The a term at 281.97 is the intercept and would be interpreted as export sales at a zero exchange rate.

The b term is −55.86 and shows the decline in export sales with a rise in the exchange rate

(f) r = −0.64
The coefficient is negative, confirming the slope of the line of best fit, but is not particularly high indicating the variation of the points on the scatter diagram form the regression line

(g) Probably not very useful, given the scatter diagram and r value, although the equation may be of some guidance in allowing management to assess the impact of exchange rates on sales levels

2 (a)

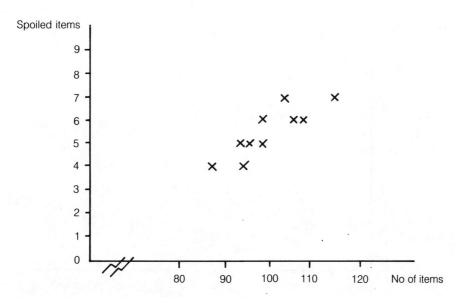

(b) Y = −6.02 + 0.116X
Where Y = no spoiled items
X = no of items

(c) a at −6.02 indicates the line crosses the X axis at a point above zero, implying that spoiled items will not occur until the number of items reaches a critical level.
b at +.116 indicates the increase in spoiled items with an increase in the number of items—here at a rate of 11.6%

(d) +0.856 showing a strong positive correlation

(e) $1 - \dfrac{6(22.5)}{10(10^2 - 1)} = +0.864$

(f) It depends on the use to which the information will be put. The product moment is useful for assessing predictions. The rank is useful if we wish to see if there is any link between a typist's overall productivity when compared to other typists and the number of spoiled items

Solutions to Chapter 17 questions

ANSWERS TO EXERCISES

1   (a)

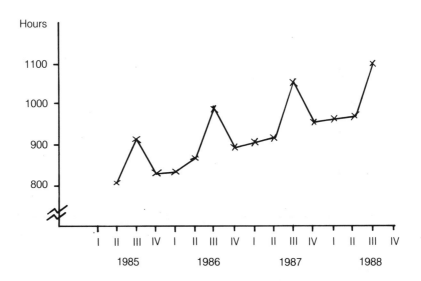

(b)   Over such a short time there would be little difference. The graph indicates a fairly stable trend so the additive model would be adequate

(c)   Trend

1985	2	
	3	
	4	855.5
1986	1	873
	2	890.5
	3	905.125
	4	918.5
1987	1	932.75
	2	948.25
	3	963
	4	976.5
1988	1	989.25
	2	
	3	

(d)   Seasonal factors

I	−30.4
II	−30.5
III	88.8
IV	−27.9

(e)   The third quarter regularly requires more part-time hours. This covers the summer period so perhaps the part-time hours are required to cover for full time staff on holiday.

(f)   The trend is reasonably linear so simple extrapolation gives:

$$\frac{989.25 - 855.5}{10} = 13.38$$

This would give a trend for 1989 I of:

$$989.25 + (13.38 \times 4) = 1042.77$$

The seasonal factor is -27.9 so the forecast would be $1042.77 - 27.9 = 1014.87$

2   (a) and (b)

		Actual	Forecast $\alpha = 0.3$	Forecast $\alpha = 0.9$
Day	1	50	50	50
Day	2	52	50	50
Day	3	48	50.6	51.8
Day	4	54	49.8	48.4
Day	5	49	51.1	53.4
Day	6	48	50.5	49.4
Day	7	51	49.8	48.1
Day	8	53	50.2	50.7
Day	9	49	51.0	52.8
Day	10	47	50.4	49.4

(c)   The choice of α makes the forecast more, or less, responsive to the forecast error

(d) $\alpha = 0.3$ is probably better. α at 0.9 makes the forecast too sensitive to the last forecast error and the forecasts fluctuate considerably from period to period

Solutions to Chapter 18 questions

ANSWERS TO EXERCISES

1

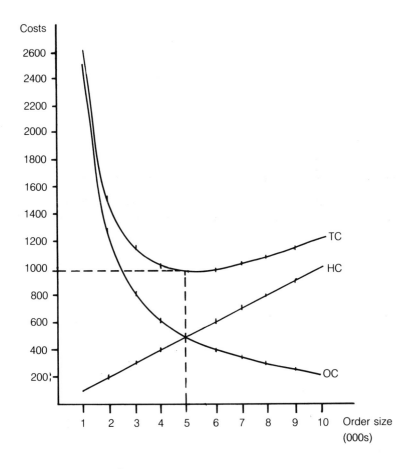

2   D = 4000
O = 25
H = 1.25

(a) $EOQ = \sqrt{\dfrac{2(25)(4000)}{1.25}} = 400$

(b) $\dfrac{4000}{400} = 10$ orders

(c) $0 = 30$

$EOQ = \sqrt{\dfrac{2(30)(4000)}{1.25}} = 438$

Solutions to Chapter 19 questions

ANSWERS TO EXERCISES

1 $P = 100$
$i = 0.07$

(a) $t = 1$
$V = 100(1 + 0.07)^1 = 107$
Interest $= 107 - 100 = 7$

(b)   If $t = 5$ $V = 131.08$
If $t = 4$ $V = 122.50$
Therefore interest at end of year $5 = 131.08 - 122.50 = 8.58$

Total interest $= 131.08 - 100 = 31.08$

2   (a) $APR = \left(1 + \dfrac{0.07}{4}\right)^4 - 1 = 0.0719 = 7.19\%$

(b) $APR = \left(1 + \dfrac{0.07}{12}\right)^{12} - 1 = 0.0723 = 7.23\%$

(c)   Assume 365 days per year

$APR = \left(1 + \dfrac{0.07}{365}\right)^{365} - 1 = 0.0725 = 7.25\%$

3   (a) $V = 2500\,(1.1)^5 = 4026.28$

(b) $V = 2500\,(1.02)^{20} = 3714.87$

(c) $V = 2500\,(1.005)^{60} = 3372.13$

Option (a) is preferred

4   (a)   Straight Line
Current value £50000
Scrap value   £7500
Time   10 years

Annual depreciation $= \dfrac{50000 - 7500}{10} = £4250$

For annual schedule, see (c)

(b)   Reducing balance:

$r = 1 - \sqrt[10]{\dfrac{7500}{50000}} = 17.28\%$

(c)

Year	Straight Line		Reducing Balance	
	Value	Depreciation	Value	Depreciation
0	50000	4250	50000	8640
1	45750	4250	41360	7147
2	41500	4250	34213	5912
3	37250	4250	28301	4890.41
4	33000	4250	23410.59	4045.35
5	28750	4250	19365.24	3346.31
6	24500	4250	16018.93	2768.07
7	20250	4250	13250.86	2289.75
8	16000	4250	10961.11	1894.08
9	11750	4250	9067.03	1566.78
10	7500		7500.25	
		42500		42499.75

Solutions to Chapter 20 questions

ANSWERS TO EXERCISES

1   NPV Purchase at 8% = £17599.73
   NPV Purchase at 12% = £17025.95
   NPV Lease   at 8% = £17248.51
   NPV Lease   at 12% = £16149.40

   With different discount rates (and discount factors) the present values of future cash flows alter, affecting the NPV

2   (a)   NPV Supplier A = £13368.61
         NPV Supplier B = £15410.22

         Both options produce a positive NPV but that for Supplier B is higher and would be preferred

   (b)   Other factors would be:
         —reliability of the two suppliers
         —quality of services provided
         —how the respective NPVs would be affected should the rate of interest change

   (c)   With a lower interest rate both NPVs will increase but it is unlikely the relative values will change given the cash flow profile

   (d)   Supplier A IRR = 17.2%
         Supplier B IRR = 18.3%

   (e)   The IRR indicates the rate of interest which gives NPV = 0. For each supplier the IRR shows that, below this rate, the project will generate a positive NPV and, above this rate a negative NPV

Solutions to Chapter 21 questions

ANSWERS TO EXERCISES

1   (a)   £2,900.96

    (b)   £2,762.82

    (c)   £2,272.98

    (d)   £2,164.74

2   (a)   £7246.89

    (b)   £6710.08

These are the present values of the annuities

3   Interest rate of 6 per cent:

Year	Debt	Interest	Repayment	Amount owing
1	25000	1500	4025.9	22474.1
2	22474.1	1348.45	4025.9	19796.65
3	19796.65	1187.80	4025.9	16958.54
4	16958.54	1017.51	4025.9	13950.16
5	13950.16	837.01	4025.9	10761.27
6	10761.27	645.68	4025.9	7381.04
7	7381.04	442.86	4025.9	3798.01
8	3798.01	227.88	4025.9	—

Interest rate of 9 per cent:

Year	Debt	Interest	Repayment	Amount owing
1	25000	2250	4516.86	22733.14
2	22733.14	2045.98	4516.86	20262.26
3	20262.26	1823.60	4516.86	17569.01
4	17569.01	1581.21	4516.86	14633.36
5	14633.36	1317.00	4516.86	11433.50
6	11433.50	1029.01	4516.86	7945.65
7	7945.65	715.11	4516.86	4143.90
8	4143.90	372.95	4516.86	—

Solutions to Chapter 22 questions

ANSWERS TO SELF-TEST QUESTIONS

1   Hardware

2
16	8	4	2	1	
×	×	×	×	×	
1	0	1	1	1	= 23

3   American Standard Code for Information Interchange

4   Eight

5   Speed and Accuracy

6   Transistors

7   ALU, Control Unit, Primary storage

8   RAM may be written to and is usually volatile. ROM may only be read and is not volatile

9   80k–120k

10   To allow for significant data storage, and to permit data back-up

11   2400′ or 3600′

12   Bits per inch. It is misleading because it actually refers to characters/inch

13   Rotational delay, head movement, transfer speeds

14   Advantage—central control through master workstation
     Disadvantage—excessive cabling

15   To handle incoming messages and convert incoming digital messages into analogue form
     suitable for telephone transmission

ANSWERS TO EXERCISES

1   Hardware is the term given to the electronic and electromechanical devices that make up
     the physical parts of the computer system. It consists of a Central Processing Unit (CPU)
     which houses the control unit, ALU and primary store. This is supported by secondary
     storage devices such as magnetic disks and magnetic tapes. The input hardware is
     dominated by screens and keyboards whilst printers are the main form of hardcopy
     output.

Software refers to the programs and protocols that make the hardware actually work. A general distinction can be made between system software-operating systems etc and application software written in a programming language. The duplication of many of these applications has led to the widespread growth of application packages.

2   RAM stands for Random Access Memory. Data and programs used by the hardware are stored in the RAM ready for processing by the rest of the CPU. RAM can thus be written to and read by application software.

ROM stands for Read Only Memory and refers to a part of the primary store whose circuits are fixed at manufacture. Thus data can be read from the ROM but not replaced, ie, written to.

RAM is normally volatile in that its contents will be lost when the computer is turned off. ROM is not volatile.

3   A floppy disk (diskette) is a plastic disk coated with iron oxide and enclosed within a reinforcing envelope. It comes in three standard sizes—8", 5" and 3". The capacity of a floppy disk is typically in the region of 360k to 1.2Mb. It is a popular method of providing storage in microcomputer systems as well as distributing software packages. The diskette is read by a read/write head that makes physical contact with the surface of the media. In contrast a fixed disk comes within a sealed unit. It provides much larger storage than a floppy disk (typically up to 300Mb) with fast data transfer to the CPU. The disks are normally accessed by a 'flying head' that travels on a cushion of air just above the surface of the media. This reduces disk wear and the chance of data loss.

4   Most disks use a cylinder concept whereby data is stored on tracks running in concentric rings around the disk (similar to the tracks of an LP record). These disks are stacked on top of each other with each disk being accessed by a read/write head. Thus data is transferred by these heads in a 'conceptual cylinder' in that data on the same track of the different disks is accessed and transferred together.

Solutions to Chapter 23 questions

ANSWERS TO SELF-TEST QUESTIONS

1   Machine code, assembler, high level languages, fourth generation languages

2   A compiler users English-like statements compared with the symbolic and mnemonic instructions of an assembler

3   A procedural statement describes *how* something should be done.
A non-procedural statement describes *what* is required

4   Beginners All purpose Symbolic Instruction Code

5   (a)   END
(b)   PRINT
(c)   REM
(d)   GOTO 120

6   ◇

7   $2^6 = 64$

8   Easing the user/machine interface, input and output control, maintenance of accounting information, housekeeping commands

9   It fits in with organisational requirements (cost and profit centres) and it provides improved security measures

10   Real time, on-line, batch

ANSWERS TO EXERCISES

1   30   S will be allocated the value 0.2
50   P will be allocated the value 1
60   If P = 99 then the program is terminated, otherwise the program proceeds to line 80
80   E will be allocated the value 743
90   If P = 1 THEN the variable F1 will be allocated the value of E (743). If the value of P is not equal to 1 then the program simply progresses and this line is not executed
100   F2 = 743 + 0.2*(743 − 743)
130   NEW FORECAST = £Integer part of (F2 + 0.5)
NEW FORECAST = £Integer part of (743.5)
NEW FORECAST = £743

2 (a) i

A	B	C	D	E
0	0	0	30	4
120	4	3600	35	7
365	11	12175	40	9
725	20	26575	45	6
995	26	38725	50	2
1095	28	43725	999	

    ii   Successive pairs of data values are entered into D and E
         A holds the running total of $D \times E$
         B cumulates the value of E
         C cumulates the value of $D^2 \times E$
         Line 200, A/B, represents a mean of a frequency distribution
         Line 210 gives the variance of this frequency distribution

    iii Documentation would include:
          —The program logic: flow chart or Structured English
          —Program listing: the program statements given in BASIC
          —Test data showing data output from sample input
          —Other administrative arrangements such as title of the program, author,
            data, purpose, cross-references etc

  (b) i   Low level language—machine code or assembler with a one to one correspon-
         dence with machine instructions. Usually difficult to program, understand and
         debug.
             High level language—usually written in English-like statements or
         algebraic functions. Each instruction will be passed through a compiler or
         assembler which will produce many lines of machine code. High level lan-
         guages are portable across machines.

3 (b) Testing will be performed via 'desk checking' the program before entering appro-
        priate test data and checking that the results match expected output. Any errors in
        construction are colloquially called 'bugs' and are hunted out in the ritual of 'debug-
        ging'. Corrected programs are then re-tested.

  (c) Program documentation should include:
      i   Program listing
      ii   Program logic—usually represented as a flow chart or Structured English
      iii Test data and test results together with a log of that testing
      iv A title and a reference which gives some indication of how it fits into the whole
          of the program suite, and any special operating environment that it requires

5

Exercise 1

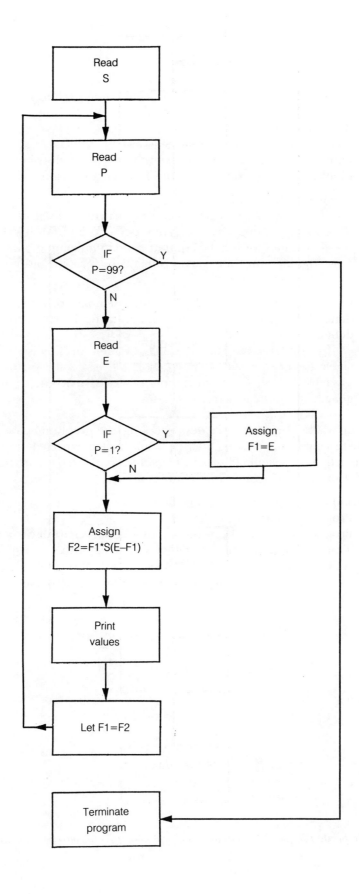

Exercise 2

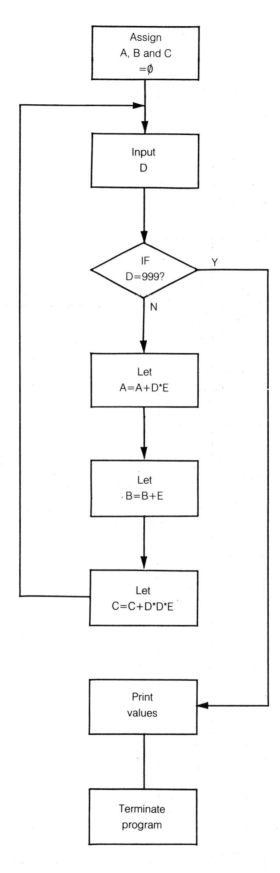

No answer is given for the Chapter 24 question as it would not reflect the variety of circumstances likely to be recorded.

Solutions to Chapter 25 questions

ANSWERS TO SELF-TEST QUESTIONS

1   Interface design and the specification of controls

2   Verification is concerned with ensuring that the correct data value has been entered into the system
    Validation attempts to ensure that the value is both accurate and meaningful through subjecting it to various checks

3   OMR, OCR, MICR, bar codes

4   Printed output

5   Impact

6   Near Letter Quality

7   A meaningless control total

8   Format, range, length, consistency

9   File dumping—copying contents of the disk onto a secondary magnetic media (usually tape)
    File generation—copying contents of a tape onto another tape which is retained as a point from which the system can be re-built

10   A group of records that is frequently assessed by the system

11   A small pointer file that holds the key field of the main file together with its physical address

12   It transforms the value of the key field into the physical storage location on the disk

13   Speed, facilities, security features, interface

14   That it fits the requirements of the organisation

ANSWERS TO EXERCISES

3   (a)   Kimball tags give product details (size, colour, price etc) attached to a piece of clothing. When a product is sold the tag is removed and sent to the data processing centre where receipts are entered via a kimball tag reader. Thus, the only variable data is the actual sale itself.

Point Of Sale terminals (POS) also precode details of products but in this instance with a bar code. This is attached to the product and the sale of that product is accompanied by passing the barcode in front of a laser reader incorporated in the POS terminal. POS terminals are often connected to a central computer hence capturing data immediately. In contrast, kimball tags are usually batched and entered at a remote central site.

4   (a)   Data validation is concerned with the accuracy of the data. It attempts to trap inappropriate entries by subjecting them to a series of validation checks. Typical examples are given in section 25.4 of the text.

              Data verification is concerned with the accurate entry of data by the data preparation operator. This is often achieved by two different clerks entering the same data and using a verification program to trap inconsistent entries. These can then be re-checked and the accurate figure entered.

    (b)   A systems analyst is concerned with understanding the business procedures of the system and identifying opportunities for profitable computerisation. These areas will be specified in detail and passed to a programmer who will use an appropriate programming language to produce a system that satisfies the analyst's specification.

5   Advantages: access to expensive expertise; access to expensive and sophisticated hardware and software; avoidance of investment needed to achieve effective internal data processing; payment only for services used.

6   A typical configuration is given in Figure 22.2 Chapter 22. A simple inventory control package could be used on this system.

7   Bar codes are held on most products giving details about product type, size, configuration, price etc. The sale of these products is notified to a central system by the act of passing the barcodes across a laser reader embedded in the Point Of Sale (POS) terminal at the 'checkout'. This permits the automatic updating of stock information, with subsequent availability of reports on stock movements, re-stocking requirements, sales analysis and supermarket branch performance.

8   (c)   Updating of a master file concerns changes to variable data—number of a product in stock, credit level of a customer, etc. File maintenance concerns changes to fixed data—creating a new product, a new customer, deleting a product, amending a customer address etc.

9   Real time processing, on-line processing and distributed processing are covered in section 23.6 of the text. Time sharing is mentioned in the context of computer bureau services in Chapter 25.

Solutions to Chapter 26 questions

ANSWERS TO SELF-TEST QUESTIONS

1   Writing, talking, data retrieval, data manipulation, image processing

2   Dedicated word processor cannot be loaded for other functions. However, it is likely to have greater functionality within the confines of word processing

3   Deletion, insertion, formatting, movement of text

4   Data Base Management System

5   Record retrieval, report presentation, query response, programming

6   Private Automatic Branch Exchange

7   13.1%

8   Computer Aided Design. A zoom facility will be used to expand the details of higher order diagrams into a detailed lower level diagram

9   Spreadsheet consolidation, formatting, graphing, programming facilities, presentation commands

10   The RAM

Additional questions

Students are encouraged to attempt these questions. However, the answers are provided only in the manual issued to lecturers. Lecturers may obtain a free copy of the manual by writing to: Sales and Marketing Department, Longman Group UK Ltd, 21–27 Lamb's Conduit Street, London WC1N 3NJ.

1   The following table shows a breakdown of the different types of employee in the Northern region for 1988 and for 1978.

	Numbers employed	
Employee category	1988	1978
Senior sales staff	95	83
Clerical staff	48	52
Junior management	8	6
Junior sales staff	20	21
Administration staff	36	24
Senior management	24	18

By constructing suitable diagrams compare the structure of employees in the Northern region and identify the major changes that have taken place over the last 10 years.

2   The table below shows total turnover by sector for the last 10 years.

MTG plc annual turnover 1978–87 by market sector
(Figures shown are in £m)

Year	Food	Clothing	Footwear	Furniture	Electrical goods
1987	13.4	87.6	5.8	23.6	31.2
1986	12.4	79.0	4.1	22.9	27.7
1985	11.5	71.5	3.6	21.5	25.9
1984	11.2	63.2	3.6	21.2	23.2
1983	10.2	56.1	3.3	20.4	19.9
1982	8.7	43.1	3.1	19.9	17.2
1981	7.6	34.5	2.9	17.4	14.3
1980	6.2	28.7	2.1	14.5	11.6
1979	5.5	21.6	1.6	12.0	7.2
1978	5.2	16.2	1.4	10.6	5.4

Source: *Company accounts*

Required:
(a)   Construct a suitable time series graph showing turnover by sector on one axis and total turnover on the other
(b)   Construct a suitable time series graph showing the percentage turnover by sector

(c)   Which of the two time series graphs do you think is better?

(d)   Do you think it would have been better to show the data in the form of a component bar chart?

3   The data below is taken from Economic Trends published by the Central Statistical Office and shows income before and after income tax in the year 1984–85 for the UK.

Income group (£s)	Before tax		After tax	
	No of people 000s	Total income £m	No of people 000's	Total income £m
less than £2000	2,778	4,630	2,778	4,630
£2000 < £3000	4,727	12,914	5,013	13,708
£3000 < £4000	3,833	14,113	4,750	17,343
£4000 < £5000	3,206	14,691	3,652	16,675
£5000 < £6000	2,386	13,155	2,908	15,989
£6000 < £7000	2,043	13,230	2,309	15,022
£7000 < £8000	1,921	14,403	1,866	13,957
£8000 < £9000	1,656	14,090	1,542	13,116
£9000 < £10000	1,329	12,571	1,351	12,809
£10000 < £12500	2,752	30,692	2,381	26,482
£12500 < £15000	1,792	24,421	1,354	18,940
£15000 < £17500	1,804	17,532	632	10,142
£17500 < £20000	662	12,330	349	6,514
£20000 < £25000	601	13,324	309	6,806
£25000 < £30000	286	7,758	116	3,141
£30000 < £35000	130	4,188	48	1,547
£35000 < £40000	71	2,635	22	827
£40000 < £50000	77	3,357	19	831
£50000 or more	81	6,292	17	1,211
Total*	31,416	236,324	31,416	199,189

* Individual figures do not sum to the totals shown because of rounding

(a)   Construct suitable Lorenz curves for the distribution of income before tax and after tax. (Note that the total income for each group is given so midpoints are not necessary in this instance)

(b)   Which distribution is more equal?

(c)   How do you explain this?

4   Refer back to question 3 above. Based on the aggregated data answer the following questions.

(a)   Calculate the mean income before tax and the mean income after tax

(b)   Calculate the median income before tax and the median income after tax

(c)   How do you explain the fact that the mean income is higher than the median in both cases?

(d)   Calculate the difference between the mean and median before tax and the difference after tax. Which difference is greater? How do you explain this?

(e)   Which measure of average would you prefer to use?

(f)   What is the average amount of income tax paid?

5   This question is based on the end-of-chapter exercises of Chapters 4 and 5.

Assume that for the data set relating to daily sales in store B an extra day's sales are added—£2,000. What effect would you expect this one extra item to have on the following statistics:
(a)   the mean
(b)   the median
(c)   the standard deviation
(d)   the quartile deviation
(e)   the coefficient of skewness?

6   Using the Consumer Price Index shown in Chapter 7 construct a deflated series for turnovers for each sector.
(a)   For the Electrical goods sector for 1987 you should have an answer of £23.6 million. How do you interpret this value?
(b)   Using the deflated series, construct a set of index numbers for turnover by sector.
(c)   Which sectors have increased most and which least?
(d)   In what ways are the impressions you get from the deflated series different from those you got from exercise 1, Chapter 7?
(e)   Using the deflated indices construct a time series graph of turnover by sector and compare it with the graph for exercise 1, Chapter 7.

7   Using the data on salary and employees used in Chapter 7 and in exercise 3, Chapter 7, calculate both a Laspeyres and Paasche Quantity index, base 1987.
Interpret the results of your indices and comment on how such information could be used by management.

8   At one of their stores MTG sells fresh bread to its customers. The quantity of bread must be ordered each day from the bakery. Each loaf costs MTG £0.40 and sells for £0.55. Due to health regulations any loaves not sold at the end of the day must be disposed of at a loss of £0.05 per loaf.
Over the last few weeks the store has monitored the number of loaves it has sold each day:

No of loaves sold (00's)	No of days
10	15
11	20
12	30
13	20
14	10
15	5

(a)   Determine the expected profit if the store orders 1,200 loaves tomorrow
(b)   Explain what the resulting monetary figure means
(c)   How can we determine the best quantity to order?

9   Head office of MTG has recently bought a consignment of 10 of the latest desk-top computers. The office manager knows from previous experience that there is a 10% chance that any one machine will develop a fault within the first 12 months and that such a repair will cost, on average, £50.
You have been asked to advise Head Office as to how much money they should allocate over the next year to fund the expected repair costs from these computers.

10   The group Chairman of MTG has asked for the PC in his office to be replaced because some part of it is always breaking down. You are currently looking at alternative replacements. One such PC comprises four components: the keyboard, the monitor, the CPU and

M

the printer. The manufacturer claims that the chance of any one of these items breaking down is only 5%.
   (a) Determine the probability that at least one part of the system will not be working at any given time
   (b) Recalculate this value if the probability of 5% is reduced to 1%.

11 Machine Y can be set to pack different average quantities. For example, rather than pack an average of 1,000g per box it could be set to pack, say, 1,100g or 950g. The company currently advertises its boxes as containing at least 1,000g and new government regulations have been introduced which mean that no more than 1% of all boxes must be under the advertised weight. If the standard deviation is 20g what average weight should the machine be set to?
   Suppose government regulations now alter the allowed percentage to 0.5%. What will the new average weight figure be?

12 An MTG store is undertaking a manpower review of its warehouse department. The department regularly receives supplies of goods that are delivered to the store. On average they receive 400 deliveries each week with a standard deviation of 35. The distribution of the number of deliveries is known to be Normal. Determine the following:
   (a) The probability that in any one week deliveries will exceed 420
   (b) The probability that in any one week deliveries will be less than 350
   (c) The probability that in any one week deliveries will be between 331 and 469
   (d) The probability that in any one week deliveries will be between 310 and 490

   Existing staff in the warehouse department total 20 and it is felt that no employee can deal with more than 24 deliveries in any one week. What is the probability that the existing staff will have to work harder than this?

13 The Sales Director of MTG has recently crashed his company car and later this week must travel to one of the stores for a meeting with the manager. He has asked you to arrange for a car to be hired for the day. You have contacted two car hire firms. Firm A will rent a car for £25 per day. Firm B will rent a car for £10 per day plus £0.10 per mile travelled.
   The meeting will take place 60 miles away.
   (a) Determine an equation representing the cost of hiring the car from each of the two firms.
   (b) Draw a graph of these two equations
   (c) Which firm would you recommend the car be hired from?

14 In Chapter 14 a profit function was given as:

   Profit $= -100 + 100X - 5X^2$

   The corresponding equation for total revenue is given by:

   TR $= 100X - 3X^2$

   (a) Given that profit is the difference between TR and TC determine the appropriate TC equation.
   (b) Plot all three equations on the same graph.
   (c) Using the roots approach determine the points where TC=TR and confirm your solution from the graph.

15 In Chapter 14 the following average cost function was used:

   $$AC = \frac{1000}{X} + 10 - 5X + X^2$$

   (a) Find the corresponding Total Cost function
   (b) Find an expression for Marginal Cost
   (c) Determine the Marginal Cost when X=5 and when X=15

(d)   Interpret your answers to (c) in a business context
(e)   Find the level of output where Marginal Cost is at its minimum
(f)   Confirm the minimum using the second derivative

16   MTG headquarters has a variety of microcomputers in use by management. For seven of the machines information has been collected on their age and the annual maintenance cost last year.

Machine	Maintenance costs £ (per year)	Age of machine (years)
A	1220	6
B	500	2
C	1800	7
D	600	4
E	1100	4
F	200	1
G	600	3

(a)   Forecast annual maintenance costs for a computer that is 5 years old
(b)   Forecast annual maintenance costs for a computer that is 8 years old
(c)   Which forecast do you think will be more reliable and why?

17   MTG has recently carried out some market research into the background of their customers and the proportion of customers who have purchased a colour TV.

Year	Average weekly income £s (1980 prices)	Proportion of customers with a colour TV
1976	123.7	32
1977	134.5	37
1978	143.9	39
1979	142.7	43
1980	142.6	47
1981	141.6	51
1982	139.3	54
1983	149.6	59
1984	158.3	63
1985	160.6	65
1986	166.6	68
1987	170.5	72

(a)   Determine an appropriate equation for forecasting the proportion of customers with colour TVs
(b)   Assess the potential accuracy of your equation
(c)   How could the equation provide information useful to management?

18 The HQ office has been monitoring its energy usage on a quarterly basis over the last 4 years. Details are given below:

Units of energy used per quarter

Year	Quarter I	II	III	IV
1985			1502	2306
1986	2513	1807	1640	2219
1987	2482	1794	1583	2248
1988	2507	1812	1575	2272

(a) Draw a graph of the data
(b) Do you think the additive or multiplicative model would be more appropriate?
(c) Estimate the trend for the model you have chosen
(d) Identify the seasonal factors
(e) What reasons can you suggest for the seasonal pattern?
(f) Forecast the energy usage for each quarter for 1989
(g) How accurate do you think your forecast will be?

19 As part of a production process the production manager is trying to schedule the manufacturing of a particular item. It is known that a total of 6,500 items will be required over the next year and the item has a holding cost of £2.50 per item per year. Set-up costs are currently £100.
     For each of the following production capacities determine the EBQ:
(a) 10,000 units
(b) 15,000 units
(c) 20,000 units

20 A company knows that it will have to replace a piece of machinery in 4 years' time, at a cost of £25,000. If the current rate of interest is 11% what sum should be invested now to generate this sum in the future?

21 The company mentioned in question 20 has decided it can only afford to invest £12,500 now to finance the future replacement of the machine. What rate of return does it require on the investment?

22 A company is considering purchasing a labour-saving piece of equipment which will cost £40,000 and have a useful life of 4 years from now. Current cost of capital is 7.5%. Purchasing the machine will allow the company to cut its workforce by 1 person. At present average annual labour costs are £10,000 per person per year and are expected to increase by 5% pa over the next few years.
(a) Advise the company as to whether it should purchase the machine
(b) At what cost of capital (%) would you change your mind about the recommendation made?

23 You have borrowed £10,000 from the bank at a rate of interest of 12%, the loan to be amortised over 10 years.
(a) Determine the annual repayments.
(b) Draw up a repayment schedule.
You wish to repay the loan via a sinking fund paying interest at 15%.
(c) Draw up a schedule of the sinking fund payments.

24 You are engaged in a discussion with your financial director concerning the merits of using magnetic tape as storage for your computerised stock control system. You are against its inclusion in the system.

Give three reasons why it may be advantageous to purchase a system using magnetic disks and three reasons why it may be disadvantageous to purchase a system using magnetic tape.

25 Construct a decision table for the following narrative:

All orders received within 7 days are automatically entered for the Grand Draw and sent a prompt-reply gift. Orders received within the next 21 days are only entered for the Grand Draw. Orders after that date are sent a letter illustrating the prizes they missed by not replying quickly enough to be entered for the Grand Draw!

26 Input design is concerned with five main tasks. Briefly explain these in the context of a payroll system.

27 Input design may be aided by following two main guidelines:

> Seek to minimise transcription
> Seek to minimise the amount of data recorded

Explain how these are followed in a bank cheque processing system.

28 A company uses a modulus 11 check digit system in its product code. An employee enters the product code 6217323. Should this be accepted or rejected?

The Chartered Association of Certified Accountants

June 1988

Level 1—Preliminary Examination
Paper 1.5

Numerical Analysis and Data Processing*

Time allowed—3 hours
Number of questions on paper—6
FIVE questions ONLY to be answered
All workings to be shown

* *From December 1988 the title of this examination will be Business Mathematics and Information Technology*

FIVE questions ONLY to be answered

1   **(a)**   A finance house has to choose between the installation of a mainframe computer with a network of non-intelligent terminals and the use of networked microcomputers with a file server.

        Required:

        What are the advantages and disadvantages of the mainframe system against the advantages and disadvantages of the networked microcomputers with a file server? (10 marks)

    (b)   The finance house has a subsidiary which has its own mainframe computer. The subsidiary leases time on this mainframe to other firms. The computer was purchased seven years ago. The subsidiary has found that the annual revenue from this machine has grown according to:

$$\text{Annual revenue (£)} = 80{,}000 + 10{,}000(1 - 5/(t + 1))$$

        where t is the number of years since purchase (so at the time of purchase t = 0)

        Required:

        (i)   **Form a table of the annual revenue for the seven years from the date the computer was purchased.** (4 marks)

        (ii)   **Show these results on a graph.** (4 marks)

        (iii) **If the computer were kept for an extremely long period of time to what value would the annual revenue tend?** (2 marks)

                                                                   (20 marks)

2   A sample of the transfer times of data from an intelligent terminal, in microseconds, are as follows:

time (microseconds)	frequency
10 and less than 20	6
20 and less than 30	12
30 and less than 35	9
35 and less than 40	12
40 and less than 45	9
45 and less than 55	9
55 and less than 65	3

Required:

(a)   **Express each frequency as a percentage of the total frequency and tabulate this data against each class**   (2 marks)

(b)   **Using the percentages found in (a) draw a histogram of the data.**   (4 marks)

(c)   **Find the mean and standard deviation of the data.**   (5 marks)

(d)   **Draw an ogive of the data.**   (3 marks)

(e)   **Using your ogive (or otherwise) find the median and semi-interquartile range of the data.**   (4 marks)

(f)   **Which measures of location and dispersion are most appropriate to this data and why?**   (2 marks)

(20 marks)

3   A survey of four companies which make similar products produced the following data on the price (p) of the products and the quantity (q) sold in three separate years.

Year		1		2		3
	p	q	p	q	p	q
Company A	2	6	3	7	3	10
Company B	4	2	4	7	5	8
Company C	4	12	6	3	5	9
Company D	8	9	7	14	9	4

Required:

(a)   **Why would an index such as a Laspeyres or Paasche be suitable as a price (or quantity) index for the above data? In what circumstances would a weighted index of price relatives be a more suitable form of index?**   (2 marks)

(b)   **Produce a base weighted aggregative quantity index for years 1 and 3 using year 2 as a base.**   (7 marks)

(c)   **Produce a current weighted aggregative price index for years 1 and 3 using year 2 as a base.**   (9 marks)

(d)   **Contrast a Laspeyres index with a Paasche index.**   (2 marks)

(20 marks)

4   A capital project costs an initial £1,000 and cash inflows and outflows over its two year life are as given below:

Year	Cash In	Cash Out
1	£800	£100
2	£800	£200

Required:

(a)   **Using discount rates of 14% and 22% find the internal rate of return of this project.**

(8 marks)

If the net cash in in year 1 is called D(1) and the net cash in in year 2 is called D(2) then the theoretical internal rate of return is given by i in the following equation.

$$D(1) (1 + i/100) + D(2) - C (1 + i/100)^2 = 0$$

where C is the capital cost of the project.

(b)   **solve this equation for (1 + i/100) using the data above and find the values of i.**

(8 marks)

(c)   **Comment on the difference between the theoretical solution for the internal rate of return and the solution you found using the interest rates of 14% and 22%.**

(4 marks)

(20 marks)

This extract from tables is for your use.

Discount Rate	14%	22%
Year 1	0.8772	0.8197
Year 2	0.7695	0.6719

5   The following is an extract from a computer program:

```
10 REM Program to work out the roots of quadratic equations
20 PRINT "Quadratic equations—finding the roots"
30 REM Inputing values of the equation and testing them
40 PRINT "Gives roots of a quadratic equation:–"
50 PRINT "                                                    ax∧2 + bx + c = 0"
60 PRINT
70 INPUT "                                    What is the value of a"; A
80 PRINT
90 IF A = 0 THEN PRINT "This is not a quadratic"
100 IF A = 0 GOTO 70
110 INPUT "                                              of b"; B
120 PRINT
130 INPUT "                                              of c"; C
140 PRINT
150 PRINT
160 REM Testing for type of roots by part under the square root
170 T1 = (B∧2 − (4*A*C))
190 REM Working out the roots by equation and
200 REM Outputing the relevant message
210 IF T1 = 0 THEN PRINT "There are two equal roots, they are:–"
220 IF T1 = 0 THEN X1 = (−B)/(2*A)
230 IF T1 = 0 THEN PRINT "                              x = "; X1
240 IF T1 > 0 THEN PRINT "There are two real roots, they are:–"
250 IF T1 > 0 THEN X1 = (−B + SQR(T1))/(2*A)
260 IF T1 > 0 THEN X2 = (−B − SQR(T1))/(2*A)
270 IF T1 > 0 THEN PRINT "                  x = ";X1;" and x = "; X2
280 PRINT "Do you want to find the roots to another quadratic"
290 INPUT "                            answer Y or N"; A$
300 IF A$ = "Y" GOTO 20
310 IF A$ = "y" GOTO 20
320 IF A$ = "N" GOTO 370
```

```
330 IF A$ = "n" GOTO 370
340 PRINT
350 PRINT "Answer Y or N"
360 GOTO 280
370 END
```

The program is used to solve the quadratic equation

$$2x^2 - 5x + 2 = 0$$

Required:

(a)   Trace the action of the program for lines 40 to 150.   (5 marks)

(b)   What are the values for X1 and X2 in lines 250 and 260?   (4 marks)

(c)   What is the output of the program between lines 210 and 270?   (2 marks)

(d)   What possibility for the value of T1 has been omitted between lines 210 and 270?   (2 marks)

(e)   If you wished to solve another quadratic and answer "y" to the question in lines 280 and 290 which of the statements in lines 290 to 330 has effect? What is that effect?   (2 marks)

(f)   If you answered "COFFEE" to the question in lines 280 and 290 what would be the effect on the program?   (5 marks)

(20 marks)

6   (a)   Explain, as if to a layman, what the following terms mean and outline their use in a business environment.

    (i)   Electronic Point of Sale (EPOS).   (5 marks)

    (ii)   Bar code   (5 marks)

(b)   The accounting function of a firm has to award the employees' bonus for the firm. Previously it has been awarded on the average monthly earnings over the quarter (3 month period) prior to the bonus payment. During the quarter leading to the next payment there was a 10% pay rise after the first month. The computer system only provides the average earnings for the quarter. The firm has a new policy for awarding payment. The new policy is to award payment on the basis of current monthly pay.

For one group of employees their average pay was £900 per month.

What is their current monthly pay?   (7 marks)

(c)   The accounting function of the firm has been asked to prepare a forecast of the pay based on quarterly average earnings for the last two years using the method of moving averages.

Explain why in producing a quarterly centred trend five consecutive quarterly figures are used.   (3 marks)

(20 marks)

End of Question Paper

Authors' model answers to this examination paper are on page 349.

Authors' model answers to June 1988 Numerical Analysis and Data Processing Paper

1 (a) The mainframe solution permits:

Advantages

i   centralised control by an established, dedicated data processing section.
ii   access to a considerable amount of power which may be reflected in the speed and functionality of the software.
iii   Adoption of proven hardware technology backed up by the support of large manufacturers.

Disadvantages

i   Centralised control may lead to reduced opportunities for the development of departmental computing. A network solution provides an opportunity for decentralising information systems.
ii   Certain types of software (such as spreadsheets) consume a lot of computing resource and are difficult to support with a mainframe. Networks give local dedicated processing.
iii   Mainframes are expensive and usually incur high numbers of staff, operations and maintenance costs. Networks should be cheaper to run as long as training and control is properly carried out. However, an absence of standards and the relatively small company size of most network suppliers means that they are often unreliable and poorly supported.

(b) i

t	Annual revenue	
0	40000	$= 80000 + 10000(1 - 5/(0 + 1))$
1	65000	
2	73333.33	
3	77500	
4	80000	
5	81666.67	
6	82857.14	
7	83750	

ii

Annual revenue—mainframe system

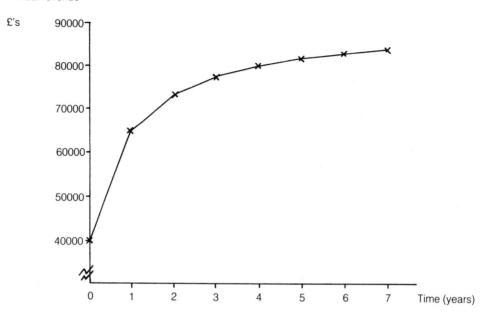

Annual revenue

£'s

iii   From the function given it can be seen that as t increases then 5/(t + 1) will tend
to move to zero. So as t increases the second part of the function will get closer
and closer to +10000. Hence, the value for all the function will get closer and
closer to 80000 + 10000 = £90,000.

2   (a)

Time	Frequency	%
10 < 20	6	10
20 < 30	12	20
30 < 35	9	15
35 < 40	12	20
40 < 45	9	15
45 < 55	9	15
55 < 65	3	5
Total	60	100%

(b)

Percentage histograms: transfer times

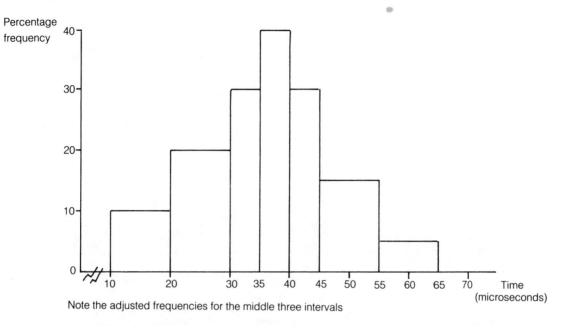

Note the adjusted frequencies for the middle three intervals

Note that because of unequal intervals in the frequency table in part (a) it is necessary to adjust the height of the three central intervals (using a standard width of 10 microseconds).

(c)   The appropriate calculations are shown in the table below:

Time	Midpoint x	f	fx	x^2	fx^2
10<20	15	6	90	225	1350
20<30	25	12	300	625	7500
30<35	32.5	9	292.5	1056.25	9506.25
35<40	37.5	12	450	1406.25	16875
40<45	42.5	9	382.5	1806.25	16256.25
45<55	50	9	450	2500	22500
55<65	60	3	180	3600	10800
Total		60	2145		84787.5

$$\text{Mean} = \frac{2145}{60} = 35.75 \text{ microseconds}$$

Standard deviation =

$$\sqrt{\frac{84787.5}{60} - 35.75^2} = \sqrt{135.0625} = 11.622 \text{ microseconds}$$

(d) and (e)

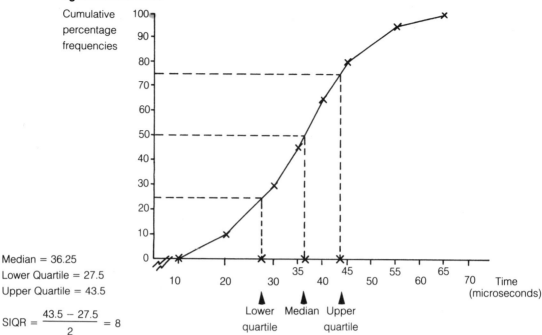

Ogive: transfer times

Median = 36.25
Lower Quartile = 27.5
Upper Quartile = 43.5

$$\text{SIQR} = \frac{43.5 - 27.5}{2} = 8$$

The diagram shows the cumulative percentage frequencies which is better for estimating the quartiles than using the cumulative frequencies.

(f)   In this case the data shows no signs of extreme values or skewness so the mean and standard deviation are to be preferred. They will not be distorted by extreme values and use all the data.

3   (a)   An aggregate index is obviously called for in this problem—aggregating prices or quantities over the 4 companies.

(b)   A Laspeyres index is required. We are told to use year 2 as the base. The weights will be the prices as a quantity index is required.

If we denote the following variables:

p_1 prices in year 1
q_1 quantities in year 1

p_2 prices in year 2
q_2 quantities in year 2

p_3 prices in year 3
q_3 quantities in year 3

We require the following:

$$p_2 q_1 = 161$$
$$p_2 q_2 = 165$$
$$p_2 q_3 = 144$$

$$\text{Index for Year 1} = \frac{p_2 q_1}{p_2 q_2} \times 100 = \frac{161}{165} \times 100 = 97.57$$

$$\text{Index for Year 3} = \frac{p_2 q_3}{p_2 q_2} \times 100 = \frac{144}{165} \times 100 = 87.27$$

(c)   A Paasche index is required, but this time as a price index.

Using the same notation as before we have:

$p_1q_1 = 140$
$p_2q_1 = 161$
$p_3q_3 = 151$

Index for year $1 = \dfrac{p_1q_1}{p_2q_1} \times 100 = \dfrac{140}{161} \times 100 = 86.95$

Index for year $3 = \dfrac{p_3q_3}{p_2q_3} \times 100 = \dfrac{151}{144} \times 100 = 104.86$

(d)   A Laspeyres index uses one set of weights for all the calculations which makes both the calculations and the data collection relatively easy. The problem with the Laspeyres index is that in using only one set of weights, these will become outdated over time and will fail to reflect changing patterns.

In contrast, the Paasche index uses fresh weights each period. This ensures that the index keeps up to date with changing patterns but makes the index more difficult and expensive to calculate.

4   (a)   To find the IRR we require the NPV for two different rates of interest. The net cash flows for the project and their discounted values are shown below:

Rate = 14%

Year	Net cash flow	Discount factor	Discounted cash flow
0	−1000	1.0000	−1000
1	700	0.8772	614.04
2	600	0.7695	461.70
Total	300		75.74

Rate = 22%

Year	Net cash flow	Discount factor	Discounted cash flow
0	−1000	1.0000	−1000
1	700	0.8197	573.79
2	600	0.6719	403.14
Total	300		−23.07

Using the interpolation formula we have:

$$14\% + 8\left(\frac{75.74}{75.74 + 23.07}\right) = 14 + 8(.7665)$$

$$= 14 + 6.132 = 20.132\%$$

giving the IRR = 20.1%

(Alternatively we could have drawn a graph to interpolate.)

(b)   Let $X = (1 + i/100)$

$D(1) = 700$
$D(2) = 600$
$C \quad = 1000$

giving:

$$700X + 600 - 1000X^2 = 0$$

This is a quadratic equation and we require the two roots. Solving gives:

X1 = 1.2
X2 = −0.5

The negative root has no meaning in the context of the question so we have:

X = 1.2 = 1 + i/100

1.2 − 1 = i/100
0.2 = 1/100

giving i = 20%

(c) the difference between the answer to part (b) and part (a) arises because:
—the interpolation formula is a linear approximation only
—the method of graphical interpolation gives rise to the usual inaccuracies of graphs and diagrams.

5 (a) Lines 40–60   display the purpose of the program
Line 70   asks for the input of a
Line 90   If a = 0 then the input is rejected
Line 100   Redirects program control to line 70 and hence requests another value for a
Lines 110–150 Request input for values of b and c

(b) X1 = 2
X2 = $\frac{1}{2}$

(c) The roots of the quadratic equation. For example, either there are two real roots which are, for example:

$$X = 2 \text{ and } X = \tfrac{1}{2}$$

or there is an equal root which is, for example:

$$X = 3$$

(d) T1 < 0

(e) Line 310. Program control will be returned to line 20 and output

Quadratic equations—finding the roots etc

(f) Line 350 will have effect and a request will be issued to "Answer Y or N"

6 (a) i   The Electronic Point of Sale terminal has developed from the humble cash register. Articles purchased by a shopper are passed across a laser reader which identifies the product bar code and calculates the amount payable. Products which do not have a bar code (such as fresh vegetables) are input directly from the keyboard. The terminal produces an itemised bill for the shopper as well as giving sales analysis by product type, group and store.

ii   Most organisations need to record information about important products or users of their systems. This information is frequently stored as a code—a membership number for a library, a product code for a particular article. A bar code stores such information as a set of bars or lines which are imprinted or embossed onto an appropriate media—a library card, the product container, etc. Data concerning a transaction (a member borrowing a book, a product being sold) is recorded by passing the bar code across a bar code reader which transmits this information directly into the computer system.

(b) Let X = earnings in Month 1

Earnings in Month 2 = 1.10X (a 10% rise)
Earnings in Month 3 = 1.10X

Earnings over the 3 months = X + 1.1X + 1.1X = 3.2X

Average earnings per month = $\dfrac{3.2X}{3}$

We know that 900 = 3.2X/3 so solving gives:

$$2700 = 3.2X$$

$$X = 2700/3.2 = 843.75$$

therefore the current rate of pay per month is:

$$843.75 \times 1.10 = £928.12$$

(c) We have to use a set of 5 quarterly figures in order to centre the moving average on the middle of the period—on the third quarter of the five in this case.

Information technology terms

ALU. Arithmetic and Logic Unit. The part of the CPU that performs arithmetic and comparisons. Contains areas of storage, called registers, which hold intermediate additions.

Analogue. Analogue computers store continuous values with different values being represented by physical differences in the voltage level.

ASCII. American Standard Code for Information Interchange. A seven bit code for storing data.

Assembler. Programs written with mnemonic or single word instructions which are translated into machine code statements by an assembler.

Bar code. A unique code recording data about a product, object or person. The code is read by passing a light pen across the code. A method of direct input into the computer system.

BASIC. Beginners All purpose Symbolic Instruction Code. A high level computer language.

Binary system. A notation with a base of 2 whereby each number is worth twice that of the immediate right hand value. For example:

$$\frac{1101}{1+8+1\times4+0\times2+1\times1} \ = \ 13$$

Bit. A binary digit, 0 or 1.

Bus network. A transmission line (often axial cable) to which may be attached various devices.

Byte. A combination of 8 bits is a byte, where each byte represents a unique value, letter or symbol.

COM. Computer Output into Microfilm.

Compiler. A piece of software that converts source code statements into object code.

Computer. Any device capable of accepting data automatically, applying a sequence of processes to this data, and supplying the results of these processes.

Control unit. The co-ordinating part of the CPU. The circuitry it contains controls and co-ordinates the other components of the CPU.

CPU. Central Processing Unit. Comprises three sections, the control unit, arithmetic and logic unit and primary storage.

Data base. A shared centrally controlled collection of data used in an organisation.

Data element or item. A piece of information held in the system. For example, surname is a data item. These data items will be grouped into logical record structures.

DBMS. Data Base Management System. A software package that organises the data in the data base and provides access to the data for different programs and users.

Decision table. A grid model showing the relationship between conditions and the possible actions that result from each combination of these conditions.

Dialogue. The conversation that takes place between the computer user and the application software. The dialogue can be structured in three complementary ways—menus, form fill and question and answer sessions.

Digital. Digital computers store specific discrete values of 0 and 1 where each combination of these binary digits (bits) represents a value, letter or symbol.

EBCDIC. Extended Binary Coded Decimal Interchange Code. An eight bit code for storing data.

Electronic mail. The computer-based capture, transmission and delivery of text.

Fax. Facsimile transmission (FAX) permits the fast transmission of images.

File. A set of data values for a record. For example, the employee file will be made up of record structure information about each employee:

```
                          data items
         Surname     Forename    Sex    Date of Birth ← record structure
         Crawford    Martin      M      07/02/48 ← record
a file   Mills       Mary        F      13/01/46
         Slack       Harry       M      11/02/47
```

Floppy disk. This is a plastic disk coated with iron oxide and enclosed within a reinforcing envelope. Common sizes are 3″, 5¼″ and 8″ with capacities ranging from 360k to 1.5Mb.

Flowchart. A diagrammatical way of showing the structure of a problem or a program.

Fourth generation language. A term that covers a variety of software. It is usually distinguished by the presence of:
(a) an accessible query language for the construction of enquiries by user personnel
(b) a report generator
(c) a non-procedural programming language.

Gigabyte. 1024Mb (1Gb).

Hard copy. A permanent physical record of data output from the system. Usually produced by a printer or a plotter.

Hardware. The various electronic and electromechanical devices that make up the physical parts of the computer system. This will typically consist of secondary storage devices (such as hard disks), central processing unit, input and output devices (eg, VDUs, printers, keyboards).

High level languages. Programs are written in English-like statements producing a source code which is *compiled* into an object code and linked into *machine code*. Some of these languages are *interpeted* rather than compiled but the principle of accessible statements remains the same. BASIC is an example of a high level language.

Hit ratio. This measures the activity on a file in a particular run or time period. It is expressed as:

$$\frac{\text{Number of records assessed}}{\text{Number of records in the file}} \times 100 = \quad \%$$

Impact printer. An impact printer creates characters through direct contact between the printing mechanism and the paper. Typical printing mechanisms include:
  (a) dot matrix, where a character is formed from a pattern of dots
  (b) daisywheel, where a character is selected from a fully formed embossed character set.

Interpreter. A piece of software that converts each source code instruction directly into machine code.

Keyboard. The usual method of data input. Usually contains a standard typewriter layout, a numeric keyboard, function keys and cursor control keys.

Kilobyte. 1024bytes (1K).

Kimball tag. A small tag, used primarily in the garment trade, to record details about the goods it is attached to. It is detached on the sale of the product and passed through a kimball tag reader.

Linker. A piece of software that converts object code statements into machine code.

Machine code. Programs written in machine instructions which are directly executable by the CPU.

Magnetic disk. A secondary storage device with data stored on tracks. Most disks have a number of disk platters with each plotter having a read/write head.

Magnetic tape. A secondary storage device where data is represented by bit patterns across the tape. 6250 of these characters can be stored per inch in the best quality tape and the tape is on a reel 2400′ or 3600′ long.

Megabyte. 1024kbytes (Mb).

MICR. Magnetic Ink Character Recognition. A specialised form of character recognition. MICR readers magnetise and recognise the ferrite impregnated ink used in the characteristic MICR font.

Multiplexor. A device which controls and co-ordinates digital messages and converts them into analogue form for transmission along the telephone lines.

Network. A network is the inter-connection of individual computers. A network can span many continents (a Wide Area Network—WAN) or be restricted to an office floor, block, campus etc (a Local Area Network—LAN).

Non-impact printer. The character is formed by a printing mechanism that does not come into physical contact with the paper. Light is an example medium, used in laser printers.

OCR. Optical Character Recognition. OCR readers interpret printed characters and automatically convert them into their digital equivalents.

OMR. Optical Mark Recognition. OMR readers recognise hand or machine printed marks on forms, and automatically convert them into their digital equipment.

Operating system. A piece of software that sits between the hardware and the application programs. It effectively organises and controls the performance of the hardware with the objective of maximising hardware efficiency without compromising the friendliness of the interface. MS-DOS (PC-DOS) and UNIX are representative operating systems.

PABX. Private Automatic Branch Exchange.

Primary storage. Data must be available in the CPU before it can be manipulated. It may be read into RAM and may also contain ROM for particular purposes.

Program. A set of instructions which directs the computer through the steps necessary to perform a specified task.

RAM. Random Access Memory. Data may be read and written from this area. Usually volatile.

Record. A set of associated data items. For example, surname, forename, address, sex etc will make up the record structure of an employee file. Individual values of those items will constitute a record, see File.

Ring network. All the devices are connected in a loop.

ROM. Read Only Memory. Data can be read but not written to this area. Usually non-volatile.

Secondary storage. The main form of data storage. The majority of an enterprise's data will be stored on secondary media whilst it is not needed in the CPU. Tape and disk are typical secondary storage media.

Software. The instructions, programs, protocols and procedures that enable the hardware components to function correctly. This will include operating systems, compilers, programming languages and application packages.

Software package. A generalised program designed to support a common application area, for example, payroll, stock control, accounts, ledgers etc.

Spreadsheet. A software package that permits the creation of data models using powerful arithmetic functions. These models usually permit 'what if?' analysis, showing the effect of changes in chosen variables.

Star network. This has a network controller or file server at the hub of the network with all other devices connected to this.

Structured English. A formalised set of English statements for describing sequence, selection and repetition problem constructs.

Transcription. A term normally applied to the process of transcribing 'human readable' format to 'computer readable' format through keyboard entry. Data verification and validation are both ways of trapping transcription errors.

Transfer rate. The speed of transfer of data from secondary storage to the CPU.

VDU. Visual Display Unit. A video monitor typically capable of displaying up to 25 lines of 80 characters. Special high resolution monitors are normally used for applications which require a large amount of graphical display and manipulation.

Word processing. The manipulation, editing, storage and printing of text.

Index